Joseph C. Wil:
CAMI

Teacher's Resource Manual

WORLD
TAPESTRIES

An Anthology of Global Literature

GLOBE FEARON EDUCATIONAL PUBLISHER
A Division of Simon & Schuster
Upper Saddle River, New Jersey

ESL Consultant: Jacqueline Kiraithe-Córdova, Ph.D.
Coordinator of Spanish and TESOL Areas
Department of Foreign Languages and Literatures
California State University at Fullerton

Director of Editorial and Marketing, Secondary Supplementary: Nancy Surridge

Project Editor: Carol Schneider

Editors: Karen Bernhaut, Amy Jolin, Lynn Kloss

Editorial Support: Stephanie Cahill, Keisha Carter, Ann Clarkson, Jennifer McCarthy, Elena Petron, Laura Ring

Editorial Assistants: Brian Hawkes, Kathleen Kennedy

Editorial Development: McCormick Associates, Forest Hills, New York

Market Manager: Rhonda Anderson

Production Director: Kurt Scherwatzky

Manufacturing Buyer: Tara Felitto

Production Editor: Rosann Bar

Production Assistant: Heather Roake

Interior Design and Electronic Page Production: Pat Smythe

Electronic Page Production: Margarita Giammanco, Joan Jacobus, Elaine Kilcullen, José López, Jonathan Nathan, Mimi Raihl

Art Direction: Joan Jacobus

Photo Research: Jenifer Hixon

Cover: BB&K Design Inc.

Cover Illustration: John Jinks

ISBN: 0-8359-1823-8

Printed in the United States of America
1 2 3 4 5 6 7 8 9   01 00 99 98 97

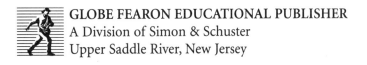

GLOBE FEARON EDUCATIONAL PUBLISHER
A Division of Simon & Schuster
Upper Saddle River, New Jersey

Contents

Contents: Themes

Contents: Genres

NONFICTION

Speech

Essays

Autobiographies

Program Philosophy and Rationale

World Tapestries is a collection of stories, poems, plays, and essays written by or about the people of the various world cultures so often forgotten in typical histories and anthologies. As a collection, these works counter the common misconception that "literature" comes only from the Western literary canon.

Much of the literature with which Westerners are most familiar is based on a literary tradition that stretches back to Greece, Rome, and the Middle East. Ours is a vivid canvas, embroidered with threads from many lands and, like so many of the arts, interwoven with the values, issues, and questions that are still central to our identity.

Many literary traditions around the world, however, do not draw upon this familiar context. The influences in their writing are vastly different, yet the central issues they present are familiar: They consider their origins and seek to understand their world; they offer spiritual insights and advice for day-to-day living; they give voice to their people in attempts at self-definition; and they respond both to the pleasures and the pains of life.

Even though these writers have not always enjoyed widespread popularity, their work lives on and even thrives. Some writers in this collection are familiar to us today; others are not as well known. *World Tapestries* includes the works of both, but there is a definite emphasis on the unheard voices-the writers so often overlooked in standard literature anthologies.

This book takes an inclusive approach. We have sought out unheard voices, yet never compromise in the quality or accessibilty of the selections. While acknowledging and celebrating the differences among world cultures, we have emphasized the commonality and humanity these voices share.

World Tapestries is a book of literature that reflects the evolution of our modern world and the voices and cultural heritages that shaped it. It is also your book and your students' book. It is a collection in which students will find works that are enjoyable to read and that will open the door of the mind a little wider. It is our hope that as they think, talk, and write about the new voices reflected in these selections, students will find their own voices as readers, writers, and members of the global community.

We have also followed an approach to teaching literature that acknowledges the importance of the reader, the writer, and their respective cultures. We have operated on the assumption that the readers of this text (you and your students) are important in determining the value of what has been read. We also believe that the writers and artists included in this collection, along with their cultures and traditions, have merit in their own right and deserve attention.

The selections in *World Tapestries* offer not only an opportunity for self-exploration, but also an opportunity for inquiry into what it means to write from a particular cultural perspective. Together with your students, you will gain insight into cultures that have been disenfranchised, that yearn for democracy, or that struggle to maintain their traditional culture within a pluralistic society. The artwork that appears with the selections and in "The Art of Tapestries" will further enhance your students' understanding of these myriad cultures. As they come to accept alternative perspectives, your students will also increase their understanding of themselves as readers, as human beings, and as member of the world community.

The selections in *World Tapestries* are arranged geographically and include background information about the author and the culture represented by each work. This background information, called "Reading the Selection in a Cultural Context," helps students consider the people and culture that so greatly influence any piece of writing. Literature is never produced in a vacuum; the writer and the writer's world shape what is written. Any student who has ever written a personal essay or created a piece of fiction knows how much of him or herself went into the process. The works they will read in *World Tapestries* are no different; they cannot be separated from the authors and cultures that gave them life.

Students' understanding of the significance of the author's culture and personal life in his or her writing can be enhanced with a consideration of the literary genre and techniques that the author chose to tell his or her "story." To aid in this approach, we have included model lessons, as well as questions and exercises, that guide students toward a deeper reading of the text.

We have also raised questions that point the students toward a consideration of both the commonalities and the uniqueness of world cultures. Our world grows smaller–yet wider–with each passing day as technology dissolves the barriers of distance. We are rapidly becoming the "global village" heralded at the birth of the modern telecommunications age. We have much to learn from our fellow villagers, both about the richness of their particular cultures and the richness of our common identity as human beings. Literature such as that found in *World Tapestries* is an integral part of that learning process—a process that will take on even greater importance in the years ahead as our interaction with our global neighbors grows as never before.

Our choice of the title *World Tapestries* is symbolic of the world view engendered by this approach to literature and learning. A tapestry is made from threads of different colors and textures stitched in distinct patterns and designs. When viewed up close, one can appreciate the intricacies of the detailed stitches, the uniqueness of their texture. It is not until one steps back and views the tapestry as a whole, however, that the full picture emerges. Only then can we appreciate the true beauty of the image created by those many intricately connected threads.

Similarly, the selections in this volume and the cultures from which they come are undoubtedly unique. Yet, at the same time, they reflect the universal human struggles and values that unite all cultures across time and space. We need only step back a bit to see how each unique voice contributes to and enriches the entire World Tapestry.

The *World Tapestries Teacher's Resource Manual* amplifies this global approach to literature and learning. It features a variety of ways to explore texts, their writers, and readers. It suggests imaginative ways of helping students enter into the cultures they encounter through the selections and presents ways of assessing student understanding and learning. This book should not be seen as a prescription, but rather as a set of suggestions from fellow teachers. You know your students best. Feel free to adapt what is in these pages to your specific classroom needs. Above all, enjoy the exploration as you and your students enter the worlds of the tapestries. We think you'll agree that sometimes the most beautiful images are found in unexpected places.

SCOPE AND SEQUENCE OF SKILLS

	Reading Level	Literary Skills	Critical Thinking Skills
UNIT 1: AFRICA AND THE MIDDLE EAST SE pp. 2–5 TRM pp. 2–3		Evaluating primary sources in history	Comparing historical events across world regions as displayed on a time-line
Chapter 1: Africa SE p. 6 TRM pp. 4–6		Exploring the history of African Literature	Analyzing the effect of colonialism
"Sundiata: An Epic of Old Mali" SE pp. 7–18 TRM pp. 7–9	Average	Recognizing elements of an epic; identifying similes and metaphors in an epic; identifying details that suggest cultural values; analyzing characterization	Analyzing key elements in an epic; drawing conclusions about characters and values suggested in an epic; comparing and contrasting legends; discussing the elements in epics
"Owner of the Sky: Olorun the Creator" SE pp. 19–22 TRM pp. 10–12	Easy	Identifying elements of a creation story; analyzing cause-effect relationships in a myth	Analyzing the effectiveness of a myth; drawing conclusions about cultural details; comparing and contrasting myths; discussing creation stories from different cultures
"The Sea Eats the Land at Home" "Song for the Sun that Disappeared Behind the Rainclouds" SE pp. 23–26 TRM pp. 13–15	Easy	Recognizing sensory details in poems; understanding how the connotations of words affect meaning; making connections between sensory details and poetic settings and themes	Analyzing the effect of sensory language; making inferences about a culture through details in a poem; describing one's own emotional reaction to poems
"The Prebend Gardens" "Interior" "All That You Have Given Me, Africa" SE pp. 27–31 TRM pp. 16–18	Challenging	Analyzing authors' purpose for writing; analyzing uses of poetic language; developing an awareness of the roots of a literary movement in Africa	Comparing and contrasting authors' techniques; drawing conclusions about a culture from poetic details; comparing and contrasting nationalistic poems; evaluating traditional poems, songs, or anthems from different cultures
"The Toilet" SE pp. 34–42 TRM pp. 20–22	Average	Identifying the characteristics of first-person narrative; analyzing point of view in a story; evaluating the effectiveness of an author's narrative techniques	Analyzing story details that relate to the theme of privacy; making connections between cultural details and story details; applying the theme of pursuing a dream to views of ambition in one's own culture; responding to ideas that relate to the theme of privacy

Vocabulary Skills	Communication Skills	Global Diversity Skills	Cross-Curricular Skills
	Understanding the cultural foundations of literature	Analyzing the cultural impact of historical events	Geography: Using a map to identify sources of literature
	Understanding the significance of storytelling on literature	Looking for evidence of the fight for equality in literature	Art: Examining the connections between art and literature
Scanning for words relating to character traits; using context clues	Writing a news story or political documentary: drawing conclusions about desirable qualities in a leader; evaluating the qualities of present-day leaders	Identifying qualities of character that a society values; analyzing the significance of traditional storytelling to African societies	History: Early history of the Mali Social Studies: Social role of the *griot* and of historical oratory Speech: Purposes of oral transmission of history
Scanning for words that apply to the creation process; using context clues	Retelling a scene from a different point of view: analyzing a character's behavior, actions, and words; making inferences about a character	Recognizing recurring themes in the creation stories of different cultures; examining historical information in myths	Social Studies: Yoruba religious beliefs
Making predictions based upon vocabulary; using context clues	Writing sensory details: envisioning or recalling the effects of an event; using descriptive details	Analyzing characteristics of a traditional African culture; recognizing cross-cultural themes	Geography: Geographical features of Ghana Social Studies: Polytheism; the roles and powers of the gods
Scanning for words relating to geographical and cultural setting; using context clues	Writing an expository essay: comparing and contrasting national poems and anthems; debating: evaluating peers' work; composing dissenting viewpoints; working in cooperative groups	Developing an awareness of Sub-Saharan black African experiences and beliefs; recognizing the universal theme of love of homeland	Art, Music, and Drama: The importance of nationalistic arts movements History: African colonialism and freedom movements Social Studies: Preservation of national culture
Making predictions about the meanings of words; using context clues	Speaking: discussing one theme of the story; evaluating the effects of segregation	Analyzing the effects of apartheid; developing an awareness of cultural conflict within the black South African community	Family Life: Parent-child and sibling relationships; self-esteem Social Studies: The role of domestic labor in class distinctions History: Apartheid; freedom movements

	Reading Level	Literary Skills	Critical Thinking Skills
"A Chip of Glass Ruby" SE p. 43–54 TRM pp. 23–25	Average	Analyzing the use of internal and external conflict in a story; interpreting symbolism in the context of a story's conflicts	Drawing conclusions and making inferences about a story's characters; evaluating the relevance of cultural details to a story's conflicts; synthesizing: applying the theme of political activism to views of political activities in one's own community
"Marriage Is a Private Affair" SE pp. 55–62 TRM pp. 26–28	Easy	Identifying internal and external conflict in a story; recognizing the tone of a story; identifying resolution of conflict	Analyzing how an author's attitude is revealed; making connections between cultural details and a story's conflicts; applying a character's problems to a personal situation
"The Dark Child" SE pp. 63–71 TRM pp. 29–31	Average	Analyzing the purposes of dialogue in a story; making connections between dialogue and plot and between dialogue and conflict	Identifying story details that suggest conflict; making connections between dialogue and cultural views about family life; relating dialogue to personal experience
"The Chair Carrier" SE pp. 72–78 TRM pp. 32–34	Challenging	Analyzing a story's setting (time); identifying irony in a story; evaluating the ending of a story	Analyzing story details that lead to an ironic ending; analyzing and evaluating a narrator's changing feelings; drawing conclusions about culture from story details; applying story details to one's own experiences
Chapter 2: Middle East SE pp. 79 TRM pp. 35–37		Exploring the history of Middle Eastern Literature	Analyzing the impact of African culture on the Middle East
"The Marks of the Wise Man, of the Half Wise, and of the Fool" SE pp. 80–82 TRM pp. 38–40	Challenging	Recognizing elements of didactic literature; analyzing the moral of didactic literature	Analyzing poetic details that relate to the theme of wisdom; drawing conclusions about cultural values; applying a poetic message to one's own life
"The House on the Border" SE pp. 83–91 TRM pp. 41–43	Easy	Recognizing elements of satire in a story; analyzing the ways in which an author uses satire	Selecting story details that suggest an author's attitude; making connections between a political setting and a character's emotions; applying story details to one's own experience

Vocabulary Skills	Communication Skills	Global Diversity Skills	Cross-Curricular Skills
Categorizing words that reflect the character's attitudes toward political activism; identifying words as positive or negative according to connotation	Writing a character sketch: analyzing a character's actions; making inferences about a character based on the reactions of others	Analyzing the effects of religious beliefs; analyzing the effects of apartheid	History: Apartheid and the freedom movements in South Africa Social Studies: Daily life in a racist society; the nature of political protest; Indian cultural distinctions
Scanning for words relating to marriage; using context clues	Writing a descriptive essay: analyzing a character's feelings and behaviors; evaluating a character's actions	Developing an awareness of cross-cultural marriage; analyzing the effects of cross-cultural marriage	Family Life: Parent-child relationships; husband-wife relationships; the role of grandparents in African culture Social Studies: Cultural groups in Nigeria
Locating definitions in footnotes; making predictions about a story's plot and setting from vocabulary clues; using context clues	Writing a paper of comparison and contrast: evaluating tone; supporting opinions with examples from the text	Recognizing cross-cultural emotions; analyzing African customs and family traditions	Family Life: Parent-child relationships; family traditions History: French colonialism in Africa Social Studies: The changes in education over time
Scanning for unfamiliar words; using context clues	Writing an expository essay: drawing conclusions from a story's details; developing an interpretation about an unknown detail in a story; supporting an interpretation with details from the story	Analyzing the nature of duty as a literary theme; analyzing the clash between ancient and modern traditions in Egypt	History: Ancient Egypt; modern Egypt; Egyptian peasantry Social Studies: Life in a large, modern city; employer-employee relationships; the continuing influence of one's historical heritage
	Discussing poetic similarities between Arabs and Israelis	Recognizing similarities between everyday events in all cultures	Social Studies: Analyzing the impact of political and religious conflict on the region
Scanning for words relating to wisdom and foolishness; classifying words as suggesting wisdom or suggesting foolishness	Writing a paper of contrast: analyzing information about different time periods	Comparing and contrasting ideas within the Muslim culture; analyzing the Islamic concept of wisdom	Government: The nature of leadership History: The rise of Sufism Social Studies: Islamic mysticism
Scanning for words relating to a story's theme; using context clues	Writing a "Dear Abby" letter: analyzing the central conflict of a story; constructing a response	Becoming aware of the blended themes of absurdity, injustice, and resignation in Islamic literature; making connections between story details and the political situation in Turkey	Government: Bureaucracy Geography: Maps and boundary lines Social Studies: Urban apartment life; crime and the justice system

	Reading Level	Literary Skills	Critical Thinking Skills
"4 + 1 = 1" SE pp. 94–99 TRM pp. 45–47	Challenging	Selecting details that illustrate various purposes of dialogue; identifying external and internal dialogue	Analyzing a main character; making connections between story details and the society in which the story is set; comparing and contrasting dialogue in stories; applying a story situation to a personal situation
"A Lover from Palestine" **"Warmth of Blood"** SE pp. 100–103 TRM pp. 48–50	Challenging	Identifying similes and metaphors in a poem; making connections between figurative language and poetic main ideas; synthesizing: suggesting alternative similes and metaphors to express an idea	Analyzing how poetic details suggest an author's emotions; making connections between poetic details and a political setting; evaluating poetic comparisons; applying poetic details to one's own experiences
"In This Valley" **"Once a Great Love"** **"Late in Life"** SE pp. 104–107 TRM pp. 51–53	Average	Analyzing hyperbole in poems; making connections between hyperbole and an author's emotions; evaluating hyperbole	Analyzing main ideas in poems; analyzing poetic details that reveal autobiographical information; comparing and contrasting love lyrics
"You Can't Fool Menashe" SE pp. 108–112 TRM pp. 54–56	Average	Analyzing characterization in a story; comparing and contrasting characters; evaluating the effectiveness of characterization	Drawing conclusions about characters; identifying story details that suggest satire; applying a theme to one's own experience
UNIT 2: **ASIA,** **AUSTRALIA,** **AND THE** **PACIFIC** **ISLANDS** SE pp. 114–117 TRM pp. 59–60		Evaluating primary sources in history	Comparing historical events across world regions as displayed on a timeline
Chapter 3: **East Asia** SE p. 118 TRM pp. 61–63		Exploring the history of East Asian Literature	Contrasting the values expressed in ancient stories to those in modern stories

Vocabulary Skills	Communication Skills	Global Diversity Skills	Cross-Curricular Skills
Defining words in context; comparing contextual definitions with dictionary definitions	Speaking: predicting new outcomes; evaluating solutions	Analyzing changes in Arabic literature; making inferences about cultural values; contrasting Arabic and American values	History: Modern Kuwait Social Studies: Employer-employee relationships; workplace relationships and ethics; factory labor
Scanning for unfamiliar words; using context clues	Writing from a different point of view: making inferences about a character's behavior, actions, and words; composing similes or metaphors	Analyzing the feelings of Arab people toward their homeland; developing an appreciation for an Arab desire for unity; analyzing the changes that have occurred in Arabic literature	Art, Music, and Drama: Love songs History: Palestine; Arab-Israeli conflicts Social Studies: Imprisonment and the justice system; freedom and love of homeland as ideals; political displacement; the Palestinian self-image
Defining unfamiliar words in context	Writing a response paper: examining a topic from a different point of view; comparing and contrasting	Developing an awareness of the chronicle of Jewish culture contained in modern Israeli poetry; appreciating imagery drawn from Jewish life and tradition	Geography: Geographical features of Palestine History: Palestine; Arab-Israeli conflicts
Categorizing words; using context clues	Writing a dialogue: satirizing an aspect of society; developing characters	Appreciating the power of Israeli humor to triumph over adversity; becoming aware of the universality of concern over status	Social Studies: Life in Israel today; standards of success
	Understanding the cultural foundations of literature	Analyzing the cultural impact of historical events on literature	Geography: Using a map to identify sources of literature
	Discussing literature as a form of protest	Exploring the importance of poetry in East Asia	Art: Examining the connections between art and literature

	Reading Level	Literary Skills	Critical Thinking Skills
"A Book of Five Rings" SE pp. 119–123 TRM pp. 64–66	Challenging	Analyzing didactic literature	Selecting details that suggest an author's attitude; applying traditional literature to modern situations; synthesizing: responding to didactic principles; applying key ideas to one's own life
"Till the Candle Blew Out" SE pp. 124–131 TRM pp. 67–69	Average	Analyzing character motivation in a story; interpreting symbols; identifying the effect of setting	Selecting story details that suggest an author's attitude; making connections between story details and cultural values; applying a character's conflict to a personal situation; evaluating the theme of a story
"The Ch'i-Lin Purse" SE pp. 132–139 TRM pp. 70–72	Easy	Analyzing the moral of a story	Drawing conclusions about an author's motivation; making connections between a tradition and cultural values in a story; applying a character's situation to a personal situation; evaluating the lesson of a story
"Hearing of the Earthquake in Kyoto (1830)" SE pp. 140–142 TRM pp. 73–75	Challenging	Analyzing point of view in a poem; speculating about changes in a poem resulting from a change in point of view	Drawing conclusions about an author's motivation; evaluating the modern relevance of a poem; applying a character's situation to a personal situation; synthesizing: describing one's own emotional reaction to a poem
"A Call to Action" "To the Tune 'The River Is Red'" SE pp. 143–146 TRM pp. 76–78	Average	Analyzing an author's purpose; analyzing comparisons in poems; analyzing persuasive devices	Speculating about choice of poetry as a vehicle for a political message; drawing conclusions about social issues from poetic details; applying the theme of political causes to personal views of activism; discussing a memorable poetic phrase or line

Vocabulary Skills	Communication Skills	Global Diversity Skills	Cross-Curricular Skills
Scanning for words relating to weapons and battle; using context clues	Listing and discussing ways to give advice	Analyzing an author's attitudes toward key aspects of his historical setting and culture; comparing and contrasting traditional American and Japanese cultural values	History: Japan during the shogunate Social Studies: Military strategy; business practices in modern Japan
Scanning for words that suggest setting; classifying words; making connections between vocabulary and themes	Discussing the nature of friendship; discussing the importance of names; comparing and contrasting characters	Analyzing the way of life in a Korean village; exploring the feelings of Koreans toward their homeland	Social Studies: Evaluating social and economic conditions; comparing Korean social structures past and present; village life in Korea; the importance of names; class distinctions; folk medicine; methods of farming rice Geography: Geographical features of Korea
Scanning for words that suggest setting; using context clues	Discussing weddings; discussing gifts as a reflection of cultural values; writing a response to a homily or a personal philosophy	Analyzing the traditional Chinese attitude toward male and female children; analyzing other Chinese customs	Art, Music, and Drama: Chinese opera; the dragon as an artistic symbol Family Life: Parent-child relationships; husband-wife relationships History: China during the Sung dynasty Social Studies: Matchmaking; Chinese wedding traditions; class distinctions
Scanning for words that suggest devastation; using context clues	Listing and discussing the value of personal possessions; discussing the results of a natural disaster; writing about emotional impact of another's grief/tragedy	Analyzing the repercussions of the Kyoto earthquake of 1830; analyzing the Japanese response to a tragedy	Environmental Science: Earthquakes Family Life: Husband-wife relationships History: The Kyoto earthquake of 1830 Social Studies: The effects of natural catastrophe upon a society
Scanning for words relating to comparisons; making connections between vocabulary and poetic themes	Discussing a quotation; discussing traditional and nontraditional roles of women	Analyzing the role of Chinese women during the Qing (Manchu) dynasty; becoming aware of the tradition of the self-sacrificing hero in Chinese culture	Government: Life under a repressive government; the need for governmental reform History: The Qing (Manchu) dynasty of China; the republican movement in China Social Studies: The role of women in society; the nature of political protest Speech: Propaganda

	Reading Level	Literary Skills	Critical Thinking Skills
"No Way Out" SE pp.147–157 TRM pp. 79–81	Average	Recognizing elements of autobiography in a selection; classifying autobiographical details as fact or opinion	Analyzing an author's purpose; drawing conclusions about political issues from autobiographical details; discussing a memorable moment or idea; preparing questions to interview a civil rights activist
"He-y, Come on Ou-t!" SE pp. 158–163 TRM pp. 82–84	Average	Analyzing the surprise ending of a story; interpreting a title; identifying foreshadowing	Drawing conclusions about an author's attitude; making connections between story details and social issues; evaluating how choices made today can affect the future; evaluating the ending of a story
Chapter 4: South and Southeast Asia SE p. 164 TRM pp. 85–87		Exploring the history of South and Southeast Asian Literature	Analyzing the impact of social conditions on literature
"Savitri" SE pp. 165–170 TRM pp. 88–90	Average	Analyzing the theme of a myth; explaining connections between characters, plot, and theme; testing for inferences of theme	Analyzing character reactions and theme; explaining connections between mythic details and religious beliefs; evaluating character traits
"This World Lives Because" "Children" "Tirumāl" SE pp. 171–175 TRM pp. 91–93	Average	Analyzing symbols in a poem: relating symbols to emotions	Selecting poetic details that suggest an author's attitude; deducing generalizations about a cultural group; applying poetic details to one's own experience
"The Tiger" SE pp. 178–184 TRM pp. 95–97	Easy	Analyzing suspense in a story; evaluating the effectiveness of suspense	Identifying story details that create an atmosphere of fantasy; relating story details to environmental issues; evaluating the two sides of a debate

Vocabulary Skills	Communication Skills	Global Diversity Skills	Cross-Curricular Skills
Scanning for words relating to conflict; classifying words as positive or negative; making connections between vocabulary and characterization	Writing a position statement or a letter to a public official: discussing a quotation; discussing the concept of free speech	Analyzing the effect of political repression upon relationships among the Chinese people; analyzing an author's perspective on cultural change	Government: Communism; the need for governmental reform History: China during the Mao Zedong era Social Studies: Political dissidence; free speech; civil rights; crime and the justice system; Chinese industry and agriculture during the Great Leap Forward
Scanning for synonyms for a key word; making connections between vocabulary and themes	Discussing a hypothetical situation	Becoming aware that people's quick solutions to difficult problems can have adverse consequences; analyzing the effects of post-nuclear devastation as a global problem	Environmental Science: Environmental preservation; disposal of toxins Government: Corruption in town government; government permits and contracts History: Japan after World War II Social Studies: The nature of an industrial society
	Discussing the importance of homeland in other cultures	Recognizing a wide array of cultures within a region	Art: Examining the connections between art and culture
Creating a list of words relating to Hinduism; classifying	Writing a collaborative response: comparing a story character with a fictional heroine	Explaining the Aryan influence on the Vedic Age in India; discussing Hinduism's teachings and place among world religions	Family Life: Husband-wife relationships; arranged marriages History: The Vedic Age of India Social Studies: Hinduism; the nature of charity work
Scanning for words that suggest goodness and positive values; explaining connections between vocabulary and poetic themes	Writing a poem: expressing a theme	Relating the use of poetry to keeping cultural traditions alive; comparing and contrasting Indian and American cultural values	Family Life: Parent-child relationships Social Studies: The nature of honor; cultural values and traditions
Scanning for environmental terms and words that suggest local color; using context clues	Creating thumbnail sketches: describing characters to create portraits	Developing an awareness of the delicate balance between Malaysian society and nature; comparing social and economic conditions in Malaysia and Singapore	Environmental Science: Endangered species; habitat destruction; the relationship between humans and nature Geography: Geographical features of Malaysia Social Studies: Village life in Malaysia

	Reading Level	Literary Skills	Critical Thinking Skills
"Forty-Five a Month" SE pp. 185–191 TRM pp. 98–100	Average	Identifying elements of plot (central conflict, story events, climax, resolution) in a story; analyzing author's attitude toward characters	Explaining how story details create a sympathetic picture; inferring connections between cultural details and story conflicts; explaining personal reactions to a given situation
"When Heaven and Earth Changed Places" SE pp.192–196 TRM pp. 101–103	Average	Describing setting in an autobiography; explaining connections between setting and character motivation	Analyzing an author's attitude and purpose; selecting autobiographical details that reveal customs; comparing a cultural group and its traditions to one's own
Chapter 5: **Australia and the** **Pacific Islands** SE p. 197 TRM pp. 104–106		Exploring the history of the literature of Australia and the Pacific Islands	Interpreting the influence of Europeans on the native people of a region
"Tangaroa, Maker of All Things" SE pp. 198–201 TRM pp. 107–109	Average	Contrasting literal and figurative language; identifying figures of speech; examining the use of metaphor in a myth; explaining connections between metaphors and images	Selecting story details that suggest a setting; explaining connections between mythic details and cultural ideas; comparing and contrasting creation myths
"Maui and the Great Fish" SE pp. 204–207 TRM pp. 111–113	Easy	Describing traditional storytelling techniques; analyzing the use of repetition in a story	Evaluating the purpose of storytelling; selecting story details that explain societal origins; applying a story situation to one's own experience
"Family Council" SE pp. 208–211 TRM pp. 114–116	Easy	Selecting elements of a personal narrative; identifying the narrator in a personal narrative; analyzing an author's purpose; examining the use of suspense to create conflict	Selecting story details that suggest cultural traditions and values; analyzing cultural views about resolving conflict; comparing and contrasting the ways two different cultures may resolve conflict

Vocabulary Skills	Communication Skills	Global Diversity Skills	Cross-Curricular Skills
Scanning for adjectives and adverbs that describe characters and action; using context clues	Writing a response: defending or refuting points made in Rao's resignation letter	Comparing and contrasting parent-child relationships in India and the United States; analyzing the conflict between cultural traditions and the need to meet the demands of the modern world	Family Life: Parent-child relationships Social Studies: The nature of education; employer-employee relationships; middle-class families in India
Classifying words as legends, foods, or customs; using context clues	Writing a response: explaining the design and purpose of including the "rice ball" legend in the narrative	Exploring the customs of village life in Vietnam; evaluating the Vietnamese peasants' feelings toward their land	Government: Life under a repressive government History: The Vietnam Conflict Social Studies: Village life in Vietnam; class distinctions; Vietnamese religious traditions; the concept of karma; methods of farming rice
	Comparing traditional story-telling to modern literature	Recognizing the differences and similarities between the values of different cultures	Art: Examining the connections between art and literature
Discussing words relating to topics and images in myths; using the dictionary to find literal meanings	Developing a statement: working with a partner to describe a target audience and the message to them	Analyzing traditional themes and characters in Polynesian mythology; identifying common elements in variations of myths from island to island	Environmental Science: Essential elements of an ecosystem; the relationship between humans and nature Geography: Location and composition of the Polynesian Islands Social Studies: Polynesian culture
Scanning for words relating to the ocean and fishing; discussing parts of speech	Writing a story: Composing a magical story about the creation of a town, state, or country	Exploring Maori creation myths; comparing and contrasting trickster figures from various cultures	Environmental Science: The relationship between humans and nature Family Life: Sibling relationships Social Studies: Maori culture; the importance of fishing to a society
Creating a web of words that suggest conflict and resolution; using context clues	Writing a response: recounting a personal situation where a family conflict was resolved	Analyzing Koori traditions concerning family relationships and nature; drawing conclusions about how a story preserves cultural traditions	Environmental Science: The relationship between humans and nature Family Life: Traditions within a family; family problem-solving; sibling relationships Social Studies: Aborigine culture; the importance of hunting to a society

	Reading Level	Literary Skills	Critical Thinking Skills
"Butterflies" SE pp. 212–214 TRM pp. 117–119	Average	Analyzing the author's attitude toward family life and values; describing the setting in a story; evaluating setting to understand a story's point	Selecting story details that create a sense of reality; analyzing cultural views about familial love; evaluating qualities of characters; relating story images to real life
UNIT 3: EASTERN AND WESTERN EUROPE SE pp. 216–219 TRM pp. 122–123		Evaluating primary sources in history	Comparing historical events across world regions as displayed on a timeline
Chapter 6: Eastern Europe SE p. 220 TRM pp. 124–126		Exploring the literary history of Eastern Europe	Examining the development of literary devices to avoid censorship
"The Servant" SE pp. 221–228 TRM pp. 127–129	Average	Identifying the historical context of a story; analyzing character motivation	Selecting story details that suggest an author's attitude; making connections between story details and historical information; applying a story situation to a personal situation
"If Not Still Higher" SE pp. 229–233 TRM pp. 130–132	Easy	Analyzing the characteristics of an author's style; comparing and contrasting character personalities	Selecting details that suggest an author's attitude; drawing conclusions about religious beliefs from story details; applying a story situation to a personal situation
"And When Summer Comes to an End" "Please Give This Seat to an Elderly or Disabled Person" SE pp. 234–236 TRM pp. 133–135	Challenging	Identifying elements of free verse; evaluating the effect of free verse elements on a poem's meaning	Inferring connections between poetic details and an author's biographical, cultural, and historical background; applying a poetic situation to a personal situation
"Random Talk" "The Heirs of Stalin" "Refugees" SE pp. 237–243 TRM pp. 136–138	Average	Identifying an author's purpose in a poem; evaluating authors' methods of achieving their purposes	Selecting story details that suggest an author's attitude toward homeland; relating an author's cultural background to a poem's content; applying a character's conflict to a personal situation

Vocabulary Skills	Communication Skills	Global Diversity Skills	Cross-Curricular Skills
Classifying words into *urban* and *rural* groups; using context clues	Writing an article: describing the New Zealand landscape and atmosphere	Analyzing Maori folk wisdom; comparing and contrasting Maori values with those of other cultures	Environmental Science: The relationship between humans and nature Family Life: Parent-child and grandparent-grandchild relationships Social Studies: Examining the assimilation of the Maori into British culture
	Understanding the cultural foundations of literature	Analyzing the cultural impact of historical events on literature	Geography: Using a map to identify sources of literature
	Analyzing the impact of censorship on literature	Understanding the impact of political systems on literature	Art: Examining the connections between art and literature
Scanning for words relating to poverty; using context clues	Writing a response: describing a personal "want"	Evaluating the relationship between servants and masters in Russia in the 1920s and 1930s	History: Post-revolutionary Russia Social Studies: Class distinctions; treatment of the elderly Speech: The power of persuasion
Comparing words that describe the differences between two characters; using context clues	Writing a response: relating the story to personal experiences	Identifying Hasidic cultural values; comparing and contrasting traditional Jewish folktales to present-day concepts of compassion	Government: The power of a rabbi in a traditional Jewish community Social Studies: *Shtetl* life in Poland; ethnic prejudices; the nature of charity work
Relating word phases to the author's message; using context clues	Writing a summary: describing author's viewpoint and message; collaborating to combine ideas	Analyzing the feelings of alienation and loss among Soviet writers; identifying words that reflect a writer's culture and experiences	Government: Communism; life under a repressive government History: The Soviet Union during the Stalin era Social Studies: The role of the artist in society
Scanning for terms relating to funerals and to warfare; making connections between vocabulary and poetic themes	Interviewing the authors: discussing the authors opinions of world leaders, war, and ultimate peace	Identifying one's ties to cultural roots during wartime; speculating about a world without war	Government: Communism History: Nazi concentration camps; the Soviet Union during the Stalin era and beyond; the reform movement in Russia Social Studies: political dissidence

	Reading Level	Literary Skills	Critical Thinking Skills
"The Bicycle" SE pp. 246–248 TRM pp. 140–142	Easy	Classifying poetic details as fantastic or realistic; drawing conclusions about an author's intent	Qualifying poetic details as suggesting an author's attitude or revealing setting; speculating about objects coming to life
"The Monster" SE pp. 249–257 TRM pp. 143–145	Average	Analyzing comparisons in an essay; analyzing mood and its overall effect	Selecting story details that suggest an author's attitude; explaining making connections between cultural details and story details; evaluating the personal effects of group opinions and peer pressure
"A Winter's Tale" SE pp. 258–262 TRM pp. 146–148	Average	Analyzing an author's purpose in creating an oath; recognizing the message of an oath	Selecting essay details that suggest an author's attitude toward war and her homeland; reflecting on a personal conflict and how it was resolved
Chapter 7: **Western Europe** SE p. 263 TRM pp. 149–151		Exploring the history of Western European literature	Evaluating the importance of Greek and Roman values on contemporary society
"The Oath **of Athenian Youth"** SE pp. 264–266 TRM pp. 152–154	Easy		Identifying details that reveal the author's purpose; drawing conclusions about societal values from an oath; applying an oath to present-day situations
"The Nightingale's **Three Bits of Advice"** SE pp. 267–270 TRM pp. 155–157	Average	Identifying narrative sequence in a folktale; analyzing the moral of a folktale	Drawing conclusions about the main idea; analyzing characterization; applying a moral or message to a personal situation
"Paying on the Nail" SE pp. 271–274 TRM pp. 158–160	Challenging	Identifying elements of a trickster folktale; analyzing the author's attitude toward honesty	Analyzing characterization; drawing conclusions about Irish culture from story details; analyzing the message of a folktale; evaluating a character's actions
"Death Seed" **"Woman, you are afraid"** **"My Mother's House"** SE pp. 275–278 TRM pp. 161–163	Challenging	Analyzing imagery in poems; recognizing conflict in poetry	Selecting poetic details that suggest emotion; recognizing elements of autobiography in a poem; applying the theme of a poem to one's own life
"Survival in Auschwitz" SE pp. 279–286 TRM pp. 164–166	Average	Analyzing elements of a personal narrative; recognizing conflict	Speculating about an author's purpose; selecting narrative details that reveal historical information; applying a character's conflict to a personal situation

Vocabulary Skills	Communication Skills	Global Diversity Skills	Cross-Curricular Skills
Classifying terms relating to realism and fantasy; relating vocabulary to character relationships; using context clues	Writing a short poem: recounting a personal adventure using imagery	Explaining the significance of poetry in Polish rural life; discussing how poetry reflects the Polish landscape	Environmental Science: Mountain goats and their habitat Geography: The Carpathian Mountains
Scanning for terms relating to and describing monsters; using context clues	Presenting personal feelings: working in a group to discuss emotions brought out by the story	Recognizing hardships that nations experience as a result of change; analyzing the feelings of loss and confusion that can result from change	History: The collapse of communism in the Soviet Union Social Studies: Urban apartment life
Scanning for nouns relating to warfare; creating webs to relate words	Writing a position paper: assessing media coverage of war; debating opposing points of view	Exploring the lives of ordinary Bosnians during a time of war; analyzing the cultural repercussions of an extended war	History: The civil war in the Balkans Social Studies: The effects of civil war upon daily life; characteristics that unify a cultural group; ethnic prejudices
	Identifying different voices as they appear in literature	Recognizing the impact of Western European values on America	Art: Examining the connection between art and literature
Scanning for words that suggest actions; using context clues	Writing an oath: composing a statement that reflects personal beliefs and cultural values	Evaluating an oath in its cultural context; comparing and contrasting "The Pledge of Allegiance" with "The Oath of Athenian Youth"	Government: The nature of democracy and of civic duty History: The structure of ancient Greek city-states
Scanning for vivid words that create clear mental images; classifying words according to their part of speech	Writing a folktale: creating a folktale with a particular moral	Identifying important values in French culture; comparing the moral of a French folktale to those of other cultures; recognizing universal themes in French folktales	Environmental Science: The relationship between humans and nature
Scanning for words that describe a character; using context clues	Summarizing ideas	Analyzing the role of folktales in Irish culture; evaluating the function of the marketplace in Irish trading	Social Studies: Village life in Ireland
Using context clues	Writing a summary of a poem: analyzing conflict and describing how imagery reveals mood and tone	Exploring the possibility of a female voice in poetry; developing awareness of cross-cultural, universal themes in women's poetry	Social Studies: Self-awareness and awareness of one's ancestry
Scanning for words relating to pain and fear; creating a word web	Expressing personal impressions and reactions to a literary piece and a historical event	Analyzing cultural biases that led to the Holocaust; understanding Hitler's influence in Europe during the 1930s and 1940s	Government: Fascism and dictatorships History: The Holocaust; the Nazi Party Social Studies: Ethnic prejudices; the concept of "ethnic purity"

	Reading Level	Literary Skills	Critical Thinking Skills
"Action Will Be Taken" SE pp. 287–293 TRM pp. 167–169	Average	Analyzing irony in a story; drawing conclusions about the author's attitude	Drawing conclusions about an author's attitude; explaining connections between story details and autobiographical information; applying a story situation to evaluating humor in a story
"The Return" SE pp. 296–302 TRM pp. 171–173	Average	Identifying examples of foreshadowing in a story; understanding how foreshadowing creates suspense	Selecting story details that relate to the theme of fear; explaining the relationship between economic realities and personal fears; applying a situation in a story to one's own life
UNIT 4: THE AMERICAS SE pp. 304–307 TRM pp. 176–177		Evaluating primary sources in history	Comparing historical events across world regions as displayed on a timeline
Chapter 8: Latin America SE p. 308 TRM pp. 178–180		Exploring the history of Latin American literature	Examining connections between art and culture
"Popol Vuh" SE pp. 309–311 TRM pp. 181–183	Easy	Analyzing the purpose of myths; recognizing elements of a myth	Selecting story details; analyzing cultural views about poverty; analyzing the theme of kindness; synthesizing: creating a personal statement about kindness
"The Great Prayer" SE pp. 312–314 TRM pp.184–186	Challenging	Recognizing concrete and abstract imagery in a poem; understanding metaphysical poetry	Comparing and contrasting an author's view of life to one's own; evaluating an author's advice; synthesizing: expressing a personal philosophy about life
"Bouki Rents a Horse" SE pp. 315–318 TRM pp. 187–189	Easy	Analyzing characterization in a folktale; identifying elements of trickster tales	Making generalizations about a folktale's audience; analyzing cultural views about families and class distinctions; evaluating the resolution to a story's central conflict
"The Street" "The Room" SE pp. 319–321 TRM pp. 190–192	Average	Recognizing mood in a poem; analyzing the way language conveys mood	Summarizing the emotional effect of a poem; making connections between an author's cultural background and a poem's content; evaluating a poem's emotional power
"Keeping Quiet" "Chilean Earth" SE pp. 322–326 TRM pp. 193–195	Average	Recognizing elements of lyric poetry; comparing and contrasting dominant emotions in poems	Analyzing an author's presence in a poem; drawing conclusions about an author's view of life; evaluating the practicality of an author's advice

Vocabulary Skills	Communication Skills	Global Diversity Skills	Cross-Curricular Skills
Scanning for words relating to feelings about employment; using context clues	Creating a comic strip: high-lighting main ideas in words and pictures	Comparing and contrasting individual and social morality in post-World War II Germany; understanding the economic repercussions of World War II on German culture	History: Conditions in Germany after World War II Social Studies: Attitudes about employment; workplace relationships and ethics; factory labor
Scanning for words relating to the term *asylum;* making connections between vocabulary and narrative themes	Writing journal entries from a character's point of view: imagining different scenarios from someone else's perspective	Understanding the role of Catholicism in Spanish culture; explaining connections between the destructiveness of war and the weakening of the human spirit	Social Studies: The importance of Roman Catholicism in Spanish life
	Understanding the cultural foundations of literature	Analyzing the cultural impact of historical events on literature	Geography: Using a map to identify sources of literature
	Identifying personal concerns as they appear in literature	Recognizing the value of ancient cultures	Economics: Examining the impact of economics and politics on literature
Scanning for words relating to building materials; classifying words as positive or negative	Writing a scene to extend the myth: creating dialogue for each character	Recognizing shared elements in creation myths from around the world; making connections between Mayan mythology and Mayan culture	History: The rise of the Maya in Latin America Social Studies: Mayan culture; class distinctions; the importance of kindness and charity toward the poor
Scanning for words that are subjects of poetic images; using context clues	Writing a message about the meaning of life: expressing a view of life from one's own or someone else's perspective	Understanding the universality of prayer	Social Studies: The role of prayer in one's life
Scanning for words that suggest cultural setting; recognizing word origins	Writing a dialogue: extending a folktale	Analyzing the blend of African and Caribbean influences in Haitian folklore; developing an awareness of the universality of the trickster in folklore	Family Life: Extended family relationships Social Studies: Village life in Haiti; class distinctions; the importance of the marketplace
Making connections between vocabulary and characterization; using context clues	Writing a screenplay: creating a suspenseful plot	Analyzing pre-Columbian influences on Mexican culture; analyzing the individual's search for identity in a changing world	Environmental Science: Links between humans and animals Social Studies: Paranoia as a psychological state
Scanning for words with literal and figurative meanings; classifying words as literal or figurative	Writing a paragraph that discusses plans for making the world a better place	Analyzing how political, social, and geographic realities affect a poet's work	Environmental Science: Ecological exploitation; the relationship between humanity and nature; the beauty of growing things Social Studies: Pacifism; the pace of modern life

	Reading Level	Literary Skills	Critical Thinking Skills
"Florinda and Don Gonzalo" SE pp. 327–334 TRM pp. 196–198	Average	Identifying elements of drama; analyzing the purposes of dialogue in a play; identifying climax and resolution in a play	Analyzing the experimental characteristics of a play; selecting dramatic details that define character; speculating about the outcome of a dramatic situation; applying a dramatic situation to a personal situation
"One of These Days" SE pp. 335–339 TRM pp. 199–201	Challenging	Analyzing suspense in a story; examining techniques for character development	Selecting story details that suggest a setting; explaining connections between story details and historical information; evaluating the actions of a character
"The Book of Sand" SE pp. 342–348 TRM pp. 203–205	Challenging	Analyzing symbols in a story; evaluating the effectiveness of symbols; synthesizing: creating personal symbols	Selecting story details that suggest an author's love for literature; analyzing ways in which cultural views might be upset by a story element; evaluating the resolution of a story's central problem
"Continuity of Parks" SE pp. 349–352 TRM pp. 206–208	Challenging	Analyzing sensory details in a story; evaluating the effectiveness of sensory details	Examining connections between story details and the nature of the reading experience; identifying connections between the plot of a story and the theme of liberation; evaluating the effectiveness of a mix of fantasy and reality
"Homecoming" "The Child's Return" "Jamaica Market" "On Leaving" "Zion, Me Wan Go Home" SE pp. 353–360 TRM pp. 209–211	Average	Analyzing standard meters in a poem; comparing and contrasting use of rhythm in poems; synthesizing: creating a rhythm to express original ideas	Analyzing main ideas in poems; comparing and contrasting poetic ideas; evaluating the appeal of a poem
Chapter 9: Canada SE p. 361 TRM pp. 212–214		Exploring the history of Canadian literature	Examining the connections between art and literature
"The Old Man's Lazy" SE pp. 362–365 TRM pp. 215–217	Average	Analyzing elements of dramatic monologue in a poem; identifying the ways character is revealed in a dramatic monologue	Explaining connections between poetic images and main ideas; drawing conclusions about cultural and political issues from poetic details; synthesizing: defending an opinion

Vocabulary Skills	Communication Skills	Global Diversity Skills	Cross-Curricular Skills
Matching words to definitions; making predictions based on vocabulary	Writing a letter: offering congratulations and advice on relationship building	Exploring cultural issues in modern Latin American drama; analyzing changing roles in Latin American society	Art, Music, and Drama: Experimental theater Family Life: Extended-family relationships Social Studies: Traditional roles of men and women
Categorizing words as they apply to characters; explaining connections between vocabulary and conflict	Writing a summary: explaining why readers identify with a character; collaborating with a partner	Analyzing the influence of culture on an author's works; explaining rural social structure in Colombian culture	Government: The power of a corrupt mayor Social Studies: Village life in Colombia; the nature of power; violence and pain as ways of enforcing control; class distinctions
Scanning for words relating to the Bible, books, and geography; using context clues	Writing an interview: developing questions to ask the author; role-playing an interview	Analyzing cultural influences on an author; examining the nature of reality as suggested by an author	Social Studies: The tradition of mystery associated with India
Scanning for words that suggest an atmosphere of suspense or fear; making predictions based upon vocabulary	Writing a new ending: extending the story to add a new surprise	Analyzing Argentinean exiles' support of individual rights throughout South America; examining the cultural basis for literary experimentation in South America	Art, Music, and Drama: Experimental fiction History: Analyzing political repression in Argentina from 1940 to 1970
Scanning for words that suggest sensory images; identifying connections between vocabulary and poetic themes	Writing a response: describing a place in the Caribbean and reasons to visit there	Examining European and African influences on Caribbean culture; analyzing the blending of many traditions to create a Caribbean identity	History: European influences on the Caribbean Social Studies: The variety of Caribbean cultures; nationalism; the continuing influence of an African ancestry
	Identifying the distinct literary voice of Canadian literature	Recognizing the value of native Canadian cultures	Science: Conceptualizing primitive printing methods
Defining words in context; making predictions based on vocabulary	Writing a story: generating ideas from a different point of view; developing a moral	Developing an awareness of the conflict between the traditional ways of native Canadian peoples and modern customs; analyzing Indian beliefs concerning the land and property rights	Environmental Science: The relationship between people and nature Family Life: Parent-child relationships; the influence of grandparents History: The role of Indian Agents in Canadian Indian history; the role of Indians in Canada today Social Studies: Ethnic prejudices

	Reading Level	Literary Skills	Critical Thinking Skills
"All the Years of Her Life" SE pp. 366–373 TRM pp. 218–220	Average	Distinguishing between round and flat characters in a story; analyzing characterization	Drawing conclusions about main ideas in a story; analyzing cultural values in a story
"Little by Little" SE pp. 376–383 TRM pp. 222–224	Average	Recognizing elements of an autobiography; evaluating the reliability of a narrator; speculating about the changes resulting from a shift in narrator	Selecting story details that suggest point of view; explaining connections between story details and cultural setting; applying text to personal experiences
"A Night in the Royal Ontario Museum" SE pp. 384–387 TRM pp. 225–227	Challenging	Analyzing the relationship between theme and symbols in poetry; identifying onomatopoeia, alliteration, and assonance in a poem	Drawing conclusions about a poetic main idea; making generalizations about a poem's audience; applying poetic details to one's own experience
"My Financial Career" SE pp. 388–392 TRM pp. 228–230	Average	Analyzing elements of humor in an essay	Selecting essay details that create a sympathetic picture; evaluating an author's viewpoint; drawing conclusions about the nature of humor

Vocabulary Skills	Communication Skills	Global Diversity Skills	Cross-Curricular Skills
Scanning for words relating to traits describing the story's characters; making connections between vocabulary and characterization	Writing a summary: analyzing a story's ending	Analyzing the cultural links between the literatures of Canada and the United States; recognizing universal elements in family relationships	Family Life: Parent-child relationships History: Canada during the Great Depression Social Studies: Life during times of economic difficulty
Scanning for words relating to medicine; using context clues	Writing a descriptive paper: analyzing and applying persuasive language	Developing an awareness of the effects of age and distance upon one's perceptions of other people and events; analyzing changing attitudes toward the disabled	Family Life: Sibling relationships; parent-child relationships Social Studies: Treatment of the disabled; the educational system of Canada
Scanning for words relating to art and death; making connections between vocabulary and poetic symbolism	Writing an essay: Discussing how the author relates images to a woman's changing role in society	Examining the diverse nature of Canadian culture; analyzing of the search for an independent Canadian literary identity	History: Symbols of world history Social Studies: The importance of preserving the past
Scanning for key words in a selection; making predictions based on vocabulary	Writing an extension: developing a topic from a different point of view; applying techniques of humor and satire	Analyzing an author's use of humor to evaluate the Canadian way of life; analyzing the influence of an academic background on an author's writing	Social Studies: Banks and banking; the role of detectives in a society

Global Diversity in the Literature Classroom

Our world is rapidly becoming the proverbial global village. Technology is breaking down the barriers of distance, bringing us all a little closer with each passing day. With our newfound closeness comes the need to focus on the common bonds and values that unite us as human beings, while celebrating the diversity and uniqueness of our respective cultures. We must see the people of the world both in the general context of the global village and in the unique context of the cultural and historical heritage from which they come.

World Tapestries reflects the theme of global diversity, aiming to stimulate students' awareness of different cultures and to help them sense what it is like to think, feel, and believe as someone else might. It is an approach that helps students to understand others and to recognize and value both the otherness and sameness of people.

A globally diverse approach to literature is built upon the premise that literary works come from authors who write from a unique cultural perspective or context that shapes their writing. Viewed this way, every text is both an individual aesthetic object and a cultural document, a part of the legacy of an individual and of a group. To understand a text, then, the reader must understand–as fully as possible–the writer and the writer's culture. Experiencing the text as the writer intended it requires that it be read in the light of what one critic called the "spirit of the age" or of the culture.

This approach broadens the student's scope of knowledge and emphasizes the significance of the student's interaction with the text. When students are given information to help them become more fully aware of the writer and his or her world, they see that each text is part of a rich and complex context. That context in turn enhances their understanding as they read. Individual interpretation occurs as the students view and interpret this context in light of their own experience of the world. In this way, students are encouraged to make connections among texts, the cultures of the writers, and their own cultures and experiences.

The global diversity approach adds questions about from whom, where, and when the text originates. The course focus is not "Reading Literature;" rather, it is "Reading Writers." The cultural identity of the writer is always examined in terms of how it may affect the writer's and the reader's perspectives on the subject. Just as important is the broader historical context that shaped that writer's cultural heritage.

World Tapestries is a collection of world literature, much of it from cultures rarely represented and by authors rarely studied until recently in U.S. schools and colleges. Reading these texts requires some understanding of the context in which the works were written.

Selections are grouped by region. Although cultures within those regions may differ dramatically, they are united by overarching themes or shared historical experiences. Each selection can be viewed as an individual piece of a larger cultural context. For example, knowing that Nigeria was a colonial possession of Great Britain and has retained some of the culture of its former ruler makes it easier for the reader to understand Chinua Achebe's "Marriage Is a Private Affair."

To look at texts as the works of human beings who have a past and a culture is to see literature, ourselves, and our cultural whole. We must acknowledge that texts build upon other texts and that texts emerge from and reshape a culture or a subculture.

To broaden their understanding of global diversity, students should be encouraged to use outside information as they read. They should be instructed to research background information on the author, to read some of the author's other works, and to consider the beliefs, assumptions, and practices of the culture from which the author comes.

Students should also be encouraged to explore their own cultures. You might consider having your students interview their parents and older relatives about the issues and themes they encounter in *World Tapestries*. For example, what do family members know of their origins, their traditions, their ceremonies? What do they remember or recall hearing about their family's experiences arriving and settling in the United States? The information they learn from such questions is personal information that will enrich each student's sense of self.

In short, the most important part of introducing global diversity to the curriculum might very well be its role as a means of opening ever wider the door to the world. *World Tapestries* will help students grow in awareness of the world outside themselves. This awareness will help them to understand and thrive in the global village in which we all live. As they answer the open-ended questions posed in this text, remember to accept and value all responses, and to encourage sharing in an atmosphere that emphasizes respect for all.

Global Diversity in *World Tapestries*

Although not every culture could be represented in a single volume anthology, *World Tapestries* has been designed to reflect the diversity of the world's population in both the literature and in the authorship. The selections reflect the notion that each person has a unique set of customs and beliefs based on ancestry; however, the commonalities in the experiences of all peoples and groups becomes evident through the thematic connections.

The literature in *World Tapestries*

- reflects the diverse and rich cultures of the world;
- represents both familiar and previously unheard voices in the literature classroom;
- is organized into four major regions and nine subregions;
- illustrates multiple perspectives on issues of major importance to the cultures it represents.

Features of the *World Tapestries* Student Edition

- Unit Opener pages provide a historical background, including time lines that provide a context in which to read the literature.
- Prereading pages provide extensive background information on each author's culture and the conditions under which the author lived.
- Motivation questions emphasize an awareness of where, when, and from whom the text originates.
- Postreading pages provide questions that broaden a student's scope of knowledge and ask the student to look at the text through his or her own cultural perspective.
- Journal writing activities provide numerous opportunities for students to respond to the text.
- Author's Craft emphasizes literary elements used by writers to develop the genres and to deliver their messages.
- Focusing the Unit pages highlight writing an essay using the stages of the writing process, model cooperative/collaborative discussion of the literature in the unit, and encourage problem solving.

- Model Lessons illustrate with sidenotes one student's critical reading of the text (a critical reading involves an awareness of the author's culture and the time period the piece was written, the author's perspective on the theme, elements of the genre used by the author, and the student's understanding of and responses to the text).
- Making Cultural Connections highlights the cultures, traditions, and heritages of the regions represented in the text.
- Making Thematic Connections draws parallels between the cultures of a region based on a unifying social or political theme.
- The Art of Tapestries features 16 pages of four-color fine art from the various regions that gives the cultural context of the selections and encourages students to think across curriculum areas.
- The Student Handbook contains a Listing of Literary Terms with definitions and a Writing Process section that outlines the stages in the writing process, as well as student essays that model the four writing process activities on the Focusing the Unit pages.

Features of the *World Tapestries* Teacher's Resource Manual

- Alternate Tables of Contents organized by region, by genre, and by level of difficulty, assist teachers in presenting the literature in ways that best meet their individual curriculum needs.
- Staff Development provides background information about the fundamentals of a globally diverse curriculum; specific information about how *World Tapestries* implements a globally diverse curriculum; assessment tips to help teachers with both formal and informal assessment; and model lessons by teachers who are currently engaged in teaching global literature in their classrooms.
- ESL/LEP activities, designed and written as an integral part of the lesson plans, are appropriate for any student who may experience difficulty with concepts that require knowledge of varying cultural, regional, or experiential elements.
- Teaching strategies and additional activities provide suggestions for presenting the Unit Openers, Chapter Openers, Making Cultural Connections, and Making Thematic Connections.
- Assessment Worksheets and Literary Skills Worksheets test students' understanding of selection vocabulary and literary skills.

Assessment Tips

In today's multicultural classrooms, there are frequent opportunities to gather evidence for assessment. The instruments for gathering evidence are varied: quizzes, papers, exams, records of reading, tapes or videotapes of discussion, performances of dramatic readings, films, games, art work and music, feedback from the students, or observations by you and others who come into the classroom. The point is not how many different ways of gathering evidence there are, but that no one kind is better than any other.

Two important facts about assessment should be remembered whenever assessment tools are designed:

- Assessment must be ongoing; it cannot occur only at isolated times during study.
- Effective assessment not only helps you to look at how the students are doing, but it also helps you to evaluate how effective you are as the teacher of the course. Consider, for example, the following eight questions that assessment should allow you to answer. (Note that four are about the students, and four are about the course.)

1. Have the students completed all the required work?
2. Has the work completed by students been of value to them?
3. Has the work completed by students been of the quality I expect?
4. Has the work completed by students shown any change over time? Are these the changes that I wanted to see?
5. How well has the program I have presented worked?
6. Has the program accomplished what I wanted it to for all students?
7. How well have the students received the program?
8. What changes could I make to improve the program's effectiveness?

What assessment tools are especially effective for multicultural programs?

Suggested below are just some means of assessment that are perhaps especially pertinent to a multicultural curriculum in general, and to *World Tapestries* specifically.

Portfolios

We recommend the creation of student and class portfolios–carefully presented and reasoned collections of the best work that the students have done. The work should show what and how they have learned about other cultures, about their own cultures, and about the literature in *World Tapestries* because it explores points of view of cultures through authorship. A class portfolio can include papers, excerpts from student journals, reading logs, tape recordings, videotapes, multi-media presentations, or perhaps a record of a game or simulation.

Many teachers have tried having students keep portfolios. The time involved in tracking and evaluating a portfolio assignment is no more than would be invested in making up and scoring a multiple-choice test, yet the results are much more valuable compared to those obtained from more traditional and sometimes more limited assessment methods. Portfolios give a comprehensive picture of what the students have learned. Portfolios allow you to study students' progress throughout the course, offering many observation points on which to base your assessment of their work. (For suggestions on how to grade portfolio assignments, see "How can I grade student work?" on page xxxviii.)

By completing a class or individual portfolio, students also participate in the task of assessment. They are given the opportunity to show you the very best of what they have learned. By talking to them about what you think ought to be learned and demonstrated in the portfolio, you help the students to set their own goals and measure their own progress. In essence, you are telling students that you are interested in them as people—in their lives in the classroom, in their growth as students. You can make this point even clearer by requesting that the students include a piece of reflective writing or a reflective tape. The reflection should consider why the various pieces are included in the portfolio and what the student thinks the pieces say about his or her growth and development as a participant in a world literature program.

World Tapestries suggests a variety of projects that might go into the portfolio, both in the Teacher's Resource Manual and in the Student Edition. For example, each selection in the Student Edition is preceded and followed by instructions for journal writing. By having students include these writings in their portfolios, you can easily see who is keeping up with the reading while also noting how the students are responding to the selections. The Teacher's Resource Manual also suggests frequent journal writing opportunities as a means of getting students to respond to the text. For example, students set personal goals before each unit, often create word banks to help with selection vocabulary, and write personal responses to selections, themes, and units.

In addition, the suggestions in certain Teacher's Resource Manual sections can lend themselves to more complex portfolio projects. For example, many resources outside of the Student Edition are suggested in the Unit Introductions and selection lesson plans found in the *World Tapestries Teacher's Resource Manual.* Students could create projects based on these outside resources, ranging from research papers to oral presentations to artistic interpretations.

You will find that portfolios work for all students, primarily because they give students a voice in their work and an opportunity to show that they can read, write, perform, and learn. One of the best portfolio projects we know of was begun by Elite Wiggington in 1966. Each year, Wiggington's ninth- and tenth-grade students, from a poor rural area in southern Appalachia, create a literary magazine called *Foxfire.* The magazine, which features many different genres, is rooted in the Appalachian environment and culture. (Periodically, the magazines are put together in book form, also called *Foxfire*, and published by Anchor Press/Doubleday, Garden City, New York. These volumes are available in most libraries. The students also do TV shows for their community cable station, create record albums of traditional music, and operate a furniture making business, all under the umbrella of The Foxfire Fund, Inc.) Through *Foxfire* the students have shown themselves as writers and transcribers of the rural culture around them. Their projects are a testimony to their ability as readers and writers. These are not all college-bound students, but they have proved themselves through this cooperative portfolio.

Examinations

A unit or semester examination is not an evil, but a real challenge for you and your class to demonstrate what has occurred. An examination should be related to your goals and allow a chance for the students to show their strengths and imagination, not just what they can recall. That is, examinations should not be limited to objective questions; they should require more from the students than a correct choice or a one-word response.

We suggest three alternatives to the traditional objective examination:

- Perhaps the best test of how well students have learned to read world literature is seen in what they say or write about a new text, one that is unfamiliar to them. For this type of examination, provide the students with a previously unread poem, short story, speech, play, or other literary form that focuses on one of the themes explored in "Making Thematic Connections." Have the students read the selection and respond to it in terms of the main ideas you have explored throughout the unit.

- Another good way to measure students' gains is to see the kinds of connections they can make among the various texts they have studied over the course. For example, an exam for Unit 1 of *World Tapestries* might ask students to discuss the similarities and differences they find between the literature of Africa and that of the Middle East.

- A third way to assess students' progress is to see what they now think of the various themes and issues that have been discussed. In order to respond to a question such as: "Do you think that European powers had an evil or a beneficial influence on Africa," students must refer to what they have read, discuss the issues they have studied, and cite specific examples to support their opinions.

Each of these approaches or a combination of them can be adapted and used in the development of a final examination or project for the students. In *World Tapestries*, you will find that many end-of-unit activities in the Student Edition can be easily reworked into effective and innovative examinations of the types suggested above.

Examinations do not have to be limited to a class period or to a scheduled examination time. Many good examinations can be what are known as "take-homes." These generally take the form of a summary paper or set of questions. The students have their books and notes available to them. The focus of the take-home examination is not on recall but on individual interpretations, applications, and syntheses of the material.

Although the issue of cheating could arise with the take-home format, it can be eliminated by the way in which the examination is set up. You might choose to allow students to work together; their shared viewpoints will be very enriching for them. You might also word the project or question so that each student must choose his or her own topic. Because some students might take advantage of the take-home situation no matter how you handle it, you might find it useful to have some part of the examination controlled–an in-class essay on a new text, for example.

Another good way of handling the examination issue is to have a performance week, during which each student presents a final project summarizing the course. The "Problem Solving" activity on the end-of-unit review page lends itself to this type of assessment. The project can take the form of a paper, an oral interpretation, a sketch or piece of art, a formal debate, and so on. The presentations should be evaluated by the rest of the class after students have developed criteria by which to judge the work. (See the section "How can I grade student work?" on this page for suggestions on these criteria.) The presentations can also be performed for a public audience; some teachers have even invited outside "juries" to enjoy the students' work.

Daily and weekly checks

Teachers often need to check whether some students have been doing the reading. The usual method is to administer some sort of post-reading test. However, in too many instances, these tests become the major focus of the course. In actuality, such tests usually are not intended as anything more than gentle reminders that students have responsibilities, too.

Alternatives to formal tests include good follow-up discussions and the occasional (not predictable!) assignment of brief in-class exercises. To combine these methods, try the use of one thought-provoking question that each person answers in writing. The question then serves as a take-off point for class discussion. The question does not have to be a typical test question. It might be a scale to rate a character or part of the action. For example, give the students a set of ten adjectives (good, strong, rigid, cruel, powerless, passive, moral, flexible, and so on) and have them rate the person or action from low to high for each quality. Sharing the ratings can serve as a springboard for discussion and other activities. The student who has not read the work will often stand out. Other examples of effective quick checks include:

- giving the students a set of pictures and asking them to select those that best illustrate the work;
- having students rate a story, play, or poem and explain why they gave it that rating;
- having students suggest alternative endings to the text.

The point is that creative post-reading exercises can both help the students get their thoughts about the text in order and help you keep track of those who seem to be falling behind. In *World Tapestries*, we provide these creative exercises for each selection in both the Student Edition and the Teacher's Resource Manual.

How can I grade student work?

The various approaches to assessment described above all need to be related to a judgment of quality. In the language arts, quality is seen both in terms of how well the students deal with the content of the course–what they have to say about what they have read and discussed–and in terms of how well they use language to express what they know. We cannot say which of these two is more important; therefore, some sort of balance between them must be made. We propose assessing several aspects of a product rather than giving a single mark. The aspects are suggested below with criteria that might be used during rating. Certainly, any criteria that you use for assessment should be shared with students so that they can perform to the best of their abilities in these areas.

Content

How well is the material covered? Is it clear? Is it interesting? What has been included? Does what is included cover the major aspects of the topic? Does the product show an understanding of what has been read or studied? Does it show a thoughtful or mature understanding? Does it show an awareness of alternative views?

Organization

Is the presentation coherent? Does it begin and end clearly? Is there sufficient development and use of specifics?

Style and tone

Does the presentation use language or the chosen medium appropriately to fit the purpose of the product? Is the style consistent throughout? Is there an effective mood presented? Does the writer/presenter appear to understand how the medium can affect the audience?

Mechanical and technical aspects

Has the writer/presenter used the medium well within the range of his or her abilities? If the product is written, has the writer used grammar, syntax, spelling, and punctuation so that the message is clear? Are these aspects in keeping with what I know is the student's potential? If the product is in another medium, do the content and organization outweigh any technical problems so that they are hardly noticeable?

Notice how the suggested criteria provide guidelines, but not prescriptive rules for good performance. They show that writing or other forms of performance are complex phenomena that need practice and that clearly are not matters of right versus wrong.

Criteria like these can also be used by the students themselves to evaluate the performances of other students. If you work with the class to explore these criteria, you can make a checklist that students can then use when they look at the performances of their classmates. Students also can use the checklist to evaluate their own work.

How do I arrive at final grades for my students?

Given all we have said about assessment, what about the final grade? Most teachers live within a system that requires that each student receive a letter or a number grade at the end of the semester. How can all that has been done be captured in a single letter or number?

The answer is that it cannot, and yet the system demands this kind of summary rating. We have found that many students understand the system, and they know how important grades can be for their future. We have also found that the best way to handle the problem is to be clear from the beginning as to what kinds of things have to be done in order to earn an A, or a 75, or whatever grade the student is interested in for the course. In this way, the grade represents the completion of a contract. The contract involves satisfactory performance on a number of tasks done both individually and in groups. The judgment of the teacher and other evaluators is a part of that contract. If the various criteria are clear and the ways in which the judges will operate are spelled out, then a complex assessment can be turned into a single grade. This is not the best summary of a student's work, and we believe that a descriptive summary or checklist should be added to it. Many schools are now operating in this way and are asking that the portfolio be carried forward by the student to the next grade level. Through this procedure, grades are given, but assessment is much broader than the grades themselves.

SAMPLE LESSON PLANS

LESSON 1

David Rowe, English Instructor, Grades 9–12
from *The House on the Border,* by Aziz Nesin

Preteaching

To prepare students for the content of the selection, you may wish to have students do one or more of the following activities:

- Divide the class into groups of 3 or 4 students. Have each group brainstorm a list of reasons why the United States has the highest crime rate of any industrialized nation. Allow 5–10 minutes of brainstorming, then ask each group to choose seven specific reasons from their lists. Have a representative from each group write their responses on the board. Discuss them in detail.

- Various groups may be responsible for the high crime rate in the United States. Ask students to evaluate the responsibility level for each of the following groups:

    1. criminals / people who commit crimes
    2. families of criminals
    3. neighbors / community members
    4. police / law enforcement officers
    5. courts / justice system
    6. prison system
    7. schools
    8. victims of crime

Have students rank the responsibility of each group on a scale of 0–10 (0 being no responsibility and 10 being complete responsibility). Students should be able to justify their ranking for each group with specific reasoning and examples. This activity may be either a group writing activity or a full-class discussion.

After completing this activity, you may wish to discuss how people avoid taking responsibility for individual or community problems. Have students hypothesize what excuses members of the above groups might use to avoid taking responsibility for our high crime rates.

Prereading

Before reading the selection, have students read the background material on Nesin. Emphasize Nesin's focus on injustice. Ask students to look for examples of injustice as they read the selection. They should consider which people or groups are responsible for the injustices they identify.

Postreading

After reading the selection, ask students to identify specific examples of injustice in the story. Then discuss with them the responsibility level of the following characters:

1. the thieves
2. the police
3. the neighbors / community
4. the owner of the house
5. the officials deciding the jurisdiction of the house
6. the husband
7. the wife

Have students rank the responsibility level of each group on a scale of 0–10 and justify their rankings with support from the text. This exercise can form the basis for a class discussion or an individual or group writing assignment.

As part of this activity, you may wish to discuss how specific characters avoid taking responsibility for the injustice in this story. Have students hypothesize what excuses members of the above groups might use to avoid taking responsibility for the couple's dilemma.

Extending the Text

Ask students to research a specific problem or injustice that interests them, such as academic cheating, underage drinking, and eating disorders. They should define the problem or injustice, identify which people or groups are responsible, and evaluate each person's or group's level of responsibility. Have them justify their evaluations with specific examples. Students can share their findings through an oral or written report.

LESSON 2

Larry O'Connell, English Teacher, Grades 9–12
from *If Not Still Higher,* by Isaac Loeb Peretz

Preparation

Divide the class into small groups. Ask each group to research one of the topics below and report their findings to the class.

- important traditions of Orthodox Jewish belief
- the significance of the Torah
- the origin of the Talmud
- the Sabbath rituals
- life on a shtetl

As an alternative, show the class the first 15 minutes of the 1970 film "Fiddler on the Roof" to aid students in picturing a shtetl as a setting. You may wish to note that the shtetl in the film has a brighter mood than the one in the story they are about to read.

Preteaching

Discuss the questions below with the class. On the chalkboard, note key words and phrases elicited from students' responses.

- What kinds of leaders are there in our culture?
- What qualities make a good leader?
- How is a religious leader different from other kinds of leaders? What qualities would a good religious leader demonstrate?

Next, present the idea of disguise to the class. Discuss reasons a person might have for intentionally hiding his or her identity. Ask: What things could a person disguise about him or herself? How do actors "put on disguises" when playing a part?

Postreading

Reminding students of their responses in the Preparation and Preteaching activities, conduct a discussion about the story. Use the following questions to help focus student's attention.

- How do we know the rabbi is a beloved leader?
- Why is the rabbi especially important to his people?
- Why are the people in the shtetl living in fear?
- How is the shtetl in the story different from the one shown in the film, "Fiddler on the Roof?"

- How is the Lithuanian man a changing or dynamic character?
- Why is it symbolic that the Lithuanian man is cold while he is hiding under the rabbi's bed?
- How is the fire a metaphor? Why is the wood described as burning "merrily?"
- The Lithuanian man implies something about the rabbi when he says, "If not still higher." What can we infer from this?
- What reasons could the rabbi have for performing his act of kindness?

Mention to the students that tone in a story is the author's attitude toward a character or subject. Divide the class into groups and review specific words the author associates with the Lithuanian man and the rabbi. How can we determine the author's attitude toward the rabbi? the Lithuanian man?

Finally, list the following themes on the board:

- An outsider can challenge the beliefs of a community.
- Anonymous giving is the highest form of charity.
- Kindness gives hope to human suffering.
- Fear and doubts darken people's lives.

Ask students to choose the theme that they believe best indicates the point the author is trying to make about human nature or life in general. Have them defend their choice in a brief essay.

Extending the text

You may wish to have students do one or more of the following activities:

- Ask students to create an album of good deeds by cutting out articles from newspapers and magazines. Display the collections in a prominent place in the classroom.
- Assign an essay in which students discuss the meaning of the saying, "It is better to strike a match than curse the darkness." Students may explain how the question relates directly to the story or they may cite examples from the news, history, or their own experiences to support their interpretation.

LESSON 3

Criselda Villarreal, Reading Teacher, Grade 8
from *One of These Days,* by Gabriel García Márquez

Preparation

Prepare a bulletin board with a map of Colombia and the title of the story, "One of These Days" by Gabriel García Márquez. As you proceed with the lesson, students may wish to add newspaper articles, stories, and pictures to it that discuss recent events in Colombia.

Motivation

To motivate and interest students in Colombian culture, you may wish to:

- Play Colombian or South American music softly in the background as you introduce the lesson. For example, *Musique de Colómbia* by Musique Du Monde (Buda Records).

- Display South American handicrafts or artifacts in the classroom. Encourage students to examine and discuss the materials on display.

Preteaching

To assess prior knowledge and prepare students for the content of the story:

- Have students brainstorm a list of what they know about Colombia. Ask: What kind of government exists today? What is the economic situation there?

- Have students read newspapers and listen to the world news on television. Tell them to pay attention to what is currently happening in Colombia politically, economically, and socially. Ask students to bring relevant articles or summaries of news programs to class and post them on the bulletin board.

Postreading

You may wish to have students do one or more of the following activities. Some may be appropriate for either small-group or individual work.

- Divide the class into small groups of 2-3 students. Ask them to work together to rewrite the story, giving it a contemporary setting. Students can share their stories with the class by reading them aloud.

- Challenge students to write an essay about the character they identify with the most. Tell them to support their choice with specific reasons and examples.

- Have students work in pairs to design and build a diorama of an important scene from the story. Ask students to write a brief summary describing the scene represented.

- Discuss with students how *One of These Days* is an excellent example of conflict. Ask students to reflect on an occasion when they were strong-willed about a decision they had made. Have them write a personal narrative in the same suspenseful style as Márquez uses.

- Encourage students to brainstorm a list of questions they would ask Aurelio or the mayor, if they had an opportunity to interview one of these characters. Pairs of students might then role-play the interview with one student assuming the voice of the character and the other playing the reporter.

The Art of Tapestries

In "The Art of Tapestries," students will explore the links between visual and written creative expression. In addition, the artifacts, paintings, sculptures, prints, and ceramics on these pages provide an understanding of the world's cultural richness.

INTRODUCING THE ART OF TAPESTRIES

Providing Motivation

Before the class looks at the art insert in the Student Edition (pp. A1-A16), you may wish to use the following ideas to spark students' interest and help them forge connections between the art and the literature.

•Read the following quotation to students.

"Not long ago I happened to visit an exhibition of modern pictures. It was held in Pittsburgh and almost every nation was represented. As I looked at those pictures I felt that I could see through them, into the minds of the nations which had created them."

Calvin Coolidge

Ask: What is this speaker saying about the relationship of art to culture? Do you agree with what he is saying? Why or why not? As a class, discuss what art can tell us about the way people lived and their values. Point out the Egyptian wall painting on page A1 and ask students what hints it provides about life in ancient Egypt. For example, students might suggest that the mural shows the importance of such daily tasks as farming and harvesting. Invite the class to brainstorm what a similar wall painting about their lives might look like.

• On the board write this question:

Why do people around the world create works of art such as paintings and sculptures? Have students work in pairs to write their responses. Each student should brainstorm at least three responses to the question. When students have finished writing, have partners

exchange ideas. Partners should look for similar ideas in each other's work and together decide on several reasons why the creation of art transcends cultural differences. As a class, explore these ideas and examine what they suggest about the importance of art in people's daily lives as well as to their culture.

BRIDGING THE ESL/LEP LANGUAGE GAP

A number of the terms in these pages are likely to be challenging for second-language speakers. To help students with their pronunciation and comprehension, present students with the following questions.

1. What questions should you ask yourself as you look at each piece of art? (What do I see? What does each work show me about the artist and his or her culture?)
2. What are "hieroglyphics"? (an ancient Egyptian alphabet made of pictures)
3. Who are the Luba? (a tribe in Zaire)
4. What is an "ancestral story"? (a story about the tribe's culture and history)

Have students find the answers to these questions as you read aloud the captions on page A1. Ask students to follow along in their books.

Then create the following chart on the board to preteach challenging vocabulary. Partner ESL/LEP students with a native speaker to find the definition of each word. Encourage teams to use context clues, as well as dictionaries, as they fill in the chart.

Term	Definition	Page
plaque		A2
sophisticated		A2
contemporary		A2
sultan		A4
reign		A5

As students read, encourage them to add any other words they do not know to their charts.

CROSS-DISCIPLINE TEACHING OPPORTUNITIES

Social Studies Have students look at the painting *The Bolshevik* on page A11. This painting, like many others in Russia during the 1920s, idealizes Communist philosophy. Ask: Why do you think Communist leaders would encourage artists to idealize their philosophy? What kind of effect do you think this painting would have had on citizens of the Soviet Union? Then have students work in small groups to research other paintings to see if and/or how historical events affected them.

Literature After students study the early Egyptian wall painting, explain that ancient Egyptians bound together the folktales and legends of several civilizations that had lived in the Nile Valley before Egypt was unified around 3100 BC. From these time-honored tales, the Egyptians wove a complex network of myths around their chief god, Ra (or Re).

Ancient Egyptians believed that Earth arose as a hill from the ocean Nun. As a phoenix, Ra dispersed the darkness. His offspring were Shu, the god of air, and Tefnut, the goddess of water. Each day, the sky goddess Nut gave birth to the sun once again. The sun rose as Khepri, a giant scarab beetle. Invite

students to look through *World Tapestries* to find an origin myth from another culture and compare and contrast it to the beliefs of the ancient Egyptians.

Language Arts Draw students' attention to the woodcut *Woman Reading a Letter* on page A7.

The artist, Kitagawa Utamaro (1754-1806), was one of the most famous woodcut designers of the 18th century. His techniques spread to Europe, where they were an important influence on the French Impressionists. This picture, as with so many of Utamaro's works, is a bit mysterious: What does the letter say? Have students solve this mystery by writing the message that the woman is receiving in her letter.

Science Draw students' attention to the Indian miniature on page A8 and the bronze sculpture and gouache painting on page A9. To help students probe the connection between Indian culture and art, you may wish to ask the following questions:

- Why is the woman in the miniature on page A8 riding on Leo the lion?
- Why would Siva the destroyer need many arms? Study the sculpture on page A9 as you make inferences.
- What do you learn about Indian lifestyles from the painting on page A9?

Tell students that in addition to the information about mythology and lifestyles they inferred from this art, Indian culture has deep roots in medical advancements. For example, the ancient Hindus practiced plastic surgery before AD 1000. They worked with steel surgical instruments and used alcohol to dull the senses. Invite students to work in small groups to find other notable scientific advances from nonWestern countries. When possible, students should also find the names of the scientists responsible for these advances.

Lesson Plans

1

Africa and the Middle East

In Unit 1, you will explore the rich heritage of Africa and the Middle East. The literature of this region reveals the writers' deep connection to their cultural roots. It also shows the diversity of the writing produced in the cradle of civilization.

UNIT OBJECTIVES

Literary

- to explain how narrative forms such as epics, myths, autobiographies, and short stories can effectively convey cultural beliefs and values
- to show how authors have used the genre of poetry to convey a nation's cultural richness

Historical

- to compare and contrast the cultural traditions of Africa and the Middle East
- to understand how historical experiences influence the literature of a region

Cultural

- to compare and contrast traditional and contemporary cultural values in Africa and the Middle East
- to understand how the history of Africa and the Middle East is reflected in their literature today

UNIT RESOURCES

The following resources appear in the Student Edition of *World Tapestries*:

- a **portfolio of culture-related art**, Art of the Tapestries, pages A2–A5, to build background, activate prior knowledge, and generate writing ideas about the unit cultures.

- a **unit overview**, pages 2–5, to provide historical background about Africa and the Middle East, including an African's perspective on the colonization of his country by Europeans.

- a **time line**, pages 4–5, to help students place the literary works in their historical context. You may wish to have students refer to the time line before they discuss each work.

- the **Focusing the Unit** activities at the end of the unit, page 113, to provide a cooperative/collaborative learning project on the theme of "Africa and the Middle East," a writing project, and a problem-solving activity in which students analyze one or more of the situations described in Unit 1.

INTRODUCING UNIT 1

Providing Motivation

Before students begin to read the unit overview in the Student Edition, you can spark their interest in the cultures of Africa and the Middle East with some of the following activities:

- Divide the class in half. Have each group brainstorm answers to one of the following questions.

    Why would European powers be so eager to colonize Africa and the Middle East in the 19th century?

    What do you think were some of the effects of European colonization in Africa and the Middle East?

When each group is finished, have them present their results to the class in the form of a panel discussion. Students can verify their responses as they read the Unit Opener.

- Read the following quotation to students:

> The struggle of the younger generation of men and women to attain their domestic freedom to shape their own lives mirrors or parallels the nation's struggle to achieve political independence and to free itself from the shackles of outworn and debilitating, almost medieval, conventions and world outlook in a gigantic endeavor to belong to the modern world.
>
> [M.M. Badawi, *The Egyptian Bulletin*, June 1982]

Explain to students that the quotation is from a contemporary journal, *The Egyptian Bulletin*, describing the writer's view of life in Egypt today. Ask: In moving toward the future, what customs and traditions of the past should people retain? Why are these aspects of a person's heritage important? Discuss the tension that might arise between the old and new ways. Invite students to speculate how this tension might be revealed in the literature in this unit.

- Use the time line for the following activity. Arrange students in small groups. Assign one portion of the time line to each group and have them discuss the cultural events in their assigned era.

Cross-Discipline Teaching Opportunity: Unit Culture

Remind students that Africa and the Middle East have a rich cultural heritage that manifests itself in many ways today. From the development of number systems and coinage to map making and exploring, the people of the "Fertile Crescent" have changed our world in a far-reaching manner. Collaborate with a social studies teacher to examine the different cultural contributions of people from Africa and the Middle East to the world. Some of the areas you might wish to explore include:

- music
- art
- food
- agriculture
- clothing
- celebrations
- dance
- storytelling
- science
- government

Discuss with students the different cultural contributions from this region. Challenge students to draw parallels between the history of Africa and the Middle East and that of modern America, focusing on the cultural aspects.

Setting Personal Goals for Reading the Selections in Unit 1

Have students keep a copy of the following chart in their journals or notebooks. Provide class time every few days for students to review and expand their charts. Encourage them to add topics of their own.

Africa and the Middle East			
Topic	What I Know	What I Want to Learn	What I Have Found Out
Historical ties between Africa and the Middle East			
Cultural ties between Africa and the Middle East			
Reasons for colonialism			
Effect of colonialism			
African culture			
Middle Eastern culture			

1 Africa

CHAPTER PREVIEW

Africa			
Selections	**Genre**	**Author's Craft/Literary Skills**	**Cultural Values & Focus**
from *Sundiata: An Epic of Old Mali* pages 7-18	epic	the epic	the importance of heritage
"Owner of the Sky: Olorun the Creator" retold by Virginia Hamilton, pages 19-22	creation myth	cause and effect	the origin of a culture
"The Sea Eats the Land at Home," Kofi Awoonor; "Song for the Sun that Disappeared Behind the Rainclouds," an oral poem of the Khoi pages 23-26	poetry	sensory details	the role of nature in human affairs
"The Prebend Gardens," "Interior," Léopold Sédar Senghor; "All That You Have Given Me, Africa," Anoma Kanié, pages 27-31	poetry	nationalism in poetry	the richness of African life
MAKING CULTURAL CONNECTIONS: Africa and the Middle East, pages 32-33			
"The Toilet," Gcina Mhlope, pages 34-42	short story	point of view	equality and civil rights
"A Chip of Glass Ruby," Nadine Gordimer, pages 43-54	short story	conflict	equality and civil rights
"Marriage Is a Private Affair," Chinua Achebe, pages 55-62	short story	conflict	the clash of old and new values
from *The Dark Child*, Camara Laye, pages 63-71	autobiography	dialogue	the importance of education in modern Afican life
"The Chair Carrier," Yusuf Idris, pages 72-78	short story	irony	respect for authority

ASSESSMENT

Assessment opportunities are indicated by a ✔ next to the activity title. For guidelines, see Teacher's Resource Manual page xxxvi.

CROSS-DISCIPLINE TEACHING OPPORTUNITIES

Speech   To help students understand the importance of the African tradition of storytelling to the preservation and transmission of cultural values, invite them to select another African story to share with to the class. Storytelling will also help students become aware of the variety and richness of the African oral tradition. Arrange students in small groups and help them select a tale. Possibilities include the Ashanti tale, "Anansi and His Visitor, Turtle," the Hausa tale, "The Rubber Man," and the Yoruba tale, "Omi and the Great Bird." To help students make their oral presentations, describe how storytellers use repetition, chanting, and musical cadence as both memory aids and performance tools. Consider videotaping the performances and placing them in an oral history section of the classroom. Students can find other authentic African folktales in *The Fire on the Mountain and Other Ethiopian Stories* (Holt, 1950); *Best-Loved Folktales of the World,* edited by Joanna Cole (Doubleday, 1982); and *Beat the Story-Drum, Pum-Pum,* retold by Ashley Bryan (Atheneum 1980).

Science   In addition to its rich literary heritage, Africa is famous for its wildlife. Sheep, goats, horses, and camels are found in North Africa; the Ethiopian zone, in contrast, is famous for its great variety of distinctive animals and birds. These include the zebra, giraffe, buffalo, elephant, rhinoceros, lion, leopard, cheetah, jackal, and various types of apes and monkeys. Have students work with a science teacher to explain how the climate and topography of Africa support its distinctive wildlife.

History   In the late 18th century, the search for new markets stimulated an age of exploration. The French began their conquest of Algeria and Senegal in the 1830s; by the 1850s, a systematic conquest of tropical Africa was well underway. Invite students to work with a history teacher to prepare maps of Africa in 1800, 1850, 1900, 1950, and the present to trace the history of African colonialism.

SUPPLEMENTING THE CORE CURRICULUM

The Student Edition provides humanities material related to specific cultures in Making Cultural Connections: Africa and the Middle East on pages 32 and 33 and in The Art of the Tapestries on pages A2-A5. You may wish to invite students to pursue the following activities outside of class:

- By the mid-1980s, almost all of Africa was independent. The young African states faced a variety of major problems. Among the most important were the political and cultural effects of the creation of a nation-state. Most African countries retained the frontiers drawn by the 19th-century European diplomats and administrators. Ethnic groups may be divided by national boundaries, but loyalties to their groups can often be stronger than ties to the state. Have students discover which regions in Africa are currently undergoing conflicts between tribal loyalties and national boundaries. Students can show their findings on a map or other visual display.

- Many beautiful stamps are issued by the African countries. Sometimes these special stamps are created to raise funds for the countries as well as to be used as postage. Invite students to look in stamp books to find African stamps they think are especially attractive. Students can photocopy these stamps, color them, and mount them to create their own stamp albums.

- The art of Africa illuminates the rich history, philosophies, religions, and cultures of the continent. The history of African art spans many centuries. For example, among the most ancient of these arts are the rock paintings and engravings from the Tassili and Ennedi in the Sahara, which date from 6000 BC. Other examples of early work include the terra-cotta sculptures created by Nok artists in Nigeria between 500 BC and AD 200. Have students work in small groups to create a time line showing the great periods in African art.

INTRODUCING CHAPTER 1: AFRICA

Using the Chapter Opener

Write the following terms on the board: *storytelling, Negritude, colonialism*. Call on volunteers to define the words. As students respond, point out that all these terms are integral to Africa's history and culture, the focus of this chapter. Then read to students the following quotation:

> Culture is the sum of all the forms of art, of love and of thought, which, in the course of centuries, have enabled man to be less enslaved.
> *André Malraux* (1957)

Ask students: What do you think Malraux means when he says culture enables people to free themselves from enslavement? (He is talking about culture and the arts as ways of freeing the mind and spirit.)

Explore with the class Africa's vast cultural diversity and richness and the many different forms it takes. Possibilities include literature, art, music, dance, textiles, and storytelling.

✔ Developing Concept Vocabulary

You can use a word web to help students understand the different forms of written and oral expression found in the African literary tradition.

Write the phrase *African literature* on the chalkboard. Have students work in teams to brainstorm a list of the different types of African literature they will read in this chapter. Write the responses on the board to create a class diagram like the one shown below.

To encourage discussion, invite students to preview the Table of Contents to find the different genres in this chapter.

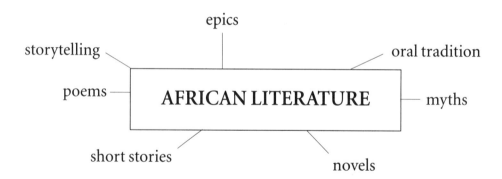

ASK:

- How might the traditional African culture support storytelling and poetry?
- Why would short stories be an important form of literature in Africa?
- What values might creation myths preserve in Africa?

from *Sundiata: An Epic of Old Mali*

edited by D. T. Niane (pages 7–18)

OBJECTIVES

Literary

- to identify the elements of an epic
- to demonstrate how traditional storytelling conveys cultural beliefs and values

Historical

- to explain the historical importance of a storyteller in African culture groups
- to show that traditional stories provide historical information

Cultural

- to identify human qualities that a society values
- to explain the significance of traditional storytelling to African societies

SELECTION RESOURCES

Use Assessment Worksheet 1 to check students' vocabulary recognition, content comprehension, and appreciation of literary skills.

 Informal Assessment Opportunity

SELECTION OVERVIEW

When the empire of Ghana collapsed at the end of the 12th century, the small kingdom of Sosso took over Ghana. Sumanguru, the leader of Sosso, then sought to take over the kingdom of Mali. To clear the way for his becoming king, Sumanguru exiled Sundiata Keita, the young prince and sole heir to the Mali throne.

In 1235, eighteen-year-old Sundiata returned to fight Sumanguru. Sundiata's army defeated the Sosso army in a series of battles. With the death of Sumanguru, Sundiata took the throne that was rightfully his. Sundiata Keita was the first of many great Mali kings. The Mali empire, at its peak, controlled most of West Africa.

In this selection, an African griot, or storyteller, describes the childhood hardships of Sundiata Keita. The story ends when Sundiata shows the strength and perseverance that he would use as the king of the mighty Mali empire.

ENGAGING THE STUDENTS

Ask students to respond to the following questions: What qualities should a great leader possess? What actions does a good leader take? What leaders today possess the qualities you think are desirable?

Allow students five minutes to compose answers. Then have volunteers share their responses. Lead the class to create composite answers for the questions. You may wish to put both questions and composite answers on the board.

BRIDGING THE ESL/LEP LANGUAGE GAP

The difficulty level of the selection vocabulary may present problems for students in following the story's action. Read the selection aloud with students, encouraging them to identify each important event as it occurs. As they do so, create a timeline on the board.

Have the students work together in small groups to fill in details for the plot outline on the board. Encourage them to refer to the text. When they have completed the timeline, discuss with them how much the details enhance the plot.

✔ PRETEACHING SELECTION VOCABULARY

Explain to students that the upcoming selection recounts the childhood of a great African leader, as well as the political plots and manipulations of the leader's relatives. Have students scan the footnoted vocabulary to find and classify three kinds of words: those that could relate to good characters or actions (*exemplary*,

7

valorous); those that could relate to bad characters or actions, (**innuendo**, *diabolical*, **malicious**, *irony*, *derisively*, **humiliated**) and those that are neutral (**infirmity**, *inquisitive*, *blandly*, *discreetly*).

The words printed in boldfaced type are tested on the selection assessment worksheet.

PREREADING

Reading the Epic in a Cultural Context

Explain that an African epic, just like an African myth, has definite purposes. (See Guidelines for Going Back Into the Text: Author's Craft on this page.) Tell students that in this selection they will learn about the early history of the Mali culture, as well as the background of a historical Mali leader.

Focusing on the Selection

Have students quickly scan the list of qualities generated earlier (Engaging the Students). Ask them to select which qualities, if any, should or might show up during childhood. After students have volunteered opinions, challenge them to identify the childhood characteristics of Sogolon Djata, the Mali leader, as they read.

POSTREADING

The following activities parallel the features with the same titles in the Student Edition.

Responses to Critical Thinking Questions

Possible responses are:

1. The Sundiata legend "builds up" Sundiata's inability to walk and details the treatment he had to endure so that the climax of the excerpt—his pulling himself up to stand—will be as spectacular as possible. There seems to be an instructive purpose as well: in spite of his apparent "handicap," he is destined for great things, and nothing can interfere with that destiny.

2. Desirable attitudes and qualities include physical perfection and strength, physical and mental liveliness, verbal ability, control of appetites, modesty, and amiability.

3. Student responses will indicate prior knowledge, as well as the ability to draw on and apply data from other disciplines to language arts. Responses should also indicate an awareness that the incidents exemplify desirable qualities and attitudes. Possible answers might include: the Arthurian

legends; Scarface and Sweet Medicine, two Native American heroes; Quetzalcoatl, a Mayan god-king; Paul Bunyun; Odysseus; and Beowulf.

☑ Guidelines for Writing Your Response to "Sundiata"

Have students share their journal entries. As an alternative writing activity, suggest that students work in small groups to draw present-day parallels to the political intrigue occurring in the Sundiata legend. Caution students to use a news report style that presents several points of view rather than sensationalism. Student groups might also enjoy recasting the selection as a contemporary political documentary for television or radio. Have student groups share their completed works and discuss how well each group fulfilled the assignment.

☑ Guidelines for Going Back Into the Text: Author's Craft

Remind students that an epic has multiple purposes: 1) to teach a cultural group's history and rules of behavior; 2) to stir feelings of cultural pride; 3) to enable a *griot* (storyteller) to recount a group's history in a manner that demonstrates his memory and story-telling abilities. List these purposes on the board as headings. As students volunteer answers to the questions in the Student Edition, work with them to enter each answer under the appropriate heading.

Possible answers to questions in the Student Edition are:

1. "The future springs from the past"; "God has his mysteries which none can fathom"; "Each man finds his way already marked out for him and he can change nothing of it"; "The silk-cotton tree emerges from a tiny seed"; "great trees grow slowly but they plunge their roots deep into the ground"; "the snake has no legs yet it is as swift as any other animal that has four."

2. "what three-year-old is not the despair . . . joy"; "a lion that crawls on the ground"; "the right hand of some mighty king"; "has the seed [Sundiata] germinated?"; "stiff-legged king"; "son of misfortune"; "young lion [Sundiata]"; "steps were those of a giant"; "the lion has walked."

3. Sundiata is always described in terms of the lion, "the king of beasts" or "the king of the jungle"; he overcomes his disability with one powerful act born of his spirit's determination; after he stands, he is so strong that he uproots an entire tree and brings it to his mother. The climax also hints that Sundiata has

simply been biding his time, that he follows "the beat of his own drum" and no one else's.

4. when the bar of iron that he uses as a crutch twists into the shape of a bow

5. Sundiata's strength appears to be the paramount quality prized by the Mali. Sundiata's father is cautioned against impatience and advised to accept the gods' mysterious ways. At the conclusion, the griot enumerates the qualities of a good wife and mother as displayed by Sogolon Kedjou: modesty, long-suffering, patience, humility, and respect towards one's husband. The queen mother embodies qualities the Mali appear to consider undesirable; she is proud, jealous, malicious, diabolical, derisive, and spiteful.

6. The selection's conclusion repeats the part that destiny plays in man's life; Sundiata is described as being "as popular as he had been despised"; the people practice some political "20-20 hindsight," recalling that as great as Sogolon Kedjou's suffering was on her son's behalf, so great shall be Sundiata's glory.

✔ FOLLOW-UP DISCUSSION

Use the questions that follow to continue your discussion of the excerpt from the epic *Sundiata*. Possible answers are given in parentheses.

Recalling

1. What is the relationship of the griot to the Sundiata legend? (He and his ancestors have always been in the service of the Keitas of Mali.)

2. What aim does the griot declare in reciting the Sundiata? (to teach kings the history of their ancestors so that it can serve as an example)

3. How old was Sundiata when he finally started to walk? (seven years old)

Interpreting

4. How does the griot prepare his audience for Sundiata's inevitable and unavoidable greatness? (He introduces the tale with a "build up": "ancestor of the great Mali, the story of him who, by his exploits, surpassed even Alexander the Great . . . shed his rays upon all the countries of the West . . . the man of many names against whom sorcery could avail nothing.")

5. What is the purpose of the repetition of the exclamation "How impatient man is!"? (The sentence reminds the audience that humans have very little, if any, control over matters that affect them; everything that occurs is the gods' will, and men have no business questioning or grumbling.

6. What does the griot mean when he says, "The future springs from the past"? (The griot teaches kings the history of their ancestors so that the lives of the ancients can serve as an example.)

Applying

7. What historical information does the legend impart? (the historical beginnings of the kingdom of Mali; Sundiata's childhood infirmity; the political position of the Doua griots; Mali leader Sundiata Keita was strong and popular with the people, exactly the kind of leader who should—and did—lead the Mali ascent to greatness.)

8. Who or what plays the role of the griot in our present-day society? How might the goals of these current storytellers differ from earlier ones? (Students may suggest that historians, biographers, and the media have taken the role of the griot. Today's storytellers seem less concerned with being the memory of mankind or the preservers of truth. Instead, their primary goal seems to be a monetary or sensationalistic one.)

ENRICHMENT

Students will benefit from viewing the videocassette *Caravans of Gold and Kings and Cities*, available from Zenger Media, 10200 Jefferson Boulevard, Room 922, P.O. Box 802, Culver City, CA 90232, (800) 421-4246.

Owner of the Sky: Olorun the Creator

retold by Virginia Hamilton   (pages 19–22)

OBJECTIVES

Literary
- to identify the elements of a creation myth
- to recognize the use of cause and effect in a creation myth

Historical
- to demonstrate that traditional stories can explain events in nature
- to demonstrate that traditional stories can contain historical information

Cultural
- to appreciate an example of African oral tradition
- to recognize recurring themes in differing cultures

SELECTION RESOURCES

Use Assessment Worksheet 2 to check students' vocabulary recognition, content comprehension, and appreciation of literary skills.

 Informal Assessment Opportunity

SELECTION OVERVIEW

The creation myth of "Owner of the Sky: Olorun the Creator" comes from Africa's rich store of traditional oral literature. This enormous collection includes not only myths but also legends, allegories, parables, tales, songs and chants, poetry, proverbs, riddles, and theater—all carefully memorized and performed from generation to generation.

The label "myth" in no way connotes a fairy or folk tale. Myths, along with legends, are the two genres considered true historical narratives of African cultures. Myths report the history of the time *before* human times began; legends report the history of human times.

The "time before human times," of course, is the era of creation. Like myths in other societies, African creation myths teach the religious beliefs of a particular cultural group about the group's own creation. For example, Olorun is the high deity of the Yoruba people; therefore, this myth presents some religious beliefs of the Yoruba cultural group. Because myths are expressions of a cultural group's religious beliefs, their purpose is to give spiritual strength and guidance.

Creation myths are a form of African prose narrative, along with legends, folktales, anecdotes, and jokes. There are more prose narratives collected than any other kind of African oral literature. Most of the collected creation myths share similar basic plots and in-

cidents. The differences in myths are attributable to the reworking done by the "composing" African cultural group so that each myth closely fits and mirrors the group's ways of life.

In this selection, the author tells how Olorun, with the help of Great God, created the earth and its inhabitants.

ENGAGING THE STUDENTS

Write the following question on the board: How was Earth created? Remind students that two major kinds of theories exist explaining Earth's creation: scientific and religious. Encourage them to volunteer what they know of these various theories. Discuss student responses, jotting on the board any that are appropriate. Explain that "Owner of the Sky: Olorun the Creator" offers one explanation of how the world came to be. Encourage students to be alert to similarities to creation stories with which they are familiar.

BRIDGING THE ESL/LEP LANGUAGE GAP

Because the vocabulary of this selection is simple and the plot structure is clear and easy to follow, the selection provides a good opportunity for limited

English speakers to take part in the class discussion about this myth. It also provides an excellent "stage" for the presentation of creation stories from many cultures. Ask students to consider the following questions as they read:

1. What qualities does Olorun possess that make him a god? Great God?

2. How is the world created? How are human beings created?

3. What kinds of "goods" do Olorun and Great God give humans?

4. How long does creation of the world take?

5. What is the purpose of the day following the four days of creation?

6. What form does Great God's jealousy take?

Discuss answers after students have read the myth. Encourage students—particularly limited English speakers—to share any similar stories they know.

☑ PRETEACHING
SELECTION VOCABULARY

Ask students to scan the selection for words that apply to the creation process. Make a list of words and phrases on the board (for example, *watery*, **waste**, *marsh-waste*, *no solid land*, **plant their feet**, *threw the earth out*, *scratch the soil*, **solid and true**, **Chameleon**, *plenty wide*, *plant trees*, *feed humans*, **give them goods**, *people's parts out of earth*, *still figures to life*).

The words printed in boldfaced type are tested on the selection assessment worksheet.

PREREADING

Reading the Myth in a Cultural Context

Help students read for purpose by reminding them that every culture has tales that explain the beginning, or origin, of the cultural group itself, as well as various forces of nature and natural phenomena. Have them look for the origins that this myth explains.

Focusing on the Selection

Ask students to consider why every culture seems to be curious about how its existence began. Allow students several minutes to formulate and write explanations to the question. Call on students to share their reasoning. Then have them keep the question in mind as they read the creation myth.

POSTREADING

The following activities parallel the features with the same titles in the Student Edition.

Responses to Critical Thinking Questions

Possible responses are:

1. The tale explains how and why land was created; who created human beings and how; how human dwellings were created; and how humans received many of the material things necessary for living.

2. The Yoruba appear to have had a fairly well-developed culture with a sophisticated religion. The Yoruba have close ties to the physical world and a highly developed sense of observation. They have a central governing city named Ifé, built in a climate where rain occurs, and they harvest their foods from the trees and other plants around the city.

3. Responses will reflect students' understanding of "Owner of the Sky: Olorun the Creator," as well as their prior knowledge and ability to draw comparisons and contrasts. Sample answer: God in Jewish and Christian creation stories is all-knowing, just as Olorun is. The Judeo-Christian God also made earth, all that is in it, and humankind. However, the Judeo-Christian God took six days to create the earth and rested on the seventh. God's helpers are archangels and angels, rather than other lesser gods.

☑ Guidelines for Writing Your Response to "Owner of the Sky: Olorun the Creator"

Have students share their journal entries. As an alternative writing activity, suggest that students work in pairs to retell a scene from the myth using the viewpoint of the scene's main characters: the pigeon, hen, Chameleon, or Great God. Remind them that they should use simple yet elegant language, as does the original story. When students have finished, have pairs read their tales and ask the class to discuss how the student myths sound as they are read aloud. Encourage students to listen for well-crafted phrases, sentences, and paragraphs.

☑ Guidelines for Going Back Into the Text: Author's Craft

Point out to students that their daily lives are propelled by cause-effect relationships. Have students volunteer examples of such relationships, for example, changing classes because the bell rings, taking a test at the end of a unit, missing the bus because you forgot to set the alarm, etc. Challenge students to think of causes and effects from other curriculum areas and/or from the news.

Possible answers to the questions in the Student Edition are:

1. Because they must spread the small amount of earth around to cover a large space.

2. Because Olorun wanted to know when the earth's condition was right for people.

3. Because it was the first city ever created by Olorun.

4. The myth contains many cause-effect relationships; accept any that students offer in a correct cause-effect format. Sample responses: Olorun and the other gods often came to earth because they wanted to play; human beings could not come to earth because no dry land existed; Olorun sent Great God to earth because he wanted Great God to make dry ground.

✔ FOLLOW-UP DISCUSSION

Use the questions that follow to continue your discussion of "Owner of the Sky: Olorun the Creator." Possible answers are given in parentheses.

Recalling

1. How did the gods get to earth? (by sliding down spider silk)

2. What two conditions of the earth made it fit for people to live on? (The earth was wide and dry.)

3. Why was Great God jealous of Olorun? (because Olorun had the supreme power to bring humans to life)

4. What other natural occurrence is explained in this myth? (The myth suggests the Chameleon's ability to change colors was the result of his leaving the heavens and walking the land that Great God made.)

Interpreting

5. What actions of Olorun demonstrate that he did not completely trust Great God? (sending Chameleon to earth to check Great God's work; putting Great God to sleep while he brought humans to life)

6. What do you think is the significance of the myth's last paragraph? What might be the "mark" of Great God? (The mark of Great God might be the Yoruba explanation for people who are physically or mentally challenged.)

Applying

7. What cultural needs are fulfilled with this particular creation myth? (how the "first" city of Ifé came to be; how Olorun's "special" people, the Yoruba, were created and came to be in Ifé)

8. How does this myth compare to a creation story from your experience? (Answers will vary based on students' literary and cultural experiences.)

ENRICHMENT

Students will benefit from exploring *History and Culture of Africa*. The CD-ROM is available from Franklin McNeal, LTD., P.O. Box 2335, Smyrna, GA 30081-2335, (800) 358-8302.

The Sea Eats the Land at Home
by Kofi Awoonor

Song for the Sun that Disappeared Behind the Rainclouds
an oral poem of the Khoi   (pages 23–26)

OBJECTIVES

Literary

- to recognize sensory details and appreciate their effects
- to understand how the connotations of words affect the impact of sensory details

Historical

- to become acquainted with some ideas of "second-generation" African authors
- to realize that the oral tradition of storytelling remains strong in many African countries

Cultural

- to describe some characteristics of a traditional African culture
- to recognize cross-cultural themes

SELECTION RESOURCES

Use Assessment Worksheet 3 to check students' vocabulary recognition, content comprehension, and appreciation of literary skills.

✔ Informal Assessment Opportunity

SELECTION OVERVIEW

Born on March 13, 1936, Kofi Awoonor began life as George Awoonor-Williams. At that time, Ghana was called the Gold Coast and was part of the British Commonwealth of Nations. In post-graduate studies at universities in Ghana, London, and New York, he earned a M.A. in Modern English and a Ph.D. in Comparative Literature. He has pursued a university career and has also directed the Ghana Film Industries Corporation.

Using imagery from the African oral tradition in his poetry, Awoonor aims to bring to the rest of the world his memories and feelings about the landscapes and seascapes of his childhood. He succeeded with his very first book *Rediscovery* (1964).

In this selection, the two poets use poetic devices to explain nature—floods in the first poem and sunshine after a rainstorm in the second.

ENGAGING THE STUDENTS

Ask students what kind of climate and geography they usually associate with Africa. List student responses on the board. Then explain that many people think only of the Sahara Desert when they think of Africa. Let students reread the words and phrases listed on the board and decide whether they share that perception. Explain that the poems they are about to read will present a different picture of African weather and geography.

BRIDGING THE ESL/LEP LANGUAGE GAP

Students may find the vocabulary, as well as the extended metaphor and use of personification, difficult to understand. Read and discuss each poem separately.

"The Sea Eats the Land at Home": Expand the preteaching of the selection's vocabulary to include the sentence, "The sea eats the land at home," and the phrase "the angry sea". Write both on the chalkboard. Discuss the meaning of the verb *eat* and the adjective *angry.* Explain that the author thinks of a hungry, angry animal as he watches the sea flood his village. Ask them to describe or pantomime the actions of a very hungry and angry animal eating. Read the poem aloud for students. Have them read the poem again in pairs and identify phrases that tell what happens as the sea acts like a hungry, angry animal.

"Song for the Sun that Disappeared Behind the Rainclouds": Also expand the preteaching of this selection's vocabulary. Discuss the meaning of the verb *disappear.* Have students brainstorm all the things that happen during a severe rainstorm. List students' suggestions on the board. Have students also tell what happens when the rain ends during the day and at night. Again, read the poem aloud for students and then pair them. As they reread the poem, have them look for phrases that poetically describe the occurrences listed on the board. Ask them to share poems or folk sayings from their native cultures that may describe rainstorms or that explain why these weather events occur.

☑ PRETEACHING SELECTION VOCABULARY

On the board, write the following words and phrases: *wood floating from the* **hearth**, *cries and shouts of* **mourning**, **eternal** *sounds of the sea, lost and scattered* **dowry**, **lamentations** *of frightened villagers.* Ask students to speculate about the events that the poems might describe, using the vocabulary in the phrases. Add their suggestions to the board.

The words printed in boldfaced type are tested on the selection assessment worksheet.

PREREADING

Reading the Poems in a Cultural Context

Help students read for purpose by asking them how they would feel if their own homes and those of their neighbors were destroyed by a flood. Discuss emotions that they think are typical of people faced with natural disasters. Ask them to consider whether such feelings might differ from culture to culture.

Focusing on the Selection

Ask students to name different kinds of storms that involve water. Write their suggestions on the board. Challenge them to rank the storms in order from "least damaging/most helpful" to "least helpful/most damaging." Ask them to determine where they would place the storms described in the poems.

POSTREADING

The following activities parallel the features with the same titles in the Student Edition.

Responses to Critical Thinking Questions

Possible responses are:

1. The language describes very exact sights, sounds, and feelings that would occur with a flood.

    For example, details from "The Sea Eats the Land at Home" might include:
    Sight — destroying the cement walls, carried away the fowls, the cooking pots and ladles; goats and fowl were struggling in the water.

    Sound — wails and the mourning shouts of the women, weeping mournfully; lap-lapping of the bark water at the shore; sobs and the deep and low moans; the eternal hum of the living sea.

    Touch — two children shivering from the cold; cold Sunday morning; lap-lapping of the bark water at the shore.

    Emotion — it is a sad thing to hear (the calls of the women); ancestors have neglected; gods have deserted; storm was raging; angry water; the cruel sea has taken away their belongings.

2. In both poems, details suggest that the villagers live simply. They cook with firewood in fireplaces, they raise goats and poultry; they use baskets and pots for holding and carrying things; their religion includes the worship of ancestors and a number of gods.

3. Answers will vary. Student responses should indicate an awareness that their experiences and those of the villagers are similar.

☑ Guidelines for Writing Your Response to "The Sea Eats the Land at Home" and "Song for the Sun . . ."

Encourage students to share their journal entries with a partner. As an alternative writing activity, have students work in pairs to compose sensory details that might be included in a newscast of a flood or that could be part of a poem about the villagers' relief in "Song for the Sun . . . ."

✔ Guidelines for Going Back Into the Text: Author's Craft

Remind students that sensory details make a writer's experience real to the reader. Explain that a poet also uses sensory details to present a picture that will evoke a particular emotion.

Encourage students to examine the choice of details and language that the poets include in the poems. Ask them to think about what emotion the poets might have wanted to evoke and how the sensory details chosen enhance that emotion.

Possible answers to Student Edition questions are:

1. It came one day at the dead of night; sending it back by night ("The Sea…"); he walks along the Milky Way and collects the stars. ("The Sun…")

2. Verbs describing the sea's actions: running in and out, collecting, eats, destroying, carried away, taken away. Verbs describing the villagers' reactions: calling on all the gods, shivering, weeping mournfully.

3. Nouns naming the sounds that can be heard: wails, morning shouts, sobs, deep and low moans, eternal hum of the living sea; the human sounds are sad and despairing. The sound of the sea *seems* uncaring because it continues throughout the storm and drowns out life in the village.

4. Results of the rainstorm: darkens, turns black, extinguishes; God's search for the stars: sparkles, collects, piles, overflows.

5. Both stars and lizards are small; neither lizards nor the stars' light could be contained or kept in the pot. The lizard image changes the feeling from the opening one of dread and unhappiness to one of relief and humor. The image also normalizes the experience; instead of being a frightening situation, the storm takes on the more common characteristics of a woman cooking.

✔ FOLLOW-UP DISCUSSION

Use the questions that follow to continue your discussion of these poems. Possible answers are given in parentheses.

Recalling

1. Where are these villages located? (near an African seacoast and/or some other area where rain is frequent) How do you know that neither village is affected by the Sahara Desert? (because both are experiencing weather events not typical of a desert) How do either or both poems challenge the stereotypical "view" of Africa? (Both are about water, a natural commodity that many believe is in short supply in Africa.)

2. What adjectives does Awoonor use to describe the sea and the sea's sound? (He describes the sea as "living" and its sound as "eternal.")

Interpreting

3. What phrases does Awoonor use to personify the sea as a hungry animal? (it is in the town, running in and out, eats the land at home, carried away the fowls, and goats and fowls were struggling)

4. How do you know that the villagers in both poems regard the flood and the rainstorm as supernatural events under the control of the gods? (In "The Sea…," the villagers call on the gods but believe that they have deserted them; in "Song for the Sun…," the villagers believe that God has heard their cries when the rainbow and then stars and starlight appear.)

5. How does the choice of language enhance the poems' emotions? (Lead students to understand that the language of both poems is highly connotative. For example, to support the phrase "sad thing," Awoonor uses words and phrases that are "charged" with negative feelings such as mourning, wails, shivering, hands on her breast, lost her joy.)

Applying

6. Why do you think Awoonor described this disastrous event from his past? (Students should realize that living through a disaster most often remains a clear, indelible memory.)

7. What generalities about human emotions in the face of "nature's fury" can you make from these poems and your own experiences? (Students should address the commonality of human helplessness in the face of natural disasters.)

8. What generalities can you make about the villagers' emotions in "Song for the Sun…" after the rainstorm? (Students should be aware of the commonality of the emotion that follows a frightening event.)

ENRICHMENT

Students will discover the diversity throughout modern-day Africa by exploring *Africa Trail*. The CD-ROM is available from National School Products, 101 East Broadway, Maryville, TN 37804-2498 (800) 627-9393.

The Prebend Gardens/Interior
by Léopold Sédar Sénghor

All That You Have Given Me, Africa
by Anoma Kanié (pages 27–31)

OBJECTIVES

Literary
- to analyze author's purpose; to become aware that poets often write for nationalistic purposes
- to observe how authors choose images and language to convey their thoughts, feelings, and culture

Historical
- to develop an awareness that many Africans rebelled against European thought and learning
- to develop an awareness that African authors began a literary movement to instill pride in African blacks

Cultural
- to develop an awareness of the inheritance of which Sub-Saharan black Africans are proud
- to recognize that love of one's homeland is a common cultural theme

SELECTION RESOURCES

Use Assessment Worksheet 4 to check students' vocabulary recognition, content comprehension, and appreciation of literary skills.

✔ Informal Assessment Opportunity

SELECTION OVERVIEW

Both Sénghor and Kanié wrote in French, one of the three European languages whose widespread use in Africa reflect Africa's colonization by the European powers. (The other two are Portuguese and English.) French was the language of the first contemporary African literature movement that appeared early in the 20th century.

Sénghor spearheaded the movement protesting French rule and the French policy of assimilation. In 1947, Sénghor and brothers-in-arms Aime Cesaire of Martinique and Leon Damas of French Guinea founded Presence Africaine, Africa's leading literary journal. A year later, Sénghor published *Anthologie de la novelle poesie negre et malgache* (Anthology of the New Negro and Madagscan Poetry), a book that heavily influenced the formation of the Negritude movement.

In 1960, Sénghor was elected as the first president of the Republic of Senegal.

Many critics were skeptical that the French language could adequately convey the mystique of African life. They found, however, that Sénghor was able to capture the essence of African existence, particularly in the structure and rhythm of his poetry. Of his ability to blend the French language with African rhythms, Sénghor said, "We [Africans] are the leaven that the white flour needs."

In these poems, the poets show their appreciation and love for the beauty of Africa, their homeland.

ENGAGING THE STUDENTS

Challenge students to list short descriptive phrases that capture the sights, sounds, smells, and feelings they have about their native homeland. To help students get started, you might suggest that they recall the lyrics to patriotic songs and national anthems.

Ask students to share the phrases, songs, or anthems that they think best capture the flavor of their homeland.

BRIDGING THE ESL/LEP LANGUAGE GAP

Note: Because the language in "All That You Have Given Me, Africa" is difficult, you may wish to use the Recalling and Interpreting questions under *Follow-Up Discussion* at the end of this lesson to further students' understanding.

Read the poem aloud and have students listen, without following along in their texts. Ask them what phrases or images struck them in particular. Write the students' answers on the board; explain any vocabulary that students don't understand. Then read the poems aloud again.

Have students work in small groups of three or four to determine what the poets are describing and what emotions they are feeling. Ask: What words or phrases do you know that name these emotions? Help students build a word bank of terms, such as homeland, patriotism, nationalism, and so forth.

When students have completed their analysis, discuss the following lines from "All That You Have Given Me, Africa" as a class: "And I go forward/Praising my race which is not better/Or worse than any other." Have groups compile a list of the things the poets describe in recalling their homelands. Then have the groups share their discoveries with the class.

☑ PRETEACHING SELECTION VOCABULARY

Ask students to identify a geographical location in Africa that might be suggested by the following terms: *misted lagoons, dark pigments etched in skin, golden savannahs, rugs and furniture from Timbuktu, lamenting European colonialism, indelible traditions* and *customs from our ancestors.* Allow students to share their opinions. Then locate Timbuktu on the classroom map. Ask students which vocabulary words, if any, they could use in the phrases they wrote earlier. Suggest that they add phrases using the words *pigments, lamenting,* and **indelible**.

The word printed in boldfaced type is tested on the selection assessment worksheet.

PREREADING

Reading the Poems in a Cultural Context

Point out that the poets who composed these poems wanted to stir national pride in fellow Africans, as well

as criticize European actions that they believed were harmful to Africa. Challenge students to look for words and phrases that fulfill both goals.

Focusing on the Selection

Ask students to predict how their own nationalistic feelings are similiar to or different from what they think the poets' feelings will be. Write their predictions on the board. After students have discussed the poems, return to their predictions. Ask them to consider whether love of one's homeland is natural; have them support their opinions with material from their own writing or from the poems.

POSTREADING

The following activities parallel the features with the same titles in the Student Edition.

Responses to Critical Thinking Questions

Possible responses are:

1. Both poets identify the beauty of their lands and their peoples.

2. Kanié speaks about the music and dancing that are an important part of African cultures and refers heavily to his country's past history and European influences on it. Sénghor talks about the Prebend Gardens, which citizens of his country apparently walk through and enjoy. He focuses on the Arab-Moslem decor of the homes in his land, as well as African masks, acknowledging both African and Arab influences.

3. Responses will indicate students' knowledg of their native cultures, as well as their understanding of the poet's aims. Guide students in discussing the universality of patriotic feelings.

☑ Guidelines for Writing Your Response to "All That You Have Given Me, Africa," "Prebend Gardens," and "Interior"

Have students share their journal entries with a partner. As an alternative writing activity, ask them to decide how effective they think nationalistic poems and songs are. Have students write and share their opinions with the class. Then ask the class to work together to compose a "ruling" that expressses the class's position on or evaluation of nationalistic poems and songs. If a dissenting opinion exists, allow students to work together to formulate a composite dissenting "challenge."

☑ Guidelines for Going Back Into the Text: Author's Craft

Ask: What words or phrases most effectively convey the poets' pride in their country? As students respond, remind them that the poets want Sub-Saharan African people to feel pride not only in their beautiful continent, but also in their survival under oppression.

Possible answers to Student Edition questions are:

1. Effective desriptions of physical objects could include "All That You Have Given Me, Africa": lakes, forests, misted lagoons, savannahs gold, your beasts that men call wicked, your mines, clear horizons; "Interior": sparkling soft carpets, Moorish cushions, dark, heavy furniture, authentic primitive masks, solid walls, black, brown, red, red as African soil.

2. Effective examples of poetic language that creates positive feelings for African history and traditions are "All That You Have Given Me, Africa": music, dances, all night stories around a fire; pigments of my ancestors, indelible in my blood, a step that is like no other, bear it with pride, praising my race, clear horizons, heaven-given task; "Prebend Gardens": a muted trumpet; "Interior": bathe in an African presence, authentic, friendly lamp, tenderness, obsession, Oh! red as African soil.

3. Effective examples of poetic language that create negative feelings about the "outside" French culture include "All That You Have Given Me, Africa": hip broken under the weight of time, feet large with journeys, health no more to be lost; beasts that men call wicked, obsession of a hostile world, suffering for lost paradises, an unforgiving hand; "Prebend Gardens": Lamenting and searching its way in some lost clearing in me.

☑ FOLLOW-UP DISCUSSION

Use the questions that follow to continue your discussion of these poems. Possible answers are given in parentheses.

Recalling

1. In addition to Sub-Saharan black African culture, what other culture is especially mentioned? (Spanish Arab or Moor) in which poem? ("Interior")

2. What are pigments? (substances in cells that give color to skin)

3. What African countries are specifically mentioned? (Guinea, Congo) What city? (Timbuktu)

Interpreting

4. What does Kanié mean by saying that his skin is etched with pigments of his ancestors, which are indelible in his blood? (that the physical characteristics of his cultural group come from a long line of ancestors as illustrious and respected as those of any other race)

5. To what journey in Kanié referring? (the trips of enslaved Africans to other parts of the world)

6. In "Prebend Gardens", what symbol does Senghor use for his African identity? (trumpet) Africa's past greatness? (lost clearing)

7. What has wounded his African sense of self, caused it to lament and search, and send out a muted note? (colonization and poor rule by European powers)

Applying

8. How could these poems raise pride in one's culture? (They speak of the beauties of Africa and the pride of peoples that no foreign power has been able to conquer fully.)

9. How do these poems indicate or imply that foreign rule is bad for Africa? (The poems refer to hurtful actions and methods that the colonial leaders have imposed on Africa and its culture groups.)

ENRICHMENT

Students may benefit from viewing *Africa: Its People and Promise,* available from Zenger Media, 10200 Jefferson Boulevard, Room 922, P.O. Box 802, Culver City, CA 90232, (800) 421-4246.

OBJECTIVE

Overall

- to discover the connections between famous monuments in Africa and the Middle East and the cultures of these lands

Specific

- to analyze the contrast between traditional and modern ideas in "Marriage Is a Private Affair" and *The Dark Child*
- to examine how different Middle Eastern cultures regard the Wailing Wall and other aspects of their homeland as shown in "A Lover from Palestine" and "In This Valley"
- to explore how the cruelty of prejudice in places like Goree Island and South Africa is reflected in "The Toilet" and "A Chip of Glass Ruby"

ENGAGING THE STUDENTS

On the board write the following question:

Why do we treasure national monuments?

Allow students a few minutes to brainstorm a list of famous monuments that are important to Americans. Next ask the class: Why do we feel so strongly about these monuments? How do they show pride in our history and culture? Then invite students to study the photographs of the Nile River, the Wailing Wall, and Goree Island on pages 32 and 33 and discuss how they represent Middle Eastern culture.

BRIDGING THE ESL/LEP LANGUAGE GAP

Have students make a chart of words that describe these monuments. Under each column, students should list words that tell more about the monument. They can start by looking through the feature, then brainstorming additional terms.

EXPLORING LANDMARKS

The Nile is the longest river in the world. From Lake Victoria in central Africa, it flows a distance of 4,160 miles. Through Uganda, Sudan, and Egypt to the Mediterranean Sea. During the 20th century, several dams were built to harness the waterpower of the Nile, including the Makwar Dam (now called Sennar Dam) and the Aswan High Dam.

Encourage students to discover more about the Nile River. The following are suggestions for activities, ranging in difficulty from least to most challenging.

- Have students look at the map of Africa on page 2 of the Student Edition. Have them list the countries through which the Nile flows, its point of origin and the sea into which it empties. Explain to students that much of Africa and the Middle East is desert. Ask them to speculate on the role the Nile River plays in this region.

- Have groups of students work collaboratively to research the Aswan High Dam and its impact on the environment in the Nile River Valley. Have students list the advantages and disadvantages of the Dam. (Advantages: supplies hydroelectric power and water for irrigation; disadvantages: traps silt that once renewed Egyptian farm soil.) Then stage a debate in which one group defends the building of the dam and the other defends the farmers who object to it.

- Have students write a brief research essay in which they compare and contrast the role of the Nile in ancient civilizations to its role in the present day.

LINKING LITERATURE, CULTURE AND REGION

Guidelines for Evaluation: Sample Answers

In *The Dark Child*, the contrast between traditional and modern machines is shown by the mother crushing millet with a pestle and mortar as she is told that her son will travel by airplane to France. In "Marriage Is a Private Affair" his son's marriage conflicts with a father's traditional beliefs.

The speaker in "A Lover from Palestine" is passionate about Palestine, "the light of my heart/The salt of my bread." The speaker in "In This Valley" is also deeply connected to his homeland, a place of hope, "of starting afresh without having to die first."

The narrator in "The Toilet" fights to get her education and escape from the second-class status of apartheid. Mrs. Bamjee in "A Chip of Glass Ruby" is arrested when she fights against apartheid.

The Toilet

by Gcina Mhlope   (pages 34–42)

OBJECTIVES

Literary

- to identify the characteristics of first-person narratives
- to analyze how point of view influences the development of ideas in a personal narrative

Historical

- to understand South Africa's apartheid policy
- to examine how apartheid influences the social, economic, and political lives of people in South Africa

Cultural

- to discuss the effects of apartheid on all South Africans
- to present relationships and conflicts within the black South African community

SELECTION RESOURCES

Use Assessment Worksheet 5 to check student's vocabulary recognition, content comprehension, and appreciation of literary skill.

 Informal Assessment Opportunity

SELECTION OVERVIEW

Apartheid is a term for the former government policy of "separate development" in South Africa. The word comes from the Afrikaans language and translates literally as "apartness."

White South Africans, descendants of Dutch, German, French, and British colonists, established the policy in 1948 to maintain white supremacy. All South Africans were classified into four groups: whites (about 13 percent); blacks (about 77 percent); coloreds (those of mixed descent, about 8 percent); and Asians (about 2 percent).

Ten African cultural groups were officially recognized by the white-dominated government. The government set up "homeland" areas within South Africa for each group and forced the black population to resettle. Black South Africans bitterly resented this because it broke up the black population and reduced their effectiveness as a political force.

In addition, the government imposed strict housing segregation on black South Africans who worked in white areas. Other laws included certain occupational restrictions, segregation of all public facilities, prohibition of racial intermarriage, and requirements that all blacks carry "passes" when in white areas.

In the early 1990s, apartheid began to crumble, but only after decades of fierce fighting on both sides, international condemnation, and embargoes on South African trade. With the end of apartheid, black South Africans gained the right to vote. In 1994, they exercised that right for the first time, helping to put Nelson Mandela into office as the first black president. In 1996, a new constitution took effect, declaring black and white South Africans equal.

In this selection, the main character finds an unlikely place to call her own. When confronted by the fact that this place isn't hers, she accepts it and moves on with her life.

ENGAGING THE STUDENTS

On the board, write the following phrases: *American society, you, your parents, your peer group.* Ask students to discuss how much influence each person or group listed should have on an individual's selection of a career. Work with the class to put the items in the list in order from most to least influential. Tell students that in the upcoming selection, the main character faces conflict from within herself as well as from the three other groups listed on the board. Challenge students to determine as they read which conflict influences the main character most.

BRIDGING THE ESL/LEP LANGUAGE GAP

The language in the selection is clear and straightforward, and the context for British terms is rich. Students may be able to add considerably to the class's understanding and empathy for the main character, particularly if the governments in their native lands are repressive. Encourage students to share as much appropriate information as they are able about government involvement in an individual's life.

Those from countries in which tradition and family desires play important roles in career selection for young people may also be able to enhance this area of American students' understanding. Encourage them to draw comparisons and contrasts between the narrator's situation in the selection and similar situations in their native countries as well as in the United States.

☑ PRETEACHING SELECTION VOCABULARY

Vertically list the following selection vocabulary on the board: *Johannesburg, matric exams, domestic worker, alternative, knocked off, boutiques, premises.* Ask students to make "educated guesses" based on what has already been presented and discussed, as to how these words may fit into the selection. Jot opinions beside each vocabulary word. Encourage students to note how close their predictions come to the words' meaning in the actual story.

The words printed in boldfaced type are tested on the selection assessment worksheet.

PREREADING

Reading the Story in a Cultural Context

Help students read for purpose by challenging them to watch for details that describe the kind of society in which the author lives. Students should address such topics as the author's living quarters and how she must control her behavior.

Focusing on the Selection

Ask: Which challenge facing the character seemed most familiar to you? least familiar? Have students support their opinions with examples from the text, constructing a Venn diagram to compare and contrast

the author's career situation to that of a young person in contemporary American society. When the diagram is completed, have students use the data to help them formulate answers for the postreading questions.

POSTREADING

The following activities parallel the features with the same titles in the Student Edition.

Responses to Critical Thinking Questions

Possible responses are:

1. The author finds the public toilet relatively clean, dry, and sheltered from the wind. She also likes the fact that the booth is very small and gives her a feeling of privacy. These qualities make her think that she has been very "lucky" to have found the toilet, because it seems that it had been made to "fit me alone."

2. The author portrays South African society as repressive to South African blacks by her choice of detail, rather than any direct comments. The author seems to accept her position in the repressive society, while making it clear that she dislikes it. Certainly, she never openly condemns it. Students might also infer that she is in conflict with her own culture group as well as with white South African society because she pursues her interest in writing and acting despite disapproval from her family.

3. Answers will vary according to students' personal experiences. However, their responses should reflect an awareness that the author's mother and sister disapprove of her goals for different reasons. They might compare or contrast their experiences with the authors', pointing out how young people often must battle for personal identity on many fronts.

☑ Guidelines for Writing Your Response to "The Toilet"

Have students share their journal entries with a partner. As an alternative activity, students may want to discuss Gcina Mhlope's ability to make the best of an intolerable situation. Share with them the explanation of South Africa's apartheid policy under the heading "Selection Overview." Ask: What was the aim of white South Africans in instituting apartheid? Call on students to share their comments. Then discuss with students how segregation injures all culture groups in a society.

✔ Guidelines for Going Back Into the Text: Author's Craft

Help students understand that the selection's first-person point of view gives it a much stronger impact than would a third-person point of view. Point out that the author is a black South African who lived under apartheid. Ask them to consider whether the author's matter-of-fact tone increases or decreases the reader's reaction to the injustices of apartheid.

Possible answers to Student Edition questions are:

1. Mhlope presents conflicts with her family matter-of-factly, providing details that clearly spotlight the heart of the conflict. For example, her mother feels her education will be wasted unless she pursues a "respectable" career, such as teaching or nursing. Her sister is not interested in her notebook. She thinks she should learn to cook, sew, and knit so she will make a good wife.

2. Mhlope's belief that her sister "hates" her may be somewhat exaggerated, though her sister is undoubtedly angry at her behavior the night she is late. However, Mhlope's "second thoughts"—that her sister was worried for her as well as scared of her employers—are probably correct, for her sister does assume that Mhlope will continue to live with her in her room. Mhlope reports that Madam scares her because her smiles seem so friendly, yet she doesn't want to extend any social courtesies to the author. She doesn't call the dogs off right away, allowing them to intimidate the author, and she doesn't offer to let the author wait in her sister's room.

3. Students' responses will reflect their ability to empathize with the narrator. Challenge students to support their opinions with examples from the text.

✔ FOLLOW-UP DISCUSSION

Use the questions that follow to continue your discussion. Possible answers are given in parentheses.

Recalling

1. How do you know that the narrator is in conflict with her own cultural group or at least that of her family? (The first four paragraphs detail the feelings of the author's mother and sister.)

2. How does Gwendolene reinforce the idea that the author is at odds with many other girls her own age? (Gwendolene can't understand Mhlope's desire to read rather than meet boys.)

3. What feelings prompt the author to start writing? (boredom with the love stories she reads, fond memories of writing poetry and stories in school)

Interpreting

4. What is surprising about the fact that a "public toilet" becomes a "private place" for Mhlope? What is the significance of the fact that the bathroom is apparently unused by black South Africans? (A public bathroom usually has people going in and out; this one appears to be used so infrequently that Mhlope feels comfortable choosing it for privacy. It appears that black South Africans may refuse to use the separate public facilities available to them.)

5. What is the significance of the dogs owned both by Madam and the family next door? (The dogs appear to be guard dogs, kept to alert white South Africans of anyone on their property.)

6. What is the significance of the selection's last sentence, "Slowly I walked over to a bench nearby, watched the early spring sun come up, and wrote my story anyway"? (In that sentence, the author underscores the determination to "do something different." She appears to reject having to live in hiding, and, literally and symbolically, decides to "come out into the sunshine.")

Applying

7. What do first-person accounts such as "The Toilet" provide that a third-person view might not? (Guide students to understand that first-person accounts can provide personal insights and accurate recollections of people living through historically important times.

8. Imagine that you live in a society as repressive as Gcina Mhlope's. How might you handle and respond to the kinds of controls that you read about in "The Toilet"? (Answers will vary. Ask students to support their responses.)

ENRICHMENT

Students may enjoy reading the books *Women in Africa*, Volumes 1 and 2, available from Social Studies School Service, 10200 Jefferson Boulevard, Room 12, Culver City, CA 90232, (800) 421-4246.

A Chip of Glass Ruby

by Nadine Gordimer (pages 43–54)

OBJECTIVES

Literary

- to understand conflicts portrayed in a short story
- to differentiate between internal and external conflict

Historical

- to develop an awareness of methods used to fight South Africa's apartheid policy
- to demonstrate various attitudes and actions in response to South Africa's apartheid policy

Cultural

- analyze various ways in which religious beliefs can affect believers
- to understand the effects of apartheid on individuals within South African society

SELECTION RESOURCES

Use Assessment Worksheet 6 to check students' vocabulary recognition, content comprehension, and appreciation of literary skills.

 Informal Assessment Opportunity

SELECTION OVERVIEW

Like Gcina Mhlope, the author of "The Toilet," writer Nadine Gordimer also grew up in South Africa. As a white South African, Gordimer came to hate the apartheid system and used her writing to expose its injustices to the world. Through her characters, Gordimer examines the complex human emotions and tensions generated by the apartheid system.

"A Chip of Glass Ruby" is among the works produced by Gordimer that demonstrates her belief that, as Mrs. Bamjee explains it, "We [South Africans] all have the same troubles." As Gordimer matured, she became convinced that every ethnic group in South Africa, including whites, suffered from apartheid. This belief became such a pervasive theme in her later works that her writings were often banned in her homeland.

Considered an accomplished short story writer as well as a reputable novelist, Gordimer has had her fiction published in such American periodicals as the *Atlantic*, the *New Yorker*, and the *Yale Review*.

In this selection, a mother of five is jailed for helping print anti-apartheid pamphlets. Her husband realizes how her selflessness makes her a special woman.

ENGAGING THE STUDENTS

On the board, write this quote from the selection: "We've all got the same troubles." Tell students that the selection takes place in Johannesburg, South Africa, the same setting as the previous selection, "The Toilet." Ask students to recall from "The Toilet" some of the troubles that the quote might refer to. List student responses on the board. Explain that in Gordimer's story, one character "takes on the system." Ask students to be alert for additional troubles engendered by South Africa's apartheid system as they read the selection. As they identify these problems, add them to the list on the board.

BRIDGING THE ESL/LEP LANGUAGE GAP

The vocabulary and the religious concepts in the selection may present difficulty for some students, and they may need to read the selection twice. At the beginning of the selection, explain that Mr. Bamjee is the main character and that everything is seen and felt through his eyes.

Help students scan the selection to find the behaviors expected from a good Moslem woman. (Depending on the level of the students, you may want to read these sentences and paragraphs aloud to them.) Write these on the board as students locate them.

Tell students that Mrs. Bamjee practices the "spirit" as well as the laws of her religion, and ask them what this might mean. What Moslem rules for womanly behavior does Mrs. Bamjee follow? What "spirit" is she following when she becomes active in the protests against apartheid?

Ask them to pay attention to how the religious concepts they found and discussed earlier relate to each character. Suggest that they ask themselves as they read: Why does conflict arise between Mr. and Mrs. Bamjee if she is behaving as a good Moslem wife should?

✔ PRETEACHING SELECTION VOCABULARY

Point out that people of the same family or culture group may respond differently to political situations. Their personal beliefs may shape their attitudes and actions. On the board, list the following selection vocabulary words: *confident, flattered, suspicious, persist,* **disarmed,** *resentment,* **morose,** *accusing,* **scandalous,** *rebellious,* **bewildered,** **reproach,** *maddened,* and *desperately.* Tell students that the two main characters in this story have very different attitudes about political activism. Challenge students to categorize vocabulary words into those relating to positive attitudes and those relating to negative attitudes.

The words printed in boldfaced type are tested on the selection assessment worksheet.

PREREADING

Reading the Story in a Cultural Context

Help students read for a purpose by asking them to consider the importance of religious beliefs in the selection. Discuss Mrs. Bamjee's apparant perception that religious beliefs should manifest themselves in the believer's actions. Encourage students to also examine the obvious fact that everyone who knows Mrs. Bamjee perceives her positively, while Mr. Bamjee apparently doesn't.

Focusing on the Selection

Have students jot down in their notebooks their agreement or disagreement with the opening comment: "We've all got the same troubles." Ask them to address the issue of when political action becomes necessary, pointing out that they are nearing the age

when they are most likely to become politically involved. Challenge them to focus on this question: When should the injustices suffered by one person or group become my concern? Tell students to save their writing and compare their ideas with Mr. and Mrs. Bamjee's as they read "A Chip of Glass Ruby."

POSTREADING

The following activities parallel the features with the same titles in the Student Edition.

Responses to Critical Thinking Questions

Possible responses are:

1. Gordimer uses details designed to show specific characteristics, thoughts, and emotions of both Mr. and Mrs. Bamjee. Mrs. Bamjee is cheerful, caring, and concerned. She smiles at her husband's objection to the duplicator, immediately makes a place for it in the house, carries on her duties as wife and mother while she runs off leaflets, always explains her activities to her husband, and remembers birthdays and other important events. Mr. Bamjee is worried, frightened, and confused; he walks heavily, refuses to "see" what his wife is doing, dozes to escape, complains about Mrs. Bamjee's behavior but can't find any real fault, and finally can only admit that she is "different."

2. In traditional Moslem culture, the role of the woman is to care for the family and the home. The fact that Mrs. Bamjee is also politically active and interacts with men who are not family members makes Mr. Bamjee nervous and unhappy.

3. Student responses will reflect their knowledge of the political issues of the community, as well as the similarities or differences between their community and the Bamjee's. Students should provide specific examples of activities they would and would not support.

✔ Guidelines for Writing Your Response to "A Chip of Glass Ruby"

Have students share their journal entries with a partner. As an alternative writing activity, suggest that they write character sketches of Mr. and Mrs. Bamjee based on the characters' actions, as well as the reactions of others to them in the story. Others include the children, the neighbors, and political activists in the area. Call on volunteers to share their character sketches with the rest of the class.

☑ Guidelines for Going Back Into the Text: Author's Craft

Ask students to identify the conflicts in the selection, telling which conflict is external and which is internal. Question them as to the outcome of each conflict: was it resolved or not? What makes them think the way they do? Suggest that they also compare the conflicts in this selection with those in "The Toilet": How is Mrs. Bamjee like Gcina Mhlope? How is Mr. Bamjee like Mhlope's mother and sister? What force in both stories causes an external conflict?

Possible answers to the questions in the Student Edition are:

1. Mr. Bamjee appears to experience the greatest internal conflict because the author includes many details describing his feelings of dismay and confusion, as well as the things he does to ignore the situation around him. Mrs. Bamjee appears to be experiencing the least internal conflict because her political activity doesn't interrupt her daily routine at all.

2. The glass ruby chip is an external sign of the traditional beliefs of Mrs. Bamjee's children in India. Apparently, Mrs. Bamjee experienced some inner conflict with traditional Moslem belief when she first moved to Johannesburg. Her removal of the chip symbolizes the resolution of her inner conflict and her break with tradition.

3. The movement of South Africa's black citizens to overturn the government's apartheid policy; Mr. Bamjee is frightened that he will somehow be implicated in his wife's activities or that something horrible will happen that will dramatically change his life.

☑ FOLLOW-UP DISCUSSION

Use the questions that follow to continue your discussion of "A Chip of Glass Ruby." Possible answers are given in parentheses.

Recalling

1. Why are the Bamjee children aware of the difference in opinion between their father and mother? (The family lives in such a small house that privacy is unknown.)

2. What are some actions that black South Africans were taking to prompt the government into changing its apartheid policy? (tearing up their passes, presenting themselves for arrest, having "sick days," and handing out protest literature)

3. What overwhelming change happened in the house with Mrs. Bamjee's arrest? (The house, once bustling with activity, became very quiet.)

Interpreting

4. What does Mr. Bamjee mean by his opening remark, "Isn't it enough that you've got the Indians' troubles on your back?" (He implies that the Indians are just as persecuted as the black South Africans.)

5. What is the significance of Mrs. Bamjee's trembling hands when she opens the door to the South African police? (She is as deeply afraid of the consequences of her actions, but she has been hiding her fear.)

6. What is significant about Mrs. Bamjee's telling her husband to go to the engagement party? reminding her daughter not to forget Mr. Bamjee's birthday? (Mrs. Bamjee appears to be truly selfless; even at the moment of her arrest or during her hunger strike at the jail, she thinks of others' feelings.)

Applying

7. What do you think Nadine Gordimer is saying about the South African policy of apartheid and its effects on all classes of South Africans? (She appears to be saying that apartheid affects everyone negatively, whether South Africans protest or try to ignore the system.)

8. If Mrs. Bamjee is released from prison and allowed to return home, do you think her behavior will change? Why or why not? Will Mr. Bamjee be different? (Answers will vary.) Students may point out that Mrs. Bamjee's impulses will remain the same but that her behavior could change; she might be more careful. Since Mr. Bamjee seems to understand his wife better by the end of the story, he might be more supportive.

ENRICHMENT

Students may benefit from viewing *Women in the Third World* from the Global Links series, available from Zenger Media, 10200 Jefferson Boulevard, Room 922, P.O. Box 802, Culver City, CA 90232, (800) 421-4246.

Marriage Is a Private Affair

by Chinua Achebe   (pages 55–62)

OBJECTIVES

Literary

- to identify external and internal conflicts in a story
- to recognize the author's attitude toward the themes of tradition and change

Historical

- to understand how European colonialism affected Africa's culture groups
- to build awareness of the challenges Africans faced as their societies changed

Cultural

- to be aware of the difficulty that culture groups experience during colonization
- to understand some effects of cross-cultural marriages

SELECTION RESOURCES

Use Assessment Worksheet 7 to check students' vocabulary recognition, content comprehension, and appreciation of literary skills.

 Informal Assessment Opportunity

SELECTION OVERVIEW

Chinua Achebe wrote and published his first novel, *Things Fall Apart,* in 1959. His work introduced serious social and psychological analysis into Nigerian prose. The novel tells the story of an Ibo warrior who rigidly identifies with his traditional culture during the early days of colonization. This identification keeps him from developing the mental flexibility necessary to adapt to changing conditions.

The novel won international recognition and set the theme for much of Achebe's early work. He explored the diverse ways that Africans responded—or didn't—to the challenges that European colonialism presented as well as the consequences of those responses. His second novel, *No Longer At Ease,* investigates a young African idealist who is incapable of choosing between the modern standards of moral judgment learned at a European school and those demanded by his traditional culture. *Arrow of God,* his third novel, portrays a village high priest who, by acknowledging the weaknesses of a traditional outlook, finds himself betraying the villagers' trust.

Achebe began to change the focus of his writing during the 1960s, as Nigeria faced overwhelming political problems and intercultural feuding. *A Man of the People,* published in 1966, portrays a corrupt Nigerian politician. This novel brought the author further international acclaim. Many hailed him as "the most notable English-speaking novelist in modern-day Africa" for his skillful exploration of individual character and ethical problems in fictional terms.

In this selection, a father exiles his son because he marries a girl from another culture group. The father refuses to see either his son or his son's wife until the wife writes to him about his grandchildren.

ENGAGING THE STUDENTS

Give students five minutes to write on this topic: Why do some parents or elderly relatives react negatively when a son or daughter marries someone of a different background?

When they have finished writing, discuss their answers. Ask volunteers to share their thoughts. Then explain that in this selection, they will read about one father's reaction to his son's marriage to a girl from a different culture.

BRIDGING THE ESL/LEP LANGUAGE GAP

Vocabulary and time changes in the selection may present some difficulties; however, the theme and plot will be familiar. Read the selection title aloud, and help students read the first scene through the father's letter. Ask students to predict several directions the plot could take. Write their suggestions on the board.

At each scene change, encourage students to re-evaluate their predictions and change them if they wish. At the selection's end, discuss the accuracy of students' predictions and how familiarity with the theme helped them make their predictions.

☑ PRETEACHING SELECTION VOCABULARY

Challenge students to create an idea or word web around the emotions and attitudes that can accompany an engagement and marriage. Then write the following words from the selection on the board: *vehemently, dissuasion, commiserate, implore, remorse.* Tell students that these words are related to the father's attitude toward the engagement and marriage of his son. Ask students to speculate about the challenges the relationship between father and son might face.

After students have read the selection, discuss how the words actually apply to the father's opposition to his son's marriage.

The words printed in boldfaced type are tested on the selection assessment worksheet.

PREREADING

Responding to Literature: Modeling Active Reading

"Marriage Is a Private Affair" is annotated with the comments of an active reader. These sidenotes, prepared to promote critical reading, emphasize the cultural content of the piece, address author values, call attention to literary skills, invite personal response, and show how the selection is related to theme. If you have time, read the entire selection aloud as a dialogue between reader and text. Encourage students to discuss and add their own responses to the ones printed in the margins. Model these skills by adding your own observations, too.

Reading the Story in a Cultural Context

Point out to students that the father sees his son's marriage as a rejection of both religious teachings and the traditions of the culture group. Help students to read for pupose by asking them to consider when a cultural tradition should be changed. Ask students whether they think Nnaemeka is rejecting his cultural heritage when he refuses to marry the woman his

father chose. Why or why not? Have students discuss when they think a cultural tradition should be changed or discarded.

Focusing on the Selection

Ask students to consider why the young people of so many cultures seem to accept quickly the Western idea of marrying for love. Ask: Why do you think Americans consider being in love so necessary to getting married? Why do some other cultures value the parents' role of choosing a spouse for their child? Do you believe that love can grow after an arranged marriage?" As they read, have students consider how cultural traditions can affect even "private affairs."

POSTREADING

The following activities parallel the features with the same titles in the Student Edition.

Responses to Critical Thinking Questions

Possible responses are:

1. The author is aware of Okeke's prejudices but appears to understand them, for he presents the old man in a kindly light, fully explaining why he feels as he does. Also, when he describes Nnaemeka's feelings for his father, Achebe is careful to show that the son, too, understands his father's feelings and behavior. The couple accepts Okeke's prejudices but works to overcome them.

2. The Ibo (and perhaps the other culture groups, too) appear somewhat intolerant of intermarriage between culture groups. The older people in the villages obviously follow traditions, while the younger people in the cities appear to be changing their beliefs. However, all groups represented in the story view marriage seriously and want to begin married life with the blessing of parents and friends.

3. Answers will vary depending on the students' experiences. Guide students to discuss ways in which such a situation might be handled.

☑ Guidelines for Writing Your Response to "Marriage Is a Private Affair"

Have students share their writings with each other. As an alternative writing assignment, students may want to describe how they would explain Okeke's feelings and behavior to his two grandsons. Do they think the parents should have told the two boys about their grandfather? Why?

☑ Guidelines for Going Back Into the Text: Author's Craft

Put the headings *internal conflict* and *external conflict* on the board. Have students identify each kind of conflict from the selection. Point out to students that, because *conflict* means a struggle or fight, the opponents in this selection use "weapons." Explain that even though the weapons in this conflict are beliefs and behaviors, they can still "wound" the mind and heart.

As they return to the selection, have students identify the weapons that are used by the opponents in each conflict.

Possible answers to the questions in the Student Edition are:

1. The characters in the selection are torn between their deep love for each other and the expectations that their cultural traditions demand.

2. The Ibo believe that parents should arrange a child's marriage; that a good wife should be Christian, quiet, and one who has housekeeping skills. Apparently, the Ibo also believe that the more formal education a woman has, the less skilled she will be as a housekeeper.

3. The conflicts are finally resolved through the patience and understanding of Nnaemeka and Nene and the gradual acceptance of the marriage and grandchildren by Okeke. Nene, in particular, goes out of her way to break through the prejudices of her husband's culture group.

☑ FOLLOW-UP DISCUSSION

Use the questions that follow to continue your discussion of "Marriage is a Private Affair." Possible answers are given in parentheses.

Recalling

1. Why does Nene think that Okeke will eventually accept the marriage? (She thinks this because he loves his son and wants his happiness.)

2. Why does Nnaemeka consider his father's choice of a wife unsuitable? (He remembers her as being physically large and not very smart. Furthermore, he does not love her.)

3. Why does Okeke never learn of his son's happiness in marriage? (He has such fierce feelings about it that no one will venture to tell him. He refuses to allow his son to visit during his leaves.)

Interpreting

4. How does the author let the reader know that the prejudices displayed by Okeke are not confined to the Ibo alone? (Nnaemeka tells Nene that if her father were alive, he wouldn't be any more understanding about the marriage than his father.)

5. What beliefs of the author's are apparent in the selection? (Some traditions cause unhappiness because they are based on prejudice and intolerance—these traditions need to change; and the best way to change intolerance and prejudice is to reach out with patience and understanding.)

6. Why does Okeke decide to meet his grandsons? (Nene's letter gives him a good excuse finally to change his mind. He realizes that he has accomplished little by excluding Nnaemeka from his life, and he wants to know his grandsons.)

Applying

7. What lessons does this selection have for today's parents and children? (Lead students to understand how unexamined cultural beliefs and traditions can often cause conflict between generations and cultural groups.)

8. What does the selection say about cultural differences? (Guide students to understand that respect and understanding for one another's cultural backgrounds leads to tolerance and acceptance of diverse beliefs.)

ENRICHMENT

Students will benefit from viewing *The Two Rivers* by Mark Newman and Edwin Wes. The video is available from First Run Icarus Films, 153 Waverly Place, New York, NY 10014, (800) 876-1710.

from *The Dark Child*

by Camara Laye   (pages 63–71)

OBJECTIVES

Literary

- to appreciate an author's use of dialogue to develop character
- to analyze how dialogue contributes to the plot

Historical

- to demonstrate the changes in African society brought about by foreign control
- to contrast the educational opportunities available to different generations of Africans

Cultural

- to recognize emotions common to many cultures
- to describe some African customs and family traditions

SELECTION RESOURCES

Use Assessment Worksheet 8 to check students' vocabulary recognition, content comprehension, and appreciation of literary skills.

✔ Informal Assessment Opportunity

SELECTION OVERVIEW

Although Camara Laye's first two books were nonpolitical, his third had a definite political aim: to expose and condemn the harsh methods of the regime in Guinea.

Guinea gained full independence from France in 1958, and a native named Sekou Toure became head of the new government. Toure and the *Parti Democratique de Guinee* (Democratic Party of Guinea) took almost complete control of the economy and attempted to establish a socialist state. Throughout the 1960s and early 1970s, Toure jailed most of his opponents, crushing all objections to his policies. In the late 1970s, Toure relaxed some political restrictions and released political prisoners. Economic problems, however, continued to keep many Guineans in extreme poverty.

Laye escaped to neighboring Senegal in 1965 and the next year published his third novel—and first protest—*Dramouss* (*A Dream of Africa*). He never returned to Guinea; he died in Senegal in 1980.

In this selection from his novel, *The Dark Child*, the author gives an autobiographical account of his decision to leave Africa to study in France.

ENGAGING THE STUDENTS

On the board, write this question: How should parents act when children are leaving home for an extended period of time?

Remind students that such an event can signal many things to a parent: that the child is growing up and becoming independent or that the parents, who are getting older, may or may not have fulfilled all of their ambitions. Challenge students to be as fair as they can to both parties involved in this dilemma. Point out that most children, no matter how old they are, want to feel that their parents will miss them when they leave home.

BRIDGING THE ESL/LEP LANGUAGE GAP

Most students should have little difficulty identifying with the selection's situation, even though some vocabulary may present a challenge. Encourage volunteers to share with the class when and how their cultures acknowledge that a child is an adult and ready to leave the family.

You may wish to construct a chart from student information that shows the culture, preparation in childhood for the event, ceremonies or celebrations for the event, the parents' roles in decision-making, and expected or acceptable parental behavior.

At the selection's end, have students complete the chart with data from the selection.

✔ PRETEACHING
SELECTION VOCABULARY

Write the following phrases on the board: *ecstatic greetings of welcome home*, **blithely** *accepting a college scholarship, discussed on the house's* **veranda**, *angrily pounding* **millet** *with a* **pestle and mortar**. Underline the vocabulary words and suggest that students locate definitions in the footnotes. Ask students to predict the setting and the plot's central conflict from the vocabulary clues. Jot their predictions on the board.

The words printed in boldfaced type are tested on the selection assessment worksheet.

PREREADING

Reading the Story in a Cultural Context

Help students read for purpose by asking them to consider the selection from the perspective of a young adult about to leave home and go out on his or her own. Ask them to consider how a parent's actions and reactions might affect the young person's emotional state and ability to enjoy a new experience.

Focusing on the Selection

Ask students to write about a recent time in their lives when they left their families for an extended period of time: summer camp, a trip to visit relatives, a trip with a school or community association, and so on. Ask them to recall how they felt and how their parents acted before they left. Ask them to compare their own experiences with the author's as they read.

POSTREADING

The following activities parallel the features with the same titles in the Student Edition.

Responses to Critical Thinking Questions

Possible responses are:

1. Laye wants to go away to school; his mother wants him to remain at home. His father also wants him to remain at home, preferring that Laye not go so far away for an education, but he realizes that his son must go. The mother and father disagree and apparently have always disagreed about where and how their son will be educated.

2. The father appears to have the final word in any decision, although the mother's feelings and thoughts receive a great deal of consideration. It is a son's responsibility to care for his elderly parents, particularly his mother. The father hints at a religious belief that a man's destiny is decreed by the gods. Village life appears to be simple, as in other selections: The author speaks of living in a hut, and his mother crushes millet by hand with a mortar and pestle.

3. Student responses should indicate an awareness that conversations can reveal people's emotions, thoughts, actions, and the events that shape them.

✔ Guidelines for Writing Your Response to *The Dark Child*

Have students share their journal entries. As an alternative writing activity, have students compare and contrast any two parents from the African selections they have read. Ask students to address the following concerns in their comparison: Do the authors present a fair picture of the parent? How are the parents alike/different in their feelings for their children? What are the parents' reactions to the changes happening around them? Remind students to support their opinions with examples from the selections. When students have finished writing, have them share their comparisons. As a class, have them address the question: How are these parents alike/different from the parents in your culture?

✔ Guidelines for Going Back Into the Text: Author's Craft

Have students locate in the Prereading section the phrases that describe Camara Laye's prose: *simple language, graceful charm,* and *an aura of dignity and sincerity*. Ask students to decide, as they review the selection, if these three qualities are represented in the author's dialogue.

Possible answers to Student Edition questions are:

1. The opening conversation when Laye reveals that he received a scholarship; the conversation between Laye and his father later that night after the welcome home festivities.

2. The conversation the next day when Laye and his father confront the mother while she is preparing dinner.

3. When his mother begins weeping and says, "You won't leave me alone, will you? Tell me you won't leave me all alone."

✔ FOLLOW-UP DISCUSSION

Use the questions that follow to continue your discussion of *The Dark Child*. Possible answers are given in parentheses.

Recalling

1. Where has Laye been? (away at school in Conakry)

2. What does the director need before he can begin the process of getting Laye's scholarship? (the consent of Laye's father)

3. How did Laye's father know that his son would leave the village? (by watching his son's enjoyment for learning)

4. Why does Laye's mother claim that her son should stay with her? (He has already been away too often and too long, he won't be able to take good care of himself, he'll get sick, and she'll be left alone.)

Interpreting

5. What does Laye's father mean when he says, "Even if we both go we'll be outnumbered." (He means that his wife's arguments and emotions will be difficult to withstand.)

6. What does Laye's mother mean when she says, "Do you [her husband] want to drive me out of my mind? I'll certainly end up raving mad...." (that she will miss her son and spend her time worrying about all the things that could happen to him)

7. What are the "wheels within wheels" that Laye talks about? (the events and decisions that people make that affect their lives and the lives of others)

8. What does the author mean when he answers Marie's question at the selection's end, "I don't think so [that I'm glad to be going]"? (He means that he is anxious about leaving home and being on his own.)

Applying

9. Do you think the apprehensions of Laye's mother are justified or not? Support your answer. (Students' answers will vary, but should indicate their awareness that Mrs. Laye's reaction to her son's adulthood and departure for college is a common parental reaction.)

10. Does a child have a responsibility to care for a parent, as Laye's mother seems to believe, or is it the child's responsibility to be educated and take his or her place in the world? Support your answer with specific examples. (Students' answers will vary, but they should show an understanding of both sides of the issue. A compromise position might indicate that a child needs to get an education so that he or she is better able to care for the whole family. Students may also point to cultural differences that determine a child's role in his/her family.)

ENRICHMENT

Students will benefit from viewing *South Farewell, GDR* by Licinio Azevedo. The video is available from First Run Icarus Films, 153 Waverly Place, New York, NY 10014, (800) 876-1710.

The Chair Carrier
by Yusuf Idris (pages 72–77)

OBJECTIVES

Literary

- to analyze a short story that converges and juxtaposes two periods of time
- to identify irony in modern Egyptian prose

Historical

- to evaluate a story set in both ancient and modern times
- to compare and contrast modern and ancient customs and attitudes

Cultural

- to observe the cultural values of ancient Egyptian peasantry
- to observe a clash between ancient and modern Egyptian customs

SELECTION RESOURCES

Use Assessment Worksheet 9 to check students' vocabulary recognition, content comprehension, and appreciation of literary skills.

 Informal Assessment Opportunity

SELECTION OVERVIEW

Like London, Rome, and New York, modern Cairo is so large and congested that even the strangest and most preposterous events can occur on the streets without a flicker of recognition or interest from the passing crowd. This is the Cairo in which Yusuf Idris sets his short story "The Chair Carrier." Rather than the tale of a modern rickshaw owner, which the title suggests, it is simply an account of the confrontation between a narrator and an Egyptian peasant who, for no discernible reason, is carrying a gigantic chair through the center of town.

In this selection, the narrator comes across a man who has been carrying a chair for thousands of years. The man is searching for his uncle, the person who ordered him to carry the chair.

ENGAGING THE STUDENTS

Ask the class if any of them has ever seen episodes of *The Twilight Zone* or *Sliders*. In both of these television shows, people cross back and forth between ancient and modern times. Ask students what kinds of events and characters they would expect to encounter in such a setting. Allow students a few moments to speculate. Then explain that the selection they are about to read takes place in ancient and modern Egypt at the same time.

BRIDGING THE ESL/LEP LANGUAGE GAP

Although "The Chair Carrier" is not difficult to read, ESL/LEP students may have trouble with some of the vocabulary and allusions. To avoid difficulty, group students in small groups of four or five, and direct them to read silently one paragraph or conversation at a time. Have group members take turns explaining what they understand and asking for the meanings of words or expressions they cannot grasp. Encourage ESL/LEP students to keep a notebook of new words for later reference.

✔ PRETEACHING SELECTION VOCABULARY

Have students scan the selection and jot down any words or references they're not familiar with. Point out that in addition to ordinary words, they will encounter words from Egyptian history (*hieroglyphics*), English words from the nineteenth century (*runnels, rivulets, amidst, untoward*), Latinate words (*institution, procession, prostrated, sacrifices*), and British spellings (*honour*). Suggest that students make lists, classifying each word under an appropriate head and writing the meaning after each one. Draw their attention to these words: *prostrated, conjuring, untoward,* **contemplate, archaeology,** *mouthed, hieroglyphics,* *descendants, porter,* **inclination***, token, authorization, honour,* **cartouche***, exasperation,* **topple***.*

The words printed in boldfaced type are tested on the selection assessment worksheet.

PREREADING

Reading the Story in a Cultural Context

Help students read for purpose by discussing people and events they have learned about while studying ancient and modern Egypt. Point out that modern Egyptian writers would be familiar with these ideas and would be as likely to write about them as Americans might be to refer to the Revolutionary War and George Washington. Students who are especially interested in history (or Egypt) should be encouraged to contribute their knowledge to the discussion.

Focusing on the Selection

Direct students to note the differences in time, customs, and attitudes between the narrator and the chair carrier. Point out that many of the things they don't understand about each other can be traced to their backgrounds.

POSTREADING

The following activities parallel the features with the same titles in the Student Edition.

Responses to Critical Thinking Questions

Possible responses are:

1. The following details set up the ironic ending: the discovery of the announcement telling the chair carrier to put his burden down; the discovery of Ptah Ra's signature and cartouche on the announcement; and the sense of joy the narrator feels about what he supposes will happen.

2. Students should mention the peasants' devotion to duty, their fear of angering their employers, and their respect for authority. Accept other reasonable responses.

3. At the beginning the narrator is interested in the phenomenon of the porter but cares little about him personally. As the story continues and he understands the weight of the chair and the unbelievable length of time the porter has carried it, he begins to sympathize with him. The narrator makes the reader share his feelings by the excitement he shows at the hope that the burden can finally be laid aside.

☑ Guidelines for Writing Your Response to "The Chair Carrier"

Have students choose someone with whom to share their journal entries. As an alternative writing activity, ask students to explain what they think the "token of authorization" was that might have finally allowed the porter to put the chair down.

☑ Guidelines for Going Back Into the Text: Author's Craft

Discuss with students the meaning of *irony*: a figure of speech in which a character's intent or a twist of plot is shown in words and actions that carry a meaning opposite to what is intended or expected.

Point out that what the narrator learns about the chair carrier throughout the story leads the reader to expect that the chair can finally be put down. However, since the chair carrier can't read the order he carries and since the narrator can't provide a token of authorization, the porter continues on his way. Note for students that such ironic endings (as opposed to the satisfying endings in more traditional works) have become common in modern literature.

Possible answers to the questions in the Student Edition are:

1. It is ironic—unless it is an example of extraordinary devotion to duty—that the porter refuses to put the chair down "till the order comes from Ptah Ra." Any ordinary (modern) worker would be more than happy to be rid of it and would probably say so. The narrator also comments on the awe and amazement he felt when he saw the chair, wanting to prostrate himself before it in worship. Ironically, nobody else notices it.

2. The most important example of situational irony occurs when the narrator notices an order fastened to the chair telling the porter to take it to his own home and enjoy it. Because he cannot read and can't (or won't) take the narrator's word for it, the porter continues to carry the chair—perhaps forever.

3. The story's ending is not satisfying because the porter's conflict is not resolved. Accept other reasonable responses.

☑ FOLLOW-UP DISCUSSION

Use the questions that follow to continue your discussion of "The Chair Carrier." Possible answers are given in parentheses.

Recalling

1. In addition to its size, what else does the narrator notice about the chair? (It has a fifth leg, which is actually the thin body of the chair carrier.)

2. How long has the porter been carrying the chair? (by his own estimation, thousands of years)

3. What ironic situation pulls the narrator into the porter's story? (He is the only one on the street—or in all of Cairo—to notice the porter.)

Interpreting

4. Why do you think that the narrator is the only one to notice the porter? (It makes it possible for the writer to tell the story; others may be too busy to notice "miracles.")

5. Why is the announcement or order attached to the chair so important to the story? (It represents a possible solution to the porter's problems, but since he won't accept it, the order sets up the ironic ending.)

6. Why does the writer describe the porter as the fifth leg of the chair? (It makes the chair the most important thing and the porter only the means by which the chair gets around. This is also an example of irony.)

Applying

7. Write a different ending for the story. Is your ending more or less effective than the original? Why? (Students' endings might be more satisfying, but they would be less effective in continuing the theme of irony. Accept other reasonable responses.)

8. How do the beliefs and customs of the chair carrier compare to those of most Americans today? (Students may note that most Americans don't feel a sense of duty to authority figures to the extent that the chair carrier does. Accept all reasonable responses.)

ENRICHMENT

Students may enjoy viewing *Egypt: Cradle of Civilization*. This video is available from Encyclopedia Britannica Educational Corporation, 310 South Michigan Avenue, Chicago, IL 60604, (800) 554-9862.

RESPONSES TO REVIEWING THE REGION

1. Sample answer: In *Sundiata*, the author shows great respect for African culture by preserving epic stories of Africa's past. In Kofi Awoonor's poem, "The Sea Eats the Land at Home," the poet shows his respect by expressing his sorrow that the villagers' rich culture is being destroyed by forces beyond their control.

2. Sample answer: Authors reveal their feelings about their country through the subjects they choose. In "Interior," the poet shows great love for Africa by citing some of the beautiful products produced there: "Moorish cushions / Musky fragrances." In the story *Sundiata*, D.T. Niane shows admiration for Africa's past in his atttempts to preserve epics and origin stories.

3. Sample answer: Like Sogolon's son in *Sundiata*, I also had a difficult childhood because I learned to walk and talk very late. I began life at a disadvantage, but like Sundiata, I made up for lost time.

✔ FOCUSING ON GENRE SKILLS

Gcina Mhlope uses several elements of autobiography in "The Toilet." First, "The Toilet" told from first-person point of view. Second, it describes key events from Mhlope's life. Among these events are her going to Johannesburg for the December holiday, getting a temporary job in a clothing factory, and seeking refuge from the rain and cold in the toilet. Select another autobiography such as *The Dark Child* and have students identify point of view and the key events in the writer's life.

BIBLIOGRAPHY

ACHEBE, CHINUA. "Marriage Is a Private Affair." In *Girls at War and Other Stories*. London: William Heinemann, Ltd., 1972.

GORDIMER, NADINE. "A Chip of Glass Ruby." In *Selected Stories*. New York: Viking Penguin, 1961.

IDRIS, YUSUF. "The Chair Carrier." In *Arabic Short Stories* translated by Denys Johnson-Davies. Berkeley, CA: University of California Press, 1983.

KANIÉ, ANOMIA. "All That You Have Given Me, Africa." In *The Penguin Book of Women Poets*. London, England: A Penguin Books Limited, 1980.

LAYE, CAMARA. *The Dark Child*. New York: Farrar Straus & Giroux, 1954.

MHLOPE, GCINA. "The Toilet." In *Somehow Tenderness Survives: Stories of Southern Africa*. Edited by Hazel Rochman. New York: HarperCollins Publishers, 1988.

2 Middle East

CHAPTER PREVIEW

Middle East			
Selections	Genre	Author's Craft/Literary Skills	Cultural Values & Focus
"The Marks of the Wise Man, of the Half Wise, and of the Fool," Rumi, pages 80-82	poetry	didactic poetry	the nature of true wisdom
"The House on the Border," Aziz Nesin, pages 83-91	short story	satire	dispute over borders
MAKING THEMATIC CONNECTIONS: Reflections of the Past, pages 92-93			
"4+1=1," Ismail Fahd Ismail, pages 94-99	short story	dialogue	conflicts between workers and management
"A Lover from Palestine," Mahmud Darwish; "Warmth of Blood," Ali al-Sharqawi, pages 100-103	poetry	figurative language	love of homeland, Palestine
"In This Valley," "Once a Great Love," "Late in Life," Yehuda Amichai, pages 104-107	poetry	hyperbole	love of humanity
"You Can't Fool Menashe," Ephraim Kishon, pages 108-112	short story	characterization	conflicts over social status

ASSESSMENT

Assessment opportunities are indicated by a ☑ next to the activity title. For guidelines, see Teacher's Resource Manual, page xxxvi.

CROSS-DISCIPLINE TEACHING OPPORTUNITIES

Social Studies To help students understand the chronology of the development of the three religions highlighted in this feature, present them with this information:

- Judaism was founded about 4,000 years ago by the Hebrew leader Abraham, who lived sometime between 2000 and 1500 BC.
- Christianity was founded about 2,000 years ago by Jesus Christ, who lived from c. 7 BC to c. AD 30.
- Islam was founded about 1,400 years ago by the prophet Muhammad, who lived from about AD 570 to 632.

Then have students work in small groups to construct a time line of major historical events showing when each religion was established and when each founder lived. The completed time line will enable students to place the religions in their historical context.

Math Most Western nations now use the Gregorian calendar, which is based on the 365.242 days the earth takes to revolve around the sun. The Hebrew and Muslim calendars, in contrast, are based on the moon. The Hebrew calendar periodically includes an extra month, known as "First Adar"; the Muslim calendar adds an extra day to the last month in some years to ensure that the first day of the new year coincides with the new moon. The Hebrew calendar dates from 3761 BC, the supposed year of the creation of the world. The Muslim calendar dates from AD 622, the year in which Muhammad moved from Mecca to Medina. Work with the math teacher to have students construct a calendar that reflects the Gregorian, Hebrew, and Muslim calendars for one solar year.

Geography Every Muslim is supposed to make a pilgrimage (known as a *hajii*) to Muhammad's birthplace, the holy city of Mecca in Saudi Arabia. Students can work with a geography teacher to map out routes to Mecca from different cities in the Middle East.

SUPPLEMENTING THE CORE CURRICULUM

The Student Edition provides materials related to a unifying theme in Making Thematic Connections: Reflections of the Past on pages 92 and 93. You may wish to invite students to pursue the following activities outside of class:

- Some of the most familiar sayings in English come from the Bible. Here are a few of the most famous: *Pride goeth* before destruction, and a haughty spirit *before a fall* (Proverbs 16:18); Come not near me, for *I am holier than thou* (Isaiah 65:5); He kept him as *the apple of his eye* (Deuteronomy 32:10). Invite students to select a famous saying from the Bible, analyze its meaning, and explain why it has become so important to American culture.

- The Muslim month of Ramadan — the holy month in which the Koran was revealed to Muhammad — is a time of fasting and atonement. During this period, no Muslim may drink, eat, or smoke between sunrise and sunset. Have students find the most sacred days in the Christian and Jewish calendars and compare and contrast all three holidays. Then ask students to find out when these holidays will be observed this year.

- Students may not be familiar with all the words that have entered English from Arabic. Here is a partial list: *admiral, albacore, alchemy, alcove, algebra, algorithm, alkali, almanac, amber, apricot, ariel, arsenal, caliber, camphor, carafe, carat, cipher, cotton, elixir, garble, hazard, henna, lute, marabou, monsoon, mosque, nadir, ream, saffron, sequin, sheik, shrub, sultan, tamarind, tariff, tarragon, tartar, zenith.* Students can work in teams to define each word and use it in a sentence.

INTRODUCING CHAPTER 2: MIDDLE EAST

Using the Chapter Opener

On the board, write these terms: *Judaism, Christianity,* and *Islam.* Call on volunteers to define the words. As they respond, point out that all three of these religions began in the Middle East, the region they are going to study in this section. Then read this quotation to students:

> All religions must be tolerated . . . for . . . every man must get to heaven in his own way.
> Frederick the Great (1740)

Discuss the conflicts in the Middle East over the issues of religion and territory. Remind students that the Arabs protested bitterly in 1948 when the State of Israel was proclaimed. Explore the continuing hostilities in the region by asking students to share what they know about recent current events and issues related to the Middle East.

✔ Developing Concept Vocabulary

You can use a cluster diagram to help students understand the implications of the term *Middle East.* Write the term on the chalkboard. Call on volunteers to list words they associate with the term. Join the responses with lines (see sample cluster diagram below).

To spark discussion, point out that *Middle East* encompasses many different cultural and religious groups. For example, clashing religious beliefs in the Middle East have led to great strife.

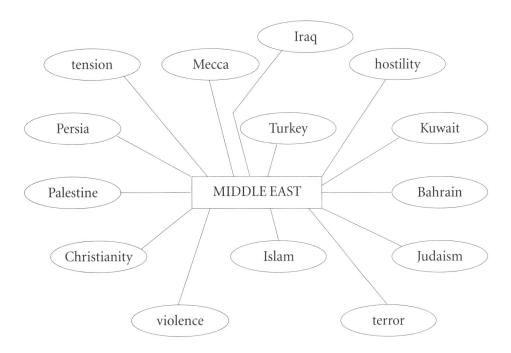

ASK:

- How do you define the *Middle East?*
- What do you think is the most important aspect of the Middle East — religion, culture, government, or something else? Why?
- How would you describe the mood or feeling of the region? What creates this mood?
- Would you like to visit the Middle East? Why or why not?

from the *Masnavi*

The Marks of the Wise Man, of the Half Wise, and of the Fool

by Rumi (pages 80–82)

OBJECTIVES

Literary

- to understand Rumi's beliefs about wisdom and its role in people's lives
- to understand the purpose of didactic literature

Historical

- to note the historical significance of the *Masnavi* in the thirteenth century
- to examine the influence of the Sufi sect

Cultural

- to compare Rumi's ideas with those of other Muslims
- to understand the Islamic concept of wisdom

SELECTION RESOURCES

Use Assessment Worksheet 10 to check students' vocabulary recognition, content comprehension, and appreciation of literary skills.

 Informal Assessment Opportunity

SELECTION OVERVIEW

This excerpt from the *Masnavi* sounds much like the Book of Wisdom from the Old Testament. Both focus on acquiring wisdom to find the straightest path to God, and both describe the attributes of wise people and fools.

The *Masnavi* is unique, however, in asserting that only through the acquisition of wisdom can people know the difference between right and wrong. It was specifically to gain wisdom that the Sufi, a Muslim sect led by Rumi, prayed while whirling about. The dizziness caused by these movements was thought to raise the Sufi to a higher level of consciousness, one that brought them closer to God.

In this selection, Rumi describes the characteristics of the wise, the half wise, and the fool. By seeing themselves in the descriptions of the latter two, readers are encouraged to seek the enlightenment of the former.

In this selction, the poet describes the qualities that make a person wise, half wise, or a fool.

ENGAGING THE STUDENTS

Ask students to write for five minutes on this topic: A truly wise person lacks for nothing, material or spiritual.

Discuss students' ideas. Some may disagree with the statement, believing that wisdom can bring spiritual richness but not necessarily material wealth. Those who agree, however, may observe that wisdom offers happiness and fulfillment that material wealth could never provide. Ask: How is wisdom rated today, on a scale of one to ten? How are material goods rated on the same scale? How can we account for the difference?

BRIDGING THE ESL/LEP LANGUAGE GAP

The language in this selection is not difficult, but ESL/LEP students might have trouble understanding words with a standard definition and an additional metaphoric meaning. *Torch,* for example, means both a physical light and the spiritual light of wisdom. Since the selection is brief, you may want students to read and comment on it as a class. Encourage students to make lists of words that have meanings on both concrete and metaphoric levels.

☑ PRETEACHING
SELECTION VOCABULARY

Explain that the words below might be used in reference to wise people and fools. Challenge students to divide the words into two lists: one that describes wise people and another that describes fools. Note that some words might be appropriate for both lists.

ashamed	**blind**	*light*
great	***illuminated***	*small*
alive	*dead*	*leader*
director	*perfect*	***degradation***
desert	***despairing***	*lamp*
halting	*wanders*	

The words printed in boldfaced type are tested on the selection assessment worksheet.

PREREADING

Reading the Author in a Cultural Context

Help students read for purpose by asking them to think about the value cultures place on wisdom. Remind students that Rumi wrote the *Masnavi* to provide guidance for his followers to attain wisdom. Ask: Is wisdom a virtue prized only in the eastern half of the world? Explain. How might a culture show that it values wisdom?

Focusing on the Selection

Have students create a list of images that they associate with each of the following: a wise person, a somewhat wise person, and a fool. After they have read the selection, have them compare their images with those Rumi uses in his descriptions.

POSTREADING

The following activities parallel the features with the same titles in the Student Edition.

Responses to Critical Thinking Questions

Possible responses are:

1. The true wise man possesses an inner light that guides his own actions as well as those of his followers. The half-wise man is wise in the sense that

he knows he lacks true wisdom but works to achieve it with the guidance of the truly wise. The fool wanders aimlessly about, not knowing where he is going and too embarrassed to admit he is lost.

2. the desire for wisdom without a wish for material goods; the reaching of a higher plateau of awareness than others strive for; being totally unafraid while under the protection of God; not fearing death because death brings the wise man even closer to God

3. Students might suggest that continuing their education is a way to apply Rumi's message. Students might also suggest that young people can use the guidance of older and wiser people, such as their parents, grandparents, and teachers.

☑ Guidelines for Writing Your Response to "The Marks of the Wise Man, of the Half Wise, and of the Fool"

Have students share their journal entries with partners. As an alternative writing activity, have students consider the differences in the ways a devoted Sufi might search for wisdom and the ways many modern people might do so.

☑ Guidelines for Going Back Into the Text: Author's Craft

Have students list some didactic works that they have read or that were read to them as children. What are some of the aphorisms in these works? What are some of the morals they learned from them? How do the morals compare to those Rumi puts forth in this selection? Point out that Rumi describes the three kinds of men more from a spiritual angle than from a practical one. However, it is still possible to discern the kinds of actions that each of the three would be likely to practice. Invite students to name specific daily values and actions that would "mark" each kind of person.

Possible answers to the questions in the Student Edition are:

1. Rumi compares the wisdom of the wise man to a torch that lights him up inwardly and guides him in making right decisions.

2. The half wise has the wisdom to know that he is not yet wise but that if he clings to the words of the wise man and follows his light, he can acquire it.

3. The wise man protects and guides his followers, nurturing them and sharing his light with them.

4. The half wise and the fool both can gain wisdom by rejecting their current life in order to enter the spiritual life of the truly wise.

✔ FOLLOW-UP DISCUSSION

Use the questions that follow to continue your discussion of "Marks of the Wise Man, of the Half Wise, and of the Fool." Possible answers are given in parentheses.

Recalling

1. How does the wise man guide and lead a caravan? (by using the light of wisdom)

2. Why doesn't the fool desire to seek wisdom? (He is ashamed to follow the footsteps of the guide.)

3. What finally happens to the fool who remains a fool? (He makes a last attempt to spring forward, but fails to spring ahead toward wisdom.)

Interpreting

4. What is Rumi's most common metaphor for wisdom? Give examples for the possession of wisdom and the lack of it. (Light, which helps a person to "see" on many levels, is the metaphor. *Torch, lamp, illuminated, sight, guide; blind, dead, shadow* are examples of wisdom and the lack there of.)

5. Why don't true seekers of wisdom fear death? (because death is not an evil thing; in fact, it is the means by which they can reach the highest levels of wisdom)

6. According to Rumi, what is the good side of being blind? (The kind of blindness to which Rumi refers is a precursor of wisdom. The half wise is blind in that he does not yet possess the light of wisdom, but if he clings to the wise man, he will eventually lose his blindness and have a light of his own.)

Applying

7. How do you know that the wise man may not always have been enlightened? (Lines 22 and 23 suggest that before becoming wise, a man will be half wise, and finds the sense "to rise up out of his degradation.")

8. Name some people of your own time who are truly wise. What actions do they perform to prove this? In what ways do they guide others by their light? (Responses will vary; accept reasonable responses.)

ENRICHMENT

Students may benefit from viewing *Ancient and Modern: The Fall and Rise of the Middle East.* This video is available from Zenger Media, 10200 Jefferson Boulevard, Room 922, P.O. Box 802, Culver City, CA 90232, (800) 421-4246.

The House on the Border

by Aziz Nesin   (pages 83–93)

OBJECTIVES

Literary

- to understand the author's use of satirical humor
- to appreciate the author's methods of developing characters

Historical

- to understand how a bureaucratic government impacts the lives of common citizens
- to recognize how oppressive governments influence the literary forms used by writers of the country

Cultural

- to recognize that absurdity and injustice coupled with resignation are pervasive themes in Islamic literature
- to recognize that the characters' collaboration with the thieves is a metaphor for the uneasy peace the author enjoys with the Turkish government

SELECTION RESOURCES

Use Assessment Worksheet 11 to check students' vocabulary recognition, content comprehension, and appreciation of literary skills.

☑ Informal Assessment Opportunity

SELECTION OVERVIEW

Faced with a government that has both educated him and punished him unjustly, Turkish author Aziz Nesin can react to it only through satire. Because of his shrewdness in describing characters and constructing plot, Nesin has largely escaped the punishments imposed on other talented Turkish writers. Perhaps because of this ability alone, people from many countries have access to his works.

The topic of this selection may both anger readers and make them laugh. Recognition of an unfair situation may make readers angry. At the same time, the humor is inescapable, and even the most reluctant reader will enjoy the sense of camaraderie that forms between the renters and the thief.

ENGAGING THE STUDENTS

Have students write for five minutes on this topic:

To see the humor in one's life, a person has only to stand in line in a government office.

When they have finished writing, lead a guided discussion on the topic. Ask students who are comfortable with responding to share their thoughts with the class. Encourage them to describe frustrating but humorous events that happened as they or their families came head to head with government bureaucracy. Explain that the story they are about to read involves citizens who learn to survive within a government much more repressive than their own.

BRIDGING THE ESL/LEP LANGUAGE GAP

Because of the author's simple, straightforward style, students will face few really difficult words. In fact, television alone may have already taught them words such as *precinct* and *jurisdiction*. Keeping this in mind, you may want students to list the words they do not know from the first page. List the most common words on the chalk board and have a discussion to arrive at an accurate definition for the context of the story. Encourage ESL/LEP students to keep running lists of such new words.

☑ PRETEACHING SELECTION VOCABULARY

Tell students that the story they will read explains what happens when a Turkish family comes face-to-face with the bureaucracy of the local police department. Have students skim the story, selecting words relevant to this theme and listing them in a column labeled A. Other words not directly related to the topic go into column B. The final groupings may look something like this:

A	B
precinct	*avid*
chief	***fazed***
jurisdiction	***nocturnal***
gendarmerie	*conceivable*
commandant	*basso profundo*
restricting	*dilemma*
sue	*emboldened*
collaborate	*affably*
authorities	*futile*

The words printed in boldfaced type are tested on the selection assessment worksheet.

PREREADING

Reading the Story in a Cultural Context

Help students read for purpose by asking them to consider what options people have when faced with bureaucracy under a repressive society, and a free society. As students read, have them jot down actions that might result from the former. When they finish reading, have them jot down choices that a member of any free society might have.

Focusing on the Selection

Remind students that *satire* is a written form of ridicule blended with humor. The point of satire is to improve the person or institution being ridiculed. Challenge students to note how the author makes the police seem outwardly cooperative, yet also stupid, bungling, and frustrating. Then ask them to notice ways in which the renters appear innocent of any wrongdoing themselves.

POSTREADING

The following activities parallel the features with the same titles in the Student Edition.

Responses to Critical Thinking Questions

Possible responses are:

1. Nesin allows the characters to reveal their own feelings by describing them as *annoyed, furious,*

ferocious, or *calm* and by having them *yell, bump into walls,* and *cackle.* Nesin makes both the narrator and the first thief particularly sympathetic because the narrator is so serious about the problem and the thief is so matter of fact and friendly.

2. the apparent unwillingness of any of the divisions to work with the others and their apparent satisfaction with the status quo

3. Accept responses describing situations similar to those in the story and providing ways of solving each problem.

✔ Guidelines for Writing Your Response to "The House on the Border"

Have students share their journal entries with partners. As an alternate activity, ask students to write "Dear Abby" letters that explain either the problem in the story or a similar problem they have encountered. Have students trade papers and write the appropriate advice column.

Guidelines for Going Back Into the Text: Author's Craft

Explain to students that satire is closely related to irony and often uses irony to accomplish its purpose. By showing the opposite view as absurd, vicious, or inhumane, satire and irony try to persuade the reader to do or believe something.

Possible answers to the questions in the Student Edition are:

1. Although most of his satire is directed at those in the government, in this case the local and state police, he also pokes fun at the narrator and his wife, the neighbors, and the thieves.

2. The renters believe they should be protected from thieves. The three police departments, however, feel satisfied with their jurisdictions, and none of them wants one more. The attitude of the thieves seems to be to "take advantage of the situation while you can."

3. The ending adds to the satire in the story because now the renters are like the thieves. Although they are now in a sense criminals, they can't be prosecuted because no police department has authority over them.

✔ FOLLOW-UP DISCUSSION

Use the questions that follow to continue your discussion of "The House on the Border." Possible answers are given in parentheses.

Recalling

1. Why couldn't the renters get the police to arrest the thief in their house? (They were not in anyone's jurisdiction.)

2. Why were the renters so afraid that the thief, whom they had tied up, would become sick? (They were afraid that some harm might come to him on their property and that he might sue them.)

3. What was funny about the renters' first encounter with the thief? (The husband got tangled in the phone cord while trying to find the light switch. The thief obviously knew the house much better than the narrator and his wife.)

Interpreting

4. How does the attitude of the thief add to the satire in the story? (He is so friendly to the renters and so much at ease because he knows he can't be prosecuted.)

5. Aziz Nesin was jailed several times because his works "criticized the state." What does he do in "The House on the Border" to make sure he wouldn't be jailed for writing it? (He doesn't name a city or country; he doesn't let the renters criticize the police too harshly; he adds humor to mitigate his satire; and he ends the story in as agreeable a way as possible.)

Applying

6. Suppose you were in the same predicament as the renters. What would you have done about it? Why? (Accept reasonable responses.)

7. Do you believe that the renters should be free from prosecution at the end of the story? Explain. (Students may suggest that since they were in no one's jurisdiction when they were robbed, they were still in no one's jurisdiction when they joined the thieves.)

8. Do you think the author believes that the renters have acted morally, especially since no one would help them? Explain. (This is a difficult judgment. Nesin is trying to show that the renters reached a compromise with the thieves that they could live with, but in no way does he suggest that they were morally right in doing so.)

ENRICHMENT

Students will benefit from viewing *South: The Singing Sheikh* by Heiny Srour. The video is available from First Run Icarus Films, 153 Waverly Place, New York, NY 10014, (800) 876-1710.

INTRODUCING THE THEME

Explain to the class that folklore comprises all the writings and traditions that are passed down through the ages. As a class, create a chart showing the most common types of folklore and the characteristics of each one.

To make the chart, list all the types of folklore in the left column. Arrange students in pairs and have them read the Thematic Connection. Tell them to fill in the right side of the chart with the characteristics of each type of folklore. Students can also draw on their previous reading as they complete the chart. Below is a sample chart:

FOLKLORE	CHARACTERISTICS
folktales	passed on orally
	help define a culture's ideals and values
myths	stories from ancient days
	explain aspects of life and nature, including the origin of Earth
	often involves the exploits of gods and heroes
legends	stories about the past, may have basis in fact
	often contain incredible feats of strength or supernatural beings
fables	teach a lesson about people, often in a stated moral
	often have animals that talk and act like people

You can use the following discussion prompts to help students connect the chart to the unit theme and their own reading experiences.

Discussion Prompts

- What does folklore teach us? (Possible responses: the beliefs and values of different cultures, ways to cope with problem situations, ideal behavior, and attitudes)
- Why do people like to read folklore? (Possible responses: These tales stimulate our imagination, entertain us, and teach us important lessons.)

BRIDGING THE ESL/LEP GAP

The references to different countries and types of folklore may be difficult for ESL/LEP students. To help students sort the information, pair ESL/LEP students with proficient speakers. Direct each team to read "Reflections of the Past" and write down at least five questions they have about the information presented.

When everyone is finished reading, have the groups exchange papers to answer another group's questions. Students can find answers by using context clues or by consulting outside references.

COMPLETING THE ACTIVITY

Explain to students that every folktale has a *plot*, or arrangement of events in the story. Tell the class that plots have a beginning, middle, and end. Describe how writers arrange the events of the plot to keep the reader's interest and convey the theme.

After students write their individual folktales and read them aloud to their groups, direct each group to create a collaborative version, with a tightened plot that is unified and logical. As they revisit their stories, students might make plot diagrams or flow charts to help them arrange the events in the best possible way.

Once each group has read its completed folktale aloud, they might be compiled into a class folktale collection.

4 + 1 = 1

by Ismail Fahd Ismail (pages 94–99)

OBJECTIVES

Literary

- to read a modern Arabic short story that uses the stream-of-consciousness technique
- to observe the use of both external and internal dialogue

Historical

- to appreciate the blending of centuries-old Arab consciousness with a modern Western genre
- to note the changes that have occurred in Arabic literature since the time of *The Thousand and One Nights*

Cultural

- to identify and appreciate an example of human compassion among the Kuwaiti working class
- to contrast the Arabic sense of loyalty to others with Americans' more independent spirit

SELECTION RESOURCES

Use Assessment Worksheet 12 to check students' vocabulary recognition, content comprehension, and appreciation of literary skills.

 Informal Assessment Opportunity

SELECTION OVERVIEW

Born in 1940, Ismail Fahd Ismail is an established Kuwaiti novelist, short story writer, literary historian, and cinematographer. Although he began by writing short stories, he experimented with other genres as well.

What makes Arab writers distinctive is the combination of events that dominated their history. Most great Islamic literature was written during the Middle Ages. After that time, however, because of wars and occupation, little true Arab literature was produced. Islam had no Renaissance, no Reformation, and no period of Enlightenment, which in the West produced a wealth of literature. Instead, the body of uniquely Arab works jumped eleven centuries—from the writing of *The Thousand and One Nights* to the present.

Distinctly modern, Ismail Fahd Ismail's writing focuses on the working class and their lives of unrewarding labor. Still, he shows their capacity for grace and compassion.

In this selection, a cleaner in a factory thinks he has broken an expensive piece of equipment, only to find out that it wasn't him at all.

ENGAGING THE STUDENTS

Write this statement on the chalkboard: Many people live lives of quiet desperation.

Ask students whether they think this is true, especially with the seemingly limitless possibilities and choices available today. Discuss whether the choices are open to all, and if not, what it means for those who don't have them.

BRIDGING THE ESL/LEP LANGUAGE GAP

Some students may have difficulty with the flow of the story and may not be able to distinguish the external dialogue from the internal dialogue in the mind of the central character. Try pairing ESL/LEP students with fluent readers, who can help them decide who is thinking or saying what. Another possibility might be to stage the story as a drama and have ESL/LEP students follow the dialogue in their books. Afterward, ask students what clues in the story helped them to distinguish between the external and the internal dialogue.

✔ PRETEACHING
SELECTION VOCABULARY

Share with students that the story they will be reading involves workers in a nondescript factory. The vocabulary words in this selection reinforce the concept of keeping to a routine. List the following words on the board, asking students to look for them as they read and try defining them in the context of work: *disciplined*, *paralyzed*, *all-pervasive*, *dismay*, *imperative*, *tense*, *current*, *stupefied*, *panic*, *din*. Then, when the reading is finished, have students check to see whether their definitions are similar to those in the dictionary.

The words printed in boldfaced type are tested on the selection assessment worksheet.

PREREADING

Reading the Story in a Cultural Context

Have students read for purpose by discussing how the Arab workers treated the cleaner. As they read, each student should try to identify an Arab cultural trait that Western workers may or may not share.

Focusing on the Selection

Have students consider how the internal dialogue helps to build tension in the story. Ask students how the situation in the cleaner's mind differs from that of the other workers' points of view.

POSTREADING

The following activities parallel the features with the same titles in the Student Edition.

Responses to Critical Thinking Questions

Possible responses are:

1. The main character is humble and adept at his job but easily alarmed, confused, and frightened when things go wrong. When the break occurs in a piece of machinery, he immediately takes the responsibility and says, "Why didn't I look behind me?", "I'm an idiot!", and "What have I done?" Accept other reasonable responses.

2. The workers seem to know their own jobs but are frightened and don't know what to do when something goes wrong. Those in charge of production, however, can go beyond fear to try to remedy a bad situation. Both of these examples

point to a rigidly structured society in which all the power rests with the leaders.

3. The suspense tales of Edgar Allan Poe and the stories of O'Henry contain good examples of external and internal dialogue. Students' examples should be similar. Their reactions to using dialogue this way should be logically explained and supported.

✔ Guidelines for Writing Your Response to "4 + 1 = 1"

Have students choose partners with whom to share their journal entries. Discuss the feelings of panic and worthlessness experienced by the cleaner when the machines go down, and the feelings of gratitude and relief he must have felt when they are fixed. As an alternative writing activity, have partners decide what would happen if a similar situation occurred again in the factory. Would additional workers step in to change things, or would events simply be repeated? Have them explain their decision.

✔ Guidelines for Going Back Into the Text: Author's Craft

Explain to students that stream of consciousness is a writing style that tries to depict the random flow of thoughts, emotions, memories, and associations rushing through a character's mind. Then guide the class in a discussion about ways in which various authors handle external and internal dialogue. Suggest that they compare dialogue in novels or stories they've read with Ismail Fahd Ismail's approach. Which approach do students think makes it easier on readers? Which approach is most effective? Which ones use the stream of consciousness technique?

Possible answers to the questions in the Student Edition are:

1. The first concerns of the workers when the machine breaks are what the factory owner will say and whether their jobs are in jeopardy.

2. The worker who shouted to the cleaner to finish his job is the first to show compassion for him.

3. The compassion spreads when the other workers begin to smile at the cleaner, act friendly, and speak encouragingly to him.

4. The last worker to show compassion is the one who asks the cleaner why he was just standing there. This worker gives him a friendly shove and comments that the cleaner hadn't been the one who broke the machine.

✔ FOLLOW-UP DISCUSSION

Use the questions that follow to continue your discussion of "4 + 1 = 1." Possible answers are given in parentheses.

Recalling

1. Why did the machines in the factory suddenly stop working? (The cleaner thought he had smashed something with his broom handle, but there may have been another, or an additional, reason that is not mentioned.)

2. What do the workers do at first when the machines stop? (They worry about themselves; think about the factory owner; look for a scapegoat—the cleaner.)

3. How do the workers' attitudes change when the machinery is fixed? (They heave sighs of relief, go back to their work, and speak kindly to the cleaner.)

Interpreting

4. What might be the significance of the title? (It may stand for the four workers and the cleaner. Together, they aren't a group of five workers; instead, they represent the single, united effort necessary to keep production going. Accept other reasonable responses.)

5. What do the cleaner's thoughts and actions just after the machines break reveal about him? (His thoughts reveal confusion, embarrassment, and concern over the future of his job. His actions reveal that he is stunned into silence and is approaching despair.)

6. If the workers at first view the cleaner as a scapegoat, what do their subsequent actions show? (that they are relieved and don't need a scapegoat any longer; that they are sorry for blaming him)

Applying

7. If the title refers to the factory workers at the time the machine breaks, how might it be changed to reflect the situation at the end of the story? Why? (It could be changed to "6" to indicate that at the end of the story, the workers feel a new togetherness.)

8. Rewrite part of the middle of the story to include description, external dialogue, and a more common way of showing the cleaner's thoughts. Compare the new version to Ismail Fahd Ismail's story. What does the new version lack? (a sense of the confusion of words and actions swirling through the factory and around the perplexed cleaner)

ENRICHMENT

Students may benefit from viewing *Cultures Around the World.* The video is available from Social Studies School Service, 10200 Jefferson Boulevard, Room 12, Culver City, CA 90232, (800) 421-4246.

A Lover from Palestine
by Mahmud Darwish

Warmth of Blood
by Ali al-Sharqawi   (pages 100–103)

OBJECTIVES

Literary

- to become familiar with themes in contemporary Arabian poetry
- to understand and appreciate the use of simile and metaphor in Middle Eastern poetry

Historical

- to understand the point of view of Arab peoples uprooted from their native lands
- to understand the changes that have occured in Arabic literature as a result of historic events

Cultural

- to understand the passion of the Arab peoples for their homeland
- to appreciate the Arabs' own view of themselves: that they, their loved ones, and their country are one and the same

SELECTION RESOURCES

Use Assessment Worksheet 13 to check students' vocabulary recognition, content comprehension, and appreciation of literary skills.

 Informal Assessment Opportunity

SELECTION OVERVIEW

The height or "flowering" of Arabic literature occurred during the Middle Ages, when the Arab peoples of various nations were one in tradition. However, during the nineteenth century, in the parts of the Arab Empire that were colonized by Westerners, everything changed. Literature became less traditional, less formal, and perhaps even less Islamic. The old ways, though respected, gave way to Arab nationalism and a fierce longing for freedom.

Modern Arabic poetry, especially that written after 1946 when the state of Israel was carved out of lands then held by Arabs, reflects and intensifies the themes of aggression, love, and a desire for peace. Both Ali al-Sharqawi and Mahmud Darwish borrow "Western" free verse and figurative language, but shape them with their own uniquely Arab vision. Prepare students for this unusual blend of Western techniques and Eastern themes as they read these two short selections.

In this selection, the two poems are filled with a sense of longing. The two poets are deeply affected by the fact that their homeland, a land that is important to their religion and heritage, has been taken away from them.

ENGAGING THE STUDENTS

Have students imagine they are uprooted from their homes for political reasons. Remind students to think about a parallel event in American history—the political takeover of Native American lands and the subsequent relocation of Native Americans on reservations. If students are having difficulty, ask them to think about how they would feel if their homes were destroyed by widespread fire, storm, or flood. Because their familiar surroundings—the neighborhood, old friends, and sense of ownership and belonging—are gone, they are exiles who cannot go back. Ask: How would you feel in this situation? What would you want? What would you do?

Explain to students that this same sense of loss is a deep-felt theme in modern Arab poetry. Many writers, in fact, feel the loss so strongly that they think of their homes, their families, and their friends as part or extensions of themselves. This is what students will encounter in the selections.

BRIDGING THE ESL/LEP LANGUAGE GAP

Share with students that like modern poetry everywhere, these poems contain many images and a great deal of figurative language. Suggest that instead of trying to grasp the meaning of each poem at the outset, they read them silently several times noting such ideas as *cold / prison / woollen garment / warmed / comrades / memories / branches / embrace*. Point out that although the ideas don't seem to make sense together, there are relationships among them.

Have students discuss the ideas in small groups with one or two ESL members in each group. Suggest that they ask, for example, how the concepts of *branches* and *embrace* can possibly be related. (As they grow, tree branches reach out and encounter other branches, where they touch one another in a kind of embrace.) Afterward, all students may be open to a discussion of each poem's meaning.

☑ PRETEACHING SELECTION VOCABULARY

Ask students to make lists from the poems that include words new to them, as well as old words with new spellings or meanings (such as *stoked* and *ember*, or *woollen* for *woolen*). Be sure they know the meanings of these words: *woollen, embrace* (n.), **stoked, radiant,** *ember, clasp* (v.), *vision, reined in* (v.); *harbor, orphan,* **wilderness,** *garments,* **orphanhood,** *misery,* **restore.**

The words printed in boldfaced type are tested on the selection assessment worksheet.

PREREADING

Reading the Poems in a Cultural Context

Help students read for purpose by asking them to imagine themselves in each poet's place. As they read, encourage them to try to feel a little of the loss, helplessness, and abandonment that both writers experience.

Focusing on the Selections

Suggest to students that they note how the two poems are alike and different. For example, they might note how the concepts of love, memories, and dreams are handled in each poem.

POSTREADING

The following activities parallel the features with the same titles in the Student Edition.

Responses to Critical Thinking Questions

Possible responses are:

1. Darwish refers to his country as an orphan. He needs it as much as light and salt when deprived of both. Ali al-Sharqawi says that Palestine's songs, his memories, and the hope of freedom can make him warmer than clothing could.

2. that Palestine no longer belongs to the Palestinian Arabs and that unless the people win it back in war, it will probably never be theirs again

3. Ali al-Sharqawi states that to him, anyplace but home is a cold prison cell. Mahmud Darwish views all the world except his homeland as a desert wilderness and himself as an orphan with nowhere to go. Whichever comparison students prefer should be supported with logical reasons.

☑ Guidelines for Writing Your Response to "A Lover from Palestine" and "Warmth of Blood"

Have class members share their journal entries with partners or in small groups, explaining the personal situations that prompted them to choose one experience over the other. As an alternative writing activity, ask pairs of students to write a poem from the Israeli point of view. What might it feel like to be forced to give up your homeland after enduring the persecution of the Holocaust? Challenge students to use at least one simile or metaphor in their poem.

Guidelines for Going Back Into the Text: Author's Craft

Remind students that readers often have to work hard to understand poetry. This effort is necessary because poetry is brief, and ideas must be compressed into "shorthand" to get everything in. Similes, metaphors, and other figurative language are types of shorthand. Once students understand the figurative language, the meaning of the poem will become clearer.

Possible answers to the questions in the Student Edition are:

1. Darwish's single simile is "like an orphan," in which the poet compares himself to an abandoned child running after his departing mother. Darwish's metaphors include describing Palestine as a land covered with thorns, as a shepherd without sheep, and as once a garden but now a wilderness. The old Palestine is a place of light where one had a zest for life. Al-Sharqawi's single simile is "like an ember," in which he compares his beloved's words about home to a burning coal. His extended metaphor compares living away from one's homeland to being in a cold jail cell, in which the only things that keep him warm are his memories, the songs of home, and his dreams of being free.

2. The similes and metaphors reinforce the sense of longing, loss, and despair that lie at the heart of both poems.

3. Metaphors that suggest loss and longing include the image of the orphan hopelessly chasing his departing mother; the image of a homeless person crying out in misery; and the image of a prisoner in a cold jail cell with nothing but memories and hopes to warm him. Whichever figure of speech students choose as the "best," they should support with specific reasons. Students' own similies or metaphors should suggest the same ideas and should relate to the chosen poem.

✔ FOLLOW-UP DISCUSSION

Use the questions that follow to continue your discussion of "A Lover from Palestine" and "Warmth of Blood." Possible answers are given in parentheses.

Recalling

1. Why doesn't the prisoner in "Warmth of Blood" want a woollen garment to keep him warm? (because his memories and dreams are all the warmth he needs)

2. To whom is Darwish speaking in the verse beginning "You are Palestinian in looks"? (both to his beloved and to his homeland)

3. Who is the "you" in Ali al-Sharqawi's poem? (a loved one and the lost homeland, Palestine)

Interpreting

4. Why do you think al-Sharqawi views freedom as an ember and not as a live coal? (He must view the idea of freedom for the Palestinians as a nearly impossible goal. Although he has not given up the idea completely, he is pessimistic about his people's ability to achieve it.)

5. What is al-Sharqawi's "flowing sorrow"? (his tears)

6. What do you think Darwish means by saying "Restore to me my color"? (He may mean both the healthy color in his cheeks, as well as the colors of the Palestinian flag flying over his homeland.)

Applying

7. An *allusion* in literature is a reference to a person or event in history or lines from another piece of literature. Why might critics see biblical allusions in the second verse of "A Lover from Palestine"? (Students, even those of diverse religions or no religion, might be familiar with parts of the Bible either from personal experience or from allusions in other literature. Discuss with the class the following allusions as they relate to the poem: thorns choking out the life of good seeds; a shepherd whose sheep have been taken away; and a garden and gardener replaced by strangers.)

8. Do you think al-Sharqawi can keep his dream of freedom alive? Explain. (By using "reined in" in line 15, the poet suggests that he has to make a conscious effort to concentrate on it. Perhaps it can be a practical goal as long as he can make that effort.)

ENRICHMENT

Students will benefit from viewing the video *Homeland: Israel and Palestine,* available from Encyclopaedia Britannica Educational Corporation, 310 South Michigan Avenue, Chicago, IL 60604, (800) 554-9862.

In This Valley, Once a Great Love, and *Late in Life*

by Yehuda Amichai (pages 104–107)

OBJECTIVES

Literary

- to appreciate the message of contemporary Israeli poetry
- to recognize the figurative language that is a hallmark of Amichai's poetry

Historical

- to recognize both ancient and modern Jewish history as expressed through poetry
- to understand the poet's historical references to the Old Testament and to ongoing Arab-Israeli confrontations

Cultural

- to understand that the poetry of modern Israel carries within it the chronicle of the Jewish people
- to recognize and appreciate imagery drawn from centuries of Jewish life

SELECTION RESOURCES

Use Assessment Worksheet 14 to check students' vocabulary recognition, content comprehension, and appreciation of literary skills.

 Informal Assessment Opportunity

SELECTION OVERVIEW

Jews from all over the world had been settling in the Middle East for years. In 1948, when by edict of the United Nations a portion of Palestine was designated the new Jewish homeland, the flurry of immigrations became a flood. Since that time, Arabs and Jews have constantly been at war.

These three poems have all grown out of the conflicts of that war. In them, Yehuda Amichai expresses both the religious Jew's love of his faith and his people, as well as the secular Israeli's love for his new land and for the special people in his life. All of these are shadowed by the war that no one ever seems to win or lose. As students read, encourage them to keep a running list of references to war, love, and loss as modern Israelis experience them.

In these poems, the central themes are love and loss. Have students note the distance the poet feels from these women.

ENGAGING THE STUDENTS

Tell students that Israeli poets today tend to be less religious and more secular than those of the past. Even the most secular Israeli poems, however, depend a great deal on Jewish history and the Old Testament for their spirit and allusions. Ask volunteers to name some of the themes in Old Testament history and write them on the board as they are given. Challenge students to match these themes and the references noted above with those in Amichai's three poems. Remind them that the love theme may be represented by love for the land and love for the nation, as well as love for a particular person.

BRIDGING THE ESL/LEP LANGUAGE GAP

Amichai's conversational style should prove easy for all to understand, but ESL/LEP students may be puzzled by some of the images, such as that of the dead but still writhing snake or the eyeglasses described as the reins on a horse. This group of students may be best served by your reading and interpreting the poems with the whole class. Afterward, if necessary, have each ESL/LEP student work with an English-proficient partner to clarify some of the more difficult imagery.

✔ PRETEACHING SELECTION VOCABULARY

Before students read, watching for the imagery mentioned above, call attention to the following words:

filtered, **spectacles**, *twisting*, *reins*, **profiles**, *souvenir*, **afresh**, **destined**. Suggest that they use context clues in the poems to try and decode the meanings for themselves. Point out that the full meanings of several words can only be determined from context.

The words printed in boldfaced type are tested on the selection assessment worksheet.

PREREADING

Reading the Poem in a Cultural Context

Help students read for purpose by reviewing Israeli history from 1948 to the present, documenting the wars and important confrontations in which Israelis have been involved. Point out that these troubles, along with the stresses of building and rebuilding Israeli cities, have, in large part, shaped the modern culture of the nation.

Focusing on the Selections

As they read, have students ask themselves what kinds of love Amichai discusses in each poem. Students should be aware that when the poet talks about a love or a lover, he may be referring to his people, his religion, or his land.

POSTREADING

The following activities parallel the features with the same titles in the Student Edition.

Responses to Critical Thinking Questions

Possible responses are:

1. "In This Valley" speaks eloquently of Amichai's love for his homeland. When he writes "And there are loves which cannot/be moved to another site," he refers to moving parts of Israel elsewhere to appease the Palestinians. "Late in Life" and "Once a Great Love" both center on his love for a person, but each one, like the "wild woman wearing spectacles" seems also to be an extension of his homeland.

2. His poems are full of allusions to finding love, losing love for a long time, and sometimes finding and losing the same love again, with constant war as the dividing factor in each case.

3. Many American and English poets, such as Herrick, Donne, Shakespeare, Keats, and Edgar Allan Poe, wrote about love for people. However, unlike Amichai's poems, their work did not usually include love for their nation or their land at the same

time. Poets, such as Boris Pasternak (Russia), Anna Akhmatova (Russia), and Nguyen Thi Vinh (Vietnam), who grew up in war torn countries or lived through wars, wrote poetry that parallels Amichai's work. Accept reasonable responses to the question about students' favorite images.

✔ Guidelines for Writing Your Response to "In This Valley," "Once a Great Love," and "Late in Life"

Have students share their journal entries in small groups, referring to particular lines in Amichai's poetry to support their opinions and interpretations. As an alternative writing activity, ask pairs of students to choose one of the three poems and write a response to it from the Arab point of view. Partners can share their poem with the class, who can then discuss how the thoughts and feelings are both similiar to and different from Amichai's poetry or their classmates' poems.

Encourage group members to respond positively to others' examples of figurative language.

✔ Guidelines for Going Back Into the Text: Author's Craft

Remind students that exaggeration, or *hyperbole*, is made to order for love poems, because love calls forth such deep emotions. Ask the class to think of love poems and songs they know in which hyperbole is clearly used. As examples are given, write them on the board, asking students how they know that each example is an exaggeration.

Possible answers to the questions in the Student Edition are:

1. Sensory details: twisting like a snake hacked apart; someone standing in a desert; a valley carved out by the waters over many years; voices of men and machines; loves which must die like a piece of furniture in a razed house; a breeze that passes through a valley to cool someone's forehead

    Similes: "… like someone standing in/the Judean desert, looking at a sign …"; "… like an old clumsy piece of furniture …"; "… like the breeze" that cools a desert; "… like a snake cut in two …"; "… as a souvenir …"

    Metaphors: "… those elegant reins of your eyes …"; "… But this valley is a hope/of starting afresh …"

2. **Hyperbole**: (words suggesting the exaggeration are underlined) "…till <u>almost nothing remained</u> …"; "After that <u>you broke your whole face</u> …"; "Once a great love <u>cut my life in two</u> …"; "Thus I

remember your face <u>everywhere</u> …"; "which many waters/carved out in <u>endless</u> years …" Accept reasonable responses, in which students identify the kinds of emotion each one expresses.

3. Accept all reasonable responses.

✔ FOLLOW-UP DISCUSSION

Use the questions that follow to continue your discussion of "In This Valley," "Once a Great Love," and "Late in Life." Possible answers are given in parentheses.

Recalling

1. Amichai says "Things like to get lost and get/found again by others." But who "love to find themselves"? (only human beings)

2. What must happen to "loves which cannot/be moved to another site"? (They must die where they stand.)

3. What happened to the woman to whom Amichai says he came "late in life"? (She left him again.)

Interpreting

4. Why does the author say that he came to his love "filtered through many doors/reduced by stairs"? (He may be referring to his age or to loves or experiences from the past which were opened like doors and then closed before he met his current love. "Reduced by stairs" may carry the same meaning.)

5. What is the meaning of the image in which Amichai's love "broke (her) whole face/into two equal profiles: one/for the far distance, the other for me—/as a souvenir." (He refers to the spectacles mentioned in verse two. Depending on the eyeglass prescription, one of a person's eyes may need help seeing things nearby; the other, objects at a distance. The woman showed two profiles, one for the vision in each eye.)

6. In what way can a great love "cut my life in two"? (The speaker may have two loves or responsibilities, each of which requires intense concentration. He may be referring to his life with the woman he loves and his life in the army. Each is completely separate from the other, resulting in a life "cut in two.")

Applying

7. At the end of "In This Valley," Amichai refers to the valley as "a hope/of starting afresh … of loving without forgetting the other love." What two loves do you think he refers to? How do you know? (He may refer to his love for a woman and his love for his country. In peacetime, which is a way of starting afresh, he doesn't have to love only one at a time.)

8. Compare the loves in "Once a Great Love" and "In This Valley." If they are two women, which do you think the poet loved more? Why? (Accept reasonable responses as long as they are developed fully.)

ENRICHMENT

Students will benefit from viewing *Backgrounds: A Brief History of Israel and the Arab/Palestine Conflict* by Barbara Pfeffer. The video is available from First Run Icarus Films, 153 Waverly Place, New York, NY 10014 (800)876-1710.

You Can't Fool Menashe
by Ephraim Kishon (pages 108–112)

OBJECTIVES

Literary

- to examine the ways in which the author develops his characters
- to appreciate the author's use of satire

Historical

- to recognize how Ephraim Kishon's stories reflect contemporary Israeli society
- to understand the concerns of members of Israel's artistic community

Cultural

- to appreciate how the art of writing humor transcends time and place
- to recognize that concern over status is a universal quality

SELECTION RESOURCES

Use Assessment Worksheet 15 to check students' vocabulary recognition, content comprehension, and appreciation of literary skills.

✔ Informal Assessment Opportunity

SELECTION OVERVIEW

Like the Kuwaiti writer Ismail Fahd Ismail, Ephraim Kishon is an unusual success story. Both writers emerged from a historical background that did not outwardly nourish their talents. Yet Ismail Fahd Ismail became a novelist, short story writer, literary historian, and cinematographer in a country that had just jumped eleven centuries into the modern era. Similarly, Ephraim Kishon drew from his nation's history of sorrow and war to become a journalist, playwright, theater producer—and its premier humorist.

"You Can't Fool Menashe" is a satirical study of status consciousness. The plot centers on the absurd notion that someone could be an intuitive social barometer.

In this selection, Menashe is described as a master of gauging a person's status. Have students notice the different ways in which Menashe greets the three other characters.

ENGAGING THE STUDENTS

Direct students to write for five minutes on the following topic. Contrast two kinds of comedy: physical comedy, in which the characters do silly things and fall down a lot; and intellectual comedy, which exploits the humor in incongruity. Ask students to decide which kind of comedy they think is superior and to explain why.

This exercise will prepare students to understand the author's depiction of Menashe, the story's central character. When students have finished writing, lead a guided discussion on the topic. Encourage students who appreciate the second kind of comedy to give examples from movies or shows with which the rest of the class will be familiar.

BRIDGING THE ESL/LEP LANGUAGE GAP

Assemble students in small groups with one or two ESL/LEP students in each one. Direct group members to take turns reading one paragraph or dialogue at a time, explaining what is happening and asking for the meanings of words or expressions that they don't know. Encourage ESL/LEP students to keep a list of new words specifically for this selection. If possible, play a tape of the story, so that after the groups have finished reading students will be able to appreciate the story as a whole.

✔ PRETEACHING SELECTION VOCABULARY

Have students list the vocabulary words by category in their notebooks. Useful categories include:
1) made-up words; 2) words associated with facial expressions or body movements; 3) words with meanings

specific to the selection; and 4) other interesting words. Here is a list to start with, but you might want to add or delete words according to your students' needs.

1 *successometer, societymanship*

2 *trembling,* **contorted,** *superhuman,* **languid,** *nine-below-zero, cursory, deathly*

3 *barometer, wisp,* **checkered,** *murderous, subsonic, tremors, crucified, ghost*

4 *flotsam/jetsam, emigrate,* **intimation,** **offing,** *coefficient, reckoning, supersensory, beeline*

The words printed in boldfaced type are tested on the selection assessment worksheet.

PREREADING

Reding the Story in a Cultural Context

Help students to read for purpose by considering that the story takes place in an Israeli café among a group of intellectuals and writers. Ask: What kinds of topics might the characters discuss? What is important to them? Does the fact that they are Israeli characters make any difference to the story? Why or why not?

Focusing on the Selection

Point out to students that Menashe, the central character, is instantly recognizable to the other characters seated in the café. He is a stereotype of the influential theater critic, but he has an extraordinary gift—the ability to sense the success level of anyone in the room. This ability makes him funny—the satirist as well as the satirized.

POSTREADING

The following activities parallel the features with the same titles in the Student Edition.

Responses to Critical Thinking Questions

Possible responses are:

1. Kishon reveals that the characters are very self-involved and concerned about their social status.

2. Answers may vary, but students may say that he is satirizing the overly great concern over social status. One way of recognizing this concern is to

observe the absurdity of the individual who measures a person's status—Menashe.

3. Accept all reasonable responses. Students should be able to point out that satire provides a way for a society to observe itself. The use of humor is a "safety valve" that allows people to put things in perspective.

✔ Guidelines for Writing Your Response to "You Can't Fool Menashe"

Responses will vary, but the scene in the café with Tola'at Shani and the scene outside with Ervinke are perhaps the funniest. They depend for their humor on the subtle behavior of Menashe and the reactions of the characters to whom he speaks. As an alternative writing activity, ask pairs of students to create a short dialogue in which they poke fun at a failing society or a short coming of a prominent individual. Have volunteers perform their dialogue for the class.

Guidelines for Going Back Into the Text: Author's Craft

Discuss with students the importance of characterization in literature. Without strong characterization, literature rings hollow because readers do not care about what happens in a story. Point out that Kishon uses different techniques to bring his characters to life.

Possible answers to the questions in the Student Edition are:

1. Kishon directly describes and explains Menashe's words and actions. He also gives insight into Menashe's abilities through the narrator's description of his "powers." Menashe reinforces what the author and narrator have told us through his actions at the end of the story.

2. The other characters are revealed through their own words and actions—especially through their reactions to Menashe.

3. Menashe is like the other characters in that he is concerned about social status, but he is unlike them because he is able to influence or measure the status of others.

4. Answers may vary. Students may consider Menashe the most effective character because he dominates both the scene and the other characters. However, the narrator's insight into Menashe's gift also sets him apart from the rest.

✔ FOLLOW-UP DISCUSSION

Use the questions that follow to continue your discussion of "You Can't Fool Menashe." Possible answers are given in parentheses.

Recalling

1. Why is Menashe so feared by the other characters? (He has a sixth sense that tells him how socially successful each person is or will be in the future.)

2. Give one example of Menashe's behavior as it affects the narrator. (Responses will vary. One example involves the time the narrator had been invited to the United States. Menashe was so cordial to him that even though the narrator didn't know what was about to happen to him, he knew it would be good.)

3. What words and expressions does Kishon use to describe Menashe? (He is a "born barometer" and a "one-man Gallup poll.")

Interpreting

4. What is the meaning of the word *ghost* as it applies to Tola'at Shani at the end of the evening? (He is such a wreck because of Menashe's greeting and the theater manager's message that he looks as pale and insubstantial as a ghost.)

5. Why is the last scene of the story so funny? (Up to this point in the story, the narrator is merely an observer. The tables are turned when Menashe gives the narrator the cold shoulder.)

Applying

6. Have two students act out the scene in which Menashe greets Tola'at Shani at the café. One student can take the part of Ervinke while the other can give a broad, comedic version of the incident as Ervinke describes it. If possible, have two or three student pairs perform the scene. Which was the funniest? Why? (Students' interpretations will vary.)

7. Write a different ending for the story, perhaps one in which Menashe is proved wrong. What happens? Why? (Students' alternate endings will vary.)

ENRICHMENT

Students will benefit by exploring *Pathways Through Jerusalem.* The CD-ROM is available from Learning Services, P.O. Box 10636, Eugene, OR 97440-2636, (800) 877-3278.

RESPONSES TO REVIEWING THE REGION

1. Sample answer: Ismail Fahd Ismail comments on the unfair treatment of poor workers in "4+1=1." The main character, a poor cleaner, is terrified by the threat that it will take him ten years of labor to pay for a broken machine. In "You Can't Fool Menashe," Ephraim Kishon satirizes his society's concern for social standing. The character Menashe recognizes only people who are socially prominent.

2. Sample answer: Aziz Nesin uses exaggeration in "The House on the Border" to comment on official incompetence. By the end of the story, the narrator and his wife are saddled with a group of resident thieves because no officials will arrest the original robber.

3. Sample answer: "The Marks of the Wise Man, of the Half Wise, and of the Fool" taught me how to be a leader of my own "direction and light." It also helped me to differentiate between a wise person and a fool.

✔ FOCUSING ON GENRE SKILLS

Yehuda Amichai uses several elements of poetry effectively in "In This Valley." The poem is written in free verse; as a result, Amichai uses repetition and parallelism to give structure to his song about hope. Parallelism is especially striking in the final stanza of the poem.

BIBLIOGRAPHY

AL-SHARQAWI, ALI. "Warmth of Blood." In *The Literature of Modern Arabia* edited by Salma Khadra Jayyusi. London: Kegan Paul International Limited, 1988.

DARWISH, MAHMOUD. "A Lover from Palestine." In *Critical Perspectives on Arabic Literature* edited by Issa J. Boullata. Colorado Springs, CO: Three Continents Press, 1980.

ISMAIL, ISMAIL FAHD. "4+1=1." In *The Literature of Modern Arabia.* London: Kegan Paul International Limited, 1988.

KISHON, EPHRAIM. "You Can't Fool Menashe." In *More of the Funniest Man in the World.* New York: Shapolsky Publishers, Inc., 1989.

NESIN, AZIZ. "The House on the Border." In *Contemporary Turkish Literature.* East Brunswick, NJ: Associated University Presses, Inc., 1982.

Unit 1
Africa and the Middle East
Focusing the Unit   (page 113)

COOPERATIVE / COLLABORATIVE LEARNING

Individual Objective: to participate in a news conference about events in Africa and the Middle East and their effect on the area and the rest of the world.

Group Objective: to develop a presentation inspired by viewpoints expressed in the news conference.

Setting Up the Activity

Have students work in heterogeneous groups of three. Stipulate that each group member is responsible for researching and expressing an individual viewpoint in the news conference and for making a contribution to the group presentation. The suggested format for the conference is as follows: Student 1 introduces the conference; Student 2 describes specific events in Africa and/or the Middle East; Student 3 gives specific examples of how the events affected the area and the rest of the world.

When they have finished preparing, have each group present their conference for the entire class. After each group's presentation, use the questions below to discuss and evaluate their reports.

• What different social and political changes are discussed in Unit 1?

• In your group's opinion, what are some ways social and political change in one area can affect other areas?

Assisting ESL and LEP Students

To allow students with limited English proficiency more opportunity to join in a closing discussion of the unit, have them choose one selection on which to focus. Then ask them to think about the answers to these questions:

1. What change does the selection deal with?
2. Is the change social, political, or both?
3. What are the effects of the change?

Assessment

Before you begin the group activity, remind students that they will be graded on both an individual and a group basis. Without individual contribution, the group presentation will not be complete. Monitor group progress to check that all three students are contributing and that they have selected a presenter.

Time Out to Reflect

As students do the end-of-unit activities in the Student Edition, give them time to make a personal response to the content of the unit as a whole. Invite them to respond to the following questions in their notebooks or journals. Encourage students to draw on these personal responses as they complete the activities.

1. What have I learned about the attitudes of Africans and Middle Easterners toward their homelands?

2. What have I learned about cultural differences between and within areas in Africa and the Middle East?

3. What have I learned about changes that have taken place in Africa and the Middle East?

4. What effect did the changes have on the inhabitants of the countries where they took place? What effect did the changes have on the rest of the world?

WRITING PROCESS: DESCRIPTIVE ESSAY

Refer students to the model of a descriptive essay found on page 429 in the Handbook section of the Student Edition. You may wish to discuss and analyze the model essay if you are working with less experienced writers.

Guidelines for Evaluation

On a scale of 1-5, the writer has

• clearly followed all stages of the writing process.

• chosen an appropriate scene from a specific selection.

• used sensory images and details to describe the scene.

• made minor errors in grammar, mechanics, and usage.

Assisting ESL and LEP Students

You may wish to provide a more limited assignment for these students so that they can complete their first drafts somewhat quickly. Then have them work at length with proficient writers in a peer-revision group to polish their drafts.

PROBLEM SOLVING

Encourage students to use the following problem-solving strategies to analyze one or more of the tales, poems, or short stories in Unit 1. Afterward, encourage students to reflect on their use of the strategies and consider how the strategies helped in their analysis.

Strategies (optional)

1. Use a semantic map, brainstorming list, or flow chart to identify social changes and resulting problems experienced by a writer or a character. Have groups of students choose the change they most want to investigate further and the selection or selections that best shed light on the topic.

2. Use a second graphic organizer, such as a cause/effect chart or a problem/solution chart, to explore in detail the topic they chose. This graphic organizer should be used to show problems caused by social change and ideas about possible solutions.

3. Decide which topics need further research or discussion. Set up a plan that shares responsibility for doing the research and using the information to create a play, song, essay, or speech.

Allow time for students to work on their presentations.

Guidelines for Evaluation

On a scale of 1–5, the student has

- provided adequate examples, facts, reasons, anecdotes, or personal reflections to support his or her presentation.

- demonstrated appropriate effort.

- clearly organized the presentation so that problems and solutions are logical and consistent.

- demonstrated an understanding of social changes that have taken place in Africa and the Middle East and the problems that have resulted.

2 Asia, Australia, and the Pacific Islands

In Unit 2, you will discover the exciting literature and culture of Asia, Australia, and the Pacific Islands. The writing from this geographic area shows the link between place and heritage. It also provides an understanding of the cultural wealth of this region which includes, among others, the ancient cultures of China, Japan, and India.

UNIT OBJECTIVES

Literary

- to explain how narratives such as short stories, folktales, and autobiographies can powerfully convey beliefs and values
- to show how writers use poetry to express the cultural richness of their heritage

Historical

- to compare and contrast the cultural traditions of Asia, Australia, and the Pacific Islands
- to understand how historical experiences are reflected in literature

Cultural

- to compare and contrast traditional and contemporary cultural values in this region
- to understand how the cultural history of Asia, Australia, and the Pacific Islands is reflected in the literature produced in the area today

UNIT RESOURCES

The following resources appear in the Student Edition of *World Tapestries*:

a **portfolio of culture-related art**, The Art of Tapestries, pages A6-A10, to build background, activate prior knowledge, and generate writing ideas about the unit cultures.

- a **unit overview**, pages 114-117, to provide historical background about Asia, Australia, and the Pacific Islands, including comments from a member of the Ming Dynasty on China's advancement and progress.
- a **time line**, pages 116-117, to help students place the literary works in their historical context. You may wish to have students refer to the time line before they discuss each work.
- the **Focusing the Unit** activities at the end of the unit, page 215, to provide a cooperative/collaborative learning project on the theme of "Asia,

Australia, and the Pacific Islands," a writing project, and a problem-solving activity in which students analyze one or more of the situations described in Unit 2.

INTRODUCING UNIT 2

Providing Motivation

Before students begin to read the unit overview in the Student Edition, you can spark their interest in the culture of Asia, Australia, and the Pacific Islands with some of the following activities:

- Read the following quotation to students.

  When I was in England, I was once laughed at because I invited someone for a snow-viewing. At another time I described how deeply the feelings of Japanese are affected by the moon, and my listeners were only puzzled.

  Natsume Soseki

Explain to students that the quotation is from the Japanese novelist Natsume Soseki. Ask: How does this quotation illustrate some of the differences between Japanese and Western cultures? Discuss whether some cultures are more sensitive to nature than others. Then invite students to speculate how Japanese writers might show their deep feelings for nature. Ask: Do you think Americans on the whole are deeply connected to nature? Why or why not?

- Explain to students that for much of its history, China was the center of civilization in East Asia. Until the 16th century, Asia was more culturally and technologically advanced than Europe. Then write this question on the board:

    How might China's past supremacy in Asia affect the literature of the region?

Have students work in pairs. Each student should brainstorm a list of effects. Then guide partners to compare answers and compile a list to share with the class. Students can verify their speculations as they read the Unit Opener and the literature in Unit 2.

- One of every five people in the world today lives in China. Some of highest rents inthe world are found in Japanese cities because space is so scarce. The streets of Indian cities like Calcutta and Bombay overflow with homeless people. Have a group of students research the issues surrounding population growth in Asia. What are some of the problems that have arisen as a result? How are people's lives in these countries affected? How might these challenges and concerns

influence the literature of these countries? Have groups share their findings in brief oral reports.

- Use the time line for the following activity. Partner students and assign one portion of the time line to each team. Have teams research the cultural events in their assigned era and share their findings with the class.

Cross-Discipline Teaching Opportunity: Unit Culture

Remind students that Asia, Australia, and the Pacific Islands have a vast cultural heritage that manifests itself in many ways today. The Chinese, for example, used ephedrine to treat asthma 1,700 years before its discovery in the West. They were equally advanced when it came to selecting government officials. Written civil service exams were used to select Chinese civil servants as far back as the second century AD—at a time when government jobs elsewhere were largely filled by the relatives of those in power. Consider small matters relating to hygiene as well. The Japanese have used paper tissues for more than 300 years. In 1637, an English traveler wrote, "The Japanese blow their noses with a certain soft and tough kind of paper which they carry about them in small pieces, which, having used, they fling away as a filthy thing."

Work with a social studies teacher to examine the different cultural contributions of the Chinese and Japanese to the world. You might wish to explore such areas as art, medicine, architecture, and daily living. Discuss with students the different cultural contributions from this region. Guide students to draw connections between the history of China and Japan and the culture of modern America.

Setting Personal Goals for Reading the Selections in Unit 2

Have students keep a copy of the following chart in their journals or notebooks. Provide class time every few days for students to review and expand their charts. Encourage them to add topics of their own.

Asia, Australia, and the Pacific Islands			
Topic	What I Know	What I Want to Learn	What I Have Found Out
China's place in the world			
India's history			
Japan's isolation			
the importance of nature in Asian Literature			
the settlement of Australia and the Pacific Islands			

3 East Asia

CHAPTER PREVIEW

East Asia			
Selections	**Genre**	**Author's Craft/Literary Skills**	**Cultural Values & Focus**
from *A Book of Five Rings*, Miyamoto Musashi, pages 119–123	excerpt from a Samurai text	didactic writing	following a code of behavior
"Till the Candle Blew Out," Kim Yong Ik, pages 124–131	short story	motivation	the importance of respect and cooperation
"The Ch'i-Lin Purse," retold by Linda Fang, pages 132–139	folktale	the moral	the values of compassion and kindness
"Hearing of the Earthquake in Kyoto (1830)," Rai Sanyō, pages 140–142	poetry	point of view	the role of nature in human affairs
"A Call to Action," "To the Tune 'The River is Red,'" Ch'iu Chin, pages 143–146	poetry	author's purpose	revolution
"No Way Out," Harry Wu, pages 147–157	excerpt from autobiography	autobiography	freedom from political oppression
"He-y, Come on Ou-t!," Shin'ichi Hoshi, pages 158–163	short story	surprise ending	the destruction of the environment

ASSESSMENT

Assessment opportunities are indicated by a ✔ next to the activity title. For guidelines, see Teacher's Resource Manual, page xxxvi.

CROSS-DISCIPLINE TEACHING OPPORTUNITIES

Drama   Nó (or Noh) is the oldest of the three traditional forms of Japanese drama (puppet and Kabuki are the other two forms.) A combination of history, legend, and Buddhist and Shinto beliefs, Nó developed in the 14th century from dances performed at shrines. In general, Nó plays are brief and very dramatic. Like Greek drama, Nó is performed by actors wearing wooden masks. The performances are accompanied by choral speaking and music. Thousands of Nó plays were written, but only about 250 are performed today. Invite a small group of students to select a Nó play and perform it for the class. Later, students can compare and contrast the Nó play to the selections in Chapter 3, focusing on similarities and differences in topic, theme, and mood.

History   Commodore Matthew Perry (1794-1858) is best known for having opened Japanese ports to world trade. In July of 1853, Perry sailed American battle ships into Tokyo Bay. Shortly after his first meeting with Japanese officials, Perry arranged a treaty with Japan. Under its terms, American people and property were protected in Japanese waters. Perry's diplomatic achievements significantly affected Japan and its relationships to outside powers. Have students work with a history teacher to explore the effect of Perry's entry into Japan. For example, the teacher can help students locate and read diaries, journals, and letters from the era that reveal the impact of Perry's actions at home and abroad.

Art   One of the world's oldest stone gardens was created at the Zen temple of Royoanji, Kyoto, in 1490. The garden contains just 15 large stones, set in a walled area 70 feet by 30 feet. The garden represents nature in the abstract: the stones symbolize islands or mountains; the gravel stands for the sea or trees. There are no plants at all. Invite students to work with the art teacher to plan a stone garden. With the approval of the principal, students may wish to create their stone garden on school grounds for everyone to enjoy.

SUPPLEMENTING THE CORE CURRICULUM

You may wish to invite students to pursue the following activities outside of class:

- In the 12th century, Japanese Zen monks began to drink tea as a treatment for different illnesses and to keep themselves alert during long periods of meditation. The practice of drinking tea, which originally came from China, later became a stylized ceremony used to teach consideration and calmness. The tea ceremony is still performed today in Japan. Guests enter the ceremonial room on their knees through a low door and sip green tea from bowls. The precise protocol extends even to the room in which the tea ceremony takes place: traditionally, the room is square and small, about 9 feet across. Invite a small group of students to find out more about the Japanese tea ceremony and perform it for the class. Students should explain what each step in the ceremony symbolizes.

- The Long March, which took place during the 1930s, was a pivotal event in modern China's history. From October 1934 to October 1935, Mao Zedong led about 100,000 Chinese Communists more than 6,000 miles from the southeastern part of China to the north to escape the Nationalist forces of Chiang Kai-shek. As many as 80,000 people died, including Mao's two small children and his younger brother. Have students find out what effect the Long March had on Mao Zedong's rise to power and the Communist Revolution.

- The Great Wall of China was built around 215 B.C., when the first Chinese emperor used convict laborers to link stretches of older ramparts. Over 1,500 miles long, the Wall is probably the largest structure ever built. Students can create a scale model of the wall to illustrate its awesome size and political effect.

INTRODUCING CHAPTER 3: EAST ASIA

Using the Chapter Opener

Write the following terms on the board: *Buddhist*, *Confucian*, and *samurai*. Ask volunteers to define the words. As students respond, point out that all these terms are key to the history and culture of East Asia, the literature of which is presented in Chapter 3. Then read the following quotation to students:

> The Master said, 'He who rules by moral force is like the pole-star, which remains in place while all the lesser stars do homage to it.'
>
> *Confucius*

Discuss with students the perspective on leadership conveyed by Confucius's quotation. Suggest to students that as they study the selections in Chapter 3, they consider how leaders governed during different periods of Chinese and Japanese history. Ask: "Which styles of government do you think were most effective? Why?"

✔ Developing Concept Vocabulary

You can use a Venn diagram to help students understand the difference between capitalism and communism. The diagram can also help students understand how the rise and fall of communism affected the people of East Asia. Write the words *communism* and *capitalism* on the chalkboard. Create the Venn diagram by drawing intersecting circles around each word. Have students work in pairs to compare and contrast communism and capitalism. Write their responses on the board to create the Venn diagram. Below is a sample of such a diagram.

To encourage discussion, invite students to skim the selections in Chapter 3 to find out how some of the authors reacted to communism.

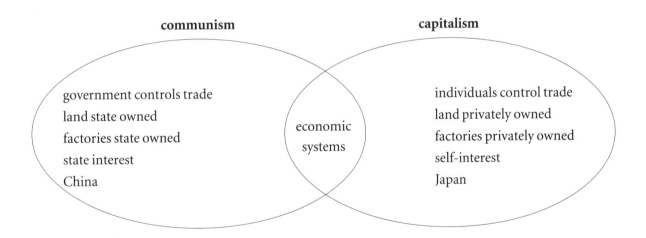

communism
- government controls trade
- land state owned
- factories state owned
- state interest
- China

economic systems

capitalism
- individuals control trade
- land privately owned
- factories privately owned
- self-interest
- Japan

ASK:

- What is the economic theory of communism? What is the economic theory of capitalism?
- How did the Communists obtain power in China? How did they keep it?
- Why do you think communism did not spread to Japan?

from *A Book of Five Rings*
by Miyamoto Musashi (pages 119–123)

OBJECTIVES

Literary

- to understand the elements of didactic literature
- to discuss the techniques used by the author to convey advice

Historical

- to trace the development of ancient Japanese class structure
- to explore the influence of Musashi's guide to strategy on contemporary Japanese business life

Cultural

- to examine the speaker's attitudes toward Kendo, the samurai, and Zen
- to compare and contrast traditional American and Japanese cultural values

SELECTION RESOURCES

Use Assessment Worksheet 16 to check students' vocabulary recognition, content comprehension, and appreciation of literary skills.

✔ Informal Assessment Opportunity

SELECTION OVERVIEW

By 1100, the rural Japanese lords had become increasingly powerful. This virtual monopoly of power helped transform Japan into a feudal society dominated by the samurai class. Included in this class were the *daimyo*, the militaristic lords, and the *samurai*, their bands of warriors. The samurai, who carried a pair of swords as a symbol of their status, followed a strict code of honor.

During the late 16th century, a great Japanese warrior named Hideyoshi conquered the feuding *daimyo* and gained control of Japan. When Hideyoshi died in 1603, Tokugawa Iyeyasu became shogun. To guard against the development of any new groups that might challenge his authority, Tokugawa attempted to prevent the development of Japanese society. The shogun himself defined all social classes, and people were not allowed to cross class lines. European merchants, also regarded as threats to the ruler's power, were driven out of the country. Christian missionaries were expelled. All Japanese ports were closed to foreign ships, with the exception of a single Dutch ship that was allowed to dock once a year. In addition, the Japanese people were not allowed to leave the island. As a result of these measures, Japan was effectively sealed off from the outside world until the middle of the nineteenth century.

In this selection, Musashi outlines his principles of fighting. Many of these principles are of a spiritual, and not physical, nature.

ENGAGING THE STUDENTS

Ask students to make a list of ten guidelines or principles by which they might live. Encourage students to draw upon their own culture's for examples. To help students get started, you may wish to present them with several examples, such as "Learn as much as you can" and "Do unto others as you would have them do unto you." When everyone has finished writing, invite volunteers to share their lists with the class. Working together, compile one list of advice with which everyone agrees. Post the list in a prominent place in the classroom.

BRIDGING THE ESL/LEP LANGUAGE GAP

It is not difficult to understand Musashi's philosophy on a literal level; however, the metaphorical and symbolic underpinnings are apt to be far more difficult for students to grasp. The author's unfamiliar style may also complicate their comprehension of this message. You can make it easier for students to understand what Musashi implies, as well as states, by familiarizing them with Musashi's writing style and preteaching challenging vocabulary. Write the following two excerpts on the board or copy them and distribute to the class.

> The bow is tactically strong at the commencement of battle, especially battles on a moor, as it is possible to shoot quickly from among the spearmen. However, it is unsatisfactory in sieges, or when the enemy is more than forty yards away...

> Moreover, in large scale strategy the superior man will manage many subordinates dextrously, bear himself correctly, govern the country and foster the people, thus preserving the ruler's discipline.

First, have ESL/LEP students work with native speakers. Ask partners to paraphrase Musashi's sentences in their own words. Allow students five minutes to write. Then have pairs of students compare their paraphrases. As a class, discuss how the paraphrases restate the writer's words and capture his meaning.

✔ PRETEACHING SELECTION VOCABULARY

Explain to students that the author teaches readers about life by using words related to weapons and battle. Read these two sentences from the selection:

> The best use of the companion sword is in a confined space, or when you are engaged closely with an opponent. The long sword can be used effectively in all situations.

Invite students to identify the two weapons referred to in this passage (companion sword, long sword). Ask volunteers to brainstorm how these swords might be the same and different. Then have students work in small groups to skim the selection to find other words that tell about warfare. (Examples include **halberd**, **sieges**, **archery**, **invincible**, **dextrously**, *battlefield*, *spear, defensive, prisoner, enemy, fortifications*, and *warrior*.) Write the words on the board. Have students copy the list and add to it as they read the selection.

The words printed in boldfaced type are tested on the selection assessment worksheet.

PREREADING

Reading the Story in a Cultural Context

Help students read for purpose by asking them to restate the writer's philosophy in their own words. Encourage students to stop reading at natural breaking points to paraphrase what they have read.

Tell students that if they do not understand a passage, they should reread it until they get the author's point. You can start them on the right track by using these questions:

- What advice does Musashi give about weapons?
- What is Musashi's advice about timing?

Focusing on the Selection

On the chalkboard, write the phrase *author's message.* Ask: Why did Musashi write this essay? Why do you think people around the world still read this essay more than three hundred and fifty years after it was written? Tell students to consider these questions as they read this excerpt from *A Book of Five Rings.* Encourage students to jot down ideas as they read.

POSTREADING

The following activities parallel the features with the same titles in the Student Edition.

Responses to Critical Thinking Questions

Possible responses are:

1. Musashi is quietly purposeful and emphatic about what he says. His devotion to his subject is clear, and he offers his advice with confidence and expertise.

2. They may conduct business enterprises like military campaigns with singleness of mind, thoroughness, timing, and strategy.

3. Answers will vary. Students should include reasons for agreeing or disagreeing with the principles.

✔ Guidelines for Writing Your Response to *A Book of Five Rings*

Students should record an example of how the use of strategic timing helped them accomplish an objective or goal. Students can share their journal entries with a partner. As an alternate follow-up activity, students can role-play the situation or event, showing how Musashi's advice about timing relates to their own life.

Guidelines for Going Back Into the Text: Author's Craft

Possible answers to the questions in the Student Edition are:

1. He repeats key concepts and words. He also separates the nine principles from the rest so that they stand out. In addition, he writes simply, directly, and forcefully.

2. He incorporates the ideals of a samurai (and of Zen), including those of excellence, honor, self-effacement, discipline, endurance, dedication, and victory.

3. He states that the person who masters timing and strategy will manage others skillfully, carry himself correctly, govern the country successfully, and care for the people wisely. He suggests that strategy and timing are not confined to the military; instead they should be practiced in all activities.

☑ FOLLOW-UP DISCUSSION

Use the questions that follow to continue your discussion of *A Book of Five Rings.* Possible answers are given in parentheses.

Recalling

1. Which weapons does Musashi say are best for use on the battlefield? (He advocates the use of the halberd and the spear.)

2. According to Musashi, why are there few schools of archery in his day? (The bow and arrow are unsatisfactory in current battle conditions, such as during sieges and when the enemy is more than forty yards away.)

3. How can a person master timing? (It can be mastered only through a great deal of practice.)

Interpreting

4. What life lesson does Musashi imply when he says, "You should not copy others, but use weapons which you can handle properly." (You should always be yourself and follow your own

talents and abilities. If you are true to yourself and your abilities, you will be a success.)

5. Why is timing so important in all things? (All human endeavors require strategy. If you do not judge the timing correctly, you cannot plan your strategy.)

6. Why do you think Musashi arranged the nine items on the list in the order he chose? (Possible response: He arranges them from most to least importance so his followers know they must master them in that order.)

Applying

7. Musashi gives a great deal of advice about the use of traditional weapons such as swords and bows. What "weapons" do people use today in business settings? (Possible responses: Physical weapons: celluler phones, computers, calculators, money, networking and so forth. Psychological weapons: cunning, power, position or status, intelligence, planning, and so forth.)

8. Do you agree with Musashi's advice that "timing is everything" in strategy? Why or why not? (Possible responses: Yes, because there is a natural rhythm to all activities. No, because a powerful creative person can manipulate timing to his or her advantage, making it simply another tool.)

ENRICHMENT

Students may enjoy viewing *The Japanese: Yesterday and Today,* available from Zenger Media, 10200 Jefferson Boulevard, Room 922, P.O. Box 802, Culver City, CA 90232, (800) 421-4246.

Till the Candle Blew Out
by Kim Yong Ik (pages 124–131)

OBJECTIVES

Literary

- to identify the motives of each character
- to describe the effect of the story's setting on its plot

Historical

- to discuss the social and economic conditions illustrated in the selection
- to compare past and present Korean social structures

Cultural

- to explore life in a traditional Korean village, especially how people helped each other
- to understand the attitude of the characters toward their homeland

SELECTION RESOURCES

Use Assessment Worksheet 17 to check students' vocabulary recognition, content comprehension, and appreciation of literary skills.

✔ Informal Assessment Opportunity

SELECTION OVERVIEW

The traditional agrarian society of the Korean countryside, steeped in Confucian beliefs, has been suddenly wrenched into the twentieth century. A little more than forty years ago, Korea lay in ruins from the Korean War. Millions of Koreans had been killed in the battles. Thirty years ago, farmers still drove bullock carts through the streets of Seoul. Then the south bank of the Han River was awash with mud. Today it has been drained and seeded with a thick crop of apartment buildings and offices. Thirty years ago, nearly all Koreans were farmers—seventy per cent in all. Today sixty-five percent of the population lives in the cities, resulting in a widespread and sudden dislocation. Twenty-five percent of all South Koreans live in Seoul, and the number continues to increase.

Centuries of adherence to Confucian values has created an authoritarian hierarchy in Korea: ruler over subject, parents over children, husband over wife, elder over younger. Even the language reflects status, with different verb endings for people of different ranks to use when speaking to each other. Only friends are equals. Almost every Korean has a group of lifelong friends to whom loyalty is as important as affection.

In this selection, the narrator and his friend try to outdo each other in an attempt to impress a girl. When the girl leaves, the two realize the pettiness of their ways.

ENGAGING THE STUDENTS

On the board, write the following question: What qualities do you look for in a friend? You may wish to use the following prompts to guide the discussion:

- How important is a similar economic background to friendship? similar values?
- What common interests do you like to share with your friends?
- Do you prefer to be friends with people of the same gender?

Write students' responses on the board. As the class discusses what they look for in a friend, have them rank their list of qualities from most to least important on a line like this:

least important   most important

1	2	4	6	7	8	9	10

BRIDGING THE ESL/LEP LANGUAGE GAP

Before students read the story, make sure that they understand that it is set in the early twentieth century in Korea. Explain that the story describes a friendship between two boys, Life-Stone and Sunny-Tiger. You may also wish to discuss different naming customs in the United States and other countries to acclimate students to the names of the characters in this story.

Then form groups of three or four students to read passages of the story individually and discuss the passages as a group. Guide students to compare and contrast Life-Stone and Sunny-Tiger, focusing on their abilities and interests. Groups can record their findings on a chart like this:

Alike	Different
both Korean boys	Life-Stone is good in art
both love Gentle-Flute	Sunny-Tiger is a musician

☑ PRETEACHING SELECTION VOCABULARY

Invite students to make a chart based on the words that describe aspects of agricultural life in Korea during the time when the story was written. Guide students to brainstorm a list of categories, such as *home, food,* and *clothing*. Then have students look through the story to find words to enter under each column. If the first column is "home," for example, possible words include **thatched**, **abode**, and *remote*. For the column labeled "food," students might list *mugwort*, **abalone**, and **sesame**. *Burlap* and *sandals* would fit in the "clothing" column. Encourage students to list at least ten words on their charts. When students have finished working, ask them the following questions to spark a discussion about the importance of specific words in the story:

- What words does the author use to describe how the people in the story live?
- Based on the story's vocabulary, would you say the author's Korean heritage is important to him? Why or why not?

The words printed in boldfaced type are tested on the selection assessment worksheet.

PREREADING

Reading the Story in a Cultural Context

Have students focus their reading by asking them to consider the importance of a story's setting on the characters and their actions. Remind students that the *setting* of a story is the time and place where the events take place. Encourage students to look for clues in the characters' speech, clothing, or means of transportation as they think about the setting.

Focusing on the Selection

After students finish reading, have them write a short dialogue between Life-Stone and Sunny-Tiger in which the two boys discuss why they act as they do. The dialogue should focus on the competition between the boys and their feelings for Gentle-Flute. When everyone has finished writing, invite volunteers to perform their dialogues for the class. Talk about what aspects of the boys' personality are revealed through the different dialogues.

POSTREADING

The following activities parallel the features with the same titles in the Student Edition.

Responses to Critical Thinking Questions

Possible responses are:

1. Kim Yong Ik describes customs, places, foods, and landscapes with warmth and pride, indicating that he has great fondness for his homeland.

2. The story suggests the values of respect, cooperation, and compassion. Respect is shown when the children are taught to bow to elderly people. Cooperation is shown as the villagers work together to clean up after the storm. Compassion is shown when the boys give up their warm overcoats to help Gentle-Flute.

3. Answers will vary. Students should include specific details in their responses.

☑ Guidelines for Writing Your Response to "Till the Candle Blew Out"

Students should recognize that the story emphasizes cooperation. This is shown when the boys work together to help Gentle-Flute, setting aside their previous competition and jealousy. In their responses, students should also explain why they agree or disagree with the story's lesson. They should consider whether individual achievement is more important than cooperation, explaining the reasons for their choice.

Guidelines for Going Back Into the Text: Author's Craft

Possible answers to the questions in the Student Edition are:

1. Life-Stone is jealous of his friend and may feel inferior because his family is poorer. Although he is

the better fighter, Sunny-Tiger admires Life-Stone, too. Both boys care about Gentle-Flute and want to please her.

2. After the storm, Gentle-Flute's mother has to take her to the city to live with relatives, and the boys are drawn together in a new way in their efforts to help her.

3. She may fear his father, or she may feel bad that Life-Stone's father isn't home very much. She may also believe that Life-Stone's father might not support her attempts to force the boy to eat.

☑ FOLLOW-UP DISCUSSION

Use the questions that follow to continue your discussion of "Till the Candle Blew Out." Possible answers are given in parentheses.

Recalling

1. Why do Sunny-Tiger and Life-Stone draw a line down the middle of the school desk they share? (The line is meant to keep each boy on his side of the desk while they work. The conflicts over space exist because Life-Stone is left-handed, and his elbow often strays to Sunny-Tiger's side of the desk.)

2. What is Life-Stone's special talent? What is Sunny-Tiger's special ability? (Life-Stone is good in art and reading aloud; Sunny-Tiger is a skilled musician.)

3. What happens to the rice harvest? (A fierce storm destroys the crops.)

Interpreting

4. A *symbol* is a person, place, or object that represents an abstract idea. What does the candle in the story's title symbolize? (Possible response: It

symbolizes Gentle-Flute, the light of their lives. When she leaves the village, the light—the candle—is extinguished. Students might also say the candle symbolizes love, hope, or youth.)

5. Why do the boys treat Gentle-Flute so well throughout the story? (Possible responses: They both love her; they feel compassion for her because they realize that her life is far more difficult than theirs.)

6. Why don't the boys fight with each other after Gentle-Flute and her mother have left the village? (Possible responses: Faced with real hardship in the example of Gentle-Flute, they may realize that their competition is petty. If the boys were fighting over Gentle-Flute's love all along, they have no reason to fight after she leaves.)

Applying

7. Many people donate goods and services to the poor. How do you think a student your age could help people who are less fortunate than you are? (Possible responses: Organize a free baby-sitting service for the siblings of a handicapped child; run errands and do simple home repairs for those who cannot do these tasks because of age or infirmity.)

8. Life-Stone and Sunny-Tiger fight like two brothers. Do you think sibling rivalry is healthy and normal? Explain. (Responses will vary, depending on students' experiences with siblings and friends.)

ENRICHMENT

Students may enjoy viewing *Korea: Past and Present.* This film explores the history, culture, and economy of this 5,000-year-old land. The video is available from Media Basics Video, Lighthouse Square, Guilford, CT 06437, (800) 542-2505.

The Ch'i-Lin Purse

retold by Linda Fang   (pages 132–139)

OBJECTIVES

Literary

- to identify a story's moral
- to understand a character's motivations

Historical

- to show how traditional stories often provide historical information
- to discuss the social and economic conditions illustrated in the story

Cultural

- to analyze the traditional Chinese attitude toward male and female children
- to identify the customs and cultural information explored in the story

SELECTION RESOURCES

Use Assessment Worksheet 18 to check students' vocabulary recognition, content comprehension, and appreciation of literary skills.

 Informal Assessment Opportunity

SELECTION OVERVIEW

Chinese literature is distinguished by two distinct literary traditions: the aristocratic and the colloquial. Aristocratic (or court) literature has an ornate style, created by historical allusions, allegories, similes, and metaphors. One of the best examples of the rich aristocratic style of writing can be found in the *Li Sao*, a long autobiographical poem by Ch'u Yuan (343–277 B.C.).

The colloquial tradition, in contrast, is characterized by simplicity of language and emotion. The folk tale "The Ch'i-Lin Purse" fits into this category. As with aristocratic literature, colloquial writing has a long history. The first colloquial literature was poetry; drama and fiction followed soon after. Later developments included short stories, folktales, and histories. Despite its heritage, colloquial literature was shunned as inferior to classical literature by the well-educated and socially prominent scholars who determined literary taste. These men favored a polished and highly ornate style of writing—not the less formal prose and poetry of colloquial writing. Their literary taste set the standard for literature for more than 2,000 years. Only in our own day have folktales received the widespread support that they deserve.

In this selection, Hsiang-ling gives a part of her dowry to another woman on her wedding day. Years later, she and her family, who have fallen on hard times, are repayed for this kindness.

ENGAGING THE STUDENTS

Poll the class on this question: If you had only one daughter, what gift would you give her for her wedding? You may wish to use the following prompts to spark ideas:

- What wedding gifts are traditional in your family? in your culture?
- Would you make or buy this gift?
- Would a daughter's wedding gift be different from a son's gift? Why? In what way would it be different?

Write students' responses on the board. Discuss the responses, guiding students to see that their choice of gifts is based as much on culture as on economics and personal taste. Tell students that a wedding gift sets off the action in the story they are about to read.

BRIDGING THE ESL/LEP LANGUAGE GAP

As with the previous tale, "The Ch'i-Lin Purse" contains vocabulary that will likely prove difficult for non-native speakers to understand. Teach students these unfamiliar words by making sets of flashcards with the vocabulary on one side and their pronunciation and identification on the other. If you wish, list the words on the board and have students make their own sets of cards. Include the following words, pronunciations, and identifications:

Teng-cho (DEHNG-joh) a small town

Hseuh (SHOO-ay) a wealthy widow

Hsueh Hsiang-ling (SHOO-ay SHEE-ahng-lihng) Hseuh's daughter

Ch'i-lin Purse (CHEE-lihn PERS) a wedding gift

hua-chiao (HWAH-jee-aw) a chair that is carried

ta-hsi-jin-tzu (tuh-shee-JOHN-soo) wedding

Lai-chou (LY-joh) a town

li (LEE) Chinese unit of distance

Yuan-wai Lu (yoo-AHN-wee LOO) a man

Have students select a partner and give each pair a set of flashcards. One student should hold up a card while the other student says the word and identifies it. Students can then switch roles. Encourage students to use the cards until they feel comfortable with the vocabulary.

You may also draw on prior knowledge of students who can explain some basics of Buddhism, or who can explain the function of family altar.

☑ PRETEACHING SELECTION VOCABULARY

Explain to students that "The Ch'i-Lin Purse" describes what happens when two brides meet on the way to their weddings. Explain that the author sets the story during the Sung Dynasty, 960–1127. Invite students to skim the story to find words that describe life in this time. Possibilities include *dowry*, **matchmaker**, **benefactor**, **Buddha**, *pavilion, governess, incense, altar*. Students can use their vocabulary words to describe life in ancient China.

The words printed in boldfaced type are tested on the selection assessment worksheet.

PREREADING

Reading the Story in a Cultural Context

Ask students to think about American wedding customs, such as the bride traveling to the wedding in a limousine and the guests giving presents to the newlyweds. Tell students to compare and contrast American wedding customs with those of the ancient Chinese as they read this story. Students can record their findings in a chart like this one:

Wedding Customs

ancient Chinese	modern American
arranged marriage	love marriage
hua-chiao	limousine
wedding procession	wedding procession
parents give gifts	parents give gifts

Focusing on the Selection

Arrange students in groups of four. After each group reads the story once through, divide the story into four sections: Hsiang-ling's life before her marriage (pages 133-134), Hsiang-ling's life when she meets the other bride (pages 134-135), Hsiang-ling's married life (page 135), and Hsiang-ling's life after the flood (pages 135-139). Have each group member pick one of the four parts to analyze. Direct students to write a brief description of Hsiang-ling's life in their part of the story. When everyone has finished, have each group collaborate on an answer to this question: How and why does Hsiang-ling change?

POSTREADING

The following activities parallel the features with the same titles in the Student Edition.

Responses to Critical Thinking Questions

Possible responses are:

1. She remembers it from her childhood as a favorite story. She wanted to share it with a larger audience because she liked it so much.

2. The *ch'i-lin* is a legendary animal from ancient times that traditionally promises a talented son. This relates to the fact that the Chinese value sons over daughters.

3. Answers will vary. Students should fully explain their actions.

☑ Guidelines for Writing Your Response to "The Ch'i-lin Purse"

Students should respond to the homily and explain whether they agree or disagree with it. They should indicate what words they try to live by. You may wish to create a bulletin board of "Words to Live By" by having volunteers write their philosophies on strips of colored paper and post them on a backdrop.

Guidelines for Going Back Into the Text: Author's Craft

Possible answers to questions in the Student Edition are:

1. Because of his embarrassment, the servent refuses to return to the store and threatens to leave. Hsiang-ling begins to feel sorry for him, takes responsibility for being difficult to please, and stops sending back the purse.

2. She realizes how lucky she is to have so much and feels sorry for the poor bride who has nothing.

3. Giving up the porridge leads to a job where she finds the purse and the woman she had given it to. Hsiang-ling is given half the woman's property; her son and husband are found. She gains the friendship of Mr. and Mrs. Lu and has the satisfaction of knowing that her acts were rewarded.

✔ FOLLOW-UP DISCUSSION

Use the questions that follow to continue your discussion of "The Ch'i-lin Purse." Possible answers are given in parentheses.

Recalling

1. Why does Mrs. Hsüeh have a difficult time preparing a dowry of wedding gifts for her daughter Hsiang-ling? (Hsiang-ling is very difficult to please; few of the gifts meet her standards, and she returns everything over and over.)

2. Why is Hsiang-ling delayed on the way to her wedding? (It is raining so hard that the footmen carrying her *hua-chiao* cannot see well enough to continue. The wedding procession is forced to seek shelter in a pavilion.)

3. To whom does Hsiang-ling give her porridge? (She gives it to a hungry old woman who reminds Hsiang-ling of her mother.)

Interpreting

4. Hsiang-ling gives her purse to the young bride but asks that her name not be mentioned. Why does Hsiang-ling choose to remain anonymous? (Possible response: She doesn't want her good deed acknowledged; she does not want the bride to feel indebted to her.)

5. Hsiang-ling had everything that a person could want, but it all vanished in the flood. What message do you think this part of the story illustrates? (Possible response: Don't take happiness for granted; it could vanish in a moment.)

6. Do you think Hsiang-ling expected to be rewarded for her several good deeds? Explain your answer. (Possible response: No. She refuses to have her name revealed to the bride. She gives the old woman her porridge simply because she is younger and she "can stand hunger a bit longer.")

Applying

7. When Hsiang-ling is sixteen years old, her mother hires a matchmaker to arrange a marriage for her. Marrying for love is a relatively new idea; traditionally, most marriages were arranged by parents or matchmakers. What might be some of the advantages of an arranged marriage? (The marriage is based on common interests and similar backgrounds; the participants and families have been carefully screened for potential problems.)

8. Do you think a child can be "spoiled"? Why or why not? (Responses will vary, depending on students' definitions of appropriate behavior and child-rearing practices.)

ENRICHMENT

Students may enjoy viewing *China: Land of My Father*. The film traces one filmmaker's search for her father's family's roots. The video is available from New Day Films, 853 Broadway, Suite 1210, New York, NY 10003, (202) 477-4304.

Hearing of the Earthquake in Kyoto (1830)
by Rai Sanyō (pages 140–142)

OBJECTIVES

Literary

- to identify a poem's point of view
- to analyze a poem for its emotional impact

Historical

- to explore how Japan was affected by the Kyoto earthquake of 1830
- to discuss how Kyoto was a unique, irreplaceable Japanese city in the 19th century

Cultural

- to explain the cultural repercussions of the Kyoto earthquake
- to discuss the Japanese response to this great tragedy

SELECTION RESOURCES

Use Assessment Worksheet 19 to check students' vocabulary recognition, content comprehension, and appreciation of literary skills.

 Informal Assessment Opportunity

SELECTION OVERVIEW

There are three main kinds of earthquakes: tectonic, volcanic, and artificially produced. Of the three, the tectonic is by far the most devastating, for it causes the greatest amount of damage and is the most difficult to predict. This type of earthquake is caused by stresses along the Earth's *plates,* the foundation of the Earth's crust. More than half of the tectonic quakes occur where the plates slide past each other. Especially active regions are the San Andreas Fault in California and the Ring of Fire along the Pacific Ocean. The Kyoto earthquake of 1830 was tectonic.

The magnitude of an earthquake is measured in several ways. The most popular method is the Richter Magnitude Scale, developed in 1935 by Charles F. Richter. This scale measures a logarithm of the altitude of the waves, as recorded by seismographs. The earthquake's magnitude is stated in whole numbers and decimal fractions. For example, an earthquake measuring 5.3 on the Richter Scale is considered moderate; strong earthquakes measure 6.0 and above. The 1923 earthquake in Yokohama, Japan, measured about an 8; about 200,000 people perished as a result of the quakes and the aftershocks.

In this selection, the poet, upon hearing that his hometown has been devastated by an earthquake, envisions the horrors his family has endured without him.

ENGAGING THE STUDENTS

Ask students: Imagine that you had a brief warning before an earthquake struck your region. You have just enough time to grab three things to take with you. What would they be, and why would you choose them? Allow students about five minutes to list their responses. Then invite volunteers to write their lists on the board. When they have finished writing, divide the list into two categories: *replaceable things* and *irreplaceable things*. Replaceable things might include toys, furniture, and appliances. Irreplaceable things might include pictures, people, pets, heirlooms, and a feeling of safety. Have students sort the class list into these categories. Then ask students these questions:

- What do you think would be the most terrible part of experiencing an earthquake?
- What do you think are the most important things to try to protect in a disaster? Why?
- Invite students to return to their lists and change any entries they wish.

BRIDGING THE ESL/LEP LANGUAGE GAP

Because poetry is meant to be heard, this selection provides an ideal opportunity to focus on listening

73

skills. This approach can teach ESL/LEP students to use oral clues to find meaning. Start by reading the poem aloud to the class. Encourage students to make notes as they listen to you read. Then ask volunteers to isolate unfamiliar words. List these on the board. Next, read the poem again, this time asking students to focus on the words listed on the board. Guide students to use clues they heard while you read to define the new words. For example, students can use the description of the devastation as a clue to define *chaos*.

☑ PRETEACHING SELECTION VOCABULARY

Explain to students that this poem describes the damage an earthquake caused in Kyoto, Japan, in 1830. Tell students that the poet's family experienced the earthquake from their home in Kyoto. Then guide students to create a word web to describe the scene after a severe earthquake like the one that struck Kyoto. Write the word "Earthquake" in the middle of the board and invite students to find words in the selection they could use to complete the web. Include at least ten empty balloons for students to fill in. Possible words include *tremors, topple, trembling, fear,* **sunder,** **beseech, cower,** *chaos,* **entreat,** *multitudes,* and **dirge.**

The words printed in boldfaced type are tested on the selection assessment worksheet.

PREREADING

Reading the Poem in a Cultural Context

Ask students to think about places in the United States that have special meaning because they are home to notable monuments, houses of worship, museums, gardens, and other cultural treasures. Possibilities might include Washington, D.C.; St. Louis, Missouri; New York, New York; and Boston, Massachusetts. Discuss with students the special meaning that these places have for their inhabitants and many other Americans. Then direct students to read "Hearing of the Earthquake in Kyoto (1830)" to see how the poet Rai Sanyō feels about his town and its destruction.

Focusing on the Selection

If you wish, have students work independently to read the poem all the way through one time to understand its main idea. Then arrange students in pairs to read the poem aloud to each other. Partners

can work together to identify the poem's speaker and point of view.

POSTREADING

The following activities parallel the features with the same titles in the Student Edition.

Responses to Critical Thinking Questions

Possible responses are:

1. The poet focuses on an important event of the time. Furthermore, because he had a home in Kyoto, he was personally affected by the tragedy.

2. Japan still has severe earthquakes, which bring with them the loss described in the poem.

3. Answers will vary. Students should give full explanations.

☑ Guidelines for Writing Your Response to "Hearing of the Earthquake in Kyoto (1830)"

Students should first list several emotions and then describe how the poet's grief affected them. Guide students to use source books, such as a thesaurus and a dictionary, to capture the precise words that describe their reactions to the poem. Students might find it easier to express their reactions by comparing their feelings to those events generated by more current events in newspapers or on television.

Guidelines for Going Back Into the Text: Author's Craft

Possible responses to questions in the Student Edition are:

1. The poet is the speaker in this poem. Readers can tell because the poet uses the first-person pronouns *I* and *my.*

2. The poem is most likely addressed to the poet's wife and children. Readers can tell because the poet wonders about their fate and refers to *you.* Students might also argue that by focusing on the particular—his family—the poet gives the tragedy a sense of the universal. He implies that the earthquake affected all families, not just his.

3. Instead of focusing on the unknown fate of loved ones, a poetic account of the earthquake written by an observer in Kyoto might describe more objectively what happened and how it affected

others. Although it might cite more specific physical results of the earthquake, it would likely lose the emotional, personal quality of Sanyo's poem.

✔ Follow-Up Discussion

Use the questions that follow to continue your discussion of "Hearing of the Earthquake in Kyoto (1830)" Possible answers are given in parentheses.

Recalling

1. How long did the earthquakes last? (They lasted from dusk to dawn for seven days and nights.)

2. Where is the poet's house located? (It is in Kyoto, on the banks of the Kamo river.)

3. How does the youngest son escape from their house? (He clings to his mother as she runs from their home.)

Interpreting

4. The poet says, "From the nest upturned though the eggs be spared." What do the nest and eggs symbolize? (The nest is the family's house; the eggs are the children, who were previously sheltered in the nest.)

5. How can you tell that the poet is not with his family during this tragedy? (First, the poem's title indicates that the poet has heard of the earthquake rather than experiencing it firsthand. Second, the line, "The mother sickens with care, bearing alone a family's burden," shows that the poet is not with his wife. Third, the lines, "I speed this letter back/And wait an answer that may never come," indicate that the poet is writing to his family to

get news of the tragedy. The line "How can I face you again" reinforces this.)

6. What is the *tone*, or overall feeling, of this poem? (On one hand, it is a dirge, or a general funeral lament, for a great tragedy. On the other, the poet's voice is highly personal, filled with guilt and worry.)

Applying

7. Do you think it would be more difficult to experience an earthquake yourself or to hear that your family was involved in an earthquake while you were away from home? How do your feelings about this compare to the poet's? Explain your answer. (Students can legitimately make a case for either side of the question, explaining why they feel as they do. They should point out that it must have been very painful for the poet to know that his family was caught in an earthquake and that he wasn't there to help them.)

8. Some places, like California's San Andreas fault and Japan's Ring of Fire, are more prone to earthquakes than other places. Why do you think some people willingly choose to live in these places? (Possible responses: These are often places of great natural beauty and are cultural centers. People may also like to dare the elements by living in dangerous places.)

ENRICHMENT

Students may enjoy viewing *San Francisco, the City that Waits to Die*, a video about earthquakes. This 57-minute color video is available from Time Life Films, 777 Duke Street, Alexandria, VA 22314, (800) 621-7026.

A Call to Action
To the Tune "The River Is Red"
by Ch'iu Chin (pages 143-146)

OBJECTIVES

Literary

- to understand the author's purpose
- to recognize devices that authors use to persuade audiences

Historical

- to understand the political and social conditions that led to revolution in China
- to discuss the emergence of feminism as a part of the revolutionary movement

Cultural

- to examine the role of women in Chinese society under the Qing (Manchu) dynasty
- to discuss the tradition of the self-sacrificing hero in Chinese culture

SELECTION RESOURCES

Use Assessment Worksheet 20 to check students' vocabulary recognition, content comprehension, and appreciation of literary skills.

✔ Informal Assessment Opportunity

SELECTION OVERVIEW

Poets have different reasons for writing. They may wish to express their feelings about a subject. They might want to tell a story. Sometimes, they simply wish to entertain. Occasionally, a poet's purpose is to persuade. Persuasive writing attempts to convince its audience to agree with the author's position on a subject.

Ch'iu Chin was a revolutionary, a feminist, and a poet whose purpose was to persuade. She was the only female leader of The Restoration Society. This revolutionary group tried to bring about reform in China. Among its goals was the education of women. Ch'iu Chin used her poetry to persuade others that a revolution was needed. She wrote poems that urged young Chinese, especially women, to become active in the reform movement.

The two poems in this selection are typical of Ch'iu Chin's persuasive poetry. In each, she tries to convince her readers that they must become heroes and lead the people. The glory of the hero, who sacrifices for the good of the country, is a traditional theme in Chinese literature. In both works, she also introduces a modern feminist note. For reform to succeed, she argues, women must take their rightful place among the nation's heroes.

The first poem bemoans the plight of China with the external threats that surround it. The second poem grieves for the dead, but at the same time asks that the struggle continue so that in the future peace will reign in China.

ENGAGING THE STUDENTS

On the board, write: "What good is the heart of a hero inside my dress?"

Explain that this is a line from "A Letter to Lady T'ao Ch'iu," another poem by Ch'iu Chin. Ask students what they think the poet might have meant in this line. Use their responses to generate a discussion concerning the traditional and non-traditional roles of women. Ask students to provide examples of women who have been successful in fields that at one time were not open to them. Ask them to consider the points raised in the discussion as they read the poems in the selection.

BRIDGING THE ESL/LEP LANGUAGE GAP

Have ESL/LEP students work in cooperative groups of three to four to answer these questions about each of the poems in the selection:

- How would you state the position with which Ch'iu Chin wants you to agree?
- What arguments does she use to convince her readers?
- What does she say will result if her readers follow her urging?

Have the groups exchange ideas in a class discussion, focusing on whether they think the poet convinced her readers of the urgent need to agree with her position.

✔ PRETEACHING SELECTION VOCABULARY

Tell students that comparisons are used in the poems to create vivid impressions in the reader's mind. Sometimes, the word *like* or *as* are used to show the comparison (simile). Sometimes, the comparison is made without using *like* or *as* to show the connection (metaphor). Discuss the following example from "A Call to Action."

"invasion" is compared to "**waves.**"

On the board, write the following terms from the poems:

the Chinese people   *sword strokes*

freedom   *free women*

Have students find the words or phrases to which these terms are compared (**swallows**, **dragons**, **perfume**, **flowers**). Call on volunteers to suggest the impressions created in their minds by these comparisons. Ask: Do you think that the poems offer a hopeful or pessimistic message about the future of China? Have students explain their reaction.

The words printed in boldfaced type are tested on the selection assessment worksheet.

PREREADING

Reading the Poems in a Cultural Context

Help students read for purpose by explaining that China is the largest country in the world in terms of population. Nearly one out of every four people on Earth live in China. Historically, China had been an extremely influential and innovative empire. However, at the beginning of the 20th century, a weak royal dynasty was resisting progressive reforms. It allowed other countries to take Chinese territory and even to dictate the nation's domestic policies. As they read the selections, ask students to consider the effect of these conditions on young, educated Chinese like Ch'iu Chin.

Focusing on the Selections

Explain to students that the phrase "jewelled dresses" is a symbol for the life led by prosperous Chinese women, whose families often sheltered them from contact with the harsh reality of life outside their homes. Challenge the class to discuss the following question: Why does Ch'iu Chin link "jewelled dresses" with "bound feet" as symbols of oppression? Discuss the responses and tell students to draw on these ideas in their journal writing.

POSTREADING

The following activities parallel the features with the same titles in the Student Edition.

Responses to Critical Thinking Questions

Possible Responses are

1. Poetry is a respected literary form in China; poetry can be very powerful. Poetry is also more indirect and compressed, suggesting a message rather than stating it. She may also have wanted to appeal to a particular type of audience.

2. Women often lived secluded and pampered lives. Some women were heroines, but that was unusual; women had deformed feet because they were bound to make them small.

3. Answers will vary. Students should describe the cause and explain how they support it.

✔ Guidelines for Writing Your Response to "A Call to Action" and "To the Tune 'The River Is Red'"

If students wish, have them share their journal entries with a partner. As an alternative writing activity, have students work in pairs to write a "thumbnail sketch" describing the kind of person Ch'iu Chin believes is a hero. Suggest that they use these questions to guide their writing: What personality traits does a hero possess? How does a hero behave? What goals does a hero hope to reach? What is more important to a hero—personal safety or the common good? Tell students to consider their responses as they write their journal entries.

✔ Guidelines for Going Back Into the Text: Author's Craft

A rhetorical question is one that the writer does not expect the reader to answer. The rhetorical question is a technique frequently used by writers whose purpose is persuasion. Ch'iu Chin uses this device in "To the Tune 'The River Is Red.'"

Some rhetorical questions need no answer. "How many wise men and heroes/Have survived the dust and dirt of the world?" is an example. Death comes to everyone; no one survives. The persuasive effect is to suggest that death is unimportant. The only immortality we can hope for is to be remembered for our deeds.

Sometimes, the writer answers the rhetorical question for the reader. Ask students to find two examples of this device in the poem. Discuss how the rhetorical questions enhance persuasion by making readers part of a dialogue with the poet instead of passive listeners.

Possible answers to the questions in the Student Edition are:

1. The poet speaks of Chinese people as swallows and China as a nest. She says that without warning, their home has become dangerous.

2. She tells scholars to throw away brushes, women to take up arms, and comrades to spare no effort to continue the struggle.

3. The revolution cast women in a new role that the poems reflect. Ch'iu Chin mentions, in particular, abuses of women in the past and dreams of freedom for them in the future. She most likely believes that women were important in bringing about change.

✔ FOLLOW-UP DISCUSSION

Use the questions that follow to continue your discussion of "A Call to Action" and "To the Tune 'The River Is Red.'" Possible answers are given in parentheses.

Recalling

1. In "A Call to Action," what can the people do together? (hold back the flooding waves)

2. In "To the Tune 'The River Is Red,'" what sounds did the swords of the heroine generals make? (They whistled like dragons and sobbed with pain.)

3. In "To the Tune 'The River Is Red,'" what will free women bear after the revolution? (brilliant and noble human beings)

Interpreting

4. In "A Call to Action," what country threatens invasion from the East? (Japan)

5. In "A Call to Action," from what continent do threats of devious plotting come? (Europe)

6. In "To the Tune 'The River Is Red,'" why do you think that the river is red? (The color of the water has turned red from the blood shed in the battle for freedom.)

7. Why are the dresses of the heroine generals stained with tears? (They are saddened by the fact that violence is necessary to achieve liberty.)

Applying

8. By using the recurring phrase "beautiful women," do you think the poet is implying that only women whose physical appearance meets some set standard are capable of becoming heroes? (Answers will vary. Guide students toward the understanding that Ch'iu Chin is saying that all women are naturally beautiful. Behaving like heroes and throwing off the symbols of oppression enhances their beauty.)

ENRICHMENT

Students will benefit from viewing *South: Female College Students in China* by Tian Zhuang Zhuang. The video is available from First Run Icarus Films, 153 Waverly Place, New York, NY 10014, (800) 876-1710.

No Way Out

by Harry Wu (pages 147–157)

OBJECTIVES

Literary

- to understand point of view in autobiography
- to analyze the author's purpose and his use of introspection

Historical

- to understand the goals and failures of China's 1958 "Great Leap Forward"
- to discuss the human rights violations of the "reform through labor" system

Cultural

- to discuss the effect of political repression on relationships among Chinese people
- to examine the author's perspective on the cultural changes

SELECTION RESOURCES

Use Assessment Worksheet 21 to check students' vocabulary recognition, content comprehension, and appreciation of literary skills.

 Informal Assessment Opportunity

SELECTION OVERVIEW

Autobiographies help us to see our lives and the world in general in sharper focus. Therefore, ***purpose*** and the use of ***introspection*** are two important considerations in autobiography. Purpose is the reason why the author wrote the work. Introspection is the examination of thoughts and feelings in order to draw conclusions about an experience.

Sometimes, the author's purpose in an autobiography is to entertain. By sharing their experiences, writers give us new insights into interesting people, places, and events. Sometimes, writers of autobiographies have a more serious purpose. They wish to inform us. These writers provide us with a unique perspective on events of social significance. By sharing their experiences, they hope to educate their readers about important issues.

The best autobiographies present the truths that the writer discovers and the significance of the events. For this reason, introspection is crucial to writing an autobiography. By examining their thoughts and feelings about events and by explaining why they choose to resolve conflicts in certain ways, they reveal who they are. This introspective process helps us identify with the author as a person. Even if we have never shared the same experiences, we may still be able to understand reactions to it or feelings about it.

In this important work, Harry Wu informs us about life in China in the 1950s. He examines his own thoughts and feelings objectively. Through his experiences, we learn the truth about the ruthless suppression of individual rights that took place under the guise of social progress.

In this selection, the narrator tries to plan an escape from Communist China. When the plan fails, he is harrassed and sent to a labor camp for dissenters.

ENGAGING THE STUDENTS

On the board, write: "Congress shall make no law. . . abridging the freedom of speech."

Call on volunteers to identify the source of this quote. After students identify it as the free speech provision of the First Amendment to the U.S. Constitution, generate a discussion about free speech. Use the following questions as prompts:

- Why is the right to free speech important?
- Should people be allowed to use the right to free speech to criticize the government?
- What could happen if people were not guaranteed the right to free speech?
- Why would a government be afraid to allow its people free speech?

79

Ask students to imagine what it would be like to live in a country where people are arrested and imprisoned for criticizing the government. After they respond, tell them that they are about to read a true story by a Chinese engineer who spent nineteen years in prison for criticizing the government. Ask them to consider the points raised in the discussion as they read.

BRIDGING THE ESL/LEP LANGUAGE GAP

The vocabulary and some of the references to political organization in the selection may present obstacles for some students. Before they begin reading, be sure they understand that "the Party" refers to the Communist Party, which controlled government at all levels. All local government officials were members of the Party. They controlled all political and economic activity through "Committees." Individuals who were accused of crimes against the state (or "the people") were often forced to attend public hearings. At these hearings, other citizens were expected to offer support for the charges by condemning the accused. Defendants, innocent or not, were expected to confess their guilt and ask for mercy.

Form mixed groups of ESL/LEP and English proficient students. Tell them to collaborate to answer these questions as they read:

- Why didn't Harry Wu see any role for himself in his country's future?

- How did he decide to resolve this conflict?

- What was the purpose of the political meeting held on October 3, 1959?

- What was its outcome?

- What was the purpose of the political meeting held on April 27, 1960?

- What was the outcome of that meeting?

✔ PRETEACHING SELECTION VOCABULARY

Have students create a chart based on words that apply to Harry Wu and his conflict. The first chart should contain words with positive or neutral connotations, such as *energetic, ambitious, technically-skilled, determination, daring,* **surveillance**, **predicament**, **bourgeois**, *caution, bold, calmly, insulted.* The second column should contain words with negative connotations, such as *rashness, overconfidence,* **furtively**, *intolerable, miserable, shaken, worried, despondency, confused,* **desolation**, *recklessly,*

loneliness, anger, fear, frantic. Explain that these words are related to the author's introspection. Discuss how the words present a complex personality with strengths and weaknesses. Ask: Does this make Harry Wu seem more believable? Why or why not?

The words printed in boldfaced type are tested on the selection assessment worksheet.

PREREADING

Reading the Story in a Cultural Context

Help students read for purpose by explaining that the human rights issues raised have contemporary significance. In this work, Harry Wu describes conditions in China in 1959 and 1960. After his release from prison, he immigrated to the United States and became a naturalized citizen. In the 1990s, he returned to China and secretly filmed proof that the brutal labor camps were still in operation. The Chinese government accused him of spying and sentenced him to 15 years in prison. The U.S. government negotiated with China, and Wu was told to leave the country. Ask: Why do you think Harry Wu returned to China and took such a risk after his earlier experiences?

Focusing on the Selection

Help students read for purpose by telling them to evaluate the author's credibility when reading an autobiography. Tell students that Harry Wu reveals strengths and weaknesses in himself when examining his thoughts and feelings. Ask: Why does Wu confess to being a thief, even though he knows he is innocent? Does this confession make his character more believable as a human being?

Challenge students with these questions: How does Wu's depiction of Comrade Ning and Wu's friend Wang add to the author's credibility? Why does Wu's depictions make us trust that he is telling the truth about what happened?

POSTREADING

The following activities parallel the features with the same titles in the Student Edition.

Responses to Critical Thinking Questions

Possible responses are:

1. He may have wanted to examine the events and their impact, as well as letting the world know about what life was actually like in China.

2. It shows that the government is still repressive and that freedom of speech remains a threat.

3. Answers will vary. Students should give reasons for the questions they would ask.

☑ Guidelines for Writing Your Response to "No Way Out"

If students wish, have them share their journal entries with a partner. As an alternative writing activity, have students work together as partners to write a letter to a public official explaining how the United States should react to China's use of labor camps to restrict freedom of speech. Use these statements as prompts for alternative positions: The U.S. should break off all diplomatic relations with China until it stops violating human rights. Diplomatic relations and open conversations are the only way to convince China that the benefits of guaranteeing human rights outweigh the disadvantages.

☑ Guidelines for Going Back Into the Text: Author's Craft

An **autobiography** is a self-written account of a person's life that focuses on the inner, private life of the author. A **memoir** is a self-written life story that emphasizes people, actions, and events that have figured prominently in the author's life. A **journal** or **diary** is a self-written record of on-going experiences kept on a regular basis for private use rather than publication. Ask students to discus how they would classify "No Way Out."

Possible answers to the questions in the Student Edition are:

1. He describes the daily life of a college student in the late 1950s, the work he did as a geology student, the political tensions on campus, the Party organization at the school, the importance of the Spring Festival, and the helplessness of anyone accused of a crime.

2. He believes his country has a terrible fate. At different times, he is scared, despondent, rebellious, and resigned.

3. If Harry Wu is an accurate example, the reform system is not very successful. Wu's views seem to have hardened, not changed.

☑ FOLLOW-UP DISCUSSION

Use the questions that follow to continue your discussion of "No Way Out." Possible answers are given in parentheses.

Recalling

1. Why does Harry Wu decide that his only hope is to flee China? (He thinks the country's situation is tragic, and he can see no role for himself in his country's future.)

2. What happens when Harry Wu asks to see the charges against him? (The Public Security Officer ignores his request.)

3. What does Harry Wu burn in the basement furnace of the dormitory? (a map of China's border with Burma that he had hidden for his escape)

Interpreting

4. Why do you think Ning treats Harry Wu kindly? (Privately, Ning, like Harry, is opposed to the abuses of the Party, but he pretends to be loyal to avoid trouble.)

5. Why does Harry Wu guide his conversations with the nurse, Li, away from political topics? (He wants to protect her. If she learns his views and continues to see him, she can be accused of associating with an enemy of the people.)

6. Why does Harry confess to being a thief even though he is innocent? (He is afraid that if the Party investigates further, they will learn of his more serious "crime"—the plan to flee the country.)

7. Why is Harry Wu insulted when he is placed in a jeep with a man arrested for theft? (The person who stole committed a real crime. Harry's only offense is to criticize the government's inefficient policies.)

Applying

8. Why do you think that the Party was afraid to let people exercise free speech? (Answers will vary. Students may suggest that if anyone was allowed to criticize the government's policies, then others might join them and oust the Party from power.)

ENRICHMENT

Students will benefit from viewing *No More Disguises* by Boryana Varbanov, Tome Sigel, and Pam Yates. The video is available from First Run Icarus Films, 153 Waverly Place, New York, NY 10014, (800) 876-1710.

He-y, Come on Ou-t!

by Shin'ichi Hoshi (pages 158–163)

OBJECTIVES

Literary

- to identify the tone of a story
- to identify the elements of a science fiction story

Historical

- to analyze how technology can adversely affect nature
- to understand how the selection reflects the effects of the nuclear bombing of Japan

Cultural

- to discuss how people's use of quick solutions to difficult problems can have adverse consequences
- to discuss the effects of post-nuclear devastation as a global problem

SELECTION RESOURCES

Use Assessment Worksheet 22 to check students' vocabulary recognition, content comprehension, and appreciation of literary skills.

✔ Informal Assessment Opportunity

SELECTION OVERVIEW

Japanese science fiction began in the 1870s when Japanese writers were introduced to the works of Jules Verne, the famous French science fiction writer. For upwards of 50 years, science fiction remained in the background of Japanese literature. Its ascent to the foreground of Japanese occurred after World War II.

There were two major reasons why this occurred: the dropping of the atomic bomb and presence of American troops in Japan.

In August, 1945, the United States dropped two atomic bombs, one on Hiroshima and one on Nagasaki. The results of these bombings were devastating. In Hiroshima alone, 70,000 people died instantly. However, this was just the beginning.

Over the next ten years, thousands and thousands people died as a result of the radiation they had been exposed to. The nature of these deaths was horrible. Painful bluish sores covered the bodies of some people. Others suffered from leukemia. Still others were born with unspeakable birth defects. Death did not come quickly for these people, instead it came slowly and painfully. For this reason, many Japanese writers

used science fiction as an outlet to help them deal with the horrors they had seen.

Another reason for the rise in science fiction's popularity was the U.S. military presence in Japan. U.S. soldiers brought many science fiction books with them. When they discarded these books they were collected and then translated. Science fiction then became an acceptable literary form in the Japanese literary community.

In this selection, townspeople find a very deep hole on the outskirts of their town. They use it for all types of waste, not thinking of the consequences.

ENGAGING THE STUDENTS

Present students with the following hypothetical situation. You are the owner of a large landfill. The NuCo (Nuclear Company) organization offers you a million dollars to use your landfill for dumping nuclear wastes. Do you accept the deal? Why or why not? In class discussion, students can consider such points as researching potential hazards and accounting for community concerns, as well as dealing with NuCo's background. Remind students to consider their responses as they read the selection.

BRIDGING THE ESL/LEP LANGUAGE GAP

Students may have trouble understanding the spelling of the words *he-y* and *ou-t* in the title and text. Explain that these spellings are stylizations to indicate how voices are echoing from the hole. Since the story has a surprize ending, LEP students will need thorough preparation to understand the twist. Create an outline of the plot on the board that can be filled in as the students read.

When they finish reading, follow up to make sure they understood the plot and the details leading up to it.

☑ PRETEACHING SELECTION VOCABULARY

On the chalkboard, write the word *greed* and draw lines from it for a webbing exercise. Guide students to skim the selection and search for words and phrases related to greed (e.g., *profits, fight for contracts*). Write student responses on the web. Challenge students to associate this vocabulary list with themes in the story, such as using easy solutions to difficult problems. When the web is finished, lead a brief discussion on how greed affects people's personalities and behaviors.

PREREADING

Reading the Story in a Cultural Context

Help students read for purpose by reminding them that many science fiction movies and television shows deal with the theme of highly industrialized societies polluting the natural environment. Guide students to recall and compare movies they have seen. They may refer to Japanese films depicting mutated creatures like the Godzilla series and films produced in other countries (e.g., *The Thing*).

Focusing on the Selection

Write the word *change* on the chalkboard and ask students to write in their notebooks one change in society they would like to see in the future. Ask for volunteers to read their responses, or have students share their an-

swers in a small group. Have one student in each group up summarize the group's ideas for the rest of the class.

POSTREADING

The following activities parallel the features with the same titles in the Student Edition.

Responses to Critical Thinking Questions

Possible responses are:

1. The author believes that it is a serious mistake. Statements such as "Safer to get rid of something one didn't understand," "The hole gave peace of mind to the dwellers of the city," and "Everyone disliked thinking about the eventual consequences" illustrate his attitudes, as does the final ironic twist of the ending.

2. Japan has already experienced firsthand the dangers of radiation. In addition, like any other industrial country, Japan must deal with these issues daily.

3. Responses will vary. Students' responses should include the causes of their decisions as well as the short- and long-term consequences.

☑ Guidelines for Writing Your Response to "He-y, Come on Ou-t!"

Challenge students to write a haiku. This poetic form, created by the Japanese, has a special pattern of three lines, consisting of a total of seventeen syllables. Lines one and three have five syllables each. Line two contains seven syllables. Students' poems could reflect the beauty of nature before and after the environment is polluted, for example.

☑ Guidelines for Going Back Into the Text: Author's Craft

Discuss with students how the story's conclusion relates to the selection's themes. Ask: Did you find the ending satisfying? Why or why not? Did the story's ending fit your own expectations? How so?

Possible answers to the questions in the Student Edition are:

1. Answers will differ. Some clues are the old man's warning, the broken rope the villagers cannot pull out of the hole, and people's not thinking about the consequences of filling in the hole with so much dangerous material.

2. Answers will differ. Students should point out that the unexpected nature of the ending gives it more force. The ironic reversal of expectations gives readers another way to look at the consequences of irresponsible behavior.

3. Answers will differ. Students should point out that Hoshi wants readers to think about the dangers of irresponsible waste disposal and about their own actions.

✔ FOLLOW-UP DISCUSSION

Use the questions that follow to continue your discussion of "He-y, Come on Ou-t!" Possible answers are given in parentheses.

Recalling

1. How deep does the scientist say the hole is? (5,000 meters deep)

2. Why are the villagers unconcerned about filling the hole with toxic waste? (They were persuaded that there would be no above ground contamination for several thousand years; they were offered a share in the profits; and it gave them a quick and easy solution to their current problems.)

Interpreting

3. What do you think the hole symbolizes? (an easy way to get rid of our problems)

4. Why do you think the hole gives peace of mind to the villagers? (It covers up their real problems. It's a matter of "out of sight, out of mind.")

5. Why does the scientist suggest that the hole be filled in? (Even though he has no foundation for his suggestion, he feels pressure by the villagers to come up with a solution because he is a scientist.)

Applying

6. What warnings does this story have for maintaining a clean and safe environment? (Answers will vary. The author suggests that we can't put off making decisions about the correct handling of pollutants. A quick fix for one part of the world may be disaster for another.)

7. What are short- and long-range solutions for keeping a safe and clean environment? (Answers will vary. Encourage as many practical and creative responses as possible. Ask students to group responses into categories.)

ENRICHMENT

Students may enjoy using the CD-ROM *Beyond the Rising Sun: Discovering Japan,* available from Social Studies School Service, 10200 Jefferson Boulevard, Room 12, Culver City, CA 90232, (800) 421-4246.

RESPONSES TO REVIEWING THE REGION

1. Sample answer: In "No Way Out" author Harry Wu was forced to follow a political doctrine he could not support. Imprisonment was the result once his escape plans were foiled.

2. Sample answer: "Till the Candle Blew Out" suggests the values of respect, cooperation, and compassion. Respect is shown when the children are taught to bow to elderly people. Cooperation is shown as the villagers work together to clean up after the storm. Compassion is shown when the boys give up their warm overcoats to help Gentle-Flute.

3. Students might select "The Ch'i-lin Purse" because of its happy ending, the reunion of Hsiang-ling with her husband and son.

✔ FOCUSING ON GENRE SKILLS

A Book of Five Rings is regarded as didactic writing because it teaches important lessons. Writing directly and forcefully, Musashi incorporates the ideals of a samurai and of Zen, including those of honor, excellence, self-effacement, and discipline. He points out that individuals can control their own bodies and conquer others. In the sentence, "You should not copy others, but use weapons which you can handle properly," he teaches that people should always be themselves and follow their own talents. Select another example of didactic writing and have students identify its lesson.

BIBLIOGRAPHY

CHIN, CH'IU. "To the Tune 'The River is Red'" and "A Call to Action." In *Women Poets of China*. New York: New Directions Publishing Corporation, 1973.

FANG, LINDA. "The Ch'i-Lin Purse." In *The Ch'i Lin Purse: A Collection of Ancient Chinese Stories*. New York: Farrar Straus & Giroux, Inc., 1995.

MUSASHI, MIYAMOTO. *A Book of Five Rings*. Woodstock, NY: The Overlook Press, 1974.

WU, HARRY and CAROL WAKEMAN. "No Way Out." In *Bitter Winds: A Memoir of My Years in China's Gulag*. New York: John Wiley & Sons, Inc., 1994.

4 South and Southeast Asia

CHAPTER PREVIEW

Literature of South and Southeast Asia			
Selections	**Genre**	**Author's Craft/Literary Skills**	**Cultural Values & Focus**
"Savitri," retold by J.F. Bierlein, pages 165–170	folktale	theme	spiritual values
"This World Lives Because," Iḷam Peruvaḻuti; "Children," Pāṇṭiyaṇ Arivuṭai Nampi; "Tirumāl," Kaṭuvaṇ Iḷaveyiṇaṇār, pages 171–175	poetry	symbols	Hindu beliefs and values
MAKING CULTURAL CONNECTIONS: Asia, Australia, and the Pacific Islands, pages 176–177			
"The Tiger," S. Rajaratnam, pages 178–184	short story	suspense	bonds between people and animals
"Forty-Five a Month," R.K. Narayan, pages 185–191	short story	plot	struggle to balance family and work
from *When Heaven and Earth Changed Places*, Le Ly Hayslip, pages 192–196	autobiography	setting	cultural importance of rice in Vietnam

ASSESSMENT

Assessment opportunities are indicated by a ✔ next to the activity title. For guidelines, see Teacher's Resource Manual, page xxxvi.

CROSS-DISCIPLINE TEACHING OPPORTUNITIES

Social Studies   To help students understand the devastating and far-reaching effect of the Vietnam War on Southeast Asia, work with a social studies teacher to give an overview of the war. Explain to students that the war had its roots in the 1940s, when a number of groups formed the Vietminh (Independence) League. It was headed by Communist guerrilla leader Ho Chi Minh. By the cease-fire in 1973, more than a million Vietnamese civilians had died; more than 6.5 million Vietnamese people were displaced.

Science   One of the world's worst natural disasters occurred in India in 1737, when more 300,000 people died in a violent earthquake.

Strong earthquakes are not uncommon in South and Southeast Asia. Have students work with a science teacher to find out how the magnitude of earthquakes is measured on the Richter Scale and the Mercalli Scale. Students can show their findings on a chart or graph that indicates the logarithmic progression of force.

Art   One of the most recognizable world landmarks is the Taj Mahal. Located in Agra, India, the building is a mausoleum of pure white marble. It was built by the Mogul emperor Shah Jahan to house the body of his beloved second wife, Mumtaz Mahal. Have students create a scale model of the Taj Mahal. Students should write a brief description of the Taj Mahal on an index card to accompany their model.

SUPPLEMENTING THE CORE CURRICULUM

The Student Edition provides humanities material related to specific cultures in Making Cultural Connections on pages 176 and 177 and in The Art of Tapestries on pages A6-A9. You may wish to invite students to pursue the following activities outside of class:

- Hinduism's most sacred text is the *Bhagavad Gita*, or "Song of the Lord." A poem of about 700 verses, it is just one section of the *Mahabharata* (Great Epic of the Bharata Dynasty), a work of about 100,000 Sanskrit couplets composed between 200 BC and AD 200. Students can read a section of the *Bhagavad Gita* and compare and contrast it to "Savitri" or "Tirumāl" to describe how they are the same and different.

- In the introduction to *The Heritage of Vietnamese Poetry*, Vietnamese writer Huynh Sanh Thong had this to say about the Vietnamese literary tradition: While Chinese poets shut themselves up in the tradition of books and had no truck with the oral tradition of peasants, Vietnamese poets moved back and forth at will between the two. They wrote for one another as members of the Confucian elite, but they also looked beyond their esoteric circle and found readers—or listeners—among the populace.

  Invite students to evaluate the validity of Huynh Sanh Thong's analysis after they read the poems in this section. Students may wish to read more Vietnamese poems to extend their knowledge.

- Observant Hindu people often have shrines with images of one or more of the thousands of gods they worship. The two major gods are Shiva (a god of violence) and Vishnu (a god of preservation). Among other gods who are widely worshipped are two of Shiva's sons: Ganesh (god of good fortune) and Karttikeya (god of war). Have students find out more about the Hindu gods and what each represents. Students can create a scroll, frieze, or display to share their findings with the class.

INTRODUCING CHAPTER 4: SOUTH AND SOUTHEAST ASIA

Using the Chapter Opener

On the board, write these terms: *epic, oral tradition, folktales.* Call on volunteers to define the words. As they respond, point out that all three of these types of literature are important in South and Southeast Asia, the region they will study in this chapter. Then read this quotation to students:

> Nonviolence is the first article of my faith. It is also the last article of my creed.
>
> *Mahatma Gandhi*

Tell students that while defending himself against a charge of sedition, Gandhi made this statement in an attempt to explain his actions. Discuss with students the philosophy Gandhi supported. Divide the class in half and have each group of students debate whether they agree or disagree with the credo of nonviolence. When, if ever, might violence be justified? Then explore with students what effect the belief in Hinduism and nonviolence might have on the literature of South and Southeast Asia.

✔ Developing Concept Vocabulary

You can use a chart to help students explore the social, economic, political, and other problems people in South and Southeast Asia face today. On the chalkboard, create a chart to analyze this issue and label the columns as shown in the sample below.

Call on volunteers to list different problems that currently challenge people in South and Southeast Asia. Enter responses on the chart. To spark discussion, point out that some problems arise from the legacy of colonialism; others, from the aftermath of the Vietnam War.

ASK:

- Most of the people of South and Southeast Asia live and work on farms. What special problems might this cause?

- Other people in this region depend on hunting for their livelihood. What problems might this cause?

- Which problems in South and Southeast Asia do you think are the most serious? Why?

- Some of the countries of South and Southeast Asia are among the most highly populated in the world. How might that affect life in those countries?

Today's Problems in South and Southeast Asia			
social	political	economic	educational
legacy of Vietnam War balancing work and family	unstable government	poverty	illiteracy

Savitri

retold by J. F. Bierlein (pages 165–170)

OBJECTIVES

Literary

- to recognize how theme is presented and developed in fiction
- to test inferences about theme

Historical

- to discuss the Vedic Age in India
- to place the *Veda* in historical context among major religious works

Cultural

- to understand the Aryan influence on the Vedic Age in India
- to discuss Hindu teachings and recognize Hinduism's place among world religions

SELECTION RESOURCES

Use Assessment Worksheet 23 to check students' vocabulary recognition, content comprehension, and appreciation of literary skills.

 Informal Assessment Opportunity

SELECTION OVERVIEW

Theme is the main idea or central message in a literary work. Some works have only one theme. Other stories have more than one theme. When a story has more than one theme, the messages are often interrelated or consistent with each other.

Readers can infer themes by looking at how the writer resolves the plot. Characters respond to conflicts by acting in a certain way. Their actions have consequences. What happens as a result of these actions are clues to the theme. "Savitri" has interrelated themes that can be inferred from the consequences of the main character's actions. Savitri marries for love and is rewarded with a happy, though brief, marriage. In return for following her husband's body to the gates of the Underworld, she is granted a wish. As a consequence of her unselfish wish, her husband is restored to life, and they live a long, happy life together.

We can also determine the theme from the lessons that characters learn. Savitri learns that love is stronger than death. She learns that those who follow the three paths to salvation, without regard to personal gain, are rewarded. The more righteous the behavior, the greater the reward.

In this selection, a young princess chooses to marry a hermit, the son of a dethroned king. Her husband "dies," but she pleas with Yama for his life, and Yama gives, not only his life, but also the kingdom back to his father.

ENGAGING THE STUDENTS

On the board, write "The first story was probably about…"

Allow students two minutes to think about how they would complete this sentence. Then discuss with them the origins and purposes of storytelling. Questions like these can stimulate class discussion: What kinds of plots and characters seem to appear over and over in stories? Why do you think people first started telling stories like these? Why do you think these kinds of stories remain so popular to this day? Tell them that they are about to read what is believed to be one of the oldest stories in world literature. Ask them to think about the discussion and decide whether the selection fits the models they described.

BRIDGING THE ESL/LEP LANGUAGE GAP

The vocabulary and the religious concepts in this myth may present difficulty for some students. Discuss the opening paragraph to give students the background of the story. Begin by describing Savitri as a woman of great wisdom and virtue. Discuss with students what this might mean in the context of Vedic culture. What kind of beliefs do they think she might have? What kind of a husband might she choose? How do they think she might act when faced with conflict? What will happen as a result of her actions?

Tell students that the main human characters in this myth are Savitri and Satyavant. Ask them to pay attention to how the paths to salvation discussed in the Student Edition (page 165) relate to each of these characters.

When the students have finished reading the selection, have ESL/LEP students work with an English proficient partner to answer these questions: Why does Savitri's father allow her to choose a husband? Why does she choose Satyavant? Why does Yama grant her one wish? Why does Yama restore Satyavant's life? Why do Savitri and Satyavant go to the highest heaven after death?

☑ PRETEACHING
SELECTION VOCABULARY

Have students create a list of words based on behavior that Hindus believe will lead to salvation (*pious*, *spiritual*, *holy*, *charity*, *wisdom*, **alms**, **ordained**, **contemplative**, *meditation*, *duty*, *compassionate*, *courage*, **equity**). When they have finished, ask the questions below to lead to a discussion of the three Hindu paths to salvation.

- Which characteristics seem most closely related to devotion?

- Which characteristics seem most closely related to knowledge or study?

- Which characteristics seem most closely related to doing what is right regardless of personal interest?

The words printed in boldfaced type are tested on the selection assessment worksheet.

PREREADING

Reading the Story in a Cultural Context

Tell students that Hinduism teaches that people achieve salvation in progressive stages. At each stage, the devout person becomes less concerned with the material world and more aware of the importance of spiritual matters. Ask students: Why does Yama tell Savitri and Satyavant that their souls will only visit his Underworld? Why are they to go to the highest heaven?

Focusing on the Selection

Help students read for purpose by asking them to consider beliefs and behavior codes that are shared by many religions and cultures around the world. Tell them to think about these questions as they read: What Hindu beliefs are mentioned that are similar to

beliefs found in other religions? What attitudes concerning correct behavior seem to have a universal cultural quality?

POSTREADING

The following activities parallel the features with the same titles in the Student Edition.

Responses to Critical Thinking Questions

Possible responses are:

1. Sample response: Kings usually choose husbands for their daughters. However, Savitri's father, recognizing her wisdom, allows her to choose her own husband. Yama is so impressed by her wisdom that he grants her a second wish and restores her husband to life.

2. Sample response: While traveling in search of a husband, Savitri spends her time helping those who are less fortunate. She chooses Satyavant, a man who would rule wisely, rather than a wealthy suitor who would bring her personal gain. When Yama says he will grant her one wish, Savitri unselfishly asks that her father-in-law again be placed on the throne occupied by an evil usurper, rather than asking to have her lover restored to life. Savitri and Satyavant live a simple, dutiful life and when they come to the throne, rule fairly.

3. Answers will vary. Possible choices include wisdom, compassion, loyalty, courage, piety, or determination. Encourage students to explain their choice.

☑ Guidelines for Writing Your Response to "Savitri"

If students wish, have them share their journal entries with a partner. As an alternative writing activity, have students work together as partners to write a paragraph comparing Savitri to a modern fictional heroine of their choice. Suggest that they compare such elements as the social setting in which each lives, the conflicts each must resolve, personality traits, lessons learned, and rewards received.

☑ Guidelines for Going Back Into the Text: Author's Craft

Personification, a type of figurative language, portrays inanimate objects or abstract ideas in human terms. In mythology, supernatural beings often appear as personifications of forces in nature or mysteries. Ask students what character in "Savitri" is an example of personification. What does this character personify? Can you explain why the expression "wrenched the soul of Satyavant from the body" is an example of personification?

Possible answers to the questions in the Student Edition are:

1. Sample response: Savitri's character demonstrates virtues that the Vedic culture valued highly. The esteem in which the gods and people hold Savitri shows the rewards that come from living a life of virtue. Savitri remains true to her principles in resolving the conflicts that arise as part of the plot. By acting the way she does, she provides an example of behavior that others who wish to achieve salvation can follow.

2. Sample response: Savitri illustrates the way of knowledge by her desire to know the answers to philosophical questions and by the years she and her husband spend in the forest acquiring wisdom. Savitri demonstrates the way of devotion by her willingness to sacrifice her own life by following her husband into Yama's realm. Savitri illustrates the way of duty by her faithfulness to her husband, her disregard for personal gain, and her unselfishness.

3. Answers will vary. Some students may suggest a moral along the lines of "virtue is its own reward." Others might write a message to the effect that true happiness is found in giving of yourself to others. Still others may choose a lesson stating that spiritual values are far more precious than material possessions. Some may stress other moral lessons that can be inferred from Savitri's exemplary life.

☑ FOLLOW-UP DISCUSSION

Use the questions that follow to continue your discussion of "Savitri." Possible answers are given in parentheses.

Recalling

1. What kind of person is Satyavant, the man Savitri chose as her husband? (He is a holy hermit who could rule wisely and understand the plight of the poor.)

2. After Satyavant's death, what amazing thing does Savitri do? (She follows Yama, the Lord of the Dead, to the gates of the Underworld.)

3. What two wishes does Yama grant Savitri as rewards for her courage and wisdom? (He restores the kingdom to Satyavant's father, and he restores her husband's life.)

Interpreting

4. Why is Savitri's decision about the kind of man she will marry surprising? (Savitri's decision to marry a holy man rather than a wealthy prince shows that, although she is young, she is more interested in spiritual matters than in material possessions.)

5. Why does Yama praise Savitri's courage? (Because of her great love for her husband, Savitri is willing to follow him to the Underworld rather than remain among the living.)

6. How does Savitri's first wish show that she considers doing the right thing more important than personal benefit? (Satyavant's father is the rightful ruler of his kingdom. The usurper's taking the throne is a wrong that should be made right. Satyavant's death at an early age, although sad and very painful to Savitri, is ordained by the gods and is part of the natural order of things. It is not a wrong that must be made right.)

Applying

7. What themes in the myth of Savitri do you think are lessons that our culture still believes are important? (Answers will vary. Some students may suggest that we still value doing what is right over personal gain. Others may suggest the theme of devotion to loved ones. Some may choose the theme that spiritual matters are more important than material possessions. Others may find other values that we share with the Vedic author of the myth.)

8. In your opinion, why is it important for cultures to have myths with heroines like Savitri, as well as myths with heroes? (Answers will vary. Some students may suggest that the importance lies in showing that men and women are equal. Others may suggest that it is important to show that women are also capable of being great leaders and performing wise and heroic deeds. Still others may suggest that it is equally important for young women and young men to have role models. Other students may find other equally valid applications of the myth.)

ENRICHMENT

Students will learn the origins and practice of Hinduism by viewing *The Hindu World*. The video is available from Coronet/MTI Film and Video, 108 Wilmont Dr., Deerfield, IL 60015, (800) 621-2131.

This World Lives Because by Iḷam Peruvaḻuti

Children by Pāntiyan Arivuṭai Nampi

Tirumāl by Kaṭuvan Iḷaveyinanār (pages 171–175)

OBJECTIVES

Literary
- to identify and analyze poetic symbols
- to discuss the emotions conveyed in these poems

Historical
- to trace the development of Tamil poetry through the ages
- to understand why these poems are considered "classics"

Cultural
- to describe how the Indian people have kept their cultural traditions alive through poetry
- to compare and contrast traditional Indian and American cultural values

SELECTION RESOURCES

Use Assessment Worksheet 24 to check students' vocabulary recognition, content comprehension, and appreciation of literary skills.

✔ Informal Assessment Opportunity

SELECTION OVERVIEW

Even though the Indian literary tradition spans a period of more than 3,500 years and the number of literary works produced by Indian writers far exceeds those of the Latin and Greek writers, people in the West generally know very little about Indian literature. In part, this is because of the sheer volume of Indian literature. Literature of the Indian subcontinent includes works written in Sanskrit, Persian, and Tamil, as well as scores of modern languages derived from these.

Ancient Indian literature took the form of myths, fables, poetry, and drama; there were no short stories or novels. Most texts, like the poems in this lesson, attempt to convey timeless truths about love, death, and humankind.

Indian culture has had a subtle yet pervasive influence on Western life. Many of India's cultural traditions have become so much a part of our lives that we do not realize they come from another country. Our number system, for example, came from India. They are called "Arabic" numbers because Arab traders brought them from India to Europe. Medical care also owes much to India because its doctors were among the first to set broken bones and recognize the importance of hygiene.

The three poems in this cluster reflect the values and beliefs of Indian culture. The first poem speaks about the importance of honorable men, the second about having children, and the third about a Hindu god.

ENGAGING THE STUDENTS

Ask: Why do people want to have children? Discuss with students some of the reasons why people are eager to have children: to continue their family line, to pass on what they have learned, to have someone to love. Tell students that one poem in this cluster, "Children," describes the warm feeling the poet Nampi has for children.

BRIDGING THE ESL/LEP LANGUAGE GAP

After students have read these three poems, ask them what they think the authors are trying to communicate. Ask: Why do you think these poets wrote these particular poems? Help students by breaking down each poem into stanzas. First, write the first stanza of "This World Lives Because" and "Children," and the last stanza of "Tirumāl" on the board or copy them and distribute to the class.

Then, as students read the stanzas, ask: How do these passages communicate ideas that are important to the author? Why do you think these ideas are important to the author? What other passages convey these ideas?

✔ PRETEACHING
SELECTION VOCABULARY

Have students create a word bank by writing all the terms in the poem that relate to goodness and positive values. Examples include *virtues, love, truth, strength,* **Vedas***, love,* **ambrosia***,* and *honor.*

Use the questions below to lead a discussion of the poets' use of these terms:

• Why do you think these writers used so many words that refer to virtuous living?

• Based on this vocabulary activity, what do you think the major themes of these poems might be?

The words printed in boldfaced type are tested on the selection assessment worksheet.

PREREADING

Reading the Poems in a Cultural Context

Help students read for purpose by asking them to list the values that can make the world a better place. Possibilities include love, compassion, patience, and belief in a higher power. Discuss how people can show these values in daily life, such as the way they treat their children, friends, and strangers. Other possibilities might include the way people worship their God and the way they pursue their goals. Ask students to discover what values from ancient India are expressed in these poems.

Focusing on the Selections

Remind students that a *symbol* is a person, place, or object that represents an abstract idea. Explain that there are universal symbols within a culture, such as a dove symbolizing peace and a rose symbolizing love. Be sure that students understand that there are also personal symbols that have meaning to only one person or to a handful of people. Then ask: Why do poets often use symbols in their writings? Discuss how symbols help poets convey much information in a compressed way. Tell students to think about how the authors of these poems describe things that are important to them by using universal symbols rather than lengthy explanations.

POSTREADING

The following activities parallel the features with the same titles in the Student Edition.

Responses to Critical Thinking Questions

Possible responses are:

1. He gives examples of their exemplary behavior and then states that they are the reason that civilization continues.

2. Readers might conclude that the Tamils loved and cherished children and saw them as a key to the meaning of life.

3. Answers will vary. Students should think of someone who is generous, kind, forgiving, courageous, and/or selfless, and explain how these qualities are reflected in their actions.

✔ Guidelines for Writing Your Response to "This World Lives Because," "Children," and "Tirumāl."

Have students share their journal entries with a partner. Or, as an alternative writing assignment, have students write a short poem that expresses a similar theme of one of the Tamil poems.

✔ Guidelines for Going Back Into the Text: Author's Craft

Solicit responses to the question about the symbolic significance of the colors in the American flag. Have students also discuss the symbolic value of the flag in general. Encourage students to think of other national or cultural symbols and to discuss their significance.

Possible answers to questions in the Student Editon are:

1. In "Tirumāl," the poet uses the heat of fire, the scent of flowers, and a diamond to describe Visnu.

2. The symbols in "Tirumāl" show great depth of feeling because they are the essence or the highest quality of the things mentioned.

3. In the poem "Children," the children represent the important things of life that go beyond money, charity, and intellectual achievements. They stand for love and the meaning of life.

✔ FOLLOW-UP DISCUSSION

Use the questions that follow to continue your discussion of "This World Lives Because," "Children," and "Tirumāl." Possible answers are given in parentheses.

Recalling

1. What four qualities of admirable people does the poet praise in "This World Lives Because"? (self-lessness/charity, forgiveness, honor, and bravery)

2. In "Children," what messy things do children do? (They "grub with mouths," "grab with fingers," and "smear rice and ghee/all over their bodies.")

3. What is the topic or main idea in "Tirumāl"? (The main idea is that the Hindu god Vishnu is the embodiment of all that is good and essential in the universe.)

Interpreting

4. In "This World Lives Because," what do you think the ambrosia in the second stanza symbolizes? (Possible responses: great riches, enormous good fortune.)

5. In "Children," why do you think the poet describes both good and bad qualities of children? (The poet is showing that despite their messiness and occasional annoying behavior, having children is still one of the most rewarding things a person can do.)

6. In "Tirumāl," why does the poet repeat the word "everything" in the final stanza? (The repetition is for emphasis. It stresses that Visnu is the entire universe.)

Applying

7. Do you think people still regard children today in the same way that the poet Nampi did in "Children"? Why or why not? (Possible responses: Yes, because some people make children the center of their lives, showering them with love and devotion. No, because some people regard children as a burden and a hardship, not a pleasure.)

8. Peruvaḷuti endorses four values in "This World Lives Because." What four values do you think are important to people today? (Possible responses: ambition, determination, love, valor, compassion, charity, forgiveness, wisdom.)

ENRICHMENT

Students may enjoy viewing *Discovering the Music of India*, a look at the history and folk traditions of India. Included are Indian songs, dances, classical music, folk music, and folk instruments. The video shows how music fits into Indian life in the past and present. The video is available from Media Basics Video, Lighthouse Square, Guilford, CT 06437, (800) 542-2505.

OBJECTIVES

Overall

- to discover the connections between famous monuments in Asia, Australia, and the Pacific Islands and the cultures of these lands

Specific

- to analyze how the political repression symbolized by China's Tienanmen Square has become a theme of Chinese literature
- to examine how the temple Angkor Wat reflects the importance of Hinduism in Cambodia
- to appreciate the Australian Aboriginals' respect for the natural world

ENGAGING THE STUDENTS

On the board write the following question: What is the most important monument in our community? First, be sure that students understand that a monument can be a building, work of art, natural feature, or historic structure. Allow students about five minutes to brainstorm a list of ideas, and then write these on the board. Next ask: What does this monument reveal about our culture? How does it mirror our important values? Have students study the photographs of Tienanmen Square, Angkor Wat, and Ayers Rock on pages 176 and 177 and discuss how these structures represent different aspects of Chinese, Cambodian, and Aboriginal culture.

BRIDGING THE ESL/LEP LANGUAGE GAP

Have volunteers point out on a map the country where each monument is located. If students are recent arrivals to the United States from Asia, Australia, or the Pacific Islands or have traveled to these locations, invite them to share what they may know about the three monuments highlighted.

The names of the monuments in this feature—*Tienanmen Square, Angkor Wat,* and *Ayers Rock*—are apt to pose difficulties in pronunciation for ESL/LEP students. Say each name and have the class repeat it after you.

EXPLORING LANDMARKS

In the 1980s, the Chinese Communists enacted major political and economic changes. These included expanding commercial and technological ties to the industrialized world and increasing the role of the free-market. Many of the people were not satisfied, however. In 1989, more than 100,000 students and workers gathered in Tienanmen Square to demand an end to restrictive governmental policies. Chairman Deng Xiaoping swiftly imposed martial law, and armed troops crushed the protesters. The death toll is estimated at 300 with 17,000 people injured. At least 10,000 dissidents were arrested; 31 were tried and executed.

- Have students write a brief research essay that compares and contrasts the Tienanmen Square incident to that of the Kent State incident in 1970. Provide resources about both events. Encourage students to discuss the similarities and differences between the roles of the military, the goal of the students, the forms of government, and outcome of the events.

LINKING LITERATURE, CULTURE, AND REGION

Guidelines for Evaluation: Sample Answers

By saying "Scholars, throw away your brushes!/Secluded women, take up arms!" Chi'iu Chin calls for people to rise up against repression. Harry Wu directly criticizes what he calls the "follies" of Chinese communism and decides to leave his homeland for freedom.

"Savitri" describes the wisdom and piety of the true believer in Hinduism, the princess Savitri.

"Tirumāl" shows the comfort such belief can bring.

The narrator in "Family Council" has a close, personal, mystical relationship to nature; she sees all things in nature as part of herself. Her beliefs reveal the native groups' respect for nature.

The Tiger
by S. Rajaratnam   (pages 178–184)

OBJECTIVES

Literary

- to understand how writers create suspense in a story
- to understand how writers reveal character in a story

Historical

- to discuss how human settlement has endangered the tiger's habitat
- to compare social and economic conditions in Malaysia and Singapore

Cultural

- to discuss the relationship between Malaysian society and nature
- to discuss the significance of the tiger in Asian lore and culture

SELECTION RESOURCES

Use Assessment Worksheet 25 to check students' vocabulary recognition, content comprehension, and appreciation of literary skills.

 Informal Assessment Opportunity

SELECTION OVERVIEW

Suspense is a feeling of strong curiosity or uncertainty about the way that events will turn out. Suspense is strongest when we care about a character. We want to see that character successfully resolve the conflict that is driving the plot. Our emotional involvement increases our anxiety about the outcome of the story.

In "The Tiger," we care about Fatima. She is young, pregnant, and alone in the forest. We identify with her fear. We understand her uncertainty, faced with the tiger's puzzling behavior. We sympathize with her desperate desire to protect the life developing within her. We admire her courage. As the plot tension grows, so does our anxiety. When Fatima escapes, we feel a rush of relief.

Our comfort is short-lived. As Fatima's concern for the tiger grows, so does our own. Like her, we are curious about its behavior. From the safety of the village, it no longer seems a menace. It did not harm her. Again, the suspense increases, but the focus of our anxiety has shifted. We have become involved with the beast. S. Rajaratnam has shown us how carefully wrought suspense can stir our emotions. He has also made us think about our relationship to the natural world.

In this selection, a tiger confronts a pregnant woman in the outskirts of her town. When the townsmen kill the tiger, they find out that the tiger had just given birth to cubs.

ENGAGING THE STUDENTS

On the board, write: "Extinction is forever."

Acknowledge that the issue of "animal rights" is a complex one. Point out that the way people view the problem depends on their perspective. People in underdeveloped countries with pressing economic needs may see the question in different terms than we do here in the United States. A Malaysian villager may not have the same perspective on tigers as an author living in the city of Singapore. Have students discuss their thoughts on the subject. Ask: Do you think that people are doing enough to prevent endangered animals from extinction? Do people and animals sometimes have competing needs? Is allowing the extinction of a species ever justified? Can it ever be harmful to the balance in nature? Tell students that they are about to read a story that asks them to draw their own conclusions about animal rights.

BRIDGING THE ESL/LEP LANGUAGE GAP

Have LEP and English proficient students work in mixed groups of three or four. Provide each group with a copy of the three selection excerpts below. Ask them to consider these questions about each excerpt: What does this passage show about Fatima's feelings toward the tiger? Are her feelings similar to or different from the other villagers at this point? Why do her feelings change?

"Fatima and the animal watched one another. She was frightened; it was suspicious." (p. 180)

"She hoped that it [the tiger] was far out of the men's reach." (p. 182)

"For a few seconds the cry of the animal seemed to fill up her heart and ears. Her face was tight with pain." (p. 183)

Use the group conclusions to generate a class discussion. Ask: What is the physical cause of Fatima's pain in the last excerpt? Is there another reason for her pain? What does this excerpt tell you about theme?

✔ PRETEACHING SELECTION VOCABULARY

Tell students that writers use environmental terms to establish the physical setting for a story. Frequently, they use words that have broad, general meanings to set the scene. Sometimes, they use words with a regional flavor. Using these kinds of words is called adding *local color*. Occasionally, they use familiar words that have a specialized meaning in a region as part of local color. Help students recognize the physical setting of "The Tiger" by guiding them in the creation of a list. The list should contain words with a regional flavor (Examples: **sarong**, **lalang**, **betel**) and words with a specialized meaning (Examples: **headman**, **mat**). (A *betel* is a climbing pepper plant whose nuts are chewed in Southeast Asia, much as we chew gum. In Malaysia, *headman* is a term for a village chief. A *mat* is a piece of woven material used as a bed.)

Have students discuss how local color adds to the atmosphere of a story.

The words printed in boldfaced type are tested on the selection assessment worksheet.

PREREADING

Reading the Story in a Cultural Context

Ask students to imagine the exact same story in a different cultural context. For example, the setting could be the western United States. The heroine is a young American woman. The animal is a wolf. Mamood and the other men are sheep ranchers. Ask them to consider whether placing the story in a different setting would have any effect on their feelings as they read. Call on students to comment and explain why or why not.

Focusing on the Selection

Help students read for purpose by asking them to consider the following questions as they read: What is the tiger looking at when it turns its eyes away from Fatima? Why does the boy say, "No wonder the beast fought so hard"? Why does the author have Fatima's birth pains start at the exact moment the tiger is shot?

POSTREADING

The following activities parallel the features with the same titles in the Student Edition.

Responses to Critical Thinking Questions

Possible responses are:

1. She cannot see or hear the village. The only sights and sounds are those of nature. She is filled with loneliness and wonder, creating the impression that she could be the only person in a strange, different world. The author describes Fatima's surroundings as a dream world. This suggests the world of the imagination in which anything is possible, including a nightmarish meeting with a tiger.

2. Human activity is threatening to destroy the environment. People must find a way to balance the need for economic development and the protection of the environment that furnishes the materials that make economic progress possible. This includes preservation of rain forests and endangered wildlife such as the tiger.

3. Answers will vary. Some students may suggest that the tiger, an endangered species, gave no indication that it would attack livestock or people. Under the circumstances, the villagers should be able to frighten it away without killing it. Others may suggest that the tiger is by nature a predator, and no one can predict the behavior of wild animals. Sad though it might be, the villagers had no choice but to kill it to protect themselves.

✔ Guidelines for Writing Your Response to "The Tiger"

Have students share their journal entries with a partner. As an alternative writing activity, have students work in pairs to create "thumbnail sketches" of Fatima, her mother, and Mamood. (Challenge them to add a portrait of the tiger as a character.) Have them do a webbing exercise to help them with their sketches. First, they should list the characters' names. Then, they should write descriptive words that come to mind when they think about that character.

✔ Guidelines for Going Back Into the Text: Author's Craft

Remind students that characters in fiction are not always human. If an animal in a story has a personality, it becomes a character. Sometimes, authors create animal characters that behave like humans so that readers can relate to them. Sympathetic characters help to build suspense. Use the following questions to stimulate discussion:

- Does the tiger in this selection behave like a tiger or like a human? Explain.
- Does this kind of portrayal strengthen or weaken the suspense? Explain.

Possible answers to the questions in the Student Edition are:

1. Answers will vary. Some students may not have expected her to drown so early in the story. Others may have been surprised that she survived, particularly if they had thought the story was entirely about her attempted escape.

2. Answers may vary. Some students may suggest that the outcome meets the reader's expectations. The tiger is a threat that the villagers have eliminated, relieving tension. Others may suggest that part of the suspense lies in the fact that the author has created sympathy for the tiger, and the reader, like Fatima, is hoping it will escape unharmed. Therefore, its death comes as a surprise.

3. During the encounter with Fatima, the tiger does not act like a predator. It behaves more like an animal warning the woman not to come near something it is protecting. It frequently looks away from her as though distracted by something else. The author suggests that there is a bond between the tiger and the pregnant woman. Fatima's concern for its safety seems to coincide with her labor pains. Accept other reasonable responses.

✔ FOLLOW-UP DISCUSSION

Use the questions that follow to continue your discussion of "The Tiger." Possible answers are given in parentheses.

Recalling

1. How does Fatima escape from the tiger? (When it turns its head away, she dives into the river and swims across to her village.)

2. Why does Fatima think that the tiger might go away if left alone? (It didn't look or act like a killer.)

3. What was the tiger protecting when the villagers found it in the lalang? (three newborn cubs)

Interpreting

4. Why was the tiger lying motionless in the grass? (It was in labor and about to give birth to cubs.)

5. Why does Fatima dare not move? (The tiger might interpret any movement on her part as a threat and attack her.)

6. Why does Fatima feel a greater fear when she realizes the tiger's growl is far away than when she was close to the animal? (She realizes that she is in the middle of the river and, in her fatigue, in greater danger of drowning.)

Applying

7. In your opinion, is the tiger's failure to run away when the villagers approach realistic? (Answers will vary. Guide students toward the understanding that most animals have a parental instinct and will fight to protect their young when threatened.)

8. Do you think the fact that the author lives in Singapore influenced his perspective on the theme of the story? (Answers will vary. Some students may suggest that a person who lives in a more urban area can have just as great an appreciation of the environment and the need to protect endangered species as those who live closer to nature. Others may suggest that it is easier for a city dweller to be sympathetic to the plight of wildlife than it is for someone whose family or livestock might be threatened by a tiger.)

ENRICHMENT

Students will benefit from exploring *Sustainable Agriculture* (Malaysia). The CD-ROM is available from Encyclopedia Britannica Educational Corporation, Attn: Customer Service, 310 South Michigan Avenue, Chicago, IL 60604-9839, (800) 554-9862.

Forty-Five a Month

by R. K. Narayan   (pages 185–191)

OBJECTIVES

Literary

- to trace the structure and events in a story's plot
- to analyze the author's attitude toward his characters

Historical

- to describe the life of a middle-class Indian family
- to explore the treatment of middle-class male bureaucrats in India

Cultural

- to compare and contrast parent-child relationships in India and the United States
- to discuss how the characters' struggle to maintain their cultural traditions while meeting the demands of the modern world

SELECTION RESOURCES

Use Assessment Worksheet 26 to check students' vocabulary recognition, content comprehension, and appreciation of literary skills.

 Informal Assessment Opportunity

SELECTION OVERVIEW

India is a country of great contrasts. On one hand, India boasts an ever-widening industrial base; on the other, the majority of the people live in poverty.

India's efforts to raise the standard of living for its citizens have been hampered by its huge population. After China, India has the second largest population in the world— over 935 million people as of 1996. Furthermore, the population is still increasing at the rate of about two percent a year or sixteen million people. Current estimates predict that India will have one billion people by the year 2000.

Monsoons and crop failures in the 1980s caused serious food shortages. As a result, India has continued to struggle to feed its huge population. Efforts to eradicate poverty have also been slowed by high rates of illiteracy and infant mortality, wavering government policies, poor internal communications, the low status of women, and conflicts between castes and religious groups. Less than half the population is literate (48%); the life expectancy is age 58 for males and 60 for females. The average farmer earns approximately $700 a year, about the amount spent for the average rural wedding. This helps to explain why Venkat Rao, a member of

India's middle class, is so fearful of losing his pay of forty-five rupees a month.

In this selection, a father from a middle-class Indian family struggles without success to leave work early to spend time with his daughter. He finally decides to make good on his promise to take her to a movie, but when he is given a raise, he breaks his promise to her to finish his work.

ENGAGING THE STUDENTS

On the board, write:

"Oh, I must go. My father will be back at home now. He has asked me to be ready at five. He is taking me to the cinema this evening. I must go home."

Explain to students that Shanta, the little girl in this story, is excited about going to the movies with her father. Ask students why children enjoy spending time with their parents. Explore the special times parents and children have together going to zoos, circuses, and restaurants. Volunteers might wish to share special times they have had with their parents on vacation, shopping, or at athletic events. Tell students that in this selection, they will read about a little girl whose father has promised to take her out for the evening.

BRIDGING THE ESL/LEP LANGUAGE GAP

To help students with their comprehension of the story, read the first two pages of the selection aloud as students follow along in their books. Carefully explain the action of the story.

After you read, present students with the following questions. Have them find the answers from their books.

1. What is the little girl's name? (Shanta Bai)

2. Who is Kamala? (Shanta's friend)

Students may also have difficulty with the author's use of British English. Explain that until 1948, India was a British colony. As a result, Indians use British words, phrases, and spellings. Point out the spelling of *coloured* in the first paragraph and explain that British spelling adds a "u" in words such as *favour* and *honour*. You may also wish to point out the use of the British English word *cinema* for the movies, *frock* for dress, and *increment* for raise.

✔ PRETEACHING SELECTION VOCABULARY

Explain to students that R.K. Narayan uses precise adjectives and adverbs to help readers visualize the way Shanta and her parents live. Discuss how he chooses each word to describe the story's setting and build the plot. Then call on students to skim the story to find precise modifiers that tell more about the characters and action. Possibilities include **laboriously, vermilion**, **wry, cynically, excruciating,** *false, petty, slightest,* and *mechanically*. Students can use these words to create a web around the phrase *middle-class Indian life.*

The words printed in boldfaced type are tested on the selection assessment worksheet.

PREREADING

Reading the Story in a Cultural Context

Help students to read for purpose by asking them to consider why Venkat Rao is so desperate to keep his job. Guide students to analyze how the author has painted a picture of middle-class life in India today by the use of precise adjectives and adverbs and phrases from British English. Ask students how they think Rao compares to many middle-class Americans today. How are they similar and different?

Focusing on the Selection

Be sure that students understand that plot is the arrangement of events in a work of literature. Describe how a plot has a beginning, middle, and end. Tell the class that the writer arranges the events of the plot to keep the reader's interest; to build the conflict; to reveal the characters' actions, thoughts, and feelings; and to convey the theme. Explain that in many stories and novels, the events of the plot can be divided as follows:

- *Exposition*: introduces the characters, setting, and conflict
- *Rising Action*: builds the conflict and develops the characters
- *Climax:* shows the highest point of the action, where the conflict comes to a head
- *Resolution:* resolves the conflict and ties up all the loose ends

Have students find places in the story that correspond to these four divisions.

POSTREADING

The following activities parallel the features with the same titles in the Student Edition.

Responses to Critical Thinking Questions

Possible responses are:

1. He shows that although Venkat Rao is weak and afraid to stand up to his manager, his reasons are very real. Rao's manager is cruel and might fire him, leaving his family without means of support. By presenting Rao's desire to spend time with his daughter and his inability to do so, the author portrays him as a real and sympathtic character.

2. The story shows a bureaucracy of exploited middle-class workers who are cowed into working long hours, taking orders, and not questioning authority for relatively low pay.

3. Answers will vary. Students should include details in their responses.

✔ Guidelines for Writing Your Response to "Forty-Five a Month"

Have students share their journal entries with a partner. As an alternative writing activity, have students write a response to Rao's resignation letter. Students can choose to either defend the manager's position or to validate Rao's points and change the system.

☑ Guidelines for Going Back Into the Text: Author's Craft

Discuss with students the difference between external and internal conflicts. Explain that in an external conflict, the main character struggles against an outside force. In an internal conflict, a character struggles with a problem within himself or herself. Ask students to identify the external and internal conflicts Rao faces in the story.

Possible answers to the Student Edition questions are:

1. Shanta's father, Venkat Rao, is torn between his duties at the office and his desire to spend time with his daughter.

2. Events that lead to the conflict include Shanta finding the cinema advertisement and asking her father to take her to the cinema and his inability to come home at five o'clock as he promised. The conflict increases as the point of view shifts and we see why Rao is delayed.

3. The climax occurs when the manager gives Rao a raise just as he is about to resign. Although he accepts the raise, Rao still faces the same conflict of not being able to balance his work and family life.

☑ FOLLOW-UP DISCUSSION

Use the questions that follow to continue your discussion of "Forty-Five a Month." Possible answers are given in parentheses.

Recalling

1. Why is Shanta impatient for school to be over for the day? (She is anxious to return home so that she can get dressed for her evening at the movies with her father.)

2. What plan does Shanta come up with to get her father to come home earlier? What is the outcome of her plan? (She decides to go to her father's office and get him. Her plan fails because she does not know the way to her father's office.)

3. What does Venkat Rao say in the letter to his boss? (Rao sends a letter of resignation. In the letter, he says that it would be better for his family to die of starvation than for him to sell his soul for forty rupees. He asks for a raise and warns his boss that

if his family dies of starvation, their ghosts will return to haunt the manager.)

Interpreting

4. Venkat Rao takes back the letter and lies about its contents. What does this action reveal about his character? (Now that he has received a raise, he is afraid of the boss and of losing his job; he places his family's welfare and security above his own need for retribution for years of mistreatment. Accept other reasonable responses.)

5. How would you describe the relationship between Venkat Rao and his daughter Shanta? (They love each other dearly. Shanta idolizes her father. Rao is trying to do the best he can for his daughter.)

6. Do you think Mrs. Rao could have helped improve the situation? Why or why not? (Answers will vary. Some students might suggest that she could have improved the situation by explaining to Shanta how hard her father works and by taking her daughter to the movies. Others may suggest that she could not have improved the situation because Shanta wanted to spend time with her father.)

Applying

7. Do you admire people like Venkat Rao? Why or why not? (Answers will vary. Possible responses: Yes, because he is sacrificing his life to provide a decent life for his family. No, because he has placed money over family responsibilities.)

8. Consider the difficult choices that Venkat Rao has to make. What choices do you think you will face in ten years? (Responses will vary, depending on students' goals. Possibilities include choices of jobs, whether to have children, and where to live.)

ENRICHMENT

Students will benefit from viewing *India,* a video about the culture of this vast subcontinent. The video is available from Zenger Media, 10200 Jefferson Boulevard, Room 922, P.O. Box 802, Culver City, CA 90232, (800) 421-4246.

When Heaven and Earth Changed Places

by Le Ly Hayslip   (pages 192–196)

OBJECTIVES

Literary

- to describe the story's setting
- to identify the author's attitude toward her culture

Historical

- to discuss the effect of the Vietnam War on the Vietnamese peasants
- to understand the importance of rice to survival in Vietnam

Cultural

- to explore the customs of village life in Vietnam
- to understand the connection Vietnamese peasants had to their land

SELECTION RESOURCES

Use Assessment Worksheet 27 to check students' vocabulary recognition, content comprehension, and appreciation of literary skills.

✔ Informal Assessment Opportunity

SELECTION OVERVIEW

In 1954, representatives from Vietnam, Cambodia, Laos, China, France, Great Britain, the Soviet Union, and the United States held a conference in Switzerland to end the French occupation of Vietnam. The leaders agreed to divide Vietnam into two countries: North Vietnam and South Vietnam. North Vietnam was to be a Communist country backed by the Soviet Union; South Vietnam was to be a democracy backed by the United States. Before the division, about a million North Vietnamese people left their homes to resettle in South Vietnam. Many were well-known writers, artists, political leaders, business people, and teachers.

Three years later, the South Vietnamese Communist rebels (the Viet Cong) and the South Vietnamese government clashed over leadership. In 1959, North Vietnam lent its support to the Viet Cong's revolt against the South Vietnamese government. The United States increased its support of the South Vietnamese. In 1975, the United States pulled its forces out of South Vietnam, and the North Vietnamese invaded the South. This resulted in the fall of Saigon and the installation of a new North Vietnamese Communist government in the South. Many people, like Le Ly Hayslip, were forced to stay in their homeland, but some found a safe haven in the United States, Norway, and other countries.

In this selection, the narrator explains the importance rice has to the Vietnamese people and the superstitions they have about it.

ENGAGING THE STUDENTS

On the board, write the following question: What aspects of the place where you live make it special to you? You may wish to use the following prompts to guide the discussion:

- How important are the foods native to your region?
- What effect does the weather have on your feelings about your community?
- What customs would you miss if you moved to a different place?

Write students' responses on the board. As the class discusses their responses, rank their list of qualities from most to least important.

BRIDGING THE ESL/LEP LANGUAGE GAP

Before students read the story, make sure they understand that it is set in Vietnam in the 1960s and 1970s. Explain that the story describes life in the midst of a war. You may also wish to discuss the difference between staple foods in the United States and other countries to acclimate students to the importance of rice in the story. Encourage students from other countries to contribute to the discussion.

Then form groups of three or four students to read passages of the story individually and discuss the passages as a group. Guide students to compare and contrast their life in the United States and/or their country of origin to the narrator's experiences in Vietnam during the Vietnam War, focusing on customs, lifestyle, and setting. Groups can record their findings on a chart.

✔ PRETEACHING
SELECTION VOCABULARY

Invite students to make a chart based on the words that describe aspects of rural culture in Vietnam during the time when the story was written. Guide students to brainstorm a list of categories, such as *legends, foods,* and *customs.* Then have students look through the story to find words to enter under each column. If the first column is "legends," for example, possible words include **rituals**, **karma**, and *ancestral*. For the column labeled "food," students might list *separation, kindle, nutrients, seedbed.* Encourage students to list at least ten words on their charts. When students have finished working, ask them the following questions to spark a discussion about the importance of specific words in the story:

- What words does the author use to describe the legends that are important in her culture?
- Based on the story's vocabulary, would you say the author's Vietnamese heritage is important to her? Why or why not?

The words printed in boldfaced type are tested on the selection assessment worksheet.

PREREADING

Reading the Selection in a Cultural Context

Have students read for purpose by asking them to consider the importance of a story's setting on the characters and their actions. Remind students that the *setting* of a story is the time and place where the events take place. Encourage students to look for clues in the characters' speech, customs, and diet as they think about the setting.

Focusing on the Selection

After students finish reading, have them write a short description of the story's setting that includes the time and place of the action. When everyone has finished writing, have students exchange papers and draw a picture of Vietnam based on their partner's description. Display the descriptions and illustrations. A follow-up class discussion might focus on the differences between Vietnam and the United States.

POSTREADING

The following activities parallel the features with the same titles in the Student Edition.

Responses to Critical Thinking Questions

Possible responses are:

1. She shows respect for the simple life and hard work, for the life-giving crops, and for the customs of her people. She wants the reader to understand that the villagers were peasants struggling to make a living from the land, and they did not welcome the war.

2. Crop failures were perceived as the fault of the people who had failed to honor ancestors; the solution was to pray and sacrifice more. Secondly, each grain of rice was a symbol of life and was therefore never wasted.

3. Answers will vary. Students should describe the customs of their families and cultures and tell why they are important.

✔ Guidelines for Writing Your Response to *When Heaven and Earth Changed Places*

Have students share their journal entries with a partner. As an alternative writing activity, ask students to work in pairs to provide a brief explanation of why Le Ly Hayslip included the legend about the rice ball in the midst of her narrative. What function does it serve? How does it help the reader to better understand how important rice is to the Vietnamese? Have students share their explanations in a class discussion.

✔ Guidelines for Going Back Into the Text: Author's Craft

Explain to students that setting helps to create the mood, or atmosphere, of a piece of literature. Lead a discussion about how the setting in this selection helps to create a specific mood. How would students describe the mood? Possible answers to the questions in the Student Edition are:

1. The setting gives a sense of the environment and customs of the family, especially the altar, family sleeping arrangements, and the hiding place. The descriptions of the water buffalo walking on rice near the house indicates the simplicity of life.

2. The fields are where the rice is grown. This is important because rice is the community's life blood.

3. The planting and harvesting cycles are at the heart of village life.

4. Land is one of the most important things to a farmer. The farmers believe that under communism their right to the land would be guaranteed. This gave a most powerful incentive for supporting the Communists.

✔ FOLLOW-UP DISCUSSION

Use the questions that follow to continue your discussion of *When Heaven and Earth Changed Places*. Possible answers are given in parentheses.

Recalling

1. What important tasks did the villages do when planting was over? (They made clothing, mended tools, found spouses for eligible children, and honored their ancestors through rituals.)

2. Why is the water buffalo important in the production of rice? (The water buffalo is used to separate the rice from the stalk.)

Interpreting

3. A *symbol* is a person, place, or object that represents an abstract idea. What does the title of this story symbolize? (It symbolizes the reversal of good and bad brought about by the upheaval of war.)

4. What purpose does the legend of the rice serve to the people in this Vietnamese village? (It explains why they have to work so hard to produce food.)

Applying

5. In what ways are the experiences of Le Ly Hayslip relevant to American teenagers today? (Her life story shows that people must work hard to succeed no matter where they live.)

6. How might life in Vietnam have been different if there had not been a war? (Lives would not have been disrupted; people would not have suffered so terribly. Without the terrors of war, the people might have learned new technology to harvest their crops.)

ENRICHMENT

Students may benefit from viewing *The Killing Fields*, starring Sam Waterston and Haing S. Ngor. This powerful film explores the war in Cambodia and the rise of the Khmer Rouge. The video is available from Media Basics Video, Lighthouse Square, Guilford, CT 06437, (800) 542-2505.

RESPONSES TO REVIEWING THE REGION

1. Sample answer: In "Forty-Five a Month," Venkat Rao is torn between his duties at the office and his desire to spend time with his daughter. His conflict is based in the realities of middle-class Indian life; most middle-class women do not work outside the home.

2. Sample answer: In "Forty-Five a Month," R. K. Narayan describes what he knows best: middle-class Indian life. The story shows a bureaucracy of middle-class workers who are cowed into working long hours, taking orders, and not questioning authority.

3. Students might ask Savitri's father why he cannot let her plan her own future.

✔ FOCUSING ON GENRE SKILLS

R. K. Narayan makes effective use of the short story form in "Forty-Five a Month" by crafting a tightly woven plot. He arranges the action to keep the reader's interest and to convey the theme. In the *exposition*, Narayan introduces the characters, setting, and conflict. During the *rising action*, he builds the conflict and develops the characters. In the story's *climax*, Rao gets a raise so he does not resign. The *resolution* ties up all the loose ends. Select another short story, such as "The Book of Sand," and have students identify plot elements and show them on a chart.

BIBLIOGRAPHY

HAYSLIP, LE LY. *When Heaven and Earth Changed Places*. New York: Doubleday, 1989.

NARAYAN, R.K. "Five a Month." In *Malgudi Days*. New York: Penguin USA, 1982.

RAMANUJAN, A.K., translator. "This World Lives Because," "Children," and "Tirumāl." In *Poems of Love and War*. New York: Columbia University Press, 1985.

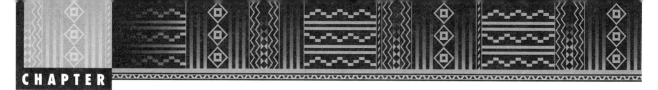

5 Australia and the Pacific Islands

CHAPTER PREVIEW

Literature of Australia and the Pacific Islands			
Selections	**Genre**	**Author's Craft/Literary Skills**	**Cultural Values & Focus**
"Tangaroa, Maker of All Things," edited by Antony Alpers, pages 198–201	creation myth	figures of speech	origin of the world
MAKING THEMATIC CONNECTIONS: Places Called Home, pages 202–203			
"Maui and the Great Fish," retold by Kiri Te Kanawa, pages 204–207	folktale	repetition	origin of the world
"Family Council," Oodgeroo, pages 208–211	short story	personal narrative	personal and mystical relationship to nature; respect for family authority
"Butterflies," Patricia Grace, pages 212–214	short story	setting	links between people and nature

ASSESSMENT

Assessment opportunities are indicated by a ☑ next to the activity title. For guidelines, see Teacher's Resource Manual, page xxxvi.

CROSS-DISCIPLINE TEACHING OPPORTUNITIES

Social Studies   John King was the first European to cross the Australian continent and survive — thanks to the compassion of the Aborigines. In 1860, King and two other explorers, Burke and Wills, set out from Melbourne on an expedition that soon ran out of supplies. Aborigines gave the men fish, but Burke lost his head and fired at the rescuers. King used his rifle to shoot birds for the Aborigines and so won their continued help. Burke and Wills died of starvation; King survived. Work with a history teacher to help students explore the relationshipbetween the Aborigines and the European explorers and settlers.

Science   In December of 1953, Queen Elizabeth's Coronation Tour of New Zealand coincided with the eruption of Ruapehu, a volcano on the North Island. On Christmas Eve, more than 600 million gallons of hot acidic water erupted from the lake surrounding the volcano, creating a murderous mudflow. Have students work with a science teacher to find out why volcanoes erupt. Students can also research whether Australia, New Zealand, and other islands in the Pacific are especially likely to experience volcanic eruptions, and if so, why.

Art   Many people think of Australia as a vast agricultural center, but the country also boasts some of the richest culture in the world. For example, Sydney, Australia, has one of the world's most famous opera houses. Opened in 1973 after fifteen years' work, it cost approximately $150 million. Students can look in travel guides to find out more about Australia's modern cultural attractions. They can present their findings in a travel brochure that persuades people to visit Australia to enjoy its cultural facilities.

SUPPLEMENTING THE CORE CURRICULUM

The Student Edition provides materials related to a unifying theme in Making Thematic Connections: Places Called Home on pages 202 and 203. You may wish to invite students to pursue the following activities outside of class:

- Just as American English has developed its own vocabulary and accents, so Australian English has developed its own special words. For example, a "lolly" is candy, "station" is a ranch, and a "sheila" is a girl. Australians also use many vivid phrases to describe people, places, and things in a uniquely Australian way. Here are three such Australian expressions that apply to people: "lower than a snake's belly," "so mean he wouldn't shout in a shark attack," and "mad as a cut snake." Invite students to work in small groups to find or create equivalents to these expressions in American English.

- The skeletons of countless sea creatures form the Great Barrier Reef, which stretches 1,250 miles along the northeast coast of Australia. It has taken about 15 million years to form this complex chain of islands and coral reefs, which cover an area the size of Kansas. A good overview of the Great Barrier Reef can be found in National Geographic's *Surprising Lands Down Under* (The National Geographic Society, 1989).

- Australia's Uluru, or Ayers Rock, is a sacred place to the country's Aborigines. The native Pitjandjara people believe that each of its features represent an important person or event in their history. One hole, for example, is believed to be the spot where a spear fell during a battle between rival clans of Aborigines. Students can find out more about this powerful national symbol in *The First Australians*, by Ronald and Catherine Berndt; *A Short History of Australia*, by Manning Clark; and *Archaeology of the Dreamtime*, by Josephine Flood.

INTRODUCING CHAPTER 5:
AUSTRALIA
AND THE PACIFIC ISLANDS

Using the Chapter Opener

On the board, write these terms: *myths*, *stories*, and *legends*. Ask students to define the words. As they respond, point out that all three of these types of literature are important to the culture of Australia and the Pacific Islands, the region they will study in this section. Then read this quotation to students:

> Myths there must be, since visions of the future must be clothed in imagery. But there are myths which displace truth and there are myths which give wings to truth.

> *William Ernest Hocking*

Explore with students how myths can capture past values as well as future expectations.

Ask: How can myths "displace the truth"? How can they "give wings to the truth"? Discuss the vital role that myths play in culture and heritage of a nation and its people.

✔ Developing Concept Vocabulary

You can use a webbing exercise to help students explore the great diversity of the literature in this chapter. Write *Australian and Pacific Island literature* on the chalkboard. Then call on students to list words they associate with each term. Link their answers with connecting lines. To get students started, write *myths*, *stories*, and *legends* on the chart and ask the following questions.

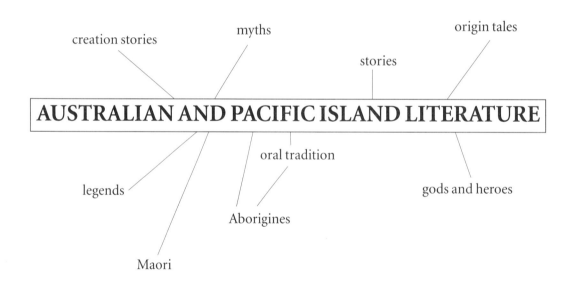

creation stories · myths · origin tales · stories

AUSTRALIAN AND PACIFIC ISLAND LITERATURE

legends · oral tradition · Aborigines · gods and heroes · Maori

ASK:

- How do you think most myths and stories were preserved through the generations in this region?

- In what ways is the literature of this region similar to the literature of native peoples in other regions of the world?

- What important cultural events do you think these myths might describe?

Tangaroa, Maker of All Things
edited by Antony Alpers   (pages 198–201)

OBJECTIVES

Literary

- to understand the difference between literal and figurative language
- to identify figures of speech and recognize their effect in a piece of literature

Historical

- to understand the location and composition of the Polynesian islands
- to discuss the settlement of Polynesia

Cultural

- to examine traditional themes and characters in Polynesian mythology
- to recognize common elements in mythological variations from island to island

SELECTION RESOURCES

Use Assessment Worksheet 28 to check students' vocabulary recognition, content comprehension, and appreciation of literary skills.

 Informal Assessment Opportunity

SELECTION OVERVIEW

Writers use two types of language. Literal language refers to the exact, factual meanings of words that are found in dictionaries. When using literal words, such as *shell, egg,* and *darkness,* writers expect that their readers will know—or can find out—exactly what they mean. **Figurative language,** on the other hand, is language used to stir the reader's imagination. Instead of presenting factual information, writers use symbols, images, and comparisons to create striking, original impressions. **Similes** and **metaphors** are two kinds of figurative language that use comparisons.

A simile compares two different things and shows the comparison by using the words *like* or *as.* Using the phrase "like an egg" to describe Tangaroa's shell is an example of a simile. It compares two different things, the shell and the egg, showing the comparison by the use of the word *like.*

A metaphor compares two different things but does not use a linking word to show the comparison. "His [Tangaroa's] ribs for the ridges" is an example of a metaphor. The author compares the crests that rise along a mountain slope to the structure of the human rib cage and its relationship to the backbone (mountain range).

In this selection, Tangaroa creates the universe with man and woman being his finishing touch.

ENGAGING THE STUDENTS

Tell students to imagine that they have spent their entire life on a small island in the middle of the ocean. The island was formed when an undersea volcano erupted millions of years ago. There is no other land in sight. Have students take two minutes to list the natural objects, plants, and animals that they see around them. When they have finished, have them write a response to this question: What kind of creation myth would you write to explain your world to others on the island? Suggest that they use the following prompts as guidelines: How did the world come to exist? Was it created with a purpose? By whom? Why? How? What images can I use to explain creation in terms others will be able to see in their minds?

Ask volunteers to read their work and use the ideas to generate a class discussion about creation myths. Tell students they are about to read one such myth from an island culture.

BRIDGING THE ESL/LEP LANGUAGE GAP

This simple but fascinating tale provides a good opportunity for limited English speakers to focus on the creation myth as a genre and on the writer's craft, especially imagery. Before they begin, make certain that they understand the cultural origins of the myth. You might have LEP students work in groups of three or four to determine the exact and relative locations of Polynesia. A world map or globe would be a helpful tool.

Ask students to consider how location might influence the choice of details in the story. Suggest they think about the following questions as they read:

- Do you know of any other creation stories from this region of the world? How are they similar to this one? How are they different?

- Do you know of any other creation stories from other regions of the world? How are they similar to this one? How are they different?

After students have read the selection, discuss these questions as a class. Encourage students—especially limited English speakers—to share their knowledge with the class.

☑ PRETEACHING SELECTION VOCABULARY

Imagery, especially metaphorical imagery, is very important to a full appreciation of this selection. While the vocabulary is familiar, it might be helpful to ensure that students have an exact mental picture of the images evoked. Have groups use a dictionary to find the literal meanings of the following words used as the subjects or images in this myth: *mountain range*, **ridges**, **scales**, **shells**, *clouds*, *flesh*, **feathers**, *guts*, *rainbows*.

Tell students to think about the imagery as they read. After reading, you might generate a class discussion about why the author of the myth compared specific subjects and images.

The words printed in boldfaced type are tested on the selection assessment worksheet.

PREREADING

Reading the Story in a Cultural Context

Help students locate Polynesia on a map while discussing the physical geography of the region. Note that these islands are relatively small in size, surrounded by large expanses of ocean, low-lying and unprotected, and isolated from other land masses. These factors make them especially vulnerable to destructive forces in nature. As they read, encourage students to compare Tangaroa, his actions, and his motivation to creators in other myths. Ask them to consider how the islands' relationship with nature influenced themes in Polynesian myths.

Focusing on the Selection

Help students read for purpose by discussing the use of the shell as an image in Polynesian mythology. Note that, according to the selection, everything in the universe has a shell. Tell students to think about the almost limitless shapes, sizes, and coloration of sea shells as they read. Ask: Why would an island culture choose the shell as an image? Why is the shell an appropriate image for the varied life found on Earth?

POSTREADING

The following activities parallel the features with the same titles in the Student Edition.

Responses to Critical Thinking Questions

Possible responses are:

1. Tangaroa uses his backbone for a mountain range and his ribs for mountain ridges.

2. All the animals (lobsters, shrimps, and eels) are edible sea creatures. This shows the importance of the ocean to a culture that arose on islands and that was dependent on the ocean for survival.

3. Answers will vary. Some students may suggest that even in cultures that believed in many gods, one god is usually credited with the creation of the universe and the life it contains. Some may suggest that creators seem to follow a common pattern in filling the void. First, they create the heavens and the earth. Then, they progress to non-living matter like rocks. Next, they create plant and animal life. Last, they create humans. Others may suggest that the makers seem to have a similar purpose: to be obeyed, worshipped, or to have their creations admired and used.

☑ Guidelines for Writing Your Response to "Tangaroa, Maker of All Things"

Have students share their journal entries with a partner. As an alternative writing activity, have students work together as partners to describe the age group for which they believe this creation myth would be most appropriate. Tell them to state at least two lessons that the target audience should learn from the tale. Ask them to explain and discuss their choice of audience (including why it would be less appropriate for either older or younger readers).

☑ Guidelines for Going Back Into the Text: Author's Craft

Unlike similes and metaphors, an apostrophe is a figure of speech that does not compare two different things. In an apostrophe, a character speaks directly to either a person who is not there or a non-living object. Writers use apostrophe to heighten dramatic effect in a work. In this selection, Tangaroa's statement, "O rock, crawl here!" is an example of apostrophe. Ask students to find another example of apostrophe in the selection. ("O sand, crawl here!")

Possible answers to the questions in the Student Edition are:

1. A shell is a protective covering in which life grows until the moment of birth. Shells are often shaped like an oval, similar to the Earth. The edge between upper and lower parts resembles the horizon. When open, light would pour in like day. When closed, it would be dark inside like night.

2. Some possible responses include: "... he took his backbone for a moutain range and his ribs for ridges that ascend." mountain range (subject) and backbone (image), ridges (subject) and ribs (image); "Of feathers he made trees and shrubs and plants to clothe the land." plant life (subject) and feathers (image); "And the blood of Tangaroa...floated away to make the redness of the sky..." blood (subject) and sky (image).

3. Students' metaphors need not be original, but they should be able to explain why each creates a vivid impression. The subject and image should be distinctly different things, not definitions or synonyms. Sample responses might include: thunder = the roar of Tangaroa's voice; lightning = Tangaroa's flashing eyes; a hurricane wind = Tangaroa's excited breath; an earthquake = Tangaroa's feet stamping in anger.

☑ FOLLOW-UP DISCUSSION

Use the questions that follow to continue your discussion of "Tangaroa, Maker of All Things." Possible answers are given in parentheses.

Recalling

1. What does Tangaroa's shell do for a long time in the lasting darkness? (It revolves in the void.)

2. What does Tangaroa do with his shell when he becomes angry? (He overturns it and raises it up to form a dome for the sky.)

3. What is it that no one can name? (the shells of all the things that are in this world)

Interpreting

4. Why does Tangaroa create the universe? (He was angry that there was nothing in the void to obey him.)

5. Why does Tangaroa keep his head sacred to himself? (The head is where the brain is located. Tangaroa wishes to remain master of the universe he has created. Therefore, he does not give up his intelligence to form part of his creations.)

6. Why is a woman the "shell" for both men and women? (Women conceive all children and protect them in the womb during the developmental stages before birth.)

Applying

7. How do you feel about the theme of creation resulting from the anger of the maker? (Answers will vary. Some students may find the concept unacceptable and prefer the theme of creation being an act of love. Others may suggest that it is acceptable as a mythical explanation for the violent forces that gave rise to volcanic islands and mountain ranges.)

8. How would you restate the message that "no one can name the shells of all the things that are in this world?" (Answers will vary. Guide students toward the understanding that this is a figurative way of praising the almost indescribable diversity found in nature.)

ENRICHMENT

Students may benefit from exploring *STV: World Geography*. This laserdisc is available from National Geographic Society, Educational Services, P.O. Box 98018, Washington, D.C. 20090-8018, (800) 368-2728.

INTRODUCING THE THEME

Begin the lesson by inviting students to make a Venn diagram comparing and contrasting the United States to a foreign country they know about. On the left side of the diagram, students should write all the ways that the United States is special. On the right side of the diagram, students should describe special characteristics of the foreign country. In the middle, students should show how the two places are similar. To help students begin, you may wish to share this sample Venn diagram that compares and contrasts the United States with the Caribbean island of Barbados:

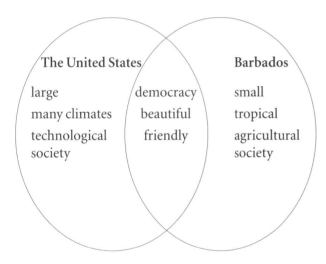

The United States — large, many climates, technological society

democracy, beautiful, friendly

Barbados — small, tropical, agricultural society

Then lead a discussion about how people feel about the places they call home. You may wish to use the following discussion prompts to help students connect the Venn diagram to the theme and to their own experiences.

Discussion Prompts

- What aspects of the United States do you like the best? (Possible responses: freedom, natural beauty, opportunities)

- What songs and symbols do you associate with the United States? (Possible responses: our national anthem, "America the Beautiful," the eagle, the flag, Uncle Sam)

- Why do you think people feel so strongly about their homelands? (Possible responses: nationalism, links to heritage, gratitude)

BRIDGING THE ESL/LEP GAP

Students from other cultures and language backgrounds can offer powerful insights into the strong feelings that people have about their homeland. Invite these students to share their feelings about moving to the United States. Pair proficient speakers with ESL students to brainstorm interview questions and then have the native speaker interview his or her ESL partner. Students may wish to discuss their sense of loyalty to their homeland as well as their feelings for their adoptive country, the United States. Invite partners to record their interviews, and place the tapes in a "Classroom History" corner.

COMPLETING THE ACTIVITY

Explain to students that one person's definition of *home* may be very different from another person's. As motivation, write poet Robert Frost's famous definition of home on the chalkboard: "Home is the place where, when you have to go there, they have to take you in." Before students write their poems or essays about home, have them create their own definition of the word. Encourage students to be as specific as possible so that their definition can be used as the basis for their writing.

When everyone is finished writing, invite volunteers to create illustrations of the home they described. Display the finished work in a prominent place so that students can compare their different interpretations of home.

Maui and the Great Fish

retold by Kiri Te Kanawa   (pages 204–207)

OBJECTIVES

Literary

- to describe the author's use of traditional storytelling techniques
- to analyze the author's use of repetition

Historical

- to understand the Maori legacy in New Zealand
- to discuss the geography of New Zealand

Cultural

- to explore Maori myths about the creation of the world
- to compare and contrast trickster figures from different cultures

SELECTION RESOURCES

Use Assessment Worksheet 29 to check students' vocabulary recognition, content comprehension, and appreciation of literary skills.

☑ Informal Assessment Opportunity

SELECTION OVERVIEW

"Maui and the Great Fish" describes how Maui catches a great fish — the South Island of New Zealand. Islands play a large role in the mythology of New Zealand because the country is comprised of four large islands and many smaller ones: North Island (44,035 square miles), South Island (58,304 square miles), Stewart Island (674 square miles), the Chatham Islands (372 square miles), the Cook Islands (93 square miles), Niue (100 square miles), and Tokelau Island (4 square miles). The Cook Islands and Niue became self-governing in 1974, although New Zealand is responsible for their defense and foreign affairs. New Zealand also administers the Ross Dependency, 160,000 square miles of Antarctic Territory.

New Zealand's first settlers were the Maoris, a Polynesian group from the eastern Pacific region. They arrived on the island's coast in the 1300s. Dutch navigator Abel Janszoon Tasman was the first European to discover New Zealand, but the Maoris would not let him land. From 1769 to 1770, British Captain James Cook explored the coasts. In 1840, British sovereignty was declared, and organized British settlement began soon after. The colony became a dominion in 1907; today, it is an independent member of the British commonwealth. Of the more than three million residents of present-day New Zealand, about 325,000 are Maori.

In this selection, Maui tricks his brothers into taking him fishing with them and catches what turns out to be the South Island of New Zealand.

ENGAGING THE STUDENTS

On the board write: *What can you catch when you go fishing?* Invite students to work individually or in pairs to brainstorm actual and fanciful things they might catch, such as fish, boots, nets, and magical genies. Write students' responses on the board. Explain that in this story, they are going to read about a Maori god named Maui who catches something quite extraordinary when he goes out fishing.

BRIDGING THE ESL/LEP LANGUAGE GAP

The author of this selection uses familiar words to tell a vivid creation story. This selection provides the opportunity for students to study the author's use of language and to expand the way they use language themselves.

Students may have been confused by the magical events in the story.

The following list identifies some events that may need additional support for an LEP student.

- The mysterious laughter they hear as they set sail
- Finding Maui hidden under the floorboards of the boat
- Maui using his magical powers to make the land seem very far away
- Maui finding a magical place to fish
- Maui hooking the land
- Maui going to make peace with the gods

Then have students list the vivid words and phrases that stood out for them. Write these on the board or on chart paper.

✔ PRETEACHING SELECTION VOCABULARY

Do a webbing exercise with students using words in the selection that relate to the ocean and fishing. Ask students to write the word *fishing* in the middle of their papers. Then have the class skim the selection and write down at least five words that show life on the sea. Examples include *fishing, seagull,* **screeching,** *paddled, anchor, nets,* **bait.**

Use the following prompts to help students analyze their webs:

- Which of your words are verbs? Which are nouns? What parts of speech are the other words?
- Which of your words do you find the most descriptive? Why?

The words printed in boldfaced type are tested on the selection assessment worksheet.

PREREADING

Reading the Story in a Cultural Context

Help students read for purpose by asking them to think about why the author recorded this myth from her childhood home in New Zealand. Discuss with students how creation myths help writers s hare their rich cultural heritage with a wider audience. As students read, have them consider what purposes creation myths might serve within their native culture.

Focusing on the Selection

Ask students to write briefly on the following question: How do you think storytellers remember the plots and details in all the different myths they tell? Discuss students' responses. Then ask students to

consider how repeated words and phrases help make it easier to remember a story.

Direct students to watch for repetition and analyze its effects as they read the selection.

POSTREADING

The following activities parallel the features with the same titles in the Student Edition.

Responses to Critical Thinking Questions

Possible responses are:

1. It recalls the Maori tales she heard as a child; she fondly remembers the sailing and fishing trips she took with her father.
2. The big fish Maui catches turns out to be a beautiful land — the South Island of New Zealand.
3. Responses will vary. Accept all reasonable and humane ideas for using magical powers.

✔ Guidelines for Writing Your Response to "Maui and the Great Fish"

Have students share their journal entries with a partner. As an alternative writing assignment, have each student write a magical story about the creation of their town, state, or country. Encourage students who have lived in other countries to write about them.

✔ Guidelines for Going Back Into the Text: Author's Craft

Remind students that the author is retelling a story she heard as a child. Explain to students that many cultures have an oral tradition, in which stories are passed on verbally rather than in writing. Have students discuss why repetition is an important technique in the oral tradition.

Possible answers to questions in the Student Editon are:

1. The repetition emphasizes that he possesses magic powers.
2. The brothers hear a noise several times and are puzzled; Maui has scared them and fooled them into taking him on their fishing trip.
3. It emphasizes that Maui is a trickster.

✔ FOLLOW-UP DISCUSSION

Use the questions that follow to continue your discussion of "Maui and the Great Fish." Possible answers are given in parentheses.

Recalling

1. Where does Maui hide so his brothers can't find him on the boat? (He hides under the floor-boards.)

2. How and why does Maui make the land seem much further away than it really is? (Maui uses his magical powers to trick his brothers so that they cannot take him home.)

3. Why does Maui go to talk to Tonganui, the son of the Sea God? (He must make peace with the gods because they are very angry with him for snagging their home on his fishing line.)

Interpreting

4. Why doesn't Maui tell his brothers about all his magical spells and magical powers? (Maui wants to keep his powers a secret from his brothers so that he can trick them.)

5. Why does Maui scare his brothers on the boat? (He wants to get back at them for trying to leave him behind; he is a trickster who enjoys playing pranks on people.)

6. What character traits do the brothers show throughout the story? (They are fearful, as shown by their reaction to Maui's tricks. They are easily tempted, as shown by their belief in Maui's promise of more fish. They are greedy, as shown by the way they try to carve up the island for themselves.)

Applying

7. How do creation myths unite people from the same culture? (These stories give people a common cultural heritage and pride in their past. They teach the values and ideals of a culture.)

8. What other aspects of the world might creation myths explain? (Natural phenomena; the origin of humans; the development of customs, institutions, and religious rites of a people; events beyond a person's control.)

ENRICHMENT

Students may benefit from viewing *Polynesians: Nomads of the Wind*. This video examines the courageous seafarers who first discovered and settled the islands of the South Seas. The video examines their culture and studies the impact of their settlement on the environment of the volcanic islands that they inhabit. The video is available from Media Basics Video, Lighthouse Square, Guilford, CT 06437, (800) 542-2505.

Family Council

by Oodgeroo (pages 208–211)

OBJECTIVES

Literary

- to recognize the elements of a personal narrative, including point of view
- to identify a writer's use of suspense to create conflict

Historical

- to trace the development of the oral tradition in Australian Aboriginal literature
- to probe the long-standing tension between Australians and Aborigines

Cultural

- to discuss traditional Koori attitudes toward family relationships and nature
- to see how literature helps preserve and honor Koori tradition

SELECTION RESOURCES

Use Assessment Worksheet 30 to check students' vocabulary recognition, content comprehension, and appreciation of literary skills.

 Informal Assessment Opportunity

SELECTION OVERVIEW

Dreamtime and *Dreaming* are direct translations from Aboriginal words, but the concept is not the same as *dreaming* in the Western sense. To the Aborigines of Australia, *Dreamtime* refers to their creation story: a long time ago, the world was a shapeless mass. Warramurrungunundji arose from the sea in female form and created the land, people, and language. Later, the giant ancestral crocodile Ginga created the rock country. The sea eagle Marrawuti planted flowers in the floodplain. Then the great spirit ancestors put themselves in specific places in the landscape, where they remain to the present day. Ginga, for example, is a rock outcrop textured like a crocodile's back. These special places are called "Dreaming sites" and still contain the power and energy of the original "Dreamtime." Finally, the ancestors charged the people to guard the land and all the creatures living on it. The Aborigines call this guardianship "looking after the country." As a result, the Dreamtime serves as a dynamic force that keeps people in harmony with their environment. These beliefs have been a part of Aboriginal culture for about 2,000 generations.

Since the Aborigines consider themselves a part of the land, they cannot understand why anyone would want to change or harm it and kill the life-force. As one of them said, "White man got no Dreaming. Him go 'nother way. . . Him got road belong himself." So strong is the Aboriginal connection to the land that

through oral history, some groups apparently still know the location of sacred sites once exposed during an ice age but now buried under the sea.

In this selection, a father presides over a family squabble. He ponders over his children's testimony and then makes a decision.

ENGAGING THE STUDENTS

On the board, write the following question: How do you solve family conflicts in your home? Have students work on their own to brainstorm a list of ways that problems are resolved in their household. Invite volunteers to share some of the methods with the class. Write these on the board or on chart paper. Discuss with students which methods work best and why. You may wish to create an advantage/disadvantage chart like the following model to organize student responses:

Method	Advantage	Disadvantage
family council	fair	takes a long time
parent decides	fast, easy	may be unfair

BRIDGING THE ESL/LEP LANGUAGE GAP

The plot of "Family Council" is easy to understand, but the unfamiliar lifestyle described and the new words presented may be difficult for many students. Be sure to preteach the selection vocabulary as follows. To help students understand Oodgeroo's theme, have them make a Venn diagram comparing and contrasting their lifestyle to the Aboriginal lifestyle described in the story. In the left circle, students should list details that describe their lives; in the right circle, they can list details about the Aboriginal lifestyle. In the middle of the diagram, students can show how the two cultures are the same. Suggest these points of comparison: *ways to resolve differences, diet, method of getting food, attitude toward nature, relationship to siblings.*

After students have read the story and completed the first draft of their Venn diagram, have them work in mixed groups of both limited and English proficient students to discuss their findings. At this point, students may need to reread the story to find other details to include on their charts. They should see that the characters in the story have a very close relationship to nature, unlike many Americans today. Students may find strong similarities in the relationships between siblings and parents.

☑ PRETEACHING SELECTION VOCABULARY

Explain to students that the author teaches readers about Aboriginal life by using words related to conflicts and resolving them. Have students create a word web by listing all the terms linked to disagreements and their outcomes found in the story and arranging them around the word "conflict." Possibilities include **arbitration, unanimously, plaintiffs, grievance,** *darkly, untrue, barged in, complaints, defense,* and **overrule.**

As a class, create a word web on the board by compiling everyone's findings. Have students add any words they did not already include to their own webs.

The words printed in boldfaced type are tested on the selection assessment worksheet.

PREREADING

Reading the Story in a Cultural Context

Help students read for purpose by having them consider how the narrator's culture is like and unlike their own. Discuss the struggle to survive as well as the conflicts among siblings. Ask: Why are hunting and fishing so important to the family? Why do the narrator's brothers and sisters resent her? What role does their father play in resolving the conflict?

Focusing on the Selection

Tell students to make a list of at least three things they learned about Aborigine culture and family from this story. When they have finished writing, ask: What are the three most important values in this family? Why? Discuss the students' responses.

POSTREADING

The following activities parallel the features with the same titles in the Student Edition.

Responses to Critical Thinking Questions

Possible responses are:

1. Aborigines resolve conflicts by working together. Every member of the family is allowed to state his or her opinion; however, the final decision rests with the father. If the other family members don't agree unanimously, they have the right to appeal for another hearing.

2. The narrator has a close, personal, almost mystical relationship to nature; she sees all things in nature as part of herself. In addition, she respects her father's authority.

3. Answers will vary. Students should include specific points of comparison and contrast in their responses.

☑ Guidelines for Writing Your Response to "Family Council"

Have students share their journal entries with a partner. As an alternative writing activity, have students write about a specific conflict that they had with a sibling or other relative and explain how it was resolved.

Guidelines for Going Back Into the Text: Author's Craft

Discuss first-person point of view with students. Explain that when a writer uses the first-person point of view, the story is from the narrator's perspective. Lead a discussion about how this account might have been different if told by another member of the family.

Possible answers to the questions in the Student Edition are:

1. The narrator is the girl that her siblings complain about because they feel she does not pull her weight when it comes to bringing home food supplies from the hunt.

2. Only a participant in the family council could know the specific complaints brought against the

narrator and the father's ruling. For example, only a participant could know that the narrator is accused of spending too much time dreaming, gathering flowers and feathers, or drawing animals in the sand.

3. The writer selected this incident because it shows a key aspect of her culture: the Aborigines' deep bond with nature.

✔ FOLLOW-UP DISCUSSION

Use the questions that follow to continue your discussion of "Family Council." Possible answers are given in parentheses.

Recalling

1. Why do the narrator's brothers and sisters call the family council? (They call it to complain that the narrator is not pulling her weight when it comes to bringing home food supplies from the hunt.)

2. What complaint does the eldest brother make in the family council? (He says that the narrator goes barging into the swamps, scaring off the birds.)

3. What are the rules of the family council? (The father is the arbitration judge. If the children do not agree with his ruling, they must oppose it unanimously and appeal for another hearing.)

Interpreting

4. How does the author create suspense in the story? (First, the narrator withholds crucial information until the very end: that she is the best fisher. Second, by having the narrator agree with the charges brought against her, the author makes the outcome of the family council uncertain.)

5. How do you think this story might have differed if it had been told from the third-person point of view? (Possible responses: Readers would have less sympathy for the narrator; the story would have been less immediate and personal.)

6. Do you agree with the father's decision? Why or why not? (Possible response: Yes, because it is fair and will reduce family conflict. It also is in keeping with the values of the family and their culture.)

Applying

7. How do you think the narrator feels about her culture? (She is very comfortable with it, for she is very close to all aspects of nature, she acknowledges her limitations, while still making every attempt to pull her weight in the family.)

8. What lessons about family and nature does this story hold for Americans today? (Guide students to understand how values such as respect for family members and nature are applicable to everyone.)

ENRICHMENT

Students may enjoy viewing *Australia's Aborigines,* a video that explores the ancient myths of Dreamtime and the extraordinary wildlife that inspires the Aborigines' sacred rock painting. The video is available from Cambridge Social Studies, PO Box 2153, Dept SS7, Charleston, WV 25328-2153, (800) 468-4227.

Butterflies

by Patricia Grace (pages 212–214)

OBJECTIVES

Literary

- to analyze the author's attitude toward family life and values
- to describe the use of setting in the selection

Historical

- to understand Maori culture in New Zealand
- to describe how the Maori were assimilated into the dominant British culture in New Zealand

Cultural

- to understand the importance of Maori folk wisdom
- to compare and contrast Maori values with those of other cultural groups

SELECTION RESOURCES

Use Assessment Worksheet 31 to check students' vocabulary recognition, content comprehension, and appreciation of literary skills.

 Informal Assessment Opportunity

SELECTION OVERVIEW

Throughout history, many native peoples have had to assimilate into the culture of other people who invaded or emigrated to their land. The Maori, a Polynesian people, settled in New Zealand as early as the tenth century. In the early nineteenth century, British missionaries and whalers established settlements and trading posts in New Zealand. These settlements were bitterly opposed by the Maori. After a series of wars and conflicts, the Maori signed a treaty with the British Empire in 1840. Great Britain proclaimed sovereignty of the New Zealand islands and agreed to respect land ownership of the Maori. In return, the Maori placed themselves under the protection of the British. The assimilation of the Maori culture into British ways is reflected in the selection. No matter how the British imposed their language, religion, customs, and values, the native Maori were able to hold on to many of their traditions and ways of life. Their strong belief in family values is probably best expressed in *aroha,* the concept of family love and respect.

Aroha is demonstrated in this selection as wise grandparents lovingly guide their granddaughter to an understanding of cultural differences.

ENGAGING THE STUDENTS

Ask students: What does family mean to you? Guide them to make a list of responses to share with their classmates. Next, pose this question: What if the con-

cept of family was declared illegal and ceased to exist? Have students share with each other how it would feel to live in this kind of world. Mention that "Butterflies" deals with the love and wisdom that grandparents offer their grandchildren.

BRIDGING THE ESL/LEP LANGUAGE GAP

ESL/LEP students may not understand the subtlety of the last line of this story. Lead a discussion with such questions as: What are butterflies born as? What do caterpillars eat? Why might a farmer dislike caterpillars? Why might a city dweller think of a butterfly as a beautiful insect instead of a pest?

When they understand the story, ask students to retell the story in their own words.

✔ PRETEACHING SELECTION VOCABULARY

Students may have difficulty identifying words related to urban and rural settings. On the chalkboard make a two-column grid labeled "Urban" and "Rural." As they read the story, guide them to find words that apply to each heading and write them in their notebooks. After students have read the stories, direct them to fill in the two columns with words

117

they have found such as *footpath*, *crossing*, and *hoeing*. Challenge students to discuss the contrasting feelings and images evoked by the words in the two columns.

The words presented in boldfaced type are tested on the assessment worksheet.

PREREADING

Reading the Story in a Cultural Context

Help students focus on the theme of assimilation by asking them these questions: What if a native people refused to assimilate into the dominant culture? What would be some of the consequences? Conduct a discussion of the pros and cons of assimilation, making sure that students incorporate examples of Maori adaptation as shown in the selections.

Focusing on the Selection

After students have completed reading the selection, have them work in pairs to draw a scene from the story, using these questions as guidelines.

• What does the setting look like?

• What colors will you use to express the various moods of the scenes?

Then have students work in small groups and arrange their drawings in a time order sequence to present a total picture of the story. Students can display their drawings and discuss how color and physical detail help to create the mood.

POSTREADING

The following activities parallel the features with the same titles in the Student Edition.

Responses to Critical Thinking Questions

Possible responses are:

1. Answers will differ. Students should mention the use of dialogue and dialect, as well as details like school lunches and schoolbags.

2. The story shows how grandparents seek to protect children while teaching them about the world.

3. Answers will differ. Student responses should show understanding, empathy, and insight into the characters' experience. Responses should note comparisons and contrasts resulting from personal experiences and cultural differences.

☑ Guidelines for Writing Your Response to "Butterflies"

Have students share their journal entries with a partner. As an alternative writing activity, challenge them to imagine they are writers for a New Zealand travel magazine and ask them to write a description of a New Zealand setting. Have volunteers read their responses aloud.

Guidelines for Going Back Into the Text: Author's Craft

Ask students to reread passages of the selection and focus on the feelings evoked by the settings. For example, a feeling of nostalgia for old-fashioned earthy values comes through in the garden setting.

Possible answers to the questions in the Student Edition are:

1. The setting is somewhat limited. The reader gets the sense that the grandparents never venture much past the crossing where their granddaughter gets the school bus. The description of the garden is somewhat idyllic.

2. The setting establishes that the Maori family lives within the white community. Without the cultural differences and misunderstandings, there would be no conflict and no wise response to the granddaughter.

☑ FOLLOW-UP DISCUSSION

Use the questions that follow to continue your discussion of "Butterflies." Possible answers are given in parentheses.

Recalling

1. What advice do both the grandmother and grandfather give the granddaughter as she leaves for school? ("Listen to the teacher. Do what she say.")

2. Who takes the granddaughter to the street crossing? (the grandfather)

3. What is the grandfather doing when the granddaughter returns from school? (hoeing around the cabbages)

Interpreting

4. Why do you think the grandparents assumed that the teacher liked the granddaughter's story? (because they were always impressed by her writing)

5. Why do you think the granddaughter's teacher is confused by her story? (While city dwellers might not perceive butterflies as destructive, farmers would.)

6. What does the last line of the story suggest about the grandfather? (that he understands the cultural differences between the teacher and his family)

Applying

7. How does folk wisdom of all cultures help people to deal with life? (Answers will vary, but encourage students to draw from their own personal experiences and those of family and friends.)

8. How do families in the United States demonstrate their love and respect for one another? (Answers will vary. Encourage students to think of times when their family members supported one another during a difficult or disappointing experience.)

ENRICHMENT

Students may enjoy viewing the video *Children of New Zealand: Living in the High Country,* available from Encyclopaedia Britannica Educational Corporation, 310 South Michigan Avenue, Chicago, IL 60604, (800) 554-9862.

RESPONSES TO REVIEWING THE REGION

1. Sample answer: The creation myths "Tangaroa, Maker of All Things" and "Maui and the Great Fish" show a specific cultural view of the creation of the world. The first myth illustrates how people isolated by great distances view the origin of their culture. Living on an island as they do, they see their god initially within a shell. They also give much attention to the creation of fish and other sea creatures. The second myth describes how Maui catches a great fish—the South Island of New Zealand. Once, again, the story of an island culture focuses on the sea.

2. Sample answer: "Family Council" shows how Aborigines resolve conflicts by working together. Every member of the family is allowed to state his or her opinion; although the final decision rests with the father. This process allowed the narrator to acknowledge her weaknesses without being punished for them and to be proud of her other talents.

3. Sample answer: In "Maui and the Great Fish," Maui scares his brothers on the boat to retaliate for being excluded. Students might cite similiar situations with their siblings.

☑ FOCUSING ON GENRE SKILLS

Creation myths explain the origin of the world within a specific culture. They unite people by giving them a cultural heritage and teaching cultural values. "Maui and the Great Fish" helped Kiri Te Kanawa remember the sailing and fishing heritage of her people. Select another creation myth, such as "Tangaroa, Maker of All Things," and have students describe how it unites people from the same culture by explaining natural phenomena, the origin of humans, particular customs, or the ideals of the writer's culture.

BIBLIOGRAPHY

ALPERS, ANTONY. "Tangaroa, Maker of All Things." In *The World of the Polynesians.* Carry, NC: Oxford University Press, 1987.

GRACE, PATRICIA. "Butterflies." In *Electric City and Other Stories.* Auckland, New Zealand: Penguin Books New Zealand Limited, 1987.

NUNUKUL, OODGEROO. "Family Council." In *Dreamtime: Aboriginal Stories.* New York: Lothrop, Lee & Shepard Books, a division of William Morrow & Co., Inc., 1972.

TE KANAWA, KIRI. "Maui and the Great Fish." In *Land of the Long White Cloud.* New York: Arcade Publishing, Inc., 1989.

Unit 2

Asia, Australia, and the Pacific Islands

Focusing the Unit   (page 215)

COOPERATIVE/ COLLABORATIVE LEARNING

Individual Objective: to create a cultural scrapbook focusing on the countries of Asia, Australia, and the Pacific Islands and to narrate a brief tour of each country. Group Objective: to develop a presentation inspired by information expressed in the scrapbooks.

Setting Up the Activity

Have students work in heterogeneous groups of four. Stipulate that each group member is responsible for researching several different countries in the cultural scrapbook and for making a contribution to the group presentation. The suggested presentation format is as follows: Student 1 introduces the scrapbook or video; Students 2, 3, and 4 describe specific nations and their people and places.

After each group's presentation, use the questions below to discuss and evaluate their reports.

- How are the countries in the scrapbooks different? How are they similar?

- In your group's opinion, how do the pictures you have selected reflect the problems and values of the nations they show?

Assisting ESL and LEP Students

To allow students with limited English proficiency more opportunity to join in a closing discussion of the unit, have them choose two selections, one a poem and one a short story, on which to focus. Then ask them to think about the answers to these questions:

1. What problem does each selection discuss?

2. How does the writer, or how do the characters, deal with the problem?

3. What social or moral values does each selection reflect?

Assessment

Before you begin the group activity, remind students that they will be graded on both an individual and a group basis. Without individual contribution, the group presentation will not be complete. Monitor group progress to check that all four students are contributing.

Time Out to Reflect

As students do the end-of-unit activities in the Student Edition, give them time to make a personal response to the content of the unit as a whole. Invite them to respond to the following questions in their notebooks or journals. Encourage students to draw on these personal responses as they complete the activities.

1. What have I learned about cultural similarities and differences between and among the nations of Asia, Australia, and the Pacific Islands?

2. What problems do the people in these areas have? Are the problems specific to their areas or are they shared by others?

3. What social values do the people of Asia, Australia, and the Pacific Islands hold important?

4. How do the social values reflect the cultures of Asia, Australia, and the Pacific Islands?

WRITING PROCESS EXPOSITORY ESSAY

Refer students to the model of an expository essay found on pages 423-424 in the Handbook section of the Student Edition. You may wish to discuss and analyze the model essay if you are working with less experienced writers.

Guidelines for Evaluation

On a scale of 1–5, the writer has

- clearly followed all stages of the writing process.

- made clear and specific references to the chosen selections.

- included details of how one selection taught something important.

- provided sufficient supporting details from the selections to prove his or her main points.

- clearly organized the paper so that the conclusion is easy to follow.

- written an opening or closing paragraph that clearly summarizes the main points of the paper.
- made minor errors in grammar, mechanics, and usage.

Assisting ESL and LEP Students

You may wish to provide a more limited assignment for these students so that they can complete their first drafts somewhat quickly. Then have them work at length with proficient writers in a peer-revision group to polish their drafts.

PROBLEM SOLVING

Encourage students to use the following problem-solving strategies to analyze one of the tales, poems, or short stories in Unit 2. Afterward, encourage students to reflect on their use of the strategies and consider how the strategies helped in their analysis.

Strategies (optional)

1. Use a semantic map or brainstorming list to identify value systems that writers focus on in the unit. Have individual students, partners, or groups of students choose the values they most want to investigate further and the selection or selections that best shed light on the topic.

2. Use a second graphic organizer, such as a problem/solution chart, to explore in detail the values and their effects on problems of the writers' time, place, and culture. Include information both from the selections and from personal experience.

3. Use the information from the graphic organizers to create a newspaper editorial, advice column, speech, or debate on the problem of leading a moral life. Set up a plan that shares responsibility for doing the research.

Allow time for students to work on their presentations.

Guidelines for Evaluation

On a scale of 1–5, the student has

- provided adequate examples, facts, reasons, anecdotes, or personal reflections to support his or her presentation.
- demonstrated appropriate effort.
- clearly organized the presentation so that problems and solutions are logical and consistent.
- demonstrated an understanding of value systems in Asia, Australia, and the Pacific Islands and their use in dealing with problems of the area, the time, and the culture.

UNIT 3 Eastern and Western Europe

Your tour around the world continues! In Unit 3, you will explore the fascinating literature and culture of Eastern and Western Europe from which so much of modern western culture springs. The experiences of these people provide strong links between homeland and heritage.

UNIT OBJECTIVES

Literary

- to explain how narratives such as short stories, essays, and autobiographies can convey a culture's beliefs and values
- to show how writers use poetry to express their values

Historical

- to compare and contrast the cultural traditions of Eastern and Western Europe
- to understand how historical experiences are reflected in literature

Cultural

- to compare and contrast traditional and contemporary cultural values in this region
- to understand how Europe's cultural history is reflected in the literature produced in the area today

UNIT RESOURCES

The following resources appear in the Student Edition of *World Tapestries*:

- a **portfolio of culture-related art**, The Art of Tapestries, pages A11–A13, to build background, activate prior knowledge, and generate writing ideas about the unit cultures.

- a **unit overview**, pages 216–219, to provide historical background about Eastern and Western Europe, including an excerpt from Marco Polo's diary that describes his travels to the Far East.

- a **time line**, pages 218–219, to help students place the literary works in their historical context. You may wish to have students refer to the time line before they discuss each work.

- the **Focusing the Unit** activities at the end of the unit, page 303, to provide a cooperative/collaborative learning project on the theme of "Eastern and Western Europe," a writing project,

and a problem-solving activity in which students analyze one or more of the situations described in Unit 3.

INTRODUCING UNIT 3

Providing Motivation

Before students begin to read the unit overview in the Student Edition, you may wish to spark their interest in the literature and culture of Eastern and Western Europe by using some or all of the following activities:

- Explain to students that Europe has had a tumultuous history, marked by fierce social, economic, and political revolutions. Among the most dramatic upheavals were the Industrial Revolution, the French Revolution, and the Communist Revolution. Then write this question on the board: In what ways might the violent revolutions in Europe affect the literature of the region?

Arrange students in small groups to speculate about the relationship between the literature and events of the time. After students have finished working, invite them to share their lists with the class. Students can verify their speculations as they read the Unit Opener and the literature in Unit 3.

- Tell students that the events that shaped Europe have had a major impact on much of the rest of the world, including the U.S. Ask pairs of students to examine the time line on pages 218–219 of the unit opener. Have each pair select at least one event they believe helped shape U.S. history or culture. For example, the quest for liberty and equality that spurred the French to overthrow their ruling nobility helped inspire the American colonies to fight for independence from the rule of British monarchy. Students should research their event's connection to the U.S. and share the findings in a brief oral report.

- Read the following quotation to students.

> Literature is the transmission of power. Text books and treatises, dictionaries and encyclopedias, manuals and books of instruction — they are communications; but literature is a power line, and the motor, mark you, is the reader.
>
> *Charles Curtis*

Ask: What does the speaker mean when he says that readers are the "motor" in literature? Explore with the class how readers are powered or driven by literature. Ask: What special information do you bring to a story, poem, or other form of literature that give spark or energy to the writer's words and ideas? List some students suggestions on the board. Discuss how all readers bring their own culture and set of values to the text. Talk about how this interaction between cultures (the reader's and the writer's) accomplishes many things. For example, it builds understanding and spreads ideas throughout the world.

Cross-Discipline Teaching Opportunity: Unit Culture

Since the accomplishments of the various European people span an astonishing length of time, students are apt to have difficulty categorizing each culture. As a result, you may wish to work with a social studies teacher to help students grasp the range of political, social, economic, and cultural events covered in Unit 3.

Ask the social studies teacher to help students examine the impact of each European historical or cultural movement on the following one. Trace the cultures and political landmarks detailed in the Unit Opener: the ancient Greeks, ancient Romans, Renaissance, Industrial Revolution, French Revolution, Bolshevik Revolution, World War II, Cold War, and breakup of the former Soviet Union.

Setting Personal Goals for Reading the Selections in Unit 3

Have students keep a copy of the following chart in their journals or notebooks. Provide class time every few days for students to review and expand their charts. Encourage them to add topics of their own.

Eastern and Western Europe			
Topic	What I Know	What I Want to Learn	What I Have Found Out
influence of Greek and Roman civilizations			
cultural achievements of the Renaissance			
results of 18th century political revolutions			
impact of communism			

6 Eastern Europe

CHAPTER PREVIEW

Literature of Eastern Europe			
Selections	**Genre**	**Author's Craft/Literary Skills**	**Cultural Values & Focus**
"The Servant," S.T. Semyonov, pages 221–228	short story	historical context	importance of personal sacrifice and selflessness
"If Not Still Higher," Isaac Loeb Peretz, pages 229–233	short story	writing style	value of compassion
"And When Summer Comes to an End ...," "Please Give this Seat to an Elderly or Disabled Person," Nina Cassian, pages 234–236	poetry	free verse	effects of being physically challenged
"Random Talk," Raisa Blokh; "The Heirs of Stalin," Yevgeny Yevtushenko; "Refugees," Ilya Krichevsky, pages 237–243	poetry	author's purpose	effects of the Russian Revolution
Making Cultural Connections: Europe, pages 244–245			
"The Bicycle," Jerzy Harasymowicz, pages 246–248	poetry	fantasy and realism	respect for the value of nature
"The Monster," Nina Katerli, pages 249–257	short story	metaphor	Russian life after the fall of communism
"A Winter's Tale," Slavenka Drakulić pages 258–262	essay	comparison	results of the ongoing war in Croatia

ASSESSMENT

Assessment opportunities are indicated by a ✔ next to the activity title. For guidelines, see Teacher's Resource Manual, page xxxvi.

CROSS-DISCIPLINE TEACHING OPPORTUNITIES

Physical Education   Explain to students that success in athletic contests was a passport to fame for the ancient Greeks. Competition was usually between individuals rather than teams, and a champion could become a hero throughout the Greek world. Success in the Olympic Games, held every four years between 776 B.C. and A.D. 393 at Olympia in the western Peloponnesus, was especially prestigious. Invite students to work in small groups to identify today's top athletes in Eastern Europe, especially Russia, Poland, Romania, and Croatia. In keeping with the cultural values expressed in "The Servant" and "If Not Still Higher," students can organize a mini-Olympics in their community to raise money for a charitable organization. Students can include some of the main events of the ancient Greek Olympics: running, wrestling, the long jump, and the discus throw. Have students work with a physical education teacher to design events that are safe as well as challenging.

Art   Work with an art teacher to give students the opportunity to examine the art of Eastern Europe. Remind students that this region of the world has an especially rich and varied artistic output. Students can consult Bruce Cole and Adelheid Gealt's *The Art of the Western World* (Simon and Schuster, 1989) and the Public Broadcasting System television show of the same name.

Science   On October 4, 1957, the 40th anniversary of the Communists' seizure of the government in the Russian Revolution, the Russians launched the first space vehicle to orbit the earth. The spacecraft was *Sputnik I*. It weighed only 185 pounds and traveled at 17,500 miles per hour — the fastest speed ever achieved by a human-made object. Have students work with a science teacher to understand the basics of air flight.

SUPPLEMENTING THE CORE CURRICULUM

- The Student Edition provides humanities material related to specific cultures in Making Cultural Connections: Europe on pages 244 and 245 and in The Art of Tapestries on pages A11–A13. You may wish to invite students to pursue the following activities outside of class:

- The world's most traveled man is the Russian cosmonaut Valery Ryumin. In October 1980, he returned to Earth from his second long-duration stay aboard the space station *Salyut 6*. He had been in space 362 days — almost a full year. During his space trip, Ryumin circled the world 5,750 times and covered 150 million miles, which is further than traveling to Mars and back. Have students work in small groups to make a poster comparing the progress of Russians and Americans in space. Based on their findings, students should draw conclusions about the importance that Russians place on space exploration. Ask students to decide what cultural values the Russian space race reveals.

- In the 20th century, as in the previous history of Eastern Europe, freedom from censorship or opression has been the exception rather than the rule. Increasingly, fewer countries in this region however, will openly admit that they are committed to a policy of religious, intellectual, artistic, or political censorship. Students can find out more about censorship in Eastern Europe in the second half of the 20th century. They can begin by reading the U.N. Charter (1945), the U.N. Declaration of Human Rights (1948), the European Convention on Human Rights (1953), and the Helsinki Final Act (1975).

- A crucial event in the history of Eastern Europe was the breakup of the former Soviet Union on December 16, 1991. The Soviet flag bearing hammer and sickle which flew over the Kremlin was lowered and replaced by the flag of Russia, ending 74 years of Communist domination. Invite students to trace the causes and effects of the end of Communist rule in Russia. Students should use newspaper and magazine articles to help draw conclusions.

INTRODUCING CHAPTER 6: EASTERN EUROPE

Using the Chapter Opener

Write the following terms on the board: *peasant, czar,* and *Iron Curtain.* Have volunteers define the words. As students respond, point out that all these terms are key to the history and culture of Eastern Europe, especially Russia. Then read the following quotation to students:

> I cannot forecast to you the action of Russia. It is a riddle wrapped in a mystery inside an enigma; but perhaps there is a key. That key is Russian national interest.
>
> *Winston Churchill*

Explore with students the perspective on the Russian national character conveyed in Churchill's famous 1939 remark. Be sure that students understand what Churchill meant by the Russian "national interest."

Ask: "What events in the 1930s do you think prompted Churchill to reach this judgment about Russia?"

✔ Developing Concept Vocabulary

You can use a Venn diagram to help students understand the interrelationship of the Russian peasants and the Russian ruling class. Write the words *Russian peasants* and *Russian czars* on the chalkboard. Create the Venn diagram by drawing intersecting ovals around each word. Pairs of students can compare and contrast serfs and their rulers.

ASK:

• Who were the Russian peasants? What kind of life do you think they had?

• What words describe Russia's rulers in the 20th century?

• What might they have had in common?

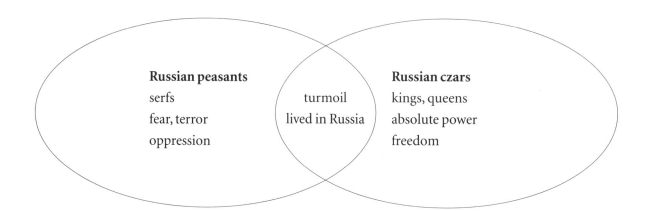

Russian peasants
serfs
fear, terror
oppression

turmoil
lived in Russia

Russian czars
kings, queens
absolute power
freedom

The Servant
by S.T. Semyonov (pages 221–228)

OBJECTIVES

Literary

- to explore the effect that historical context has on a story
- to analyze the characters' motivation

Historical

- to describe how the Russian Civil War and rise of communism affected the Russian peasants
- to discuss the desperation of the Russian working classes in the 1920s and 1930s

Cultural

- to evaluate the relationship between servants and masters in Russia during the 1920s and 1930s
- to explain how different characters do and do not show compassion

SELECTION RESOURCES

Use Assessment Worksheet 32 to check students' vocabulary recognition, content comprehension, and appreciation of literary skills.

✔ Informal Assessment Opportunity

SELECTION OVERVIEW

Russian writers reacted in different ways to the overthrow of the Czar and the subsequent rise of communism. To some writers, traditional literary forms seemed unable to express the disruption of public and private life and the collapse of institutions. These writers tried various literary experiments. Writer Dimitri Furmanov, for example, listed historical events, which he arranged according to military discipline. On the other end of the spectrum, novelist and short story writer Isaac Babel created perfectly formed stories, rich in irony. Other writers, such as S. T. Semyonov, experimented with various kinds of realism.

With the first five year plan of 1929, however, officials put an end to competing literary schools of thought. All literary activity was controlled by one administrative group, the Russian Association of Proletarian Writers (RAPP). RAPP ordered all writing to conform to the policies of the Communist party. Writers were heavily pressured to toe the line. This resulted in lockstep, formula writing, such as the melodramas set in factories and idealized villages, where people and ideas were portrayed as either black or white. In 1932, RAPP dissolved and was replaced by the Union of Soviet Writers. At first, this group seemed to promise a liberal atmosphere, but the system of control was simply more subtle.

In this selection, an out of work servant finds happiness, not in finding a job, but in allowing another servant to keep his job.

ENGAGING THE STUDENTS

Tell students to imagine the following scenario: Having graduated from high school, they are expected to be independent. Explain that they must get a job to support themselves. Unfortunately, very few jobs are available, particularly for those lacking special skills or job training. Ask students how they would go about looking for a job. To help them respond, ask them the following questions:

- Do you have any friends you could ask for work? If so, why should they help you?
- For which jobs in newspaper want ads could you qualify?
- Would you take a job from someone who needed it just as much or more than you do? Why or why not?

Explain that in "The Servant," the peasant Gerasim is desperate to find a job. However, many other people are out of work and there are very few jobs. Explain that Gerasim gets a job by having his friend arrange for an elderly servant to be fired. Invite students to predict how Gerasim might react to taking a job from someone else.

BRIDGING THE ESL/LEP LANGUAGE GAP

The Russian names in the story might be challenging for many students. To help students pronounce the words and link them to the correct characters, read the first two pages of the selection aloud as students follow along in their books.

Before you read, present students with the following questions. Encourage them to find the answers as you read aloud.

1. What is the main character's name? (*Gerasim*)

2. Who is Yegor Danilych? (*Gerasim's friend*)

Then list these other two names on the board: *Sharov, Polikarpych*. Pronounce the names for students and have them repeat each one until they are comfortable saying it. Next, ask students to choose a partner and have them create a dialogue using all four names: Gerasim, Yegor Danilych, Sharov, and Polikarpych. Guide students to use the names often in their dialogue.

☑ PRETEACHING SELECTION VOCABULARY

Have students create a word bank for this story by writing down all the terms from "The Servant" that can relate to poverty: ***downcast, charwoman, almshouse, disheartened**, peasant, want, servant, in vain*. While students are writing, use the following categories to make the columns of a chart on the board: "people," "feelings," and, "places." Call on students to fill each column with the words they have found in the story. You can use the following questions to spark discussion:

• Which words describe how poor people might feel?

• Are there any words here that you would like to be called? Why or why not?

• Which words identify locations?

The words printed in boldfaced type are tested on the selection assessment worksheet.

PREREADING

Reading the Story in a Cultural Context

Help students to read for purpose by asking them to discover why Gerasim is so desperate to find a job. Ask students how they think Russia in the 1920s and 1930s compares to the United States today. How are they similar and different? Be sure that students understand that there was no "safety net" of social services in Russia sixty years ago. There were no unemployment insurance payments, soup kitchens, or welfare benefits. Without a job, Gerasim would starve.

Focusing on the Selection

Before they read the story, invite students to write a brief paragraph describing what they think the relationship was like between servants and their employers in Russia in the 1920s and 1930s. As students read, have them compare their predictions to the reality described in the story.

POSTREADING

The following activities parallel the features with the same titles in the Student Edition.

Responses to Critical Thinking Questions

Possible responses are:

1. Semyonov reveals his disdain for the coachman, Yegor Danilych, by showing how he betrays the other servants for his personal gain. He also shows how Yegor Danilych encourages and then believes Gerasim's flattery. Finally, the author portrays Yegor Danilych negatively by showing the coachman's unfair arguments against keeping the Polikarpychs.

2. The economic situation is very fragile. There is almost no work to be had, and the elderly are completely dependent on the good will of their employers for their survival.

3. Responses will vary but should reflect students' own understanding of sacrifice. Students might cite personal, as well as public, examples of sacrifice.

☑ Guidelines for Writing Your Response to "The Servant"

Invite students to trade journal responses with a partner and discuss both the story and their entries. As an alternate writing activity, have students write four words that express their initial response to the story. Students can use those words as a jumping-off point for describing a time when they wanted something very badly.

Guidelines for Going Back Into the Text: Author's Craft

Possible answers to the Student Edition questions are:

1. During this time, young men had to serve military duty. Furthermore, the economic climate was bad for the peasant class; they could not afford to leave one job and hope to find another. Also, the elderly were not cared for by the government.

2. Responses will vary. Some students may include ideas like the following: he wanted to impress his friend with his importance; he wanted to help his friend find a job; he wanted to further ingratiate himself with his master.

3. Answers will reflect students' own reading. Young adult authors who have written historical fiction include Laurence Yep, Katherine Paterson, Yoshiko Uchida, Avi, Walter Dean Myers, and Maya Angelou, among others.

✔ FOLLOW-UP DISCUSSION

Use the questions that follow to continue your discussion of "The Servant." Possible answers are given in parentheses.

Recalling

1. Why did Gerasim lose his last job, working for a merchant? (He was called back to his village from Moscow to serve in the military. While he was gone, his boss hired someone else to fill his position.)

2. Why does Yegor Danilych say Polikarpych should be fired? (Yegor Danilych says that Polikarpych never shovels the snow on time, deserts his post while serving as night watchman because of the cold, and is too old to be a good worker. As a result, Sharov is wasting money on his servant, especially since Polikarpych will cause trouble for his master with the police.)

3. How does Mrs. Polikarpych want to take revenge on Yegor Danilych? (She wants to tell Sharov that Yegor Danilych steals hay and fodder. She wants to ruin Yegor Danilych as he has ruined them.)

Interpreting

4. Why do you think Semyonov set the story around Christmas time? (Christmas is a season of celebrating and giving.)

5. Gerasim lost his last job because he was called for military service. What does this detail add to your feelings about Gerasim and his plight? (It creates sympathy for Gerasim. He lost his job through no fault of his own. Furthermore, he was trying to serve his country, but now his country cannot even provide him with a job.)

6. What do you think the reader is supposed to learn from this story? (Possible responses: Life was very difficult in Russia in the 1920s and 1930s; compassion is an important value, especially during difficult times. Even when people feel that they are suffering, there are always others whose plight is worse.)

Applying

7. Gerasim's compassion for the old couple compels him to turn down the job. Why is compassion important? (Possible responses: Compassion creates a better world, brings happiness to everyone, and sets people apart from animals.)

8. If you had been Gerasim, would you have turned down the job? Why or why not? (Students who agree with Gerasim's actions might cite the old people's age and need; students who disagree might site Gerasim's own need for employment.)

ENRICHMENT

Students will benefit from viewing *Ten Days That Shook the World.* This comprehensive study of the Russian Revolution includes the decay of the Tsarist era, the devastation caused by World War I, and the fiery drama of 1917. This video is available from Media Basics Video, Lighthouse Square, Guilford, CT 06437, (800) 542-2505.

If Not Still Higher
by Isaac Loeb Peretz   (pages 229–233)

OBJECTIVES

Literary

- to analyze the author's style, including diction, sentence structure, and tense
- to analyze how contrasts between characters help to develop their personality

Historical

- to discuss the Hasidic underpinnings of this story
- to understand what life was like in a Jewish shtetl in Poland

Cultural

- to develop an awareness of Hasidic cultural values through reading the story
- to compare traditional Jewish folktales to present-day concepts of compassion

SELECTION RESOURCES

Use Assessment Worksheet 33 to check students' vocabulary recognition, content comprehension, and appreciation of literary skills.

 Informal Assessment Opportunity

SELECTION OVERVIEW

Isaac Loeb Peretz was a member of the Hasidic (or Chasidic) sect of Judaism. The Hasidim (the name means "the pious ones") are a mystical sect established in the 1750s by Baal Shem Tov. A strong and vibrant leader, Shem Tov stressed trust in God and believed that religious worship should be filled with joy. Jewish people soon flocked to his congregation. The established rabbinical leaders of the day strongly objected to the Hasidic breaking away from orthodox Judaism. Despite excommunication orders against the Hasidim, the group continued to grow.

Hasidic teachings are largely based on medieval Jewish mysticism. The Hasidim believe that God is everywhere—even in evil. As a result, observers must work to turn evil into good. The leader of the group, called *zaddik* ("righteous one") is respected as a mediator between the Hasidim and God. That person is also revered as a counselor and wise person. Some *zaddikim* were even rumored to have performed miracles. The Hasidim stress emotional piety and enthusiastic worship over strict disciplined study. They believe that the divine can be understood through prayer, study, contemplation, and good deeds. Hasidic teachings remain influential today in Jewish life and philosophy.

In this selection, a rabbi shows a man the true meaning of piety.

ENGAGING THE STUDENTS

Begin by asking this question: How can you tell if a religious leader is truly holy? As students respond, encourage them to give specific examples of the individual's actions to support their opinions.

When the discussion is finished, arrange students in pairs to brainstorm a list of real people they consider holy. Possibilities might include the Pope, Mother Teresa, and students' own religious leaders. Allow partners five minutes to write their responses, then call on volunteers to read their answers to the class. Write the names of the religious individuals on the board. Then discuss what qualities all of these individuals have in common.

BRIDGING THE ESL/LEP LANGUAGE GAP

To help students become accustomed to the unfamiliar terms, first discuss the setting and how the author conveys its flavor through his choice of words. Students with a Hebrew or Polish background may be able to explain some of the cultural flavor of this story

Write the following categories and words on the board. You may also wish to explore with students how these words help the time and place described in the story come alive.

People	Definitions
rabbi	(a Jewish spiritual leader; a teacher)
Lithuanian	(someone from the country of Lithuania)
Vassil	(the name the rabbi gives the widow)

Places	Definitions
Nemirov	(a Polish town)
synagogue	(a Jewish house of worship)

Things	Definitions
Gemara	(a part of the Talmud, a book of Jewish law)
groschen	(a Polish coin)

☑ PRETEACHING SELECTION VOCABULARY

The rabbi and the Lithuanian described in the story are two very different individuals. Ask students to make a two-column list of words and phrases to describe the differences. For example:

The Rabbi of Nemirov	The Lithuanian
pious	*mocking*
mysterious	*down-to-earth*
sorrowful	*contented*
introspective	*dogged*
religious	*not religious*
saintly	*everyday*
broods	*acts*
soft-hearted	*heart of cast iron*

Before students read the story, post the list in a prominent place so that they can clearly differentiate the characters. After they have completed their reading, invite students to add words and phrases that complete the characterization of the two men.

The words printed in boldfaced type are tested on the selection assessment worksheet.

PREREADING

Reading the Story in a Cultural Context

Help students read for purpose by asking them to determine the author's attitude toward the rabbi. Ask them to consider how the Lithuanian might represent the author. You may wish to guide students by using these prompts:

- How does the Lithuanian's attitude toward the rabbi change as the story progresses?
- What relationship do you see between the title and the author's attitude toward the rabbi?

Focusing on the Selection

Have students work in pairs. Assign one student in each pair to answer the three questions on page 229 of the Student Edition and to share the answers with his or her partner. Then have the second student in each pair summarize the message the author is trying to convey. Afterward, have partners collaborate to see if they agree with each other's answers. Ask students to share their answers with the class.

POSTREADING

The following activities parallel the features with the same titles in the Student Edition.

Responses to Critical Thinking Questions

Possible responses are:

1. By showing the rabbi taking care of a poor, sick widow without revealing his identity, Peretz shows him to be truly charitable and kind. We see a portrait of a man who, in spite of his own sorrow, puts others first. The doctor obviously honors and respects the rabbi, repeatedly wishing him a long life.

2. The following aspects of Jewish belief are shown: honoring the Sabbath, believing in the Torah, practicing daily prayer, and engaging in good deeds.

3. Responses will reflect students' own experiences. Students should provide as much detail as possible, responding to all parts of the question.

☑ Guidelines for Writing Your Response to "If Not Still Higher"

Have students share their journal entries. As an alternate writing activity, students can work in small groups to explain what part of the story affected them most strongly. Write the following questions on the board for groups to answer collaboratively:

- What made that specific part of the story especially meaningful for you?

- In what ways does the lesson of the story relate to your own life?

Guidelines for Going Back Into the Text: Author's Craft

Possible answers to questions in the Student Edition are:

1. The author's writing style can be described as simple, spare, and gently humorous. His use of repetition, rhetorical questions, and small asides (such as the fact that no one ever steals from the rabbi) give the reader a sense of intimacy with both the narrator and the two characters.

2. The present tense gives the story a feeling of immediacy, as though it were not a historical event that occurred in the distant past, but rather something that continues to happen.

3. Responses will reflect students' own reading. Students should provide specific examples of the ways in which the style of the two stories is different.

☑ FOLLOW-UP DISCUSSION

Use the questions that follow to continue your discussion of "If Not Still Higher." Possible answers are given in parentheses.

Recalling

1. What happens to the rabbi early every Friday morning? (He disappears, as though he melts into thin air.)

2. What does the Lithuanian discover? (He discovers that the rabbi disguises himself as a peasant, goes into the forest, chops down a small tree, and sells the wood to a poor widow for almost no money. The rabbi even lights the widow's stove.)

3. Who is Vassil? (It is the name the rabbi assumes when he disguises himself as a peasant.)

Interpreting

4. What stylistic purpose do you think Peretz had in mind when he used the Lithuanian to discover where the rabbi goes? (Because the Lithuanian is so different from the rabbi, he easily highlights and intensifies the positive qualities of the religious leader.)

5. What do you think motivates the rabbi to help the poor widow? (Possible responses: The rabbi recognizes that she is truly in need; the rabbi is a genuinely holy man who does not need or want to have his good deeds known or celebrated.)

6. What does the Lithuanian mean in the end of the story when he adds quietly, "If not still higher?" (He means that the rabbi is a true saint who has earned a place in heaven among the holiest of the holy.)

Applying

7. What lessons about compassion from this story do you think are applicable today? (Possible response: No act of compassion is too small to be important. Charitable acts provide their own rewards that go well beyond public notice or approval.)

8. How can each of us make the world a better place? (Possible responses: Even without the expectation of a reward, we can help people who are less fortunate. By being skeptical of people or ideas, we can test our beliefs and reinforce the important ones that guide our actions.)

ENRICHMENT

Students will benefit from exploring *World Religions*. The CD-ROM is available from National School Products, 101 East Broadway, Maryland, TN 37804-2498, (800) 251-9124.

And When Summer Comes to an End...
Please Give This Seat to an Elderly
or Disabled Person

by **Nina Cassian**   (pages 234–236)

OBJECTIVES

Literary

- to become aware that form conveys meaning in poetry
- to identify techniques of free verse

Historical

- to evaluate the impact of censorship and repression on Soviet writers and poets
- to recognize the tight control that Stalin had over artists and writers in the Soviet Union

Cultural

- to identify words that reflect a writer's culture and experiences
- to understand the feelings of alienation and loss among writers in the Soviet Union

SELECTION RESOURCES

Use Assessment Worksheet 34 to check students' vocabulary recognition, content comprehension, and appreciation of literary skills.

✔ Informal Assessment Opportunity

SELECTION OVERVIEW

Nina Cassian's poems can be read on two levels— a literal level and an interpretive level. On the literal level, her poems appear to be about old age or dying. A deeper analysis tells us that she is writing about the effects on her of communism, alienation, and betrayal by her country ("*...nobody offered me a seat*"). She has given up hope—communism had been the promise of a utopia, but she refers to it as "*dangerous*". She knows through her own experiences that it is like "*the world is coming to an end.*"

Writing on two levels was not something new for Cassian. Under Stalin, the government exercised tight control over Soviet writers. All authors were required to join the Union of Soviet Writers if they wanted to have their works published. Many writers were persecuted, imprisoned, or killed. Therefore, writers had to use numerous devices to elude the censors, who were literate people. Outright criticism of the regime was impossible, yet writers felt a certain urgency and obligation to expose the repressive forces of the time.

Although Cassian speaks for many repressed people, her voice is at the same time intensely personal.

In these poems, the poet feels a deep sense of loss and feels out of place.

ENGAGING THE STUDENTS

Ask students to consider this hypothetical situation as the basis of class discussion: You are a well-respected poet. You consider yourself a "voice of the people." You live in a country where a repressive government tells you what you can write about. You disagree with many of the leader's policies, and your works often express a critical viewpoint. You know that you may be punished or even killed if you continue. What are your options, and what do you think you would do?

BRIDGING THE ESL/LEP LANGUAGE GAP

Students may gain meaning through oral clues by hearing Cassian's poems read aloud. Encourage students to take notes as you read each poem.

Discuss words such as *wilderness, shrink,* and *terror* that reveal the author's message. Read the poem a second time, emphasizing the last line. Explain that *Utopia* is the name of a book written by Sir Thomas More, describing an ideal society. The word has come to stand for an ideal society that is purely visionary and cannot realistically be attained. Discuss how the poet's use of the word *utopia* helps to convey her message.

Direct students' attention to the last three lines of "Please Give This Seat to an Elderly or Disabled Person," which reads, "... although the signs of at least three major afflictions/were visible on me:/Pride, Loneliness, and Art." Ask students what they think the poet is saying and feeling in these lines.

PRETEACHING SELECTION VOCABULARY

On the board, write *entire journey, major* **afflictions,** **dignity's** *gone, web* **slabs,** **dejected** *coats, Winter Street/on the corner of* **Decline.** Call on students to speculate on the statement that the author is making in each of the poems based on these words.

The words printed in boldfaced type are tested on the selection assessment worksheet.

PREREADING

Reading the Poems in a Cultural Context

Have students work in pairs to list significant events in Nina Cassian's life. Tell students to keep this list in mind as they consider the following questions:

In "And When Summer Comes to an End...," is Nina Cassian describing what it is like to get old, or is she describing something else?

In "Please Give This Seat to an Elderly or Disabled Person," what do you think Nina Cassian is really angry about?

Focusing on the Selections

Read the poems aloud, emphasizing length of lines, sudden breaks, and positioning of words as you read. Point out the significance of the word *Art* at the end of "Please Give This Seat to an Elderly or Disabled Person." Tell students that this word is strategically placed at the end of the poem for emphasis—almost like an exclamation point. Discuss the ways in which this word gives clues to the meaning of the poem. Ask students to identify other words in the poems that give emphasis and are clues to meaning because of where they are positioned.

POSTREADING

The following activities parallel the features with the same titles in the Student Edition.

Responses to Critical Thinking Questions

Possible responses are:

1. She is old, lonely, proud, and has lead an artistic life. She has been through some terrifying winters.

2. Her background as an expelled Jew, a charity case, and an enemy of the government infuse her poems with a sense of betrayal and abandonment. Her musical background can be seen in her melodic imagery.

3. Responses will reflect students' own experiences.

✔ Guidelines for Writing Your Response to the Poems

Have students share their journal entries with a partner. As an alternative writing activity, ask students to write a brief summary of the poems, including the author's viewpoint and message. Next, have students exchange their writing with a partner. Ask them to collaborate on a single summary that includes the points they believe the poet was trying to make.

✔ Guidelines for Going Back Into the Text: Author's Craft

Discuss with students why free verse is an effective method for creating meaning. Ask them whether they think that poems with regular, rhythmic patterns are as effective as those written in free verse. Also ask them why the subjects of these poems are well-suited to free verse. (The author is crying out for recognition. She has been abandoned by her country; as an artist, she suffered under communism. Through free verse, she can emphasize the erratic nature of her past, which lacked predictable rhythms or patterns.) Possible answers to the questions in the Student Edition are:

1. Their lines have varying lengths, read almost like everyday speech, and do not rhyme.

2. By placing the word *although* at the beginning of two separate lines in "Please Give This Seat ...," Cassian emphasizes the complete lack of observance of the other passengers. In "And When Summer ...," the first three lines are long, just as the days of summer are long. The rest of the poem has very short lines, signifying the shortness of the winter days.

3. The reader gets a sense of a real person who is writing the poems. You can feel her age and loneliness and her cold. Writing them as metrical poetry would create more of a distance between the poet and the reader.

FOLLOW-UP DISCUSSION

Use the questions that follow to continue your discussion of the poems. Possible answers are given in parentheses.

Recalling

1. What are the three major afflictions the poet suffered? (Pride, Loneliness, and Art)

2. How does the poet travel on her journey? (She stands throughout the journey.)

3. Which two seasons does the poet compare? (spring and winter)

Interpreting

4. What do you think the "long journey" might be? (the poet's long life)

5. Why does she say she is "at least a hundred years older than anyone else"? (Perhaps she feels that way as a poet who has traveled and experienced a lot.)

6. What effect does winter have on her? (a loss of dignity)

Applying

7. What might spring and winter stand for in "And When Summer Comes to an End . . ."? (Winter stands for communism under Stalin; spring might represent freedom from tyranny.)

8. How does she feel about the possibility of spring ever coming? (Pessimistic; she says it is as dangerous as any utopia.)

ENRICHMENT

Students may enjoy viewing *Europe After the Cold War,* available from Social Studies School Service, 10200 Jefferson Boulevard, Room 12, Culver City, CA 90232, (800) 421-4246.

Random Talk
by Raisa Blokh

The Heirs of Stalin
by Yevgeny Yevtushenko

Refugees
by Ilya Krichevsky   (pages 237–245)

OBJECTIVES

Literary

- to identify the author's purpose for writing a poem
- to recognize the central idea of a poem
- to read a poem in cultural context

Historical

- to evaluate events related to the collapse of the Soviet Union in 1991
- to describe conditions in Hitler's concentration camps
- to describe the power of Stalin's regime in the Soviet Union

Cultural

- to recognize the importance of one's ties to cultural roots during wartime
- to discuss the possibility of a world without war

SELECTION RESOURCES

Use Assessment Worksheet 35 to check students' vocabulary recognition, content comprehension, and appreciation of literary skills.

 Informal Assessment Opportunity

SELECTION OVERVIEW

Poems about war are generally powerful and make a strong impact on the reader—which is precisely the author's purpose. However, for a truly multicultural understanding, one must go beyond how the poem makes the reader feel. One must understand where and when the text originated and the person who wrote it. The world of Raisa Blokh's "Random Talk" is a Nazi concentration camp during WWII. The world of Yevtushenko's poem is during Stalin's rule of the USSR, when the Communist party used terror to enforce its will. The context of Ilya Krichevsky's "Refugees" is modern-day Russia, when Moscow citizens set up a barricade around the parliament to protest Communist coup leaders who sought to regain their power. Understanding these contexts will lead students to a greater understanding of and appreciation for the horrors of war and tyranny that cross both physical and cultural boundaries.

SUMMARY

In these poems, fear, pain, and hardship flood the lives of each of the poets. These emotions stem from war and tyranny.

ENGAGING THE STUDENTS

Write the following quotation on the board: "I dream of giving birth to a child who will ask, 'Mother, what was war?'"

Explain to students that the quotation is from American poet Eve Merriam. Have students work in groups of three to discuss the likelihood of war becoming a thing of the past during their lifetime. A volunteer from each group can then summarize the opinions expressed and the reasons for them.

Point out that in the poems they are about to read, students will have the opportunity to discover the human spirit that remains in the face of war and tyranny.

BRIDGING THE ESL/LEP LANGUAGE GAP

These poems may be difficult for students to comprehend. In preparation for reading the poems, explain the subject matter of each one briefly. Then ask students to look for the answer to this question as they read: What does the author say about the human spirit and the will to live in the face of war and tyranny?

In preparation for reading "Random Talk," ask students what they know about Hitler, Nazism, and the concentration camps of Germany, Poland, and Austria. Do they know what kind of suffering the prisoners endured? Read the poem aloud together as a class, stopping to discuss a few lines at a time. Ask: How did Blokh's memories of her homeland bring pleasure and pain at the same time? Do similar preparation for Stalin's regime and the fall of communism in Russia in the early 1990s.

☑ PRETEACHING SELECTION VOCABULARY

Have students scan the selections and create word banks by writing all the words that relate to the categories "funerals" and "warfare". (Responses should include *bayonets, recruits, **sortie, sentries, henchmen**, soldiers, combat, prison camp, **mausoleum, pallbearer**, and coffin*.) While they are writing, use the above categories to make two columns on the board. Call on students to fill the columns with the words they have found in the text. Use the categories to discuss the questions below:

- Do the words in the word bank relating to warfare describe modern warfare? How do you know?
- Which of the word bank words are related to death?
- Based on this activity, what do you think the poems are about? Explain how you arrived at your answer.

The words printed in boldfaced type are tested on the selection assessment worksheet.

PREREADING

Reading the Poems in a Cultural Context

Help students read for purpose by asking them to consider the ties that each of the poets has to his or her homeland. Discuss how these ties led to the subject matter of each poem and its powerful message.

Focusing on the Selections

Have students work in groups of three. Assign a different poem to each of the three people in the group. After considering their poem individually, have each group summarize the poets' purposes for writing. Ask: Is there a common thread that suggests a similar purpose for writing in all three poems? (Students may suggest the desire for freedom.) Suggest that students use their responses to this question to draft a topic sentence for their summaries. Call on groups to read their summaries aloud and to discuss the various interpretations.

POSTREADING

The following activities parallel the features with the same titles in the Student Edition.

Responses to Critical Thinking Questions

Possible responses are:

1. All three believe that their homeland has been ravaged by brutal leaders but has still survived. All three have feelings of loyalty and nostalgia.

2. Blokh died in one of Hitler's concentration camps but yearned for Russia; Yevtushenko lived in the USSR during Stalin's reign of terror and fears that it may return; Krichevsky fought to protect modern-day Russia from the Communists who were trying to regain their power.

3. Responses will reflect students' own cultural backgrounds and experiences.

☑ Guidelines for Writing Your Response to "Random Talk," "The Heirs of Stalin," and "Refugees"

Have students share their journal entries with a partner. As an alternative writing activity, ask students to work in small groups, writing a response to the author of each poem. What would they say to the poet if they had the opportunity to talk with her or him? Questions like the following can stimulate class discussion.

- What message does each author have for young people and world leaders today?
- What does each author say about the effects of war and suffering?

- Can individuals react responsibly to create a world without war? Why or Why not?

Call on a representative to read each group's response. Ask: Has the world view of war changed in the 20th century? Some students may wish to consider what war will be like and how people will feel about it in the 21st century.

✔ Guidelines for Going Back Into the Text: Author's Craft

Yevtushenko said, "A poet in Russia is more than a poet." He means that a poet's job is to represent the voice of the people. Ask students to identify words in the poems that effectively express voices of the people. (Accept all reasonable answers). Possible answers to the questions in the Student Edition are:

1. "Random Talk": to place past suffering behind and to look ahead; "Stalin": to warn of a return to Stalinism; "Refugees": to inspire a fight for life in the midst of deepest hardship.

2. "Random Talk": evokes an image of a blizzard destroying old Russia, leaving emptiness behind and presenting the symbol of light as the hope for the future; "Stalin": portrays Stalin as pretending to be dead but planning to pursue his goal; "Refugees": creates images of suffering but ends with a declaration to live.

3. Responses will reflect students' opinions.

✔ FOLLOW-UP DISCUSSION

Use the questions that follow to continue your discussion of "Random Talk," "The Heirs of Stalin," and "Refugees." Possible answers are given in parentheses.

Recalling

1. Why does Blokh say in "Random Talk" that "she must live—not simply reminisce"? (Thinking about the past is not enough for her, she needs to live again.)

2. What is the greatest fear that Yevtushenko expresses in "The Heirs of Stalin"? (Stalin is not really dead and he and his followers plan to continue their reign of terror.)

3. What is the mission of the "refugees" as described by Ilya Krichevsky? (to continue to fight and to live)

Interpreting

4. What are "the pain" and "the blizzard" that Blokh refers to in "Random Talk"? (the pain of being in the camp, away from her homeland; the Holocaust)

5. Who are Stalin's heirs, and what might they do? (The heirs are his soldiers, or henchmen, who might be able to contact him and carry out his orders again.)

6. According to Krichevsky, which two possibilities lay in store for the refugees? (Some will live to tell their grandchildren about the struggle; others will die.)

Applying

7. Do you think that poetry is a good way to make a statement about oppression, struggle, and war? Explain. (Students may suggest that the sensory imagery and the personal expression of suffering can make a powerful impression on the reader.)

8. What lessons do these poems have for a world struggling with political and ethnic tensions today? (Answers will vary. Accept all reasonable responses.)

ENRICHMENT

Students might benefit from viewing *The Rise and Fall of the Soviet Union,* available from Social Studies School Service, 10200 Jefferson Boulevard, Room 12, Culver City, CA 90232, (800) 421-4246.

OBJECTIVE

Overall

- to forge links between several famous monuments in Europe and the cultures of these lands

Specific

- to make connections between Catherine the Great's Winter Palace and the lives of ordinary people who live under government repression
- to view the old town square in Warsaw and the storytelling that once took place there as reflections of the culture's values
- to compare and contrast the ruins of the Colosseum in Rome, Italy, with the ruins of modern European cities such as Sarajevo

ENGAGING THE STUDENTS

Invite students to respond to this topic:

> If we do not understand the past, we are doomed to relive it.

Allow students five minutes to write. Then invite volunteers to share their responses. Discuss with the class what they think the quotation means. Ask how we do and do not learn from our past errors. Tell students that in this feature, they will make connections between famous monuments and current-day events. Point out that they will see how some individuals and governments have failed to build on what people learned in the past.

BRIDGING THE ESL/LEP LANGUAGE GAP

Write the following questions on the board:

1. What is the Colosseum? Where is it located? (It is a huge arena in Rome, Italy.)
2. Why do you think so many people died while building Catherine the Great's Winter Palace? (The workers were treated very badly.)
3. How is Warsaw, Poland, like many European cities? (It is a blend of old and new buildings.)

Then read the selection as students follow along in their books. Ask them to focus specifically on the answers to the three questions as they listen and read.

EXPLORING LANDMARKS

The Roman Colosseum is an *amphitheater*, a spacious open-air oval or round structure. The first amphitheaters were constructed of wood; later, they were built of stone. Originally the Romans used these theaters for gladiator combats, wild beast fights, and other great spectacles. The first amphitheater was built in 59 B.C., in Rome. Several others followed until the erection of the great Roman Colosseum.

The Roman emperor Vespasian ordered the Colosseum to be built. Since it was not finished in his lifetime, his son and heir, Titus, dedicated the structure in A.D. 80. The upper part of the Colosseum was built of wood. After 223, it was replaced with stone. According to modern scholars, the Colosseum seated 50,000 people.

- Have students write a brief research essay that compares and contrasts the ruins of ancient Rome to those of another ancient civilization, such as ancient Greece, Egypt, Zimbabwe, or the Maya. Have students consider the following: What significance did these structures have to their respective cultures? What do these ruins reveal about the accomplishments and beliefs of their respective cultures? When did these civilizations rise and fall? What events led to their demise?

LINKING LITERATURE, CULTURE, AND REGION

Guidelines for Evaluation: Sample Answers

In "The Servant," the peasant Gerasim is desperate to find a job. However, the economic situation is very fragile under the repressive government and those without work have no place to turn for even basic necessities. "The Heirs of Stalin" also describes the terrible time ordinary people have under dictatorships.

By showing the rabbi taking care of a poor, sick widow without revealing his identity, Peretz shows that some people in his culture are kind and charitable. "The Nightingale's Three Bits of Advice" shows that Pourrat believes some people in his culture are foolish, gullible, and greedy. Both stories embody values or teachings of their writer's culture.

The ruins of Sarajevo add to the despair that people in "A Winter's Tale" feel about their situation.

The Bicycle

by Jerzy Harasymowicz   (pages 246–248)

OBJECTIVES

Literary

- to understand the elements of a poem
- to identify the relationship between realism and fantasy in a poem

Historical

- to recognize the importance of nature in Polish life

Cultural

- to identify the significance of poetry in Polish rural life
- to discuss how poetry reflects the Polish landscape

SELECTION RESOURCES

Use Assessment Worksheet 36 to check students' vocabulary recognition, content comprehension, and appreciation of literary skills.

☑ Informal Assessment Opportunity

SELECTION OVERVIEW

Poland, a country that is situated in Central Europe, is noted for its many colorful landscapes. In fact, the name Poland derives from the Slavic word *polane*, which means "plain" or "field." This is an appropriate description for this country of flat landscapes, gently rolling hills, and clear, blue lakes. The northern area consists of thousands of small, picturesque lakes. Sandy beaches border the Baltic Sea. Rugged mountain ranges form part of the country's southern boundary. Lumbering is the country's most important economic activity. The plains are the country's main agricultural areas. In addition to goats and sheep, animals that are prominently featured in the selection, Poland is noted for its bison, wild cats, and brown wolves.

In this selection, the author uses the imagery of Poland's landscapes and natural settings to bring life to an inanimate object—a bicycle.

In this poem, the poet weaves a fantastical story in which a bicycle joins a herd of mountain goats.

ENGAGING THE STUDENTS

Ask students: What if some of the objects in this classroom could come alive? What would they say? What would they do? How would they feel? Guide students to work in pairs, choose an object in the classroom, and write a short dialogue involving the object that has come to life. This object can relate to another object, to a person in the room, or to anyone else. For example:

> Paper: Oh, no! She doesn't like what she wrote. She's going to crumple me up and throw me away!

> Pencil: Gee, after all the work I did on you . . . I feel let down.

Mention to students that they might wish to recall their dialogues when they read the selection.

BRIDGING THE ESL/LEP LANGUAGE GAP

This poem should not be difficult for students. Guide them to work in small groups (mixing English proficient and ESL/LEP students). Tell them that this selection is a narrative poem, that is, it tells a story. Assign each group a different stanza or stanzas. Then, in each group, help students take turns summarizing, in their own words, their part of the poem's story. Finally, have groups tell, in order, the complete story of the whole poem.

☑ PRETEACHING SELECTION VOCABULARY

List on the board the following words and phrases from the selection:

bell	*nimble*
gazed	*happy*
drank	*back wheel*
silver horns	*fought*

Explain that these words are used in connection with the story's elements of realism and fantasy. Ask what these words reveal about the relationship of the bicycle to the herd of mountain goats. Encourage students to add to the list other appropriate words as they read the selection.

The words printed in boldfaced type are tested on the selection assessment worksheet.

PREREADING

Reading the Poem in a Cultural Context

Help students read for purpose by asking them to consider the poem from the bicycle's perspective. Ask them the following questions:

- How does the bicycle feel after being left behind?
- How does the bicycle feel joining the herd of goats?

Finally, ask students to describe, in their own words, the dreamlike journey of the bicycle through time and space. Have them comment on the colors and sounds they associate with the journey.

Focusing on the Selection

Have students work in small groups and draw an environmental image of one of the bicycle's adventures. Help students focus their creativity on design, colors, and realistic/fantastic images.

POSTREADING

The following activities parallel the features with the same titles in the Student Edition.

Responses to Critical Thinking Questions

Possible responses are:

1. By having the bicycle become like a mountain goat, he shows that he thinks of the bicycle as a living thing, capable of acting on its own.
2. It is mountainous and has streams and glades.
3. Responses will reflect students' own imagination. Encourage them to create a story that marries realism and fantasy.

☑ Guidelines for Writing Your Response to "The Bicycle"

Have students share their journal entries with a partner. As an alternative writing activity, have them recall a vivid memory of a personal adventure and use evocative imagery to write a short poem about the experience. Direct them to write the first draft freely and rapidly. Encourage students to draft and revise with images that refer to environment, weather, colors, behaviors, time, and space. Ask student volunteers to read their poems aloud.

☑ Guidelines for Going Back Into the Text: Author's Craft

To be sure that students understand the relationship between realism and fantasy in literature, have each student find a sentence in the selection that illustrates a realistic situation and a fantastic situation. Then have each student write a realistic or fantastic phrase or sentence on any topic. Example:

- The cup holds juice.
- The cup danced lightly with joy when it was emptied.

Possible answers to the questions in the Student Edition are:

1. The bicycle joining the herd of goats, gazing on people, fighting over a buck, rearing up at eagles, and going to heaven while being ridden by the angel of death are examples of fantasy.
2. All the natural elements, such as the goats, the snow-covered glade, the mountains, the poacher, and the sky are realistic, as is the fact that the bicycle has been left behind by a tourist.
3. To surprise readers and make them look at an inanimate object in a different light; to show the thoughtlessness of humans.

☑ FOLLOW-UP DISCUSSION

Use the questions that follow to continue your discussion of "The Bicycle." Possible answers are given in parentheses.

Recalling

1. For what did the bicycle use its bell ? (to warn the goats of danger)
2. Who shot the bicycle? (a poacher)
3. Why was the bicycle shot? (for its silver horns)

Interpreting

4. Why do you think the bicycle became the leader of the goats? (because its silver "horns" were superior to the others' horns)

5. Why do you think the author chose a bicycle to join a herd of goats? (Its structure resembles that of a goat.)

6. How does the author use imagery to transform the bicycle into a mountain goat? (Its handlebars become horns and its back wheel becomes back legs capable of rearing. It never nibbles grass or drinks from a stream.)

Applying

7. What positive role do you feel poetry plays in society? (Answers may vary. They may include: nurtures the spirit; provides freedom of expression; and helps people use and expand their minds. It may teach a lesson or provide a different way of thinking about a subject.)

8. What function do you think fantasy will have in future technology? (Answers will vary. What was once science fiction or fantasy, such as people traveling to the moon or beneath the sea or robots replacing humans for mechanical activities, has become a reality. The more we imagine, the more we can create.)

ENRICHMENT

Students may benefit from exploring *How to Read and Understand Poetry*. The CD-ROM is available from National School Products, 101 East Broadway, Maryville, TN 37804-2498, (800) 251-9124.

The Monster

by Nina Katerli   (pages 249–257)

OBJECTIVES

Literary

- to examine metaphor as a literary technique
- to recognize an author's use of details to create imagery

Historical

- to evaluate events related to the collapse of the Soviet Union in 1991
- to understand the ambivalence felt toward the decline of communism

Cultural

- to recognize the hardships that nations experience as a result of change
- to discuss how change can lead to loss of control and feelings of confusion

SELECTION RESOURCES

Use Assessment Worksheet 37 to check students' vocabulary recognition, content comprehension, and appreciation of literary skills.

✔ Informal Assessment Opportunity

SELECTION OVERVIEW

Theoretically, communism in the Soviet Union was supposed to create a society in which everyone's needs were met. What developed instead was a system of dictatorial rule by the Communist party with many serious inequities. For example, consumer goods remained in short supply for everyone except Communist officials, and most of the people lived in poverty. Domestic life was difficult—especially for the elderly, who were forced to share cramped apartments with relatives. Neighbors in city apartments often shared kitchens and bathrooms. Life was not entirely negative, however. The Soviet economic system did provide its citizens with several basic benefits: free health care, inexpensive public transportation, low rents and basic food prices, and a guaranteed job for every individual. Also, all occupations were open to women. In spite of the poverty that existed, there was a sense of stability, and people knew what to expect. With the collapse of the Soviet Union in 1991 and the decline of Communist party power, increased economic hardships and government instability have led to a sense of disorder.

In this short story, the author uses the metaphor of a monster to show the effects of communism on the Soviet peoples' lives, as well as the confusion and uncertainty that has developed after the system's collapse.

In this selection, a monster disrupts the lives of a Russian household. The monster can be interpreted as a metaphor for the effects of communism on Russian life and for growing old.

ENGAGING THE STUDENTS

Display the following statements:

1. At least my pension gave me enough money to buy food and some essentials. Now I don't even have enough money to keep from going hungry. Everything is so expensive.

2. People were always paid for their work. Now there is unemployment. Factories are shut down. You never know how much things will cost. Everything is changing. It used to be easier. You knew what to expect.

3. It's so much better now. There's a bright future for people who are better educated. Goods can now come here from other countries. Although we have to go through these difficulties, it would be terrible to go back.

Divide the class into three groups and assign a statement to each group. Tell students to discuss the statement assigned to them in terms of the recent events that have taken place in Russia. Call on a representative to summarize each group's discussion.

BRIDGING THE ESL/LEP LANGUAGE GAP

This story is about the narrator and two other women who live in an apartment in Russia with a "monster." Form groups of three to four students. Ask them to read small sections of the text to themselves and then discuss each section within their groups, looking for descriptions of the monster that reveal what it really represents.

Ask students to read the following passages in the Student Edition and to discuss the questions that follow each one:

> . . . there was nothing unusual about coming across a shaggy creature with a single crimson eye in the middle of its forehead and a long scaly tail. . . (page 250)

How does the narrator feel about the monster at first?

> . . . as the Monster grew older, he began to turn nasty, and gave us no peace. . . his eye has turned from red to a kind of dirty ginger color and his fur has gone gray; to put it in a nutshell, our Monster is getting old. (page 252)

Ask: What do you think the monster's change in appearance signifies?

> "If he was human, it would be one thing, but he's not, he's just vermin!"

> "You should feel sorry for him; after all, he's old. (pages 254-255)

Ask: What do the narrator and Anna Lvovna think of the monster now?

☑ PRETEACHING SELECTION VOCABULARY

On the board, write *monster* and ask students to describe monsters they have read about or seen on television or in the movies. Explain that in the story they will read next, a monster has taken over the lives of the narrator, her Aunt Angelina, and another woman, Anna Lvovna. Read aloud the following paragraph, listing the words in boldfaced type as you say them. The monster had a *crimson* eye. He had not caused anyone **grievous** bodily harm. Once, he had caused frogs and *newts* to appear in the bathtub and a *boil* to appear on Anna Lvovna's nose. Aunt Angelina moaned **dolefully** when the monster made them freeze. Then she began leaping about in a **frenzied** dance. Afterwards, the monster looked for his bone in **perplexity**, thrashing his **mangy** tail across the floor.

Have students locate each listed word and its definition in the footnotes on pages 249-257 of the Student Edition. Call on students to define each word.

The words printed in boldfaced type are tested on the selection assessment worksheet.

PREREADING

Reading the Story in a Cultural Context

Ask students to read for details that reveal the ways that the monster affects the women's lives and how the women feel about the monster aging. Suggest that students read to find out what ideas the monster might represent in this story.

Focusing on the Selection

Have students form pairs. One student in each pair should look for details showing that the monster represents old age; the other should look for details that show that the monster represents communism and its decline. Each should list the details that support his or her assigned role. Tell students their lists should include physical characteristics as well as behaviors, actions, and words spoken. When they have finished, ask students which characteristics and images identify the monster as representing both old age and communism.

POSTREADING

The following activities parallel the features with the same titles in the Student Edition.

Responses to Critical Thinking Questions

Possible responses are:

1. The author appears to be sympathetic to either interpretation of the monster. On one level, she presents a humorous fantasy; however, on another level, she illustrates typical attitudes toward a loss of literal or figurative power.

2. Life is difficult for these characters. They must share an apartment ("too many monsters and not enough apartments") and adjust to many changes. The monster has lost his job due to his age, has no pension, and could be evicted. When she disagrees with the monster and opposes his will, Anna Lvovna disappears.

3. Answers will vary. Many students will respond that they go along with the majority since at their age, it's difficult to be an individual. Students should explain their position in detail.

☑ Guidelines for Writing Your Response to "The Monster"

Have students share their journal entries with a partner. As an alternative writing activity, ask students to work in small groups, sharing points that struck them most deeply as they read the selection. On the board, write the following questions for the groups to answer collaboratively.

- In what ways did the monster change in the story?
- How did the women feel toward the monster at the end of the story?

☑ Guidelines for Going Back Into the Text: Author's Craft

Ask students to identify sensory details used by the author to describe the monster's appearance and his actions. List these on the board as they are given. Discuss how these details created vivid pictures in each student's mind as he or she read. Ask students to discuss how these pictures influenced their reading and understanding. Possible answers to the questions in the Student Edition are:

1. The monster may represent old age and the frustration people experience as they lose their ability to function at the same level they are accustomed to. The monster may also be interpreted as the collapse of communism, an old, worn out system that doesn't work as well as it once did. Once highly successful in controlling people, the monster now arouses only pity or derision.

2. Whether a monster growing old or a political system that is outmoded, the creature is past its prime. His shaggy fur has gone grey, his crimson eye has faded to a dirty ginger color, and he is losing the scales from his tail. No longer able to work, he sits in his room, hissing and sighing. He still attempts to exert control in mean ways (freezing his apartment mates, making them dance, etc.), but he has lost his power and is frightened when his "spell" doesn't seem to work on Anna Lvovna.

3. Answers will vary. Students might select an extinct animal, an obsolete highway, or a historic building.

☑ FOLLOW-UP DISCUSSION

Use the questions that follow to continue your discussion of "The Monster." Possible answers are given in parentheses.

Recalling

1. Who wanted the monster to be the way he used to be? (Aunt Angelina)

2. How did the monster's appearance change? (Its crimson eye turned to a dirty ginger color, his fur became gray, he stopped going to work, and he sat for days on end, sighing occasionally.)

3. What did Aunt Angelina and the narrator feed the monster? (bones and chopped meat)

Interpreting

4. Why do you think the monster wouldn't go to his job in a museum? (Students may suggest that he was reluctant to become a relic, something from the past that is meant to be viewed only with awe from a distance.)

5. How did the monster demonstrate his power? (by transforming people, by making people cold and stiff, by making animals or diseases appear, and by disrupting daily life)

6. Whether the monster was communism or old age, how did he affect the women? (They were unable to escape from him; their lives were in disorder because of his unpredictability; they accepted the unreal as being real. Aunt Angelina seems to have been genuinely fond of the monster and takes care of him. The narrator seems to have respected him, but now she feels only pity. Anna Lvovna is angry with the monster; she had accepted him when he was useful, but now regards him as vermin.)

Applying

7. How did Aunt Angelina's attitude change during the course of the story? Why? (First, she wants him back the way he had been. Toward the end of the story, she is concerned that he will go hungry. Perhaps she has resigned herself to what was ahead, or perhaps now she is totally under the monster's power.)

8. What happened to Aunt Lvovna and why? (The monster turned her into a rat. Throughout the story, she represents the voice of reason. Reason and logic prove to be her undoing.)

ENRICHMENT

Students might benefit from viewing *The Fall of Communism,* available from Zenger Media, 10200 Jefferson Boulevard, Room 922, P.O. Box 802, Culver City, CA 90232, (800) 421-4246.

A Winter's Tale
by Slavenka Drakulić (pages 258–262)

OBJECTIVES

Literary

- to understand how the author uses comparisons to convey her point
- to analyze the mood of the essay and how it contributes to the overall effect of the piece

Historical

- to describe the war in Bosnia and the effect it has on the people of the region
- to discuss how people in the West have responded to the Bosnian war

Cultural

- to explore the lives of ordinary Bosnians in a war-torn land
- to explain the cultural repercussions of an extended and bloody war

SELECTION RESOURCES

Use Assessment Worksheet 38 to check students' vocabulary recognition, content comprehension, and appreciation of literary skills.

 Informal Assessment Opportunity

SELECTION OVERVIEW

On October 15, 1991, the Bosnia and Herzegovina parliament adopted a declaration of sovereignty. This was followed shortly thereafter (on February 29, 1992), by a referendum for independence. Violent conflicts resulted, including fierce and bloody bombings. Bosnian Serbs attacked Sarajevo, the country's capital city. The Serb forces then massacred thousands of Bosnia Muslims and expelled many more non-Serbs in a policy called "ethnic cleansing."

Muslims and Croats called a cease-fire on February 23, 1994. A month later, leaders signed an accord that created a Muslim-Croat confederation in Bosnia. The Bosnian/Croatian governments linked this confederation with Croatia. Nonetheless, intense Muslim-Serb battles continued and many people died. By the summer of 1994, Bosnian Serbs controlled more than 70 percent of the country. As the fighting continued, the balance of power began to shift toward the Muslim-Croat alliance. A new round of peace talks began after NATO forces attacked the Bosnian Serbs; the siege of Sarajevo ended that September. At this point, all sides have agreed to create independent regions within Bosnia, with the Serbs controlling 49 percent of the country. However, as explained in "A Winter's Tale," peace is still a long way off in the beleaguered country.

In this selection, a Croatian writes about the atrocities that are ravaging his homeland and the inablility of words to remedy the situation.

ENGAGING THE STUDENTS

Have students consider the following situation: Imagine that you live in a country torn apart by war. What do you think you could do as one person to help end the fighting and heal your country? Allow students five minutes to write their responses, then call on volunteers to read their answers to the class.

Record students' responses on the board. Challenge students to decide how important a writer might be to bringing about peace. Focus the discussion on the power of words to heal.

BRIDGING THE ESL/LEP LANGUAGE GAP

The Balkan war is likely to be unfamiliar to many students, which could make the selection difficult for them. Before they read the story, invite students to share what they know about Bosnia and Herzegovina. Ask: What is happening today in the Balkan countries of Bosnia, Herzegovina, and Croatia? Do you know the reason why people in these countries are at war? What was the name of these three countries when they were united as one country? If students have not already done so, locate all three countries on a world map. Discuss the reasons for the war. Ask: Do you know of any similar conflicts in other parts of the world today? In the past?

SELECTION VOCABULARY

Do a webbing exercise with students using nouns that describe the situation in Bosnia and Herzegovina. First, direct students to skim the selection and list at least five nouns that refer to what is happening in the Balkans. Examples include *gulag*, *carnage*, *rations*, *refugee*, *language*, *concentration camps*, *mass rapes*, *bombing*, and *death*. Then create a web on the board using the words that students locate in the selection. You may wish to use the following questions to draw parallels between students' findings:

- How did these words help you get a mental picture of the Balkan war?
- Which words describe the mood of the time and place?
- Why might the author use these words to describe life in her homeland?

The words printed in boldfaced type are tested on the selection assessment worksheet.

PREREADING

Reading the Essay in a Cultural Context

Help students read for purpose by asking them to consider how growing up in a war-torn land might affect their own lives. Discuss such factors as physical danger, mental stress, food shortages, and educational disruptions. Also have students consider how cultural traditions, such as the celebrations of holidays, might be disrupted by war. As they read, have students consider how the war has affected Slavenka Drakulić and why she has decided not to leave her homeland for safety in Vienna, the United States, or Sweden. Guide students to see that Drakulić has placed her cultural identity over her concern for her physical and emotional safety.

Focusing on the Selection

When students finish reading, ask them to choose partners. Have the pairs work together to create a chart or Venn diagram comparing and contrasting life in the West and in the author's war-torn land. Encourage students to reread the story to find as many specific examples as possible. When they have finished, call on each pair to read their charts and discuss how the author makes her readers see the war in the Balkans from within. Guide them to see that this point of view makes the war much more immediate and emotional.

POSTREADING

The following activities parallel the features with the same titles in the Student Edition.

Responses to Critical Thinking Questions

Possible responses are:

1. She feels hopeless, despairing, and haunted. She fears that her good intentions aren't enough to help her country.

2. These threads include language, home, relatives, and friends. The author can't forget these important ties and believes that she must do something to change the status quo and preserve these threads.

3. Answers will vary. Students should describe the situation and what they did about it.

✔ Guidelines for Writing Your Response to "A Winter's Tale"

Invite students to share their journal entries. As an alternative writing activity, ask students to work in pairs to draft a position paper about the media's coverage of war and other acts of violence. Tell students to support or attack the way newspapers, magazines, and television cover these events, using specific examples to support their position. When students have completed their papers, they might stage a mini-debate to share their points of view.

Guidelines for Going Back Into the Text: Author's Craft

Possible answers to questions in the Student Edition are:

1. She says that the snow is innocent and suggests the coming of Christmas. Her day in Vienna is quiet and ordinary. In comparison, she thinks about the coming winter in Bosnia and the pain, fear, and suffering that the war will bring to Sarajevo.

2. She describes her rich Viennese breakfast of butter, bread, milk, jam, egg, and coffee and compares it to the meager daily rations (given in grams) of bread, potatoes, and rice in Sarajevo. While she will have potatoes as a side dish at lunch, only 6.5 grams of potatoes, less than a single potato, is allowed for the whole day in Sarajevo.

3. She wants to make the strength of her feelings clear. As a child, she was happy in Sarajevo even though she knew places like the United States were richer. As an adult, she wishes to be a "citizen

of any country where there is no war" and where family life and holidays can be enjoyed in peace.

☑ FOLLOW-UP DISCUSSION

Use the questions that follow to continue your discussion of "A Winter's Tale." Possible answers are given in parentheses.

Recalling

1. Where is Drakulić as she writes this essay? (She is in Vienna.)

2. What was in the packages that Drakulić got as a child from her relatives in America? (beautifully smelling soaps, cocoa, gum, stockings, razor blades, chocolates, instant coffee)

3. How does Drakulić make her living? (She is a writer.)

Interpreting

4. Why do you think Drakulić set the story during the Christmas season? (Christmas is the season of peace and hope, just the opposite of what is going on in her country. This juxtaposition shows her despair at peace ever being achieved.)

5. How can you tell that Drakulić could never give up her citizenship and move permanently to another country? (The "millions of fine threads" that link her to Bosnia; the fact that she cannot forget or relinquish her culture and heritage)

6. What is the tone or mood of this story? (The tone is despairing, sad, and mournful.)

Applying

7. Why do you think Drakulić wrote this essay? (Possible responses: To point out the terrible conditions in her country, and to underscore the need for immediate and drastic intervention)

8. What impact does the war in the Balkans have on the people of the region? (Possible responses: There are both physical and emotional hardships. Physically, people are killed and families are torn apart. Emotionally, people can become dispirited and depressed.)

ENRICHMENT

Students can benefit from viewing *Forms of Government: What's the Score?* This video is available from Cambridge Social Studies, PO Box 2153, Dept. SS7, Charleston, WV 25328-2153, (800) 468-4227.

RESPONSES TO REVIEWING THE REGION

1. Sample answer: In "A Winter's Tale," Drakulić feels words cannot stop the bloodshed in Bosnia. However, she places her cultural identity over her concern for safety. In "If Not Still Higher," Peretz admires a culture that could produce someone as saintly as the rabbi of Nemirov.

2. Sample answer: The poem "Please Give This Seat to an Elderly or Disabled Person" shows that the author lives in a culture that does not respect age or disability. The speaker has to stand during the entire journey—although she was "at least a hundred years older than anyone else on board"—because no one will give up a seat for her.

3. Disabled students might say they have also stood during a journey because no one would give up their seat to them. Unlike the poem's narrator, who silently endures this maltreatment, students might say they would complain.

☑ FOCUSING ON GENRE SKILLS

Drakulić uses many elements of *nonfiction*—a type of writing about real people and events—to describe the war in Bosnia and the effect it has on the people there. Drakulić points out the terrible conditions in her country and underscores the need for immediate and drastic intervention. She yearns to be a "citizen of any country where there is no war," where family life and holidays can be enjoyed in peace. Have students choose and read another nonfiction selection and explain what real people and events it describes.

BIBLIOGRAPHY

BLOKH, RAISA. "Random Talk." In *20th Century Russian Poetry*. New York: Doubleday, 1993.

CASSIAN, NINA. "Please Give This Seat to an Elderly or Disabled Person." In *Life Sentence: Selected Poems by Nina Cassian*. New York: W.W. Norton & Company, Inc., 1990.

DRAKULIĆ, SLAVENKA. "A Winter's Tale." In *The Balkan Express*. New York: HarperCollins Publishers, Inc., 1993.

KATERLI, NINA. "The Monster." In *Soviet Women Writing*. New York: Abbeville Press, 1990.

KRICHEVSKY, ILYA. "Refugees." In *20th Century Russian Poetry*. New York: Doubleday, Inc., 1993.

YEVTUSHENKO, YEVGENY. "The Heirs of Stalin." In *20th Century Russian Poetry*. New York: Doubleday, 1993.

7 Western Europe

CHAPTER PREVIEW

Literature of Western Europe			
Selections	**Genre**	**Author's Craft/Literary Skills**	**Cultural Values & Focus**
"The Oath of Athenian Youth," Anonymous, pages 264–266	oath	author's purpose	devotion to the state and a code of ideal conduct
"The Nightingale's Three Bits of Advice," Henri Pourrat, pages 267–270	poetry	sequence	effects of foolishness and gullibility
"Paying on the Nail," Padraic O'Farrell, pages 271–274	short story	trickster folktales	the value of honesty
"Death Seed," Ricarda Huch; "Woman, You Are Afraid," Maria Wine; from *My Mother's House*, Leah Goldberg, pages 275–278	poetry	imagery	devastating impact of war
from *Survival in Auschwitz*, Primo Levi, pages 279–286	autobiography	personal narrative	horrors of the Nazi Holocaust
"Action Will be Taken," Heinrich Böll, pages 287–293	short story	irony	struggles of the working class
Making Thematic Connections: A House Divided, pages 294-295			
"The Return," Carmen Laforet, pages 296–302	short story	foreshadowing	the demands of modern life

ASSESSMENT

Assessment opportunities are indicated by a ☑ next to the activity title. For guidelines, see Teacher's Resource Manual, page xxxvi.

CROSS-DISCIPLINE
TEACHING OPPORTUNITIES

History   Europe's literary history was greatly influenced by World War II, the greatest war in history in terms of human and material resources expended. In all, 61 countries and 1.7 billion people, three-fourths of the world's population, took part. About 100 million people mobilized for military service; the total cost was more than $1 trillion, more than all the other wars combined. The human cost, not including the six million Jews killed in the Holocaust, has been estimated at 55 million dead. Have students work with a history teacher to trace the history of World War II. Time-Life's series on World War II provides an excellent in-depth look at the conflagration. (Time-Life Books, 1981). There are 28 books in the series, each one highlighting an important aspect of the war. Titles include *Prelude to War, the Battle of Britain, The Rising Sun,* and *The Italian Campaign.* Don McCombs and Fred L. Worth's *World War II: Strange and Fascinating Facts* (Crown Publishers, 1983) is another good resource.

Science   The potato had a major impact on the history of Ireland. In the 18th and 19th century, the average Irish adult ate several pounds of potatoes a day—and little else. This nourishing staple helped sustain Ireland as its population nearly tripled from the mid-18th century to the mid-19th century. But depending on only one crop for survival was dangerous. When the potato blight hit Europe in 1845, it devestated Ireland. More than a million Irish people died from starvation and related illnesses. Another million fled to the United States and Canada —not all of them survived the ocean crossing. Have students work with a science teacher to explain the causes of the blight, based on the way that potatoes were cultivated.

Art   Work with the art teacher to give students the opportunity to study some of the most significant art work of western Europe. Remind students that the tremendous diversity in the art produced in this region reflects the diversity of cultural groups who live there. Students can start by looking at Bruce Cole and Adelheid Gealt's *The Art of the Western World* (Simon and Schuster, 1989) and the Public Broadcasting System television show of the same name.

SUPPLEMENTING
THE CORE CURRICULUM

The Student Edition provides material related to a unifying theme in Making Thematic Connections: A House Divided on pages 294 and 295. You may wish to invite students to pursue the following activities outside of class:

- Around 1500 B.C., the women of Minoan Crete had far greater rights than their contemporaries. For example, the dowry of a Minoan woman remained at her disposal and women occupied influential roles in society. Have students work with a social studies teacher to investigate the social, political, and economic rights of men and women in ancient Greece. Students can share their findings in the form of an oral report.

- The Nobel Prize for Literature is the most prestigious literary award a writer can win. Students may be interested in finding out whether any writers from Greece, France, Ireland, Italy, Germany, and Spain have won the Nobel Prize for Literature and if so, for which novels or poems. Challenge students to find out why the Russian writer Boris Pasternak declined the prize in 1958 and why French writer Jean Paul Sartre declined the prize in 1964.

- Many of Europe's most famous writers published some or all of their works under a pseudonym. Invite students to find the real names of these European writers: Maxim Gorky (Aleksei Peshkov), George Sand (Armandine Dupin), Stendhal (Marie Henri Beyle), and Voltaire (Francois Marie Arouet). See how many other pen names students can find.

INTRODUCING CHAPTER 7: THE LITERATURE OF WESTERN EUROPE

Using the Chapter Opener

On the board, write these terms from the Chapter Opener: *Renaissance, Enlightenment,* and *nationalism.* Ask students to give definitions and synonyms for these terms. Write their suggestions on the board to create a chart or web. As students respond, point out that all three terms are important to the development of the literary and cultural tradition in western Europe. Then share this quotation with students:

> Two cultures cannot exist on equal footing side by side. That is out of the question. Hellenic culture could not live under Roman influence. Roman culture disappeared. . . . The one in time must destroy the other.
>
> *Houston Stewart Chamberlain*

Divide the class in half to debate the issue that Chamberlain raises here. Guide half the class to argue that two cultures can exist side-by-side while the other half argues why they cannot. After the debate, have the class vote on the issue. Then explore with students what effect two or more equally powerful cultures existing at the same time might have on a region.

✔ Developing Concept Vocabulary

You can use a time line to help students explore the literary and cultural tradition of western Europe. Draw a line the full length of the chalkboard. Write "ancient Greece" on the left and "modern era" on the right. Divide the class into small groups and assign one major cultural, historical, or literary period to each. Possibilities include the Renaissance, Enlightenment, Nationalism, World War I, World War II, etc. Then have students fill in the cultural events of their assigned time period.

ASK:

- What were the most important achievements in art, music, and drama in your era?
- Why is your time period famous?
- Which people were best known at that time?

ancient Greece	Renaissance	Enlightenment	Nationalism	WWI	WWII	modern era
Alexander the Great	Dante's *Inferno*					
Athens, Sparta	Leonardo da Vinci					
democracy	Gutenberg printed *Bible*					
	Machiavelli's *The Prince*					

The Oath of Athenian Youth

Anonymous (pages 264–266)

OBJECTIVES

Literary

- to identify the purpose in writing an oath
- to recognize the message of an oath

Historical

- to describe elements of Athenian democracy
- to understand the roles of young Athenian men and women in their communities

Cultural

- to evaluate an oath in its cultural context
- to compare "The Pledge of Allegiance" with "The Oath of Athenian Youth"

SELECTION RESOURCES

Use Assessment Worksheet 39 to check students' vocabulary recognition, content comprehension, and appreciation of literary skills.

 Informal Assessment Opportunity

SELECTION OVERVIEW

In 500 B.C., ancient Greece consisted of tiny, scattered city-states. Because the mountainous countryside of Greece made travel difficult, the city-states remained isolated. The people's loyalty and civic pride was not to the Greek nation, but to their particular city-state. Athens was one of the first city-states to develop a democratic government. By 462 B.C., it was a direct democracy, with all citizens participating in government directly. Every year about a fifth of the adult male citizens of Athens were selected by lottery as judges, public officials, and council members. When not serving as an official, a citizen took part in the assembly—the body which changed laws, raised taxes, and decided whether to go to war. A citizen's participation in politics was considered to be as important as taking care of his own business or farm. The concept of individual responsibility in government later influenced the democracies of the United States and countries of the world.

This selection is the oath that young Athenian males took to pledge their commitment to bettering their community.

ENGAGING THE STUDENTS

Write the word *allegiance* on the board and discuss its meaning. Then lead the students in a recitation of "The Pledge of Allegiance." If necessary, post the words for students to follow:

"I pledge allegiance to the flag of the United States of America, and to the republic for which it stands, one nation, under God, indivisible, with liberty, and justice for all."

Discuss with students the meaning of the Pledge. Ask: What ideals are expressed in the Pledge? Do you think the ideals are important enough to merit your loyalty?

Suggest to students that they keep in mind "The Pledge of Allegiance" as they read this selection, "The Oath of Athenian Youth."

BRIDGING THE ESL/LEP LANGUAGE GAP

Read the oath aloud, stopping to discuss a few lines at a time. Tell students to consider the implications of this oath. Use questions like these to prompt class discussion:

- To what do the speakers pledge in the first sentence? (not to disgrace their community by any act of dishonesty or cowardice)
- To what do the speakers pledge in the second sentence? (to fight alone or with others to defend the ideals and sacred things of the community)
- What is the main pledge in the third sentence? (to keep a watchful eye on the people running the government)
- What is the last pledge of the youth? (to improve their community)

Next ask students whose first language is not English to recite the oath of allegiance of their country of origin if they know it or to bring in a copy. Students might like to provide the class with a written translation of their oath, which can be posted alongside copies of "The Oath of Athenian Youth" and "The Pledge of Allegiance."

☑ PRETEACHING
SELECTION VOCABULARY

Inform students that an oath is a pledge of action taken by an individual. Tell them that in the oath they are about to read, many actions are listed. Have students skim the selection to make a list of phrases describing the actions that are pledged. (Examples include: *never bring disgrace; never engage in any act of dishonesty or cowardice; fight for ideals and sacred things;* **revere** *and obey the community's laws;* **incite** *reverence and respect in community leaders so they will not try to* **annul** *the laws or to set them at* **naught***; improve the public's sense of* **civic duty***;* and *to work to improve their community*) Direct students to use a dictionary to find the definitions of any words they don't know. Pairs of students can then teach each other these vocabulary words.

The words printed in boldfaced type are tested on the selection assessment worksheet.

PREREADING

Reading the Selection in a Cultural Context

Help students read for purpose by asking them why someone might take an oath to his or her town, city, community, or country. Discuss ways an oath can set priorities, especially for young people. Ask: What loyalty or pride do you feel toward your community, neighborhood, town, or city? What is it about this place that brings out these feelings? Would taking a similar oath work today, or was it only effective 2,400 years ago?

Focusing on the Selection

Have students work in groups of three to consider the following questions and to give examples to support their responses: How are the priorities in this oath organized? Are individual rights given more or less importance than those of the community? Would an oath like this be possible today? Why or why not? Call on groups to summarize their responses aloud.

POSTREADING

The following activities parallel features with the same titles in the Student Edition.

Responses to Critical Thinking Questions

Possible responses are:

1. The writer shows his respect for his country by asking the youth to promise not to disgrace the country and to defend it. The writer reveals his love and reverence for his country by promising to transmit a greater, better, and more beautiful community to the next generation.

2. The oath reflects a society in which all citizens work together for the greater good of the community. The oath includes a responsibility of citizens to act as "watchdogs" over those in authority in case they do not have respect and reverence for the community's laws.

3. Responses will reflect students' own cultural backgrounds and experiences.

☑ Guidelines for Writing Your Response to "The Oath of Athenian Youth"

Have students share their journal entries with a partner. As an alternative writing activity, ask students to work in small groups to write oaths of their own. Explain that an oath is a solemn promise made by an individual to another person, a group of people, or a community. The oath that someone takes reveals what that person's priorities are. What would they set as the priorities in their oath? Which actions would they swear to take or not to take? Allow time for students to share their original oaths with the class, or display some of the more creative efforts alongside "The Pledge of Allegiance."

Guidelines for Going Back Into the Text: Author's Craft

An oath is generally written in the first person. The author's purpose in writing "The Oath of Athenian Youth" was to allow the young men to establish their values or priorities and to make a pledge to take actions that would preserve the society of Athens. Using the first person helps the author achieve this purpose.

Possible answers to the questions in the Student Edition are:

1. To ensure that young men will grow to be good citizens.

2. They promised to fight for the ideals of the community, to revere and obey the community's laws,

and to improve the public's sense of civic duty. They promised not to bring disgrace to their community and not to be dishonest or cowardly.

3. Responses will reflect students' own points of view. Accept all reasonable answers. Students should note that the purpose of the oath was to persuade Athenian youths to accept and uphold the ideals and laws of Athens.

☑ FOLLOW-UP DISCUSSION

Use the questions that follow to continue your discussion of "The Oath of Athenian Youth." Possible answers are given in parentheses.

Recalling

1. Who took this pledge? (19-year-old males who were citizens of ancient Athens)

2. Which ideals did they swear to defend? (the ideals of the community)

3. What did they promise to revere and obey? (the community's laws)

Interpreting

4. Who could not take the oath? (women of Athens, male slaves, and foreigners)

5. According to the oath, how would youths be able to create a better community than the one passed on to them? (by never disgracing the community with an act of dishonesty or cowardice; by fighting for the ideals and sacred things of the community; by revering and obeying the community's laws; and by encouraging reverence in the community's leaders)

6. Why might the youth of Athens have been expected to improve the public's sense of civic duty? (The democratic ideal was a group effort. People weren't just responsible for themselves; instead, they had an obligation to ensure that others worked toward the common goals.)

Applying

7. In what ways was the Athenian democracy not ideal? (Slavery still existed. Women were considered to be inferior, and girls did not get the same education as boys.)

8. How is democracy in the United States similar to and different from democracy in ancient Athens? (Differences: Slavery no longer exists in the U.S.; young girls get an equal education as boys; foreigners can become citizens; the U.S. has a representative government, not a direct democracy; loyalty is usually to the country, as well as to individual states. Similarities: citizens in the U.S. aspire to similar priorities of fighting for our ideals, being honest and brave, obeying the laws, watching carefully what our lawmakers do, and hoping to leave our children a better country.)

ENRICHMENT

Students may benefit from viewing *Athenian Democracy* available from Encyclopaedia Britannica Educational Corporation, 310 South Michigan Avenue, Chicago, IL 60604, (800) 554-9862.

The Nightingale's Three Bits of Advice

by Henri Pourrat (pages 267–270)

OBJECTIVES

Literary

- to trace the sequence of events in a folktale
- to identify and analyze the story's moral or lesson

Historical

- to describe the history of French folktales
- to recognize universal themes in French folktales that have endured through time

Cultural

- to recognize important values in French culture
- to analyze how the moral is universal, applicable to all people in all times and places
- to compare the moral of a French folktale to those of other cultures

SELECTION RESOURCES

Use Assessment Worksheet 40 to check students' vocabulary recognition, content comprehension, and appreciation of literary skills.

✔ Informal Assessment Opportunity

SELECTION OVERVIEW

Folklore is a term that applies to stories, songs, and poems that have been handed down from generation to generation through the **oral tradition**, by word of mouth. Since folklore was originally spoken rather than written, stories may undergo intriguing changes as each storyteller adds his or her unique twist. As a result, the same story may be subtly different in various cultures—or even in the same culture! Therefore, there are many different versions of each work, and the original writers and tellers are no longer known. In most cases, a specific story is written down only after it has been told for many, many years.

Some of the most common types of folklore include folktales, fairy tales, legends, tall tales, myths, fables, and trickster tales. "The Nightingale's Three Bits of Advice" is a classic example of a folktale. Many folktales such as this one are amusing stories that were first told to entertain people; often, they make fun of a human weakness. Most folktales contain a **moral**, a lesson about right and wrong. Sometimes, the moral in a folktale will be stated directly. Other times, readers have to infer the moral from the plot, characters, and setting. Folktales entertain people, preserve the past, and teach important lessons about behavior and attitudes.

In this folktale, a villager disregards a nightengale's advice and proves himself a fool.

ENGAGING THE STUDENTS

Have students freewrite on the following topic: "Imagine that you have captured a nightingale that can speak. It's plain to you that the bird has other magical powers as well. Would you let the bird go free? Why or why not?" Allow students five minutes to write their response, then call on volunteers to read their answers to the class. Invite students to share their reasons for keeping the bird or setting it free.

BRIDGING THE ESL/LEP LANGUAGE GAP

This story is about a man who is tricked by a magical bird. While the plot is straightforward and easy to understand, the translation contains a number of idiomatic expressions that might puzzle ESL/LEP students. First, explain that every language contains expressions, called **idioms**, that do not make literal sense. Describe how these expressions have to be taken as a whole, not word-for-word. Share and explain these idioms: "It's raining cats and dogs" (it's raining very hard) and "to catch one's eye" (to get one's attention). Then explain these idioms from the story:

idiom	meaning
the dead of the year	winter
get them into your head	understand
listened with his mouth agape	be surprised
the villager was beside himself	very angry

Ask students who speak other languages to volunteer some common idioms from their cultures, and to translate and explain them as needed. Have native English speakers also contribute some common idioms used in the United States.

✔ PRETEACHING SELECTION VOCABULARY

Explain to students that the author uses vivid words to make the action come to life for readers. Suggest that students skim the story to find words that helped them get a clear mental picture of the people, places, and action in the story. Possibilities include: ***stifle, defy, agape,*** *perch, flicks, crabapple, enormous, strangled,* ***stove-in, fluttered,*** *clogs.* Then have students sort the words according to their part of speech: noun, adjective/adverb, and verb. Students can exchange papers to check whether they correctly identified how the word is used in the story.

The words printed in boldfaced type are tested on the selection assessment worksheet.

PREREADING

Reading the Story in a Cultural Context

Help students read for purpose by asking them to see what elements of the story might explain its lasting appeal. Guide students by using these questions:

In what ways are the characters in this story memorable?

What effect might the values depicted in the story have on readers?

Why might the story's message stay with readers?

Focusing on the Selection

When students finish reading, have them select a partner. Have one student in each pair imagine that he or she is the nightingale and the other imagine that he or she is the villager. Direct each student to write a personality profile of his or her character. Tell students that the profile must contain psychological as well as physical characteristics. Afterwards, have partners

work together to summarize the differences between the two characters. When they have finished, have volunteers tell the class which character they would rather be and why.

POSTREADING

The following activities parallel the features with the same titles in the Student Edition.

Responses to Critical Thinking Questions

Possible responses are:

1. Readers can infer that Henri Pourrat believes that people are foolish if they try to reach for something that is beyond their grasp, if they cry over what they've hopelessly lost, and if they believe in fantasy.

2. The story illustrates that humans can be foolish, gullible, greedy, and ashamed. The nightingale is wise and full of cunning.

3. Responses will reflect students' own experiences. Reassure students that they do not have to reveal personal examples if they do not wish to do so.

✔ Guidelines for Writing Your Response to "The Nightingale's Three Bits of Advice"

Have students share their journal entries with a partner. As an alternate writing activity, students can work in small groups to write a folktale of their own that teaches a similar lesson.

✔ Guidelines for Going Back Into the Text: Author's Craft

Encourage students to generate other words that signal sequential order. Remind students that they can use these transitional words in their own writing.

1. The first event in the story is the villager setting out to catch small birds. He catches a nightingale.

2. The author uses the numbers **one, two,** and **three** to signal each piece of advice the nightingale gives the villager. These numbers also indicate the order in which the rest of the events in the story will occur.

3. The last event in the story is the nightingale fluttering up to the tree, leaving the villager with the knowledge that he has been a fool.

☑ FOLLOW-UP DISCUSSION

Use the questions that follow to continue your discussion of "The Nightingale's Three Bits of Advice." Possible answers are given in parentheses.

Recalling

1. Why doesn't the villager kill the nightingale? (The nightingale tricks the villager into sparing his life by promising the man three pieces of valuable advice.)

2. What three pieces of advice does the nightingale give the villager? (One, don't go after what's beyond your reach. Two, don't cry over what is hopelessly lost. Three, don't accept things that should logically defy belief.)

3. How does the villager try to trick the nightingale into coming back to him? (The villager promises the nightingale great honor, a home filled with all that birds love, and a special present of extraordinary value.)

Interpreting

4. In the first paragraph, the author writes that the villager was "lucky" because he managed to catch a nightingale. How is this statement ironic? (The villager is not lucky because the nightingale tricks him and makes the villager realize what a fool he is.)

5. How does the villager react when he learns about the huge pearl? What does this reaction reveal about him? (Possible responses: The villager gets very angy that he has freed the bird and thereby lost the huge pearl. This reaction proves that the villager is very greedy and lets his greed get the best of him.)

6. How can you tell that the villager understands the nightingale's lesson? (The villager feels "thoroughly ashamed" of himself at the end of the story. This shows that he has understood the lesson.)

Applying

7. What do you think the villager learns about himself from this experience? (Possible responses: He learns that he is greedy and gullible. He learns that he should think before he acts. He learns that he should heed good advice.)

8. Do you agree with the nightingale's advice to the man? Why or why not? (Answers will vary. Some students might disagree with the advice suggesting that people shouldn't limit themselves to only easily reachable goals. Others might agree with the advice and say that it is foolish to believe in things that do not make sense.)

ENRICHMENT

Students may enjoy viewing *Cultural Diversity*. In this video, teens of different backgrounds discuss their attitudes toward cultural differences—and much more. A Study Guide and blackline masters are included. The video is available from Media Basics Video, Lighthouse Square, Guilford, CT 06437, (800) 542-2505.

Paying on the Nail
by Padraic O'Farrell (pages 271–274)

OBJECTIVES

Literary

- to identify the author's attitude towards honesty
- to describe elements of a trickster folktale

Historical

- to understand the role of farming in Irish history and economics
- to understand the role of trading in Irish history and economics

Cultural

- to evaluate the function of folktales in Irish culture
- to evaluate the role of the marketplace in Irish culture

SELECTION RESOURCES

Use Assessment Worksheet 41 to check students' vocabulary recognition, content comprehension, and appreciation of literary skills.

 Informal Assessment Opportunity

SELECTION OVERVIEW

Historically, farming and trading have been two important interrelated components of the Irish economy. More than two-thirds of Ireland is farmland. Irish farmers raise some of the world's finest cattle and horses. Trading is a vital industry, both for imports and exports. Farms provide many products for export trade, including meats and dairy products. Other goods that Ireland exports include chemicals, computers, machinery, and textiles. In Ireland, as the selection illustrates, trading permeates much of the daily commerce and life of its citizens.

In this selection, the central character, Shynail, is a trickster trader who uses the marketplace as the setting for his business schemes.

ENGAGING THE STUDENTS

Write on the chalkboard the word *tricks*. Under the word, create a two-column grid with the headings "Help" and "Hurt." Use the words on the board to lead a class discussion on how tricks can be used for good or for bad. Ask students to recall a time in their lives when trickery was *helpful* (e.g., to trick a friend to come to his/her own surprise party), or *hurtful* (e.g., tricking friends into believing that people liked them when they really didn't). Have students answer questions like these:

- What trick did you play or was played on you?
- What were the consequences?
- Was the trick helpful or hurtful?

BRIDGING THE ESL/LEP LANGUAGE GAP

Have students in work in pairs. Match English proficient and ESL/LEP students whenever possible. Have students make a list of unfamiliar words in the selection on slips of paper. Next, have students write the meanings of the words on the other side of the slips. Collect all the slips of paper and place them in a bag that you can label "Bag of Tricks" (or create your own title). As the bag is passed around the class, have students take out a slip of paper and either describe, act out verbally, or pantomime how the word relates to the characters or setting of the story. For example, for a *blacksmith*, a student might pantomime a blacksmith working while saying, "Welcome to Mr. Shynail's blacksmith shop. How may I help you?"

✔ PRETEACHING SELECTION VOCABULARY

Guide pairs of students to make a two-column grid with the headings "Before" and "After" on a sheet of paper. In the "Before" column, they are to write at least five words that describe Shynail's character as a trickster, such as *crooked, cheating, dishonest* and ***rogue***. In the "After" column, have students come up with at least five new words from the selection that describe Shynail after he starts his blacksmith's business, such as *trusting, straight, praise*, and *favourably*.

The word printed in boldfaced type are tested on the selection assessment worksheet.

PREREADING

Reading the Story in a Cultural Context

Help students read for purpose by creating an oral folktale. Divide the class into small groups. Hold up a common classroom object, such as an eraser, piece of chalk, or waste basket. Present the groups with this task: Each group will represent a different marketplace with you as its vendors selling a common classroom object. As part of your sales pitch, make up a tale about the object's origin and use.

After the folktales have been told, lead a brief discussion about the similarities and differences among them.

Focusing on the Selection

Turn the classroom into a courtroom. ON TRIAL: SHYNAIL—GUILTY OR INNOCENT OF TRICKERY? Ask volunteers to play such roles as judge, jury members, defense and prosecuting attorneys, and witnesses who have been duped by Shynail. To begin, recreate a short scene from the selection showing one of Shynail's business ventures. Make sure that this enactment is nonjudgmental, leaving room for individual interpretations of the scene. Then, have students enact the trial. To help the trial move along, you might play the role of the judge.

POSTREADING

The following activities parallel the features with the same titles in the Student Edition.

Responses to Critical Thinking Questions

Possible responses are:

1. The folktale reveals that, until forced to do otherwise, Shynail uses his cleverness to his own advantage and at the expense of others.

2. Trading was done in a specially designated market area defined by crosses where people could expect honest dealing.

3. Responses will vary, but may include: People can attain wealth by offering a service that improves the lives of others; a negative reputation can be rescued if the dishonest person changes his or her ways; taking advantage of circumstances rather than people can be surprisingly profitable.

☑ Guidelines for Writing Your Response to "Paying on the Nail"

Have students share their journal entries with a partner. As an alternative writing activity, have students work in small groups to summarize their favorite scenes or ideas from the selection. Then have each student write an answer to this question: Do you think Shynail's blacksmith business will be honest? Why or why not? Encourage students to volunteer their responses.

☑ Guidelines for Going Back Into the Text: Author's Craft

Discuss with students how they feel about Shynail's character. Is he a moral person, immoral, amoral, or a combination of all three? Ask students to offer reasons for their responses.

Possible answers to the questions in the Student Edition are:

1. Shynail has a well-deserved reputation of being a dishonest trader. Because he's an extremely clever person, he figures out a scheme in which being honest can make him a lot of money in the long run.

2. Some students will respond that he did because he got richer than he was when he had been dishonest. Others may think that he didn't because now he will have to work harder to earn his money.

3. Responses will reflect students' own creativity.

☑ FOLLOW-UP DISCUSSION

Use the questions that follow to continue your discussion of "Paying on the Nail." Possible answers are given in parentheses.

Recalling

1. What is another name for market crosses? (nails)

2. Where do Shynail and the farmer go at the end of their journey? (to an inn)

3. What kind of trickery does Shynail use to fool the farmers? (a sleight-of-hand technique where he counts out less money than he owes)

Interpreting

4. Why do you think Shynail avoids fairs where there are marketplaces? (He is superstitious about the symbolic religious cross and fears cheating others in this environment.)

5. Why do you think the central character's name is Shynail? (He avoids or shies away from market crosses, which are also called nails.)

6. Why do you think Shynail is honest with the farmer instead of tricking him? (Shynail believes he can make even more money through his temporary honesty.)

Applying

7. Do you feel businesses today practice honest dealings? Why or why not? (Responses will vary. Encourage students to draw from their personal experiences, from articles they've read, or from films and TV programs.)

8. How do you feel society should deal with businesses that are dishonest? (Responses will vary. Ask students to provide specific examples to support their opinions.)

ENRICHMENT

Students may enjoy viewing the video *Discovering Ireland,* available from Zenger Media, 10200 Jefferson Boulevard, Room 922, P.O. Box 802, Culver City, CA 90232, (800) 421-4246.

Death Seed
by Ricarda Huch

Woman, You Are Afraid
by Maria Wine

from *My Mother's House*
by Leah Goldberg, translated from Hebrew by Robert Alter (pages 275–278)

OBJECTIVES

Literary
- to recognize types of conflict expressed in poetry
- to understand how sensory imagery contributes to tone in poetry

Historical
- to understand the obstacles that European women writers faced
- to recognize the voice of European women writers in the 1900s

Cultural
- to explore the possibility of a distinct female voice in poetry
- to recognize universal themes that exist across all cultures

SELECTION RESOURCES

Use Assessment Worksheet 42 to check students' vocabulary recognition, content comprehension, and appreciation of literary skills.

 Informal Assessment Opportunity

SELECTION OVERVIEW

Throughout history, women have had a lower status than their male counterparts and have been limited to learning practical skills such as cooking, sewing, and weaving. With increased trade sweeping across Europe between 1500 and 1800, many cottage industries developed, enabling women to become successful business owners. Some worked outside the home brewing liquor, tailoring clothes, manufacturing silk, or working as spinners. During the late 1700s, women's voices began to be heard, the most passionate being the English feminist, Mary Wollstonecraft, whose work attacked the inferior status of women. The role of women changed dramatically again during the Industrial Revolution, beginning in the 1800s, when many women were hired to work in factories and mines. During these years, the negative attitude toward women writers resulted in women such as George Eliot, the Brontës, and George Sand adopting male pseudonyms. The word *poet* had always had a masculine connotation; women's poetry was expected to be sentimental and romantic.

The three poems that follow were all written by women, who explore the universal themes of the paradox of life and death, the search for identity, and the search for our ancestoral roots.

ENGAGING THE STUDENTS

Engage students in a discussion about gender. Ask: Is there a woman's voice in literature? Are there subjects that are typically explored by women writers? Lead a discussion with students of the possibility of a female voice in literature, especially poetry. Tell students that the three poems they will read are all by European women who wrote during the early 1900s. As students read, have them consider whether they hear a "female voice" in each poem, or if they think the poems could have been written by men. Ask them to identify the elements they consider to be "female" and those that they consider to be "male" or "gender neutral." Encourage them to explain their responses.

BRIDGING THE ESL/LEP LANGUAGE GAP

Students may gain benefit from hearing the three poems read aloud. Then have LEP students work with a partner to read the poems again and explain difficult phrases such as the following:

women as forests, dark and defenseless; a man as death, sowing seeds in a field of grain; a mirror sunk in its silver frame is like a lake hiding treasures/underwater; grandmother dying in the spring of her days.

Pairs may exchange ideas about the imagery in each poem. Have them identify the imagery as strong or weak. Then have partners consider the feelings each poet is expressing through the images in her poem.

✔ PRETEACHING SELECTION VOCABULARY

List each word printed in boldfaced type on the chalkboard as you introduce vocabulary words to students. Tell them that in one poem the poet faces the fear inside herself—the fear that is inside all women. The second poem they will read is about a *reaper* with a *stern* face who *sows* the fields of grain with seeds. The last poem is about a young woman. After her grandfather died, all portraits of her grandmother had been *expunged*, or removed, from view. Although she does not *resemble*, or look like, her grandmother, she sees the grandmother's young image through a mirror— and in this way, she discovers her own beauty.

The words printed in boldfaced type are tested on the selection assessment worksheet.

PREREADING

Reading the Poems in a Cultural Context

Help students to read for purpose by suggesting they enter the world of the poet and ask themselves: How did I feel when I read the poem? What does it tell me about the world of the poet? What does it say about the poet's experiences and views of the world? What is the poet's attitude toward life and death? Tell students to consider these questions as they read.

Focusing on the Selection

Remind students that conflict is a part of everyday life. Ask students to consider in what ways conflicts in their lives have helped them to become stronger and wiser. Ask: "Do you think the conflicts in these poems leave the poet stronger and wiser?"

Copy the following chart on the chalkboard, leaving the columns under "Type of Conflict" and "Resolution" blank:

Poem	Type of Conflict	Resolution
Death Seed	internal/between narrator and death	acceptance of the life/death cycle
Woman, You Are Afraid	internal/between narrator and fear	realization of internal fears
from **My Mother's House**	internal/between narrator and memory of her ancestors	acceptance of her heritage and beauty

Divide students into groups of three, and have them complete the chart as they read the poems. (Suggested student responses are given above.) Students can then discuss their responses in their small groups or bring their reactions to a full class discussion.

POSTREADING

The following activities parallel the features with the same titles in the Student Edition.

Responses to Critical Thinking Questions

Possible responses are:

1. Wine: terror, self-realization; Huch: wonder, confusion, acceptance; Goldberg: separateness, being connected, self-acceptance

2. Responses will vary, but may include: Wine learned to overcome her fears; Huch was faced with a death in the family or her own death and came to accept it; and Goldberg was perhaps searching for her heritage.

3. Responses will reflect students' own cultural backgrounds and experiences. Guide the discussion so that students recognize that the subjects of these poems — acknowledging fear, facing death, and searching for our roots—are universal themes that exist across cultures.

✔ Guidelines for Writing Your Response to the Poems

Have students share their journal entries with a partner. As an alternative writing activity, ask students to select one of the poems and write a brief summary of it. Tell students to include in their summaries the conflict in the poem, the imagery that reveals how the poet feels about the subject, and the mood or tone of the poem. Next, have students who have written about the same poem exchange responses with one another. Ask students to collaborate on a single summary.

✔ Guidelines for Going Back Into the Text: Author's Craft

Discuss with students how the poets use imagery to express feelings and to create a tone or attitude toward the subject. (Students may suggest the following responses: Wine uses a simile to compare a woman to a forest, creates a mysterious tone, and is somewhat confessional; Huch uses a reaper to symbolize death, creates religious and personal tone, and reveals a paradox of life; Goldberg compares a mirror to a lake hiding treasures, creates a celebratory tone, and is inspirational.)

Possible answers to the questions in the Student Edition are:

1. "Woman, You Are Afraid": a forest, darkness, an animal, possibly a deer; "Death Seed": grain, a reaper sowing seeds, his stern face; *My Mother's House*: portrait in her grandfather's heart, a mirror sunk in its silver frame, a lake hiding treasures under water

2. Imagery contains multiple layers of emotion that readers grasp as they visualize and interpret the poem. Both the images and the emotions help the reader figure out the tone and the poet's purpose for writing.

3. Responses will reflect students' personal views.

✔ FOLLOW-UP DISCUSSION

Use the questions that follow to continue your discussion of the poems. Possible answers are given in parentheses.

Recalling

1. Who is the woman afraid of, according to Maria Wine? (herself)

2. Whom does the speaker in Huch's poem meet in the field of grain? (The Grim Reaper)

3. What does the speaker in Goldberg's poem discover in the mirror? (that her grandmother was very beautiful; that she shares her grandmother's inner beauty)

Interpreting

4. In Goldberg's poem, the speaker does not really see her grandmother in the mirror. What does she really see? (She sees herself as a descendant and inheritor of the grandmother's beauty.)

5. According to Maria Wine, why does the woman look like a defenseless creature? (She is afraid of her complex nature.)

6. Which words give "Death Seed" a religious tone? (blessed, Behold)

Applying

7. What do you think the title of Huch's poem, "Death Seed," suggests? (Students may respond that it suggests a paradox of the life/death cycle.)

8. What do you think the speaker in Goldberg's poem is searching for as she looks into the mirror? (a connection to her past, her roots)

ENRICHMENT

Students may benefit from exploring *Women in Literature.* The CD-ROM is available from National School Products, 101 East Broadway, Maryville, TN 37804-2498, (800) 51-9124

from *Survival in Auschwitz*

by **Primo Levi**   (pages 279–286)

OBJECTIVES

Literary

- to analyze the techniques of fiction used in a personal narrative
- to discuss the conflicts the author recounts

Historical

- to understand the Nazis' attempt to exterminate Europe's Jews during the Holocaust
- to understand how Adolf Hitler influenced other political leaders during the 1930s and 1940s

Cultural

- to explore cultural biases that led to the Holocaust
- to describe life in a Nazi concentration camp

SELECTION RESOURCES

Use Assessment Worksheet 43 to check students' vocabulary recognition, content comprehension, and appreciation of literary skills.

✔ Informal Assessment Opportunity

SELECTION OVERVIEW

Originally, the term *holocaust* referred to a religious rite in which an offering was consumed by fire. Today the term refers to any widespread destruction of life. When written as the *Holocaust*, however, it refers to the almost complete extermination of European Jews by Nazi Germany during World War II.

By September of 1941, the Jews of Europe had been forced into ghettos and marked by a yellow Star of David. That same year, the Nazis had set into motion the "final solution to the Jewish question": complete extermination of the Jewish people. Camps such as Auschwitz, Belzec, Treblinka, and Sobibor were equipped with facilities for gassing people. Auschwitz, in Poland, was the largest death camp. Unlike the others, it used quick-working hydrogen cyanide for the gassings. Although only Jews and Gypsies were killed with gas in that death camp, hundreds of thousands of other Auschwitz prisoners died from disease, starvation, or shootings. To erase the evidence of their actions, the Nazis built large crematories to incinerate the bodies.

When World War II ended, about three million Jews had died in the death camps, about a million and a half had been the victims of execution, and the rest had been killed in ghettos. After the Holocaust, the Allies established Palestine as a permanent haven for the survivors. On May 14, 1948, the Jewish community of Palestine declared its independence as the State of Israel.

In this selection Primo Levi, a well-known Jewish Italian chemist, recounts his first days in the labor camp at Auschwitz.

ENGAGING THE STUDENTS

Show students pictures of concentration camp victims or photographs of those who were liberated from the camps at the end of World War II. Describe how the Nazis systematically killed six million Jews during World War II. You may also wish to explain that even though many European Jews felt they had assimilated into gentile society, anti-Semitism was a constant fear among European Jews. Anti-Semitic groups had long harassed and vilified Jews through brutal raids called *pogroms*. Ask students: What can people do to make sure that what happened to the Jewish people at the hands of the Nazis never happens again? Write students' responses on the board, focusing on the issue of education and truth. Explain that in this selection, they will read a first-hand account of how the Jews were treated when they arrived at concentration camps.

BRIDGING THE ESL/LEP LANGUAGE GAP

The brutal realities of the Holocaust will be new to some students. The raw emotion in the essay could make this selection challenging.

Before they read the excerpt, ask students what they know about the Holocaust. Present the Prereading material in the Student Edition and the information in the Selection Overview in the Teacher's Edition to enrich their knowledge. Then read the first two paragraphs of the selection aloud. Explain the use of the British term "lorry." Be sure the students understand the details of the setting for the story.

✔ PRETEACHING SELECTION VOCABULARY

Do a webbing exercise with students using words in the selection that relate to pain and fear. First, direct students to skim the selection and write down at least five words that show terror and pain. Examples include *writhe, livid, phantoms, disconcerted, demolition*. Use the following prompts to help students analyze their webs:

- Which of your words refer to physical pain?
- Which of your words show the mood or feeling of the death camps?
- Why might the author use these words in an essay about the Holocaust?

The words printed in boldfaced type are tested on the selection assessment worksheet.

PREREADING

Reading the Autobiography in a Cultural Context

Help students read for purpose by asking them to think about why the author wrote this essay. Discuss with students how writing this personal narrative had to be extremely painful for Primo Levi. As students read, have them consider what purpose first-hand accounts of the Holocaust serve.

Focusing on the Selection

Have students do a quick freewrite on the following question: What do you learn about people from the conflicts Primo Levi describes in this selection? Tell students to consider external conflicts (between peo-

ple) as well as internal conflicts (within a person) as they write. Direct them to watch for these conflicts and to analyze their effects as they read the selection.

POSTREADING

The following activities parallel the features with the same titles in the Student Edition.

Responses to Critical Thinking Questions

Possible responses are:

1. Responses will vary but may include that Levi wished to share with the world the horrors he and others endured to prevent another Holocaust from happening again.

2. Levi tells readers that the prisoners were dehumanized. The Germans stripped them of their identities, personal belongings, clothing, hair, and even their names.

3. Responses will reflect students' own cultural backgrounds and personal values.

✔ Guidelines for Writing Your Response to *Survival in Auschwitz*

Have students share their journal entries with a partner. As an alternate activity, students can work in small groups to explain their reactions to the selection. You may wish to write the following questions on the board to spark discussion:

- What were the first words that came to mind after you finished reading this selection?
- How did you feel about the prisoners? How did you feel about the way they were treated?
- How would you feel if you were stripped of your name?

✔ Guidelines for Going Back Into the Text: Author's Craft

Lead a discussion about why Levi chose to write a personal narrative to describe this experience. Ask: How might have a fictional story or poem on the same subject been less difficult to write? Would these have been as effective? Why or why not? Guide students to recognize that these other genres often allow a writer—and a reader—to separate himself or herself from painful events. By writing this personal account, Levi brings the horrors of the Holocaust directly to the readers to make the strongest impact possible.

1. He describes the physical setting, what the prisoners were made to do, the tattoos they were given, and the conditions in the camp.

2. Levi learns that when a person is deprived of everything that contributes to his identity, he loses his sense of self and feels less than human.

3. The historian could compare this narrative with other factual accounts of concentration camps during the war. He or she could also read newspaper reports and books by historians. Another possibility is to interview other survivors.

✔ FOLLOW-UP DISCUSSION

Use the questions that follow to continue your discussion of *Survival in Auschwitz*. Possible answers are given in parentheses.

Recalling

1. In the beginning of the selection, what makes the concentration camp seem like hell to Levi? (He is tortured by thirst, but cannot drink the contaminated water; he is exhausted, but cannot sit down; he must wait for something to happen and yet nothing happens for a long while.)

2. What happens during the "second act" of the author's imprisonment? (Unidentified men come in and shave the new prisoners, but their questions still go unanswered. They are left alone in a shower room, which causes them to rationalize that they won't be killed yet.)

3. How is Levi affected by having a number tattooed on his arm? (He regards it as the real, true initiation to the camp, the ultimate reminder that he is not free.)

Interpreting

4. Why do you think the Nazis have a tap that offers only undrinkable water? (It is a form of torture designed to break down the prisoners.)

5. What is ironic about the incident with the prisoners' shoes? (It is ironic that the prisoners remove their shoes and are told to pay special attention that they are not stolen, yet all the shoes are swept away in a heap outside the door.)

6. How can you tell that Levi is suspicious of the Nazis? (He says that he "does not swallow the bait" offered by the few people who speak to the prisoners. He sees the possibility of getting a shower as a game to mock and sneer at the group. Levi believes that they will all be killed very soon.)

Applying

7. What do you think Primo Levi learned about himself and other people from this experience? (Possible responses: He learned that he is tough, intelligent, and determined to live. He learned that some people are capable of unbelievable cruelty.)

8. Do you think a situation similar to the Holocaust could occur today? What do you think people should do to prevent it? (Answers will vary. Accept all reasonable responses)

ENRICHMENT

Students can benefit from viewing *Holocaust*. This award-winning docudrama, starring Meryl Streep and James Woods, tells the story of the Holocaust from the viewpoints of two German families who struggle to survive events that are out of their control. The video is available from Media Basics Video, Lighthouse Square, Guilford, CT 06437, (800) 542-2505.

Action Will Be Taken
by Heinrich Böll   (pages 287–293)

OBJECTIVES

Literary

- to recognize the use of irony in a story
- to identify the author's attitudes toward work and bureaucracy

Historical

- to understand the effect World War II had on German industry and economics
- to understand the nature of bureaucracy in post–World War II German industry

Cultural

- to recognize the contrasts between individual and social morality in post–World War II Germany
- to recognize the universality of bureaucratic structures in the developed world

SELECTION RESOURCES

Use Assessment Worksheet 44 to check students' vocabulary recognition, content comprehension, and appreciation of literary skills.

 Informal Assessment Opportunity

SELECTION OVERVIEW

After Germany was defeated in World War II, the country was left in a state of economic depression. East Germany was controlled by the Soviet Union (now Russia), and West Germany was under the control of the United States and England. West Germany was faced with the task of rebuilding its industry, which had been virtually destroyed by the Allied Powers. Faced with the difficult decision to rebuild its former enemy, the Allies chose to help West Germany recover because a strong functioning country would contribute to the general prosperity of Western Europe. The result was such an enormous economic boom that it has been referred to as the "German Miracle." By 1949, West Germany reached its prewar levels of production, and by 1958 West Germany was the leading industrial nation in Western Europe. In East Germany, economic recovery was delayed because Russia had dismantled numerous factories and demanded huge economic reparations.

In this humorous story, Heinrich Böll shows how the bureaucracy of German industry actually hindered productivity.

ENGAGING THE STUDENTS

On the board write this quote: "Action to be effective must be directed to clearly conceived ends."

Explain to students that this quotation is by Jawaharlal Nehru, an Indian statesman. Conduct a discussion on the nature of action. Ask: What is action? What is inaction? Guide students to give positive and negative examples of action and inaction, such as, "My mom always tells me to clean up my room, but I have other things, too." Call on volunteers to act out a short scene involving action or inaction. Ask: Did the main action lead to a positive or negative conclusion? Why?

BRIDGING THE ESL/LEP LANGUAGE GAP

After students have read the story, guide them to work in small groups to create drawings that illustrate one of the following workplace settings in the selection:

- the lunchroom
- the narrator's office
- Broschek's office

167

To reinforce vocabulary, have students label each drawing with at least 5–10 words from the story. Words can include *office decor, equipment,* and *business personnel.* Encourage students to share their group drawings with classmates.

✔ PRETEACHING
SELECTION VOCABULARY

After students have read the story, have them create a vocabulary list using the following questions:

1. What are some words the narrator uses to depict his feelings when applying for the job? (e.g., *aversion, suspicious, fellow sufferers*)

2. What are some words the narrator uses to describe his feelings while working on the job? (e.g., *capacity, swarming, vigorous, energy, reluctantly*)

The word printed in boldfaced type is tested on the selection assessment worksheet.

PREREADING

Reading the Story in a Cultural Context

Help students to analyze how the author has conveyed the metaphor of the workplace in the story. Have them discuss how the way in which the character was treated symbolizes the modern rebuilding of postwar Germany. Example: Students should be able to point out that the story is an ironic exaggeration of real bureaucratic red tape, an emphasis on efficiency, and the creation of useless jobs.

Focusing on the Selection

Have students write a short, funny anecdote about a time in their lives when there was a contradiction between what was said and what was actually done. Provide an example to get them started, such as someone promising to do the dishes immediately, but being interrupted by several crises that actually cause the dishes to pile up higher and higher.

POSTREADING

The following activities parallel the features with the same titles in the Student Edition.

Responses to Critical Thinking Questions

Possible responses are:

1. Böll believes that people usually pretend to be busier than they actually are.

2. Böll may have once worked at a meaningless, bureaucratic job, or he may have been a customer frustrated with bureaucracy.

3. Responses will reflect students' own personal backgrounds. Their answers should be supported with specific examples.

✔ Guidelines for Writing Your Response to "Action Will Be Taken"

Have students share their journal entries with a partner. As an alternative activity, have pairs of students write and illustrate a comic strip that highlights the key events in the story.

✔ Guidelines for Going Back Into the Text: Author's Craft

Ask students to give examples of ironic situations from their own lives, from movies and TV shows they have seen, or from stories they have read.

Possible answers to the questions in the Student Edition are:

1. We never know what action is supposed to be taken, and nobody actually does anything except tell others to take action.

2. It is against his nature, which is to be pensive and generally lazy.

3. His job as a mourner requires him to be quite inactive. Also, he acquires the job as a result of being at the funeral of his action-oriented boss.

✔ FOLLOW-UP DISCUSSION

Use the questions that follow to continue your discussion of "Action Will Be Taken." Possible answers are given in parentheses.

Recalling

1. Where did the unemployment office send the narrator? (Wunsiedel's factory)

2. How many phones was the narrator eventually able to operate? (13)

3. What job did the narrator have for Wunsiedel's burial? (He carried artificial roses and walked behind Wunsiedel's coffin.)

Interpreting

4. Why do you think the employees have to say, "Action will be taken"? (They are programmed by

their boss. Their verbal responses cover up their inaction.)

5. How do you feel the narrator's job at the end of the story relates to his personality? (The job coincides with his pensiveness and inactivity.)

6. In your opinion, is it important to know what the factory produces? (Responses will vary, although most students will agree that the actual product is irrelevant, since the plot deals with management rather than workers.)

Applying

7. If you were independently wealthy, would you still continue to work for a living, stop entirely, or consider some other options? Why? (Responses will differ. Encourage students to be as specific as possible. Have them compare this hypothetical situation with the narrator's earlier views on work.)

8. How do you think our society would be affected if everyone shared the same philosophy as the narrator's? Why? (Responses will differ. Students may point out that driving energy and the feeling of being able to work to capacity would inprove the production of goods and the functioning of services. On the other hand, empty action and useless skills would probably be an economic disaster because nothing would get done.)

ENRICHMENT

Students may benefit from viewing the video, *Central Region,* from the European Geography Series, available from Social Studies School Service, 10200 Jefferson Boulevard, Room 12, Culver City, CA 90232, (800) 421-4246.

INTRODUCING THE THEME

Open the lesson by inviting students to list some of the ways that people can be different from each other. Give students sufficient time to list five specific ways, and then compile a class list on the board or on chart paper. The class list might look like this:

Differences

1. age
2. physical appearance
3. race
4. religion
5. cultural traditions

Then lead a discussion about what effect these differences have on the ways we interact with each other. You may wish to use the following discussion prompts to help students connect the list to the theme and their own experiences.

Discussion Prompts

- Why do you think some people find it hard to accept individual differences? (Possible responses: People tend to fear the unknown. Some people, removed from the familiar, may be anxious about losing control of a situation.)

- What conflicts might arise between people because of differences in such things as religion, customs, and race? (Possible responses: arguments, physical attacks, oppression, and even war)

- Based on its title and our discussion, what kinds of literature do you expect to read in this theme? (Possible responses: selections about conflicts that arise because of differences among people and about the ways people resolve their differences and achieve understanding)

BRIDGING THE ESL/LEP GAP

The references to countries, historical events, and ethnic groups in this theme might be challenging for many students. To help students with their pronunciation and comprehension, read "A House Divided" aloud as students follow along in their books.

After you read, present students with the following questions. Have them use an encyclopedia, almanac, or map to find answers.

1. What was Auschwitz? (a concentration camp built by the Nazis in Poland during World War II to kill Jewish people and other targeted groups)

2. Who were the Nazis? (the National Socialist German Worker Party, which seized control of Germany in 1933 under its leader, Adolph Hitler)

3. Who are Native Americans? (the first people to live in North America)

4. Where do the Maori people live? (New Zealand)

5. Where is Nigeria? (Africa)

COMPLETING THE ACTIVITY

Before students begin the activity, ask them to explain the meaning of the word *prejudice*. Have students record their definition of the term and encourage them to refer to it as they work through the activity. You may also wish to present specific historic examples of people who have struggled to overcome prejudice; for example, Dr. Martin Luther King, Jr., who promoted civil rights for African Americans through peaceful demonstrations and public speeches.

Allow groups sufficient time to choose and read their selections before they move on to complete the activity.

When each group has composed its letter and read it aloud, lead a class discussion on the effects of prejudice. Then ask students to suggest all the ways mentioned to fight it. Make a list of the suggestions and display it in the classroom.

The Return

by **Carmen Laforet** (pages 296–302)

OBJECTIVES

Literary

- to recognize the use, purpose, and effects of foreshadowing in a story
- to understand the use of the flashback technique in a story

Historical

- to understand the effects of war in Spain during the 1940s
- to describe the role of Catholic asylums in Spain during the 1940s

Cultural

- to appreciate the role of religion in Spanish life during the 1940s
- to understand the effects of war on the human spirit

SELECTION RESOURCES

Use Assessment Worksheet 45 to check students' vocabulary recognition, content comprehension, and appreciation of literary skills.

 Informal Assessment Opportunity

SELECTION OVERVIEW

General Francisco Franco (1892–1975) led a military revolt against the Popular Front government in Spain in 1936, which led to the Spanish Civil War. During this rebellion, Nazi Germany and Fascist Italy contributed troops, munitions, and airplanes to Franco's cause. The Loyalists, Franco's opposition in Spain, were joined by an International Brigade, which included volunteers from the United States. Despite protest by foreign powers and the Catholic Church, many Spanish nonmilitary sites were bombed by Germany. Pablo Picasso depicted these civilian deaths in his painting *Guernica.* The Spanish Civil War was long and bloody because German and Italian forces used Spain as a testing ground for newly expanded planes and weapons. Many innocent people suffered during these years. As reflected in the selection, the Catholic Church served as a refuge for many of those suffering from the casualties of war. During World War II, Franco was proclaimed *Caudrillo,* dictator of Spain. Free elections and most civil rights in Spain were abolished. During Franco's regime, the Catholic Church's powers were restored but limited.

In this story, an asylum run by the church helps the main character overcome some of the ravaging effects of war.

ENGAGING THE STUDENTS

Read aloud or write on the board the following quotation:

"The next world war will be fought with stones."

Explain that the quotation was expressed by Albert Einstein, Nobel Peace Prize winner. This famed physicist helped design the atomic bomb, which contributed to ending World War II. Help students respond to the quotation by having them answer the following questions: Is war ever justified to solve human problems? Why or why not? In this age of advancing technology, is there an increased danger of warfare? Why or why not?

BRIDGING THE ESL/LEP LANGUAGE GAP

While most students will understand the references to celebrating Christmas, they may have difficulty grasping the author's use of past/present frameworks to advance the plot and deepen the characterization of Julian. Have students work in groups of three and make a three-column chart with the headings "Past," "Present," and "Future." Explain to students that the story takes place in three time frames: (1) Present—

Christmas Eve in the asylum; (2) Past—Julian's flash-back to the events leading to his stay in the asylum; and (3) Future—his thoughts about returning home. Assign each group one of the time frames. After students have read the entire selection, help them focus on their particular time frame. Students are to write specific examples of the following: how the author uses the time frame to advance the plot; how she reveals the characters' outside actions and feelings; and how her attitude regarding war and its effects on families is reflected in this portion of the story.

☑ PRETEACHING
SELECTION VOCABULARY

On the center of the board, write *asylum* for a webbing exercise. Ask students to skim the selection for related words and phrases, such as *institution* and *refuge* of *salvation*. Write their responses on the board. Help students associate this vocabulary web with themes expressed in the story (e.g., people's inability to take responsibility and to face reality). When students have finished their word search, lead a discussion on how Julian's stay in the asylum affects his personality and sense of responsibility, as well as the lives and future of his family.

The words printed in boldfaced type are tested on the selection assessment worksheet.

PREREADING

Reading the Story in a Cultural Context

Help students read for purpose by asking them if they ever had to return to a familiar place after a long absence, such as returning to school after summer vacation. Have them consider how they felt about returning. (As they read about Julian's feelings about leaving the asylum to return home for good, ask them to keep their own feelings in mind.)

Focusing on the Selection

As they read the story, have students imagine that they are psychologists working on Julian's case. Guide them to come up with as many reasons as they can either for Julian to stay in the asylum or to return home. Ask students to summarize Julian's problems and make recommendations for his continued care.

POSTREADING

The following activities parallel the features with the same titles in the Student Edition.

Responses to Critical Thinking Questions

Possible responses are:

1. She suggests that they are well-founded.

2. He has a wife, mother, and children who have been relying on charity. When he returns, he must provide for them again. He is afraid that he will not be able to do this properly.

3. Responses will reflect students' own experience. Lead students to realize that often the anticipation is worse than the reality.

☑ Guidelines for Writing Your
Response to "The Return"

Have students share their journal entries with a partner. Or, as an alternative writing activity, challenge students to imagine they are Julian and write several journal entries: (1) on Christmas Eve in the asylum; (2) on the train home, (3) at home. Encourage volunteers to share their entries with classmates.

☑ Guidelines for Going Back
Into the Text: Author's Craft

Ask students to review the definition of foreshadowing on page 302 in the Student Edition. Ask them how the author uses foreshadowing to build suspense. Remind students that suspense creates strong interest for what will happen next in the story. Then ask how Laforet uses foreshadowing to prepare the reader for what will happen next.

Possible answers to the questions in the Student Edition are:

1. "The Return" can mean both a return home and a return to madness. The title hints that Julian will regress.

2. Julian thinks "it was a bad idea" to go home for Christmas, indicating that this may not be a time of celebration. He is reluctant to leave the institution, suggesting that he is not ready to resume his responsibilities. The statement that he had once been dangerous suggests that he could be again under similar circumstances. Julian's reflection

on the way things were before he was taken to the asylum indicates that his aggressive, destructive behavior could return if he isn't really cured.

3. It makes the reader want to read on to see whether Julian's fears will be realized when he returns home.

✔ FOLLOW-UP DISCUSSION

Use the questions that follow to continue your discussion of "The Return." Possible answers are given in parentheses.

Recalling

1. Why was Julian being sent home? (He was believed to be completely cured.)

2. Sister Rosa reminded Julian of whom? (his wife, Herminia)

3. What kind of job was waiting for Julian when he went home? (working in a garage)

Interpreting

4. Why do you think Julian wants to stay at the asylum longer? (The asylum offered him a sense of security. He had few responsibilities and very little pressure.)

5. Why was Mother Superior referred to as "Mother?" (She fit the image of a mother: nurturing and kind.)

6. Why was Julian anxious about returning home? (He was afraid to face up to his family responsibilities.)

Applying

7. In your opinion, do asylums help or hinder people and society? Why? (Answers will vary. Have students back up their opinions with references, examples, and facts.)

8. In your opinion, in what ways is war harmful to society? (Answers will vary. Encourage students to give specific references, examples, and facts.)

ENRICHMENT

Students may enjoy seeing the video from the European Geography Series titled *Southern Region*. The video is available from Social Studies School Service, 10200 Jefferson Boulevard, Room 12, Culver City, CA 90232, (800) 421-4246.

RESPONSES TO REVIEWING THE REGION

1. Sample answer: Primo Levi experiences great horrors in the concentration camp through no fault of his own. For example, he is tortured by thirst but cannot drink the water; he is exhausted but cannot sit down. On the other hand, the main character in "The Nightingale's Three Bits of Advice" is tricked by his own greed and foolishness. Had he listened to the nightingale, he would have been a lot better off.

2. Sample answer: The "system" in *Survival in Auschwitz* dehumanizes prisoners. The Germans stripped the Jews of their identities, personal belongings, clothing, hair, and even their names. Levi shares the horrors of the Nazi system to help prevent a similiar situation from ever happening again.

3. Some students may liken themselves to Primo Levi because he is tough, intelligent, and determined to live. Others may compare themselves to the nightingale because it is cunning and wise.

✔ FOCUSING ON GENRE SKILLS

"The Oath of Athenian Youth" uses several elements of speech. An *oath* is a solemn appeal to God or to some revered person or thing to witness one's determination to speak the truth or to keep a promise. In this speech, the speakers promise to uphold the ideals of their community. Select another speech with the same tone as "The Oath of Athenian Youth," such as the Pledge of Allegiance, and ask students to recite it aloud. Have them identify elements of speech such as tone, diction, articulation, and pitch. Guide them to analyze the elements used by the speaker.

BIBLIOGRAPHY

GOLDBERG, LEAH. "My Mother's House." In *The Penguin Book of Women Poets*. Edited by Carol Cosman, Joan Keefe, and Kathleen Weaver. London: Penguin Books Limited, 1978.

HUCH, RICARDA. "Death Seed." In *The Penguin Book of Women Poets*. Edited by Carol Cosman, Joan Keefe, and Kathleen Weaver. London: Penguin Books Limited, 1978.

O'FARRELL, PADRAIC. "Paying on the Nail." In *Humorous Folktales of Ireland*. Cork City, Ireland: Mercier Press Limited, 1989.

POURRAT, HENRI. "The Nightingale's Three Bits of Advice." In *French Folktales*. Translated by Royall Tyler. New York: Random House, Inc., 1989.

Unit 3
Eastern and Western Europe
Focusing the Unit (page 303)

COOPERATIVE/COLLABORATIVE LEARNING

Individual Objective: to participate in a panel discussion about an important social issue in Europe.

Group Objective: to develop a presentation inspired by viewpoints expressed in the panel discussion.

Setting Up the Activity

Have students work in heterogeneous groups of three. Stipulate that each group member is responsible for researching and expressing an individual viewpoint in the panel discussion and for making a contribution to the group presentation. Suggested topics are as follows: Student 1 introduces the panel and its topic; Student 2 describes the social issue and its impact; Student 3 gives a personal interpretation of the issue.

When they have finished their preparation, have each group present their discussion for the entire class. After each group's presentation, use the questions below to discuss and evaluate their reports.

- What different social issues are treated in the literature of Unit 3?
- In your group's opinion, what are some ways the social issues you focused on affected the lives of people in Eastern and Western Europe?

Assisting ESL and LEP Students

To help integrate students with limited English proficiency into a closing discussion of the unit, have them choose one selection on which to focus. Then ask them to think about the answers to these questions:

1. What social issue does the selection deal with?
2. How did the issue affect people in Eastern or Western Europe?
3. Is the issue still a matter for concern today? Explain.

Assessment

Before you begin the group activity, remind students that they will be graded on both an individual and a group basis. Without individual contribution, the group presentation will not be complete. Monitor group progress to check that all three students are contributing and that they have selected a presenter.

Time Out to Reflect

As students do the end-of-unit activities in the Student Edition, give them time to make a personal response to the content of the unit as a whole. Invite them to respond to the following questions in their notebooks or journals. Encourage students to draw on these personal responses as they complete the activities.

1. What have I learned about social issues in Eastern and Western Europe?
2. In what way do European social issues relate to issues in my own life?
3. How can people protest social injustice? What methods of protest seem most effective?

WRITING PROCESS: PERSUASIVE ESSAY

Refer students to the model of a persuasive essay found on pages 427–428 in the Handbook section of the Student Edition. You may wish to discuss and analyze the model essay if you are working with less experienced writers.

Guidelines for Evaluation

On a scale of 1–5, the writer has

- clearly followed all stages of the writing process.
- made clear and specific references to the chosen selections.
- provided sufficient supporting details from the selections to support arguments and opinions and effectively persuade the reader.
- clearly organized the paper so that the conclusion is easy to follow.
- written an opening or a closing paragraph that clearly summarizes the main points of the paper.
- made minor errors in grammar, mechanics, and usage.

Assisting ESL and LEP Students

You may wish to provide a more limited assignment for these students so that they can complete their first drafts somewhat quickly. Then have them work at length with proficient writers in a peer-revision group to polish their drafts.

PROBLEM SOLVING

Encourage students to use the following problem-solving strategies to analyze two or more of the selections in Unit 3. Afterward, encourage students to reflect on their use of the strategies and consider how the strategies helped in their analysis.

Strategies (optional)

1. Use a semantic map or brainstorming list to identify a social problem covered in Unit 3. Have groups of students choose the problem they most want to investigate further and the selection or selections that best shed light on the topic.

2. Use a second graphic organizer, such as a problem/solution chart, to explore in detail the topic they chose. Include information about the problem from the selections and ideas about the authors' use of literature to solve the problem. This graphic organizer should be used to show how writers use literature to help solve social problems.

3. Decide which topics need further research or discussion. Set up a plan that shares responsibility for doing the research and creating a news show, poem, debate, editorial, or speech presenting reactions to the problem and solution.

Allow time for students to work on their presentations.

Guidelines for Evaluation

On a scale of 1-5, the student has

- provided adequate examples, facts, reasons, anecdotes, or personal reflections to support his or her presentation.

- demonstrated appropriate effort.

UNIT 4 The Americas

The Americas include the country of Canada and the Latin American nations. Like the United States, these two regions were first populated by Native Americans, went through periods of European colonization, and won independence. Their literature reflects these and other shared influences, as well as different cultural and historical traditions.

UNIT OBJECTIVES

Literary
- to understand the parallel emergence of regional literature that defines national identities
- to evaluate the influence of the search for identity on theme and structure in the literature of the region

Historical
- to discuss how the literature reflects changing political and social conditions in the region
- to examine the relationship between the United States and the other countries of the Americas

Cultural
- to understand African and Native American influences on life and literature in the region
- to show the different European influences on life and literature in the Americas

UNIT RESOURCES

The following resources appear in the Student Edition of *World Tapestries*:

- a full-color **regional art insert**: The Art of Tapestries, pages A14-A16, to build background, activate prior knowledge, and generate writing ideas about the unit region.
- a **unit overview**, pages 304-307, to provide background about Canada and Latin America, including the effects of colonization on the region.
- a **time line**, pages 306-307, to help students place world events in their historical context. You may wish to have students refer to the time line before they discuss each work.
- the **Focusing the Unit** activities at the end of the unit, page 393, to provide a cooperative/collaborative learning project on the region, a writing project, and a problem-solving activity.

INTRODUCING UNIT 4

Providing Motivation

Before students begin to read the unit overview in the student edition, you might want to stimulate their interest with some of the following activities.

- On the board, write the following: Baseball is the American pastime. What is Canada's national sport? What is the most popular sport in Latin America? Use the answers to the questions (ice hockey and soccer) to generate a discussion about the reasons certain sports are popular in a particular region. Ask students to suggest other terms they have heard which use the adjective "American" to describe only the United States. (Examples: the American people, American foreign policy, American movies) Ask: How do you think people in other parts of the Americas feel about this? Guide them toward the understanding that those in other countries have "American" identities, cultures, and historical traditions.

- Arrange groups of four to six students around a table. Have members pass a sheet of paper and take turns writing the names of Latin American countries they know. When prior knowledge is completed, allow groups to use an atlas or encyclopedia and take turns adding more countries until their lists are complete. Then, have volunteers share with the class information that they would like to learn about the history and cultures of Canada and Latin America. Have individuals record the questions in their journals and later answer them with text information or use them for independent research projects.

- Ask: Have you read any stories or seen any movies set in Canada or in a Latin American country? If so, how would you describe each setting? What were the characters like? What was the story about? If not, what do you imagine the setting, characters, and plot would be like in these regions? How do you think stories from these regions that were written 100 years ago might be similar to or different from those written today? Encourage students to compare and contrast the real or imagined responses to the information they learn as they read the unit selections.

- Tell students that there are some similarities in the immigration patterns to the United States and other countries of the Americas. Ask: How do you think the experiences of different cultural groups in these areas compare to those of people living in or entering the United States? (Examples: Native Americans, Europeans, Africans, Asians) Discuss cultural diversity here and elsewhere in the Americas.

- Have students work in pairs or in small groups to identify any similarities among the events listed on the time line on pages 306-307. (For example, explorers came to lands already inhabited by other peoples, nations gained independence from other nations.) Ask groups to imagine what types of stories a group of people might develop when faced with situations such as these.

Cross-Discipline Teaching Opportunity: Unit Culture

Collaborate with social studies and/or foreign language teachers to explore historical and cultural extensions. For example, you might have the class create a calendar marking the birthdays of famous past and present Canadians and Latin Americans as well as the dates of historical events and cultural celebrations. Have students take turns adding information in appropriate months. A social studies teacher might discuss the implementation of the North American Free Trade Agreement and how it has affected relations between the United States and the other American nations. A language teacher might be able to enrich students' appreciation by comparing themes in the French-language literature of Canada with the text selections and/or playing recordings of Latin American poems in Spanish to give students the flavor of the original works. Ask teachers from these departments to suggest additional sources of information on the literature of the region.

Setting Personal Goals for Reading the Selections in Unit 4

Have students keep a copy of the following chart in their journals or notebooks. Provide class time every few days for students to review and expand their charts. Encourage them to add topics of their own.

The Americas			
Topic	What I Know	What I Want to Learn	What I Have Found Out
Literature as a reflection of political/social issues			
Literary themes common to the region			
Literature and the search for a national or regional identity			
Cultural/historical connections between nations in the region			

8 Latin America

CHAPTER PREVIEW

ASSESSMENT

Assessment opportunities are indicated by a ☑ next to the activity title. For guidelines, see Teacher's Resource Manual page xxxvi.

CROSS-DISCIPLINE TEACHING OPPORTUNITIES

Social Studies   To help students understand the rich history of Latin America, work with a history teacher to identify major figures from the independence movements in various countries as well as important contemporary leaders. Have interested students research the lives and accomplishments of these individuals and prepare short oral reports to the class. Students could also research the work of regional Pan-American organizations such as the Organization of American States. You could invite guest teachers to discuss contemporary political and human rights issues in Latin America, as well as new fiction and nonfiction with historical connections to this region. If possible, invite a member of a local Latin American cultural or civic association to speak to the class about the group, its role in the community, and its goals.

Art   Like the literature, Latin American art has been heavily influenced by the history of the region. Work with an art teacher to create a lesson on the social themes in the works of the three great Mexican muralists, Rivera, Orozco, and Siqueiros, and their influence on artists throughout the region. Consider having your class select one literary work that could be illustrated as a classroom mural. Small groups of students could collaborate to create a variety of scenes depicting this story.

Music   An exciting way to explore cultural heritage is through music. Work with a music teacher to identify folk songs and contemporary music with Latin American origins. Discuss the works, play recordings, and invite students to share any appropriate Latin American-influenced recordings of their own.

Geography   Have students work in pairs or small groups to select one country in the region and create a travel brochure (with map) describing the physical and cultural geography found there. Tell them to include a side trip to the home town of a famous author. Ask a social studies teacher to help you gather resource materials to assist the class in their projects.

Languages   Ask a language teacher to help the class prepare a Spanish-English glossary featuring the original titles of the chapter selections and key words from each (with a pronunciation guide.) Encourage the students to use these words in class discussions.

Economics   Work with an economics teacher to present a lesson about current economic issues in the region. Include developments of national importance in particular countries as well as cooperative efforts to improve the regional economy.

SUPPLEMENTING THE CORE CURRICULUM

The Student Edition provides materials related to a unifying theme in Making Thematic Connections: Rise of the People on pages 340-341. You might wish to invite students to pursue the following activities outside of class:

• Have students examine the painting on page 340 entitled "Birth of Class Consciousness." The caption explains that the Mexican artist Diego Rivera often deals with highly-charged political and social issues. Ask students to explain how they think the painting portrays a new awareness of class distinctions. What is the artist telling us about the plight of the common people in this painting? Suggest that students research other artists or works of art that deal with themes of social consciousness. They may select artwork that expresses the evils of oppression on human rights abuses or works that inspire by portraying people's triumphs over the forces that oppress them. Students may want to consider the Spanish artist Francisco José de Goya (1746–1828), who painted several dramatic works depicting the oppression of the Spanish people under King Ferdinand VII. Ask students to share illustrations of works they research.

- A number of the selections in the Chapter address the theme of searching for an individual identity in the modern world. Lead a class discussion about the relationship between individuals and society. Discuss rights and responsibilities. Ask students to consider concerns and values that people in Latin America might share with our society. Students who wish to explore this theme further could use library resources to find and read additional works by the authors in the chapter and others from Latin America that address similar conflicts.

- Tell students that Latin Americans are the fastest growing population group in the United States today. If possible, encourage them to explore historic or contemporary Latin American cultural influences in your area. Alternatively, they might select one region of the United States. Suggest that they work in small groups to prepare a written report. Each group member could take responsibility for one specific section. (Examples: historic influences, immigration patterns, architecture, music, economic trends)

INTRODUCING CHAPTER 8: LATIN AMERICA

Using the Chapter Opener

On the chalkboard, write: "Who are you?" Challenge students to identify the various ways in which teenagers try to establish an individual identity. Guide them toward behavioral expressions such as different hair styles and clothes, nontraditional musical forms, new cultural heroes, their own slang, entertainment in different forms and settings. Assemble as comprehensive a list as possible. Then discuss the reasons why teenagers behave this way.

Explain that, for three hundred years, Spanish ideas dominated the culture of Latin America. After the wars for independence in the 1800s, the United States heavily influenced the smaller countries of the region. In the early 20th century, the search for its own regional identity became a dominant cultural issue among Latin American political leaders and artists. Modern Latin American literature is noted for its experimentation with new forms and themes, innovation in the use of language, its unusual imagery, and its local settings. Ask: "Why do you think writers from the region would seek to express the Latin American identity in these ways?" Ask students to consider the points raised in the previous discussion as they respond. Suggest that many of the selections will be unlike literature they have read in the past, but if they think about it in the context of this activity, they may identify closely with the writers and their works.

✔ Developing Concept Vocabulary

Illustrate the concept of Latin American literature as a search for new ways to express individual identity through a simple graphic representation. On the chalkboard, draw a large tree and label it "The Individual—Me." Then draw several branches growing out from the trunk in different directions. Explain that the branches are the expression of an individual's identity. Label various branches with the names of literary elements: character, setting, plot, theme, language. Ask students to draw their own trees and label the branches with words they would use to describe how they would express their own identity in a story that they were writing. Use these questions as prompts:

- What would the main character be like? How would he or she be different from others?

- Where would the story take place? Why would the character be in that place? What feelings would he or she have about this place?

- What unusual things would happen in the story? What conflicts would the character need to resolve?

- What lesson would they like readers to learn from their story?

- How would the characters speak? Would their use of language be unusual? Why?

from the *Popol Vuh*
edited by J. F. Bierlein (pages 309–311)

OBJECTIVES

Literary

- to recognize the characteristics of myth
- to understand the story's message about the effects and rewards of kindness

Historical

- to locate Mayan culture in time and place
- to discuss the social, economic, and scientific developments in Mayan civilization

Cultural

- to recognize shared elements in creation myths from around the world
- to show how the lesson of the myth applied to the values of Mayan culture

SELECTION RESOURCES

Use Assessment Worksheet 46 to check students' vocabulary recognition, content comprehension, and appreciation of literary skills.

 Informal Assessment Opportunity

SELECTION OVERVIEW

Popol Vuh means "Book of Counsel (Instruction)." It is the sacred book of the Quiché Maya, who lived in the highland forests of Guatemala. The *Popol Vuh* is an account of this sophisticated culture's history, philosophy, religion, and mythology. The Maya devised a writing system that used hieroglyphics, or pictorial symbols, to record their beliefs and achievements. They also developed a complex social structure and formulated several abstract astronomical and mathematical theories, including the concept of zero.

There was a practical side to the Mayan theories. Priests used the mathematical formulas and astronomical observations to create calendars. With amazing accuracy, they calculated monthly and yearly cycles of change that could bring good weather, floods, or drought. This knowledge was essential to a society that relied on agriculture and trade to prosper. Engineers designed and built elaborate stone pyramids. These complexes, with rooftop temples, were used for religious ceremonies at which offerings were made to the gods.

Like virtually all ancient groups that lived close to nature, the Maya often expressed abstract knowledge in symbolic terms. The forces of nature were controlled by gods. The lessons needed for survival were taught through tales explaining how to please the gods and warning of dire consequences if the rules were ignored. These tales taken together make up a culture's mythology.

In this selection, the Maya describe the creation of man. Four gods—yellow god, red god, black god, and the colorless god—each attempted to make man. Yellow god's and red god's attempts failed. Black god made a man out of gold; the colorless god made poor man from the fingers of his left hand. Poor man brought life to the man of gold, or rich man. Forever after, rich man was to take care of poor man.

ENGAGING THE STUDENTS

Tell students that there are a number of shared elements in the mythologies of cultural groups who lived in different parts of the world. One concept found in a number of traditions is the idea of mistakes being made by the gods before they perfected the human race. Ask students: What characteristics in a creation do you think would displease a maker and lead to another attempt? What qualities in a creation do you think would please a maker? Use student responses to discuss their expectations about the message of the selection.

BRIDGING THE ESL/LEP LANGUAGE GAP

The vocabulary of this selection is not difficult; it presents a good opportunity for students to focus on the author's craft and the purpose of writing. After students have read the selection, use these questions to spark discussion:

181

- Are all the characters human beings? What kind of beings are some characters?
- What questions does the myth answer about the culture of the Maya?
- What does the myth suggest the Maya admired in human beings?
- What does the myth suggest the Maya disliked in human beings?
- What myths from other cultures have similar plots or themes?

As an alternative, have students work in groups of three or four (mixing proficient and ESL/LEP students) to discuss their answers to these questions and share information about mythology.

✔ PRETEACHING
SELECTION VOCABULARY

Have students scan the story and find four words that describe materials that the gods used to make people. Make a list of the words on the board (*clay*, *wood*, *gold*, *flesh*). After reading the selection, students may list positive and negative characteristics of the people made from each material. Encourage them to compare these lists with their expectations before reading. Use the comparisons as a basis for class discussion. You might want to focus on universal themes found in the Mayan view of social behavior.

The words printed in boldfaced type are tested on the selection assessment worksheet.

PREREADING

Reading the Myth in a Cultural Context

Explain that in one version of this tale from the *Popol Vuh*, the men of wood are attacked and burned by domesticated animals and animated utensils, such as cooking pots. The animals are angered that people treat them only as food without regard to their worth as living beings or as the saviors of their species. The utensils are outraged that the wood people misuse them and fail to care for them as natural resources. Discuss with students the values that Mayan society was conveying through this story. Ask: Do you think there is a lesson here for our culture? What modern concerns have you heard about regarding environmental issues here and in other parts of the Americas?

Focusing on the Selection

On the board, write: "If I am not for myself, who will be? If I am only for myself, who am I?" Tell students that this is from the teachings of Hillel, an ancient Jewish scholar. Ask students to write one paragraph explaining what they think this means and how it applies to social responsibilities. When they have finished, note that many people also believe Hillel first stated the rule that says you should treat others the way you would like to be treated yourself. Ask them to compare their ideas and Hillel's to those of the Mayan teachers as they read.

POSTREADING

The following activities parallel the features with the same titles in the Student Edition.

Responses to Critical Thinking Questions
Possible responses are:

1. After three of the four gods in heaven failed to create a satisfactory human being, the fourth god cut off the fingers of his left hand. These fingers became the first people.

2. Sample responses: Most people would be classified as "poor" instead of "rich." Poor people work hard and seem to have an innate kindness; the rich have a divine responsibility to take care of the poor.

3. Answers will vary and may not relate directly to story details. In the myth, the kindness of the men of flesh brings the man of gold to life; students may suggest that acts of kindness can change people's lives in dramatic ways.

✔ Guidelines for Writing Your Response to the *Popol Vuh*

If students wish, have them share their journal entries with a partner. As an alternative writing activity, have students write a short scene for an extension of the myth. Tell them to create dialogue for the "rich" man of gold in which he tells a "poor" man of flesh the lesson he has learned and how he intends to carry out the command of the gods in his life.

✔ Guidelines for Going Back Into the Text: Author's Craft

Help students distinguish between the terms *myth*, *legend*, and *fable*. Remind them that a common characteristic of a myth is the presence of supernatural beings, usually gods. Myths explain a belief, custom, or mysterious natural phenomenon. These explanations often suggest appropriate behavior, attitudes, or values.

Legends, too, reinforce values or lessons that are highly regarded in a culture. Even though the characters are mainly human beings, these people tend to have incredible skills or abilities, making them into cultural heroes. Although the plots of legends are generally associated with historical events, they do not attempt to be realistic.

Like myths and legends, fables have an instructive purpose. Most end with a stated or implied moral that teaches a lesson about life or human nature. The characters tend to be animals who have human characteristics.

Discuss familiar legends that have been the basis for books or movies, such as King Arthur and Paul Bunyan. Ask students to comment on why these men are regarded as cultural heroes.

Ask volunteers to name various animals and human characteristics sometimes attributed to them. Discuss why we might associate those traits with particular animals and how they might appear in a fable. Encourage students to give examples of familiar fables.

Possible answers to the questions in the Student Edition are:

1. Sample responses: If we have been divinely created, what are our responsibilities to our God or gods? How do our God or gods feel about us today? What is our relationship to the earth itself? How are we to treat one another? What happens to us when we die?

2. Answers may vary. Some students will point out that the Maya saw themselves as "fingers" of the "colorless lord," making people and gods similar. Other students may suggest that since three of the four gods were unable to create a proper human being, the Maya felt that they were like some gods but different from others.

3. Answers will vary. Encourage students to look for similar details in creation stories with which they are familiar. Ask them to comment on the values and answers to questions about life and social responsibilities that the various stories convey.

✔ FOLLOW-UP DISCUSSION

Use the questions that follow to continue your discussion of the *Popol Vuh*. Possible answers are given in parentheses.

Recalling

1. Why did the gods decide to create people? (They wanted to create beings that would enjoy the earth and give praise to the gods.)

2. What warms the heart of the man of gold and brings him to life? (the kindness of the men of flesh)

3. How do the gods ordain that a rich person will be judged at death? (The rich person will be judged on how well he cared for the poor.)

Interpreting

4. Why do you think that the Maya chose gold as the material from which the rich man was made? (Gold is traditionally associated with wealth in many cultures. It is the metal from which the most valuable coins and jewelry are made. It also was an abundant natural resource in the area in which the Maya lived.)

5. Why must a rich man be accompanied by a poor man to enter heaven? (The gods ordained that the rich have a responsibility to care for the poor. To enter heaven, the rich man must bring proof [the word of a poor man] that they have obeyed the gods' wishes.)

Applying

8. Do you think that the Maya would agree or disagree with the saying, "Gold can't buy happiness"? Explain your answer. (Answers will vary. Students should recognize that, in the myth, the man of gold is "cold as stone" and cannot feel joy until his heart is warmed by the kindness of the men of flesh.)

ENRICHMENT

Students may enjoy viewing the video *Ancient Maya Indians of Central America*, available from the Encyclopaedia Britannica Educational Corporation, 310 South Michigan Avenue, Chicago, IL 60604, (800) 554-9862.

The Great Prayer

by Alfonso Cortés   (pages 312–314)

OBJECTIVES

Literary

- to understand the nature of metaphysical poetry
- to examine the use of different kinds of imagery in poetry

Historical

- to examine the development of metaphysical poetry in Latin America since World War II
- to determine how political unrest may influence the form and content of poetry

Cultural

- to understand how cultural origins may influence the development of poetic imagery

SELECTION RESOURCES

Use Assessment Worksheet 47 to check students' vocabulary recognition, content comprehension, and appreciation of literary skills.

✔ Informal Assessment Opportunity

SELECTION OVERVIEW

As well as using both **concrete imagery** and **abstract imagery** in "The Great Prayer," Cortés also uses **conventional imagery** and **personal imagery**. Conventional imagery uses words in ways that create traditional, widely accepted impressions. Personal imagery uses words in ways that have special significance to a particular poet.

"Eagle of the soul" is an example of conventional imagery. Traditionally, the eagle is admired as a majestic, fiercely independent bird that can soar to great heights and accomplish mighty feats. Almost all readers will understand the comparison and agree on the associations between the human spirit and the eagle.

"Time is hunger" is an excellent example of personal imagery. It does not bring to mind the conventional picture of "Father Time," a kindly, old man with a long beard. The reader must infer the meaning of the personal image from the context of this poem. Individual interpretations may vary. Some readers may think Cortés is comparing the effects of time to the uneasy weakness that comes from lack of food. Others may think that he is suggesting that time is like a beast with an unnatural craving that devours people. Others may have different impressions.

In this poem, Cortés expresses the need for prayer to "quiet the anguish of the void" and for dreaming to take refuge from everyday life.

ENGAGING THE STUDENTS

On the board, write "Time is a thief." Have students think about this statement and spend five minutes writing what it means to them. Call on individuals to read their interpretations aloud. Discuss the responses. Next, write the word *time* on the board. Ask volunteers to share statements that they have read or heard about time. (Examples: Time flies. Time heals all wounds. Time waits for no one. Time is my ally. Time stood still. Time is money.) As phrases are offered, discuss what each statement means. Note that the idea of time can mean different things to different people and even different things to the same person, depending on the circumstances. One's concept of time is also influenced by one's culture. Ask students of different cultures to share what time means in their culture. Then, write on the board: "Time is hunger." Tell students that this is an image from the selection that they will read next. Ask them to predict what the image might mean in the context of a poem titled "The Great Prayer." Suggest that they think about the points raised as they read the work.

BRIDGING THE ESL/LEP LANGUAGE GAP

The intensely personal, sometimes highly abstract nature of the imagery in this poem will be difficult for many students, and they will need to read the poem more than once. Before the first reading, have them copy the following chart:

SUBJECT	IMAGE	READER'S IMPRESSION
time	hunger	
space	cold	
void	anguish	
dream	solitary rock	
soul	eagle	

As students read, have them record their impressions in the third column. Tell them to use the following questions as prompts: Is the image reassuring or disturbing? Why? How does the poet feel about the world around him? How does prayer help? Would he rather be alone or with others? Where does he find peace?

After they have read the poem, have students work in mixed groups of limited and proficient English speakers to discuss their interpretations of the images and the meaning of the poem. Ask them to consider the points raised as they read the poem again individually. Tell them to revise their lists, if necessary, after the follow-up reading.

✔ PRETEACHING SELECTION VOCABULARY

Tell students that the author of this selection uses imagery to create vivid impressions in the reader's mind. Imagery includes a subject and an image. To understand imagery, it is important to recognize the subject and the image. The subject is the idea or thing described. The image is the way in which the subject is described. The image creates the vivid impression of the subject. Help students scan the poem to find five words that are the subjects of imagery in the poem. (*time*, *space*, *void*, *dream*, *soul*). Ask them to name the image used to describe each subject?

Review the difference between concrete and abstract imagery. You might use questions like these to prompt class discussion:

• Which images are concrete? Which are abstract?

• Are there any images that can be interpreted as both concrete and abstract?

The words printed in boldfaced type are tested on the selection assessment worksheet.

PREREADING

Reading the Poem in a Cultural Context

Help students read for purpose by asking them to consider how the poet's personal life might have influenced this poem. Ask them to comment on what physical conditions Cortés might have lived under that contributed to the images he uses for time and space. What do you think he prayed for? What do you think his dream world was like? Why is it "solitary"?

Focusing on the Selection

Have students work in pairs. Assign one of the questions in the student edition to each partner. When they have finished working individually, ask them to collaborate to come up with a single shared response to each question. When all have finished, write on the board:

Metaphysical = beyond what we can know with the senses; outside objective experience

Challenge partners to collaborate on an answer to this question: Why is "The Great Prayer" considered to be metaphysical poetry? Discuss the responses and tell students to draw on these ideas in their journal writing.

POSTREADING

The following activities parallel the features with the same titles in the Student Edition.

Responses to Critical Thinking Questions

Possible responses are:

1. Cortés describes the "void" as a place of hunger, cold, and anguish. He urges us to bring calm to the "void" through prayer.

2. Sample response: Yes. During times of confusion or insecurity, we are more likely to feel the anguished emptiness that Cortés describes. The chance to dream away our lives (and our troubles) also may seem attractive.

3. Answers will vary. Some students may argue that dreaming is impractical, even an obstacle to dealing with real life. Other students may suggest that we achieve great things in our everyday lives because we dare to have great dreams.

✔ Guidelines for Writing Your Response to "The Great Prayer"

If students wish, have them share their journal entries with a partner. As an alternative writing activity, have students work in pairs to write about a message concerning life that is associated with another individual. The message might be inscribed on a memorial to that person, or it could be his or her words that are frequently quoted. Why is the individual remembered?

What suggestions did this person offer others about living? Why do you think it is important or good advice? What do the words mean to you personally?

☑ Guidelines for Going Back Into the Text: Author's Craft

Not meant to be taken literally as fact, **figurative language** makes comparisons. **Imagery** is one kind of figurative language that paints a word picture different from the literal dictionary definition. Ask students to identify whether the following statements are literal or figurative interpretations of the phrase "space is cold."

- Outside the earth's atmosphere, the temperature drops to extremely low levels.
- The troubled soul longs for the warmth of human understanding.

Ask volunteers to suggest literal and figurative interpretations of other expressions in the poem.

Possible answers to the questions in the Student Edition are:

1. Cortés describes time as hunger and space as cold. The first image is abstract because the reader has to think about what makes these terms equivalent. The second image is more concrete, for cold appeals to the sense of touch. (Cortés's use of the word, however, may refer to a psychological coldness.)

2. Sample response: You need to understand or remember what anguish feels like. You also need to think about what "the void" is.

3. Cortés compares dreaming to "a solitary rock" and the soul to an eagle. Both are concrete images. Cortés relates them by suggesting that just as an eagle has its nest upon a rock, the soul makes its home in dreaming; dreaming, therefore, makes it possible for the soul to be creative.

☑ FOLLOW-UP DISCUSSION

Use the questions that follow to continue your discussion of "The Great Prayer." Possible answers are given in parentheses.

Recalling

1. Why does Cortés say that we should pray? (Only prayer can quiet the anguish of the void.)

2. To what does Cortés compare the soul? (an eagle)

3. What does Cortés say is a refuge from everyday life? (dreaming)

Interpreting

4. What do you think the image of "the void" represents? (Answers will vary. Some students may suggest that the void represents a universe without meaning, the pain found in everyday life, or death. Others may suggest that the void represents the terrible loneliness of a troubled mind.)

5. How does Cortés's image of an eagle's nest suggest the heights to which the human spirit can soar? (Eagles make their nests among the highest crags of mountains. The comparison suggests that, like the eagle, the human spirit finds its home high above the petty concerns of the everyday world.)

Applying

6. In your opinion, why would those who loved him inscribe this poem on Cortés's tomb? (Answers will vary. Some students may suggest that it was done because this poem is typical of Cortés's poetry and contains the theme of his work. Others may suggest that those who loved him hope that, in death, Cortés's prayer was answered, and he found the peace that was denied him in life.)

7. What relationship do you think exists between the poetry of Cortés and the relationship between Nicaragua and the United States? (Answers will vary. Guide students toward an understanding that Cortés had an uneasy relationship with the outside world. Nicaragua has had an uneasy relationship with the United States. As an individual, Cortés could not escape the demands of the larger world except through dreaming. As a small country, Nicaragua has difficulty escaping the influence of the largest, most economically and politically powerful country in the western hemisphere.)

ENRICHMENT

Students may benefit from viewing *Nicaragua: Report from the Front* by Deborah Shaffer, Pamela Yates, and Tom Sigel. The video is available from First Run Icarus Films, 153 Waverly Place, New York, NY 10014, (800) 876-1710.

Bouki Rents a Horse

retold by **Harold Courlander**   (pages 315–318)

OBJECTIVES

Literary
- to evaluate how an author shows character through dialogue and actions
- to recognize stock characters and their uses in humorous works

Historical
- to discuss the colonial and post-colonial history of Haiti
- to relate economic conditions in Haiti to the story's theme

Cultural
- to recognize the blend of African and Caribbean influences in Haitian folklore
- to understand the universality of the "trickster" in folklore

SELECTION RESOURCES

Use Assessment Worksheet 48 to check students' vocabulary recognition, content comprehension, and appreciation of literary skills.

 Informal Assessment Opportunity

SELECTION OVERVIEW

The *trickster* is a traditional character found in the folklore of cultures around the world. He is a part of many of the oldest folktales. The trickster plays an especially prominent role in the oral traditions of African and Native American cultures. Sometimes, as in "Bouki Rents a Horse," the trickster is a human being. In other stories, the trickster is an animal. He may be a spider, a tortoise, a hare, or a jackal in African tales. In Native American folklore, the trickster also appears in many guises. They include the raven, the mink, the rabbit, and the spider. The trickster as coyote is the most common figure in North American folklore.

The trickster is a complex character. In many tales, such as this selection, the sly prankster uses deception to triumph over a stronger or more powerful figure. That character may represent oppression. Then the trickster's actions have heroic elements. In some stories, however, the trickster's unscrupulous behavior leads to his own humiliation. In those tales, the joker's defeat serves as the moral lesson. It teaches listeners how they should not behave if they want to gain the group's approval. Whether he appears as hero or villain, the trickster's exploits almost always contain a strong element of humor.

In this selection, Bouki needs to rent a horse from Toussaint. After paying Toussaint 5 gourdes in advance, Bouki finds out that he does not need the horse

after all. Ti Malice, the trickster, helps Bouki get his money back, plus some, by tricking Toussaint.

ENGAGING THE STUDENTS

Discuss with students fictional characters from books, movies, or television who "don't play by the rules" but are presented in a sympathetic light. They may include rebellious students, romanticized outlaws, and practical jokers. Ask: Who usually suffers as a result of their antics? Why do we often identify with these characters? Why is humor almost always an important element in their character? Would we sympathize with them if they hurt innocent people? At what point do you think such a character's actions go too far?

Ask students to reflect on the discussion as they read "Bouki Rents a Horse."

BRIDGING THE ESL/LEP LANGUAGE GAP

Although the vocabulary in this selection is simple, the author does not provide direct character descriptions. Instead, he shows what the three main characters are like strictly through their actions and words (the true meaning of which may not be immediately obvious.) To help students, tell them to list the names "Bouki," "Touissant," and "Ti Malice" on a sheet of paper. As they read the story the first time, have them list adjectives of their own choosing that they think apply to each character. During a second reading, tell students to underline traits they think still apply and revise or strike out others.

Encourage all students—especially limited English speakers—to share information about other tales they know that are similar to this story. Challenge students to find universal themes and values, as well as local variations and adaptations, in folklore.

✔ PRETEACHING SELECTION VOCABULARY

Remind students that Haitian culture is a blend of African, Caribbean, and French cultures. Tell them that **gourde,** the term for the Haitian unit of money, comes from a French word meaning "flask or water bottle." Challenge students to suggest reasons why this word would become a term for money in a land with a hot climate and an agricultural economy.

On the board, list the following words and definitions as they appear:

Column 1	Column 2
Malice	male child of Bouki
Madame	female child of Bouki
Bouki(no)	mischief; trick
Bouki(nette)	Mrs.

Explain that these words and suffixes found in the story also have French origins. Challenge students to match each definition with the correct word and to use each word in a sentence. Tell them to watch for each word's occurrence in the story.

The words printed in boldfaced type are tested on the selection assessment worksheet.

PREREADING

Reading the Story in a Cultural Context

Help students read for purpose by discussing "subsistence farming." Elicit the idea that subsistence farmers depend on the results of their labor to provide for the basic needs of their families. Tell students that about four out of every five Haitians are subsistence farmers. Suggest that they consider this fact as they evaluate the characters in the selection. Ask: How does Toussaint's way of earning a living differ from most Haitians? How do Moussa and Toussaint differ with respect to letting others use their animals? How does this cultural information affect your thinking about

Toussaint's behavior? Does this make Ti Malice's behavior more justifiable?

Focusing on the Selection

On the board, write this question: "Does the end ever justify the means?" Discuss and tell students to consider their responses as they read. Ask: Why do you think that culture groups have ambiguous feelings about a trickster character? Why do you think humor is usually an important element in trickster tales? If Bouki really understood exactly what the trickster was doing, would your opinion of the farmer change? How?

POSTREADING

The following activities parallel the features with the same titles in the Student Edition.

Responses to Critical Thinking Questions

Possible responses are:

1. Sample responses: The audience would recognize details from everyday Haitian life; poor Haitians might applaud a hero who got the better of someone who was putting him at an economic disadvantage.

2. Sample response: The listing of family members as possible passengers on Toussaint's horse suggests that at least some Haitians have large or extended families. Toussaint does not seem particularly wealthy, but he has a strong horse and is accustomed to charging people money. His character may suggest that in a society where most people are poor, it does not take much money for some people to set themselves over others.

3. Answers will vary. Some students may applaud Ti Malice's cleverness at getting not only a refund of Bouki's five gourdes but also ten gourdes more. Other students may be disturbed at the lie that is told to get the money back and at Ti Malice's extortion of the additional ten gourdes.

✔ Guidelines for Writing Your Response to "Bouki Rents a Horse"

If students wish, have them share their journal entries with a partner. As an alternative writing activity, have students work together as partners to write a dialogue exchange between Bouki and Ti Malice. Tell them each character should express his opinion on what to do with the extra ten gourdes. If necessary, you might use prompts: spend it on entertainment; use it to play tricks; give it back to Toussaint; pay Moussa for the use of his mule; buy a mule that Bouki could lend to other poor farmers.

☑ Guidelines for Going Back Into the Text: Author's Craft

Discuss with students the different uses of characterization in literature. Note that often writers use character to show us something surprising or insightful about human nature. Sometimes, authors use what are referred to as *stock characters*. Stock characters are types who appear repeatedly. They are instantly recognizable to the audience and their behavior is predictable. Comedy writers in all cultures have used stock characters since ancient times. Tell students to consider how Bouki, Toussaint, and Ti Malice fit the description of stock characters. Ask: With what humorous stock characters are you familiar? How does the appearance of this kind of character put an audience in a mood to laugh?

Possible answers to the questions in the Student Edition are:

1. Sample response: The first words that Ti Malice says show that the character has a plan in mind. From that point, Ti Malice takes over the story, telling the lie that will get Bouki his money back. The way in which Ti Malice keeps adding details shows that he is a master trickster, as does the smooth way in which he handles Toussaint's objections.

2. Sample response: On one hand, the name suggests power, and Mr. Toussaint certainly tries to hold power over Bouki. On the other, the name also suggests freedom, unity, and honor—words that certainly do not describe Mr. Toussaint's attitude toward his neighbors.

3. Sample response: Bouki seems a rather simple man. He fears Toussaint ("He'll charge me more than I can get for the yams!") and quickly slips into despair ("I'll never get my money back!"). He fails to respond correctly when Ti Malice first tries to involve him in the lie ("Baby?… Baby?"). When it seems that perhaps he has caught on ("Where will we put Grandmother?"), it turns out that he was taking the lie seriously ("I don't think we could have … [put] Grandmother on the horse.")

☑ FOLLOW-UP DISCUSSION

Use the questions that follow to continue your discussion of "Bouki Rents a Horse." Possible answers are given in parentheses.

Recalling

1. Why does Bouki need the temporary use of an animal? (He needs an animal to carry yams to market in the city.)

2. What does Ti Malice, by his words and actions, suggest that Toussaint's horse will be used for? (to carry his family and Bouki's, as well as several pigs)

3. What does Ti Malice say that he and Bouki will do if Toussaint tries to back out of his deal with Bouki? (They will take the matter to the police.)

Interpreting

4. Why is Bouki afraid that he will not get his five gourdes back? (Bouki knows that Toussaint takes unfair advantage of people and will not return the deposit even though Bouki no longer needs to rent the horse.)

5. What admirable trait in Bouki is revealed by his remarks about the "baby" and grandmother? (Bouki is essentially honest and did not understand that Ti Malice was lying all along.)

6. What makes Bouki, Ti Malice, and Mr. Toussaint stock characters? (All three have only one or two personality traits that can be summed up in a single phrase. None of the three change during the course of the story.)

Applying

7. In your opinion, how is the expression "You can't cheat an honest person" related to the character of Toussaint in this story? (Answers will vary. Students should recognize that if Toussaint were honest, Bouki would not have been worried about asking for the return of his five gourdes. Consequently, the farmer would not have needed the trickster's help, and Toussaint would not have been cheated out of the additional ten gourdes.)

8. How does this tale illustrate both the heroic and the unscrupulous aspects of the trickster's character in mythology? (Ti Malice performs a heroic deed by getting the honest Bouki's five gourdes returned. However, he also behaves unscrupulously by extorting from Toussaint an extra ten gourdes to which he and Bouki were not entitled.)

ENRICHMENT

Students may enjoy viewing the video *The Caribbean*, which explores this region's history and culture. This video can be obtained from Encyclopaedia Britannica Educational Corporation, 310 South Michigan Avenue, Chicago, IL 60604, (800) 554-9862.

The Street
by Octavio Paz, translated by Muriel Rukeyser (pages 319–321)

The Room
by Victor Manuel Mendiola

OBJECTIVES

Literary

- to recognize mood in a poem
- to analyze the ways in which language and setting help establish mood

Historical

- to understand how history has influenced Mexican literature
- to discuss the political instability that has troubled Mexico since the 1800s

Cultural

- to discuss pre-Columbian influences on Mexican culture
- to discuss the individual's search for identity in a changing world

SELECTION RESOURCES

Use Assessment Worksheet 49 to check students' vocabulary recognition, content comprehension, and appreciation of literary skills.

 Informal Assessment Opportunity

SELECTION OVERVIEW

Octavio Paz has written that to understand modern Mexican culture, we must understand its pre-Columbian roots. Prior to the arrival of Europeans, native peoples flourished in Mexico. These people established advanced civilizations with complex traditions. In 1521, Spanish *conquistadors* overthrew the Aztec Empire, the last of these great cultures. The Spaniards colonized the land, imposing European customs and religious beliefs on the people. Still, Mexico remains, in many ways, a country heavily influenced by its native peoples.

Today, approximately 28 percent of all Mexicans are direct descendents of native peoples. Over 60 percent of Mexico's inhabitants are *mestizo*, or people of mixed Indian and European ancestry. In Paz's writing, the Mexican people wear a "mask." To outsiders, they appear to have adopted European culture. Behind the mask, however, is the real Mexican heritage rooted in pre-Columbian Indian traditions. He is concerned with the individual's attempts to reconcile these contradictory impulses and to find a true identity. The younger writer Victor Manuel Mendiola explores a similar theme. Like Paz, Mendiola suggests that beneath a modern veneer, the individual's identity is linked to the instinctive behavior of an earlier time.

In these two poems, the poets express ways in which individuals search for identity.

ENGAGING THE STUDENTS

Tell students to imagine that they are alone in familiar surroundings. It might be their bedroom or a neighborhood street. It is night. They hear dogs barking or footsteps in the dark. They see the ordinary play of shadows. Ask: In a situation like this, do commonplace sights and sounds sometimes take on a mysterious or disturbing quality? What kinds of thoughts run through your mind at times like this? Discuss responses with the class. Ask students to consider as they read the poems the way our imagination works at such moments.

BRIDGING THE ESL/LEP LANGUAGE GAP

The language in these selections is not difficult, but the unusual arrangement of ideas in both works may present problems. You might consider pairing

190

ESL/LEP students with English proficient students to analyze the structure and the imagery in the poems.

After the first reading of "The Room," write the following sentence on the chalkboard: "Dogs are barking and something inside you—goes off with the dogs and howls." Note that this sentence expresses the main idea of "The Room." Tell partners to discuss what the poet means by this statement and how it expresses the main idea of the poem.

After the first reading of "The Street," write the following phrases on the chalkboard: "A long and silent street" and "Everything dark and doorless." Note that these introductory phrases provide the setting and establish the mood of the poem. Tell partners to discuss the action that occurs after each scene-setting phrase and what idea they think the poet means to convey.

✔ PRETEACHING SELECTION VOCABULARY

Have students scan the selections for words associated with the dogs in "The Room" and the narrator in "The Street." List the following words on the chalkboard: *barking*, **lost**, **bewildered**, *howls* (from "The Room") and **stumble**, *fall*, **rise**, **turning**, *pursue* (from "The Street"). After reading the selection, students may use these words to find similarities and differences between the dogs and the narrator. Remind them that the individual's search for identity is a main theme in both poems. Challenge them to explain how the words and phrases are related to the theme. Ask: Do you think the message in both poems is exactly the same? Is one more optimistic than the other? If so, which? Explain your answer.

The words printed in boldfaced type are tested on the selection assessment worksheet.

PREREADING

Reading the Poems in a Cultural Context

Help students read for purpose by explaining that in the early 1800s, Mexico became an independent republic. Unlike some former Spanish colonies, however, Mexico has had difficulty creating permanent political stability. Some republican leaders established dictatorships. Governments that began by adopting socialist reforms to aid the poor often became corrupt tools of the wealthy. Because of this situation, political themes frequently play an important role in Mexican literature. In addition, leading writers often hold public office. Ask: How is political activism evident in the careers of Paz and Mendiola? How would disillusionment with socialist philosophy lead writers to search for the individual's identity and place in society?

Focusing on the Selections

Tell students that a literary and artistic movement known as *Surrealism* influenced the writing of Octavio Paz. The surrealists emphasized the importance of unrestrained, instinctive, individual expression over the constraints of society. Surrealists often use dreamlike or nightmarish settings and employ unusual images. Have students work in pairs to find surrealist influences in the setting and mood of "The Street." Use partners' findings as the basis for a class discussion.

POSTREADING

The following activities parallel the features with the same titles in the Student Edition.

Responses to Critical Thinking Questions

1. Sample response: Mendiola wants us to feel that the "room," the secret place inside of us, is frightening because it can go "wild" at any time. Paz wants us to feel lonely and somewhat nervous about the "street," a real or figurative place where we are always chasing or being chased by "nobody."

2. Answers will vary. Students may suggest that the wanderings of the lost, howling dogs ("The Room") might be a relatively common sight in Mexico, and the idea of being followed in the dark ("The Street") might reflect a troubled political situation in Mexico. Some students may feel, however, that the emotions that come to light in these poems are not culturally bound—that the poems are effective because they express universal feelings.

3. Answers will vary and may be based on private emotions. Students who choose "The Room" may be aware of a "wildness" within themselves; students who respond more to "The Street" may feel that they are on an uncertain quest for something or that they, in some way, are being "followed." Some students may also point to particular phrases or images that they find powerful.

✔ Guidelines for Writing Your Response to "The Street" and "The Room"

If students wish, have them share their journal entries with a partner. As an alternative writing activity, ask students to imagine that they are writing a screenplay for a suspense movie. Tell them to write one paragraph in which they describe the setting for a scene that takes place in a hotel room at night or on a darkened street. Ask volunteers to read their entries and explain how their details help establish mood.

☑ Guidelines for Going Back Into the Text: Author's Craft

Review with students ways in which writers create mood. Note that in addition to the repetition of words and phrases, poets sometimes use alliteration to reinforce mood. The repetition of hard consonant sounds, such as the *s*, *d*, and *c* at the beginning of words, can contribute to a sense of uneasiness or dread, while softer vowel sounds are more soothing. Help students find examples of this alliterative effect in the two works. Examples from "The Street" include "stepping on silent stones" and "dark and doorless." Examples from "The Room" include "shadow of a silence" and "cold country."

Possible answers to the questions in the Student Edition are:

1. Sample response: The moods are similar in a general way, for both express an uneasiness or sense of dread. They are different in that "The Room" expresses a fear of our possible wildness, whereas "The Street" expresses a fear of failing to understand what we seek—or what may be seeking us.

2. Sample response: The repetition of *dogs* in "The Room" reminds us of the wildness that, according to Mendiola, lies hidden within each of us. In "The Street," repeating *street* emphasizes the uneasiness that Paz describes, and repeating *nobody* strengthens the feeling that we cannot find a satisfactory resolution to that uneasiness.

3. Answers will vary. For a sense of contrast, you might encourage students to describe a piece of literature with a more positive mood—perhaps a mood of joy or romance.

☑ FOLLOW-UP DISCUSSION

Use the questions that follow to continue your discussion of "The Room" and "The Street." Possible answers are given in parentheses.

Recalling

1. In "The Room," what does Victor Manuel Mendiola describe as a "cold country"? (time)

2. In "The Street," what does the "Someone behind me" do if the narrator slows down or runs? ("Someone" also slows down or runs.)

3. In "The Street," who does the man that the narrator is pursuing see when he rises? ("Nobody")

Interpreting

4. In "The Room," what do you think Mendiola is referring to with the phrase, "the farthest room of the house of you"? (the deepest recesses of the mind; the subconscious)

5. In "The Room," why do you think the person in the room closes the windows? (The person is trying to shut out the sound of the dogs barking, i.e., to ignore the instinctual call of the wild. In addition, closing the windows may offer a sense of protection or an attempt at isolation.)

6. In "The Street," who do you think "nobody" is? (Answers will vary. Some students might say that it is only the poet's imagination, literally nobody. Others might suggest that it is the individual identity for which he is searching. Still others might suggest that it is the Mexicans' pre-Columbian past from which they cannot escape.)

Applying

7. In 1968, Octavio Paz resigned as ambassador to India to protest the Mexican government's harsh treatment of student radicals. Why do you think he took that stand? (Answers will vary. Students might suggest that Paz was protesting what he saw as an infringement of individual rights or free expression. Those who found political implications in "The Street" might suggest that he was protesting government surveillance of the people.)

8. What similarities do you see between the theme of "The Room" and Paz's ideas about pre-Columbian influences on modern Mexico? (Answers will vary. Students may suggest that the dogs represent a past part of ourselves that we must acknowledge if our identity is to be complete. Others might suggest that the room represents the constraints of modern European society, while the dogs represent the pre-Columbian cultures that were more attuned to the natural environment.)

ENRICHMENT

The students may enjoy seeing *Mexico: Yesterday and Today,* which surveys the culture and politics of Mexico. This video is available from Zenger Media, 10200 Jefferson Boulevard, Room 922, P.O. Box 802, Culver City, CA 90232, (800) 421-4246.

Keeping Quiet
by Pablo Neruda

Chilean Earth
by Gabriela Mistral   (pages 322–326)

OBJECTIVES

Literary

- to identify the elements of a lyric poem
- to analyze how lyric poets create emotional responses in the reader

Historical

- to explain how Chilean political and social issues influenced Neruda's poetry
- to recognize rural Chilean social and geographic influences on Mistral's themes

Cultural

- to examine how both poets express strong feelings for the people of Chile
- to discuss the cultural values illustrated in the poems

SELECTION RESOURCES

Use Assessment Worksheet 50 to check students' vocabulary recognition, content comprehension, and appreciation of literary skills.

 Informal Assessment Opportunity

SELECTION OVERVIEW

Neruda "sings" of a simple life. He sees a world with none of the confusion caused by complex, destructive activities. This is the way to peace ("walk about with their brothers/in the shade, doing nothing"). He suggests that peace could be found by imitating the simple rhythms of nature ("Perhaps the earth can teach us…").

Mistral celebrates the natural beauty of the Chilean landscape. She "sings" of the ways it has molded the character of the people ("kneads men/their lips and hearts without bitterness"). She refers to its gentle, motherly feel ("kisses our feet with a melody/that makes any mother sigh.") She recognizes the economic needs of modern society ("Tomorrow we will open its rocks [mine the earth]"). However, she also reminds people that they must take time for the simple pleasures of nature. ("Today we need only dance!")

In the first poem, Neruda describes the peace and brotherhood that would exist if only people would keep quiet and stand still for a while. In the second poem, Mistral celebrates the beauty of Chile, the simple activities of everyday life, and freedom.

ENGAGING THE STUDENTS

On the board, write: "I'd like to teach the world to …"

Allow students two minutes to think about how they would complete that fragment to make it a topic sentence for a paragraph. Tell them that each should select one subject. Then, have them write a paragraph explaining why their choice is important. Before they begin, suggest the following questions as prompts:

- What is the most important lesson you think people should learn about life?
- How would that lesson make the world a better place?
- How would the lesson teach people to get along?
- What should people do to put that lesson into practice?

Allow five minutes for writing. Use the responses as the basis for a class discussion. Tell students to think about the discussion as they read the poems in the selection.

BRIDGING THE ESL/LEP LANGUAGE GAP

Read the poems aloud, or, if possible, play a pre-recorded reading. Have students listen without looking at their texts. After reading each poem, ask students what words, phrases, or images stood out. Write the students' choices on the board in columns under the appropriate title. Then read each poem again as students look at the text.

Have students work in mixed ESL/LEP and English proficient groups of three or four. Ask them to discuss what the items listed on the board mean in the context of the poems. Why do you think they chose the titles they did? In your own words, what lesson would each poet like to teach the world?

Have the class discuss their answers to these questions. Tell students to think about the points raised in the discussion and then read each poem again silently.

☑ PRETEACHING SELECTION VOCABULARY

Discuss with students the difference between literal and figurative language, especially as it applies to imagery in poetry. List the following words and brief literal meanings on the board:

WORD	LITERAL MEANING	FIGURATIVE MEANING
exotic	introduced from another country	excitingly different
face	the front part of the head	entire surface
truck	goods exchanged in trade	agreement; compromise
kneads	shapes with the hands	forms character
molded	to give shape to	made something what it is
kisses	touches with the lips	shows affection
light up	illuminate	bring joy to

Before reading, have students predict possible figurative meanings the words may have within the context of the poems. After reading, discuss the figurative meanings again and refine that list, if necessary.

The words printed in boldfaced type are tested on the selection assessment worksheet.

PREREADING

Reading the Poems in a Cultural Context

Help students read for purpose by telling them that both poets published their works under pen (fictitious) names. Pablo Neruda's real name was Nefitali Ricardo Reyes Baosalto. Gabriela Mistral was born Lucila Godo y Alcayaga.

Explain that authors use pen names for different reasons. Tell students that as a young man, Neruda was an anarchist (someone who is against any form of government). Anarchists often argue that governments are the cause of wars and social injustice. They believe people can resolve problems by working together as individuals. At the time, Chile was experiencing political unrest. Discuss with students why a person who urges the overthrow of government might write under a pen name.

Share with students that Gabriela Mistral spent her life working for educational and social reform in Chile and Mexico. Explain that in the Bible, the angel Gabriel (the masculine form of Gabriela) is God's messenger. A mistral is a strong, cold wind that brings a change in the weather. Discuss with students why Alcayaga might have chosen the pen name she did.

Focusing on the Selections

Have students work in pairs. Tell them to discuss the following questions: What early influences can you see in the message of this poem from Neruda's later career? What connections do you see between Mistral's poem and the pen name she chose?

POSTREADING

The following activities parallel the features with the same titles in the Student Edition.

Responses to Critical Thinking Questions

1. Yes. Both poets speak of themselves in the first person. It is as if Neruda plans to be part of the "we" who "will count to twelve/and … keep still," and Mistral is one of the dancers whose feet are brushed by the land and kissed by its melody.

2. Sample response: "Keeping Quiet" expresses a distaste for war (lines 15–17) and for hunting animals (lines 11–12), as well as a compassion for the elderly and for those who work hard (lines 13-14). "Chilean Earth" expresses a joy in natural beauty (lines 1–8) and in freedom (lines 15–17). That freedom could include freedom of expression (the "dance" symbolism that runs throughout the poem).

3. Answers will vary. Some students may suggest that the advice in "Keeping Quiet" is more practical because it is easier to follow; other students may prefer the advice in "Chilean Earth"—practical or not—because of its joy and sense of celebration.

✔ Guidelines for Writing Your Response to "Keeping Quiet" and "Chilean Earth"

If students wish, have them share their journal entries with a partner. As an alternative writing activity, allow students to select a favorite writer, public figure, or entertainer. Tell them to write one paragraph explaining what they think is the message that person would like to tell the world. Encourage them to include words, phrases, or images that recur in the person's work. Ask volunteers to read their entries and compare the subject's message to those in the poems.

Guidelines for Going Back Into the Text: Author's Craft

Discuss first-person point of view in autobiography and fiction with the students. Guide them to the understanding that in fiction, the first-person narrator is a character whose feelings are not always those of the author. Tell them that in lyric poetry, the speaker usually represents the voice of the poet.

Possible answers to the questions in the Student Edition are:

1. Sample response: Joy is the strongest emotion, as seen in lyrics such as "light up fields with song" (line 14) and "bathe its face in music" (line 17). In particular, it is a joy in the natural beauty of Chile (in lines 5–7, for example).

2. Sample response: The emotion in "Keeping Quiet" is different, even though both poems are positive. The emotion is more determined than joyful; it tries to teach rather than celebrate.

3. Sample response: The speaker of "Keeping Quiet" does seem to be "singing" to himself for much of the poem even though he refers to "we." At the poem's end, he directly addresses someone (perhaps the reader). In "Chilean Earth," the speaker may be "singing" to the other dancers; possibly she is "singing" to herself about her joy.

✔ FOLLOW-UP DISCUSSION

Use the questions that follow to continue your discussion of "Keeping Quiet" and "Chilean Earth." Possible answers are given in parentheses.

Recalling

1. In "Chilean Earth," what three features of the land does Mistral describe as "green," "blond," and "red" respectively? (orchards, grain, and grapevines)

2. In "Chilean Earth," why does the poet want to bathe the land's face in music? (because it is free)

3. In "Keeping Quiet," what does Neruda say that those who start wars would do during the lull? ("walk about with their brothers in the shade, doing nothing")

Interpreting

4. In "Chilean Earth," what does Mistral suggest that the people will do the day after the dance? (They will return to work.)

5. In "Keeping Quiet," why do you think the poet is opposed to people speaking in languages? (Language, rather than making communication between people of the world easier, is creating another barrier to brotherhood.)

6. In "Keeping Quiet," why do you think the poet says that he will go after counting to twelve? (His job is done once he has helped others begin to communicate freely. He will now leave so that his words do not interfere with the silent communication.)

Applying

7. If Neruda and Mistral were alive today, what social issue that you have read or heard about recently do you think they might write a lyric poem about? (Answers will vary. Students may suggest, based on the poems in the selection, that Neruda would write about peace in the world and Mistral would write about educational reform. Encourage them to think of others.)

8. Why do you suppose that these two writers chose the medium of poetry rather than journalism to express their ideas? (Answers will vary. Students should point out that poetry, being more indirect, is subject to personal interpretation. It would be a much safer form of expression during times of political unrest.)

ENRICHMENT

Students may enjoy viewing *The Andean Region* from the South America series, available from Zenger Media, 10200 Jefferson Boulevard, Room 922, P.O. Box 802, Culver City, CA 90232, (800) 421-4246.

Florinda and Don Gonzalo

by Luisa Josefina Hernández (pages 327–334)

OBJECTIVES

Literary

- to identify setting, plot, and character as elements of drama
- to explain how dialogue reveals character in drama

Historical

- to discuss European influences on early Latin American drama
- to recognize the use of experimental drama to explore social change in Mexico

Cultural

- to understand the cultural issues being explored in modern Latin American drama
- to discuss changing roles in Latin American society

SELECTION RESOURCES

Use Assessment Worksheet 51 to check students' vocabulary recognition, content comprehension, and appreciation of literary skills.

✔ Informal Assessment Opportunity

SELECTION OVERVIEW

During the colonial period, European models heavily influenced Latin American drama. Serious plays portrayed main characters of noble birth or heroic stature. Average people, if depicted at all, were minor characters such as servants.

Revolution swept away the political traces of colonization. It also ushered in new literary ideas expressed through experimental theater. Playwrights used unconventional techniques to explore American themes by examining the lives of average people.

Many of these striking new ideas are illustrated in *Florinda and Don Gonzalo*. The work is a short "dialogue" between average Mexicans. There are only two characters—a widowed seamstress and a mobility-impaired bachelor. The author provides no exposition to familiarize us with the characters or their world. The setting, a porch, is minimalist; no scenery distracts the audience. There are no stage directions; character is developed through dialogue alone. There is only one scene, and the action occurs in real time—the length of a conversation. The theme addresses changing attitudes about women, work, and marriage in a changing world. The conclusion, though hopeful, leaves us with as many questions as answers.

In this play, a self-sufficient widow courts a conservative and introverted old man.

ENGAGING THE STUDENTS

On the board, write:

Traditional Roles

Dating   Marriage

Allow students two minutes to list ideas they associate with traditional male and female roles in these relationships. When they have finished writing, tell them to study and evaluate their lists using the following questions as a guide: How do you think these traditional roles came about? Do you think these roles still exist today? Explain. What reasons can you think of to support preserving these roles? In what ways? What reasons can you think of to support changing or abandoning these roles?

With your discussion as a backdrop, have students reconsider and, if necessary, revise their lists. Ask them to consider these ideas as they read the selection.

BRIDGING THE ESL/LEP LANGUAGE GAP

The vocabulary in the selection should not present a significant obstacle to comprehension. However, the reliance on character revelation through dialogue, without exposition or narrative clarification, could hinder full understanding of the reversal of traditional roles. You might suggest that students ask themselves the following questions about the characters as they read: What do the characters have in common? How are they different? What do their statements reveal about each person? How do they feel about themselves? each other? How does each approach the idea of change or adventure?

After a first reading, have LEP students work with an English-proficient partner to discuss stage directions that could accompany dialogue and reveal character. Facial expression indicators might include: amused, sad, excited, hesitant, puzzled, assured. Tell them to add hand gestures and body language as well. You might encourage volunteers to read short exchanges with stage directions aloud.

✔ PRETEACHING SELECTION VOCABULARY

On the board, write the following words in a column: *Don, remedy, suitors, pessimist, consolation.* In a second column, list definitions in the following order: men courting a woman; comfort; gloomy person; title of respect; cure. Have students scan the selection and locate the sentence containing each word. Ask volunteers to read the words aloud in context and try to match vocabulary words with definitions on the board. After all the words are correctly defined, have students predict what the play will be about and how it will end. Have them confirm their predictions after reading the work.

The words printed in boldfaced type are tested on the selection assessment worksheet.

PREREADING

Modeling Active Reading

Florinda and Don Gonzalo is annotated with the comments of an active reader. These sidenotes, prepared to promote active reading, emphasize the cultural content of the piece, address author purpose, call attention to literary skills, reveal personal response, and show how the selection is related to the theme. If you have time, read the entire selection aloud as a dialogue between the reader and the text. Encourage students to discuss and add their own responses to the ones printed in the margins. Model these skills by suggesting your own observations.

Reading the Play in a Cultural Context

Help students read for purpose by discussing the importance of conservative traditions in Mexican culture. Tell them that traditions include strong family involvement in the choice of suitors, the presence of a chaperone during courtship, and male authority. Ask them to consider the cultural conflicts faced by the main characters in the selection. Ask students what they think the author is suggesting about the need for cultural as well as political change.

Focusing on the Selection

Have students work in pairs. Assign one student the role of Florinda and the other the role of Don Gonzalo. Have each student write active reading comments focusing on each character's life struggles and how those struggles shape their beliefs and behavior. When students have finished, tell them to collaborate on an answer to this question: Which character needs the other more in order to find happiness in his/her life?

Stress that there is no incorrect answer as long as pairs can support their opinion through active reading. Call on student pairs to read their answers aloud and then discuss the questions in the student text.

POSTREADING

The following activities parallel the features with the same titles in the Student Edition.

Responses to Critical Thinking Questions

Possible responses are:

1. Characters are revealed through their words alone, and there is very little action; the events in the story occur in a short span of time; the play is short; the idea that a woman would seek out and propose to a man is very unusual in Mexican culture.

2. Despite some interest in Florinda, Don Gonzalo waited a long time to talk to her because he was afraid to be daring. Furthermore, as a young man he did not challenge his beloved's decision to marry someone that her parents found more acceptable. Finally, he insists on marrying instead of just living with her. Florinda, on the other hand, takes the initiative to introduce herself and present her proposition in the same conversation. She also makes the suggestion that they need not marry before they live together.

3. Answers will vary. Some students may suggest that Florinda and Don Gonzalo will wed and be happy because Florinda is determined to make the relationship work. Other students may feel that Don Gonzalo is such a weak character (especially when compared to Florinda) that the differences between them will create problems.

✔ Guidelines for Writing Your Response to *Florinda and Don Gonzalo*

Have students share their journal entries with a partner. As an alternative writing activity, ask students to imagine that they are a friend of Don Gonzalo's who has heard about his good fortune. Tell them to write a friendly letter, congratulating him and offering him advice on how to make the relationship a rewarding experience for both parties.

✔ Guidelines for Going Back Into the Text: Author's Craft

Explain that experimental dramatists often use symbolism to convey their themes. Plot incidents, setting, even characters may be more symbolic than realistic. Remind students that Mexican literature often reflects social and political changes occurring there. Use the following questions as the basis of a class discussion about symbolism: Do you think the plot is realistic? How do you think it may be symbolic of cultural changes taking place in Mexico? What symbols can you find in the setting? What might the opposite sides of the street symbolize? What do you think Don Gonzalo crossing the street with Florinda could mean? What do you think the author may be suggesting about Mexican traditions by portraying Don Gonzalo confined to a wheelchair? Possible answers to the questions in the Student Edition are:

1. Florinda's words reveal that she is strong-willed and that she believes in making things happen. She also is determined to have her way and is not afraid of what people will think. Don Gonzalo's words show him to be pessimistic and rather bored with life, unsure of himself, and somewhat fearful about the future.

2. The climax occurs when Florinda proposes that Don Gonzalo comes to live with her. The situation is resolved when Florinda and Don Gonzalo agree to marry and Florinda wheels him across the street.

3. Answers will vary. Many students will feel that Florinda, especially, has been outspoken; however, some students may wonder what more she might have to say about statements such as "We widows are very difficult to please" and "... in order to be happy it's necessary to have humility." Students also might feel that Don Gonzalo has not said very much; they might want to know more about why his brother considers him "somewhat of a nuisance" or how he has come to be such a pessimist.

✔ FOLLOW-UP DISCUSSION

Use the questions that follow to continue your discussion. Possible answers are given in parentheses.

Recalling

1. Why does Don Gonzalo believe that his family does not have time to talk to him? (He believes that he is somewhat of a nuisance.)

2. Why does Florinda believe that curiosity is important in life? (it is the source of many discoveries)

3. What was Florinda's real intention in coming to visit Don Gonzalo? (to take him home with her)

Interpreting

4. Why do you think that Florinda works longer hours when a holiday draws near? (She is not paid unless she works and wants to earn extra money so that she can afford to take time off on the holiday. Another possibility is that people may want new clothes or home decorations for a holiday, thus increasing her business.

5. What do you think might be symbolized by the fact that Don Gonzalo concentrates on books rather than on watching people? (He finds comfort in books and is afraid of contact with the real world of the street.)

6. How does Don Gonzalo's reaction to Florinda's proposal show that he believes in tradition more than she does? (He is determined that they should follow tradition and get married rather than live together.)

Applying

7. How do you think the character of Florinda and the relationship between her and Don Gonzalo illustrate the changing role of women in society? Support your answer with examples from the play. (Answers will vary, but students might note that in this relationship, the traditional roles are reversed. Florinda is the breadwinner. She takes the initiative by courting him. She is the one in charge, guiding him and reassuring him as they venture out into the world of reality).

ENRICHMENT

Students may benefit from viewing *Latin American Lifestyles,* which explores everyday life and culture in Mexico, Central America, and South America. This video is available from Social Studies School Service, 10200 Jefferson Boulevard, Room 12, Culver City, CA 90232, (800) 421-4246.

One of These Days

by Gabriel García Márquez (pages 335–339)

OBJECTIVES

Literary

- to analyze the effects of suspense in fiction
- to understand the techniques the author uses to develop the protagonist and the antagonist in a literary work

Historical

- to examine the effects of civil war and political conflict in Colombia
- to discuss the impact of the post World War I economic depression on Colombia

Cultural

- to discuss the cultural influences on the author's works
- to recognize the rural social structure in Colombian culture

SELECTION RESOURCES

Use Assessment Worksheet 52 to check students' vocabulary recognition, content comprehension, and appreciation of literary skills.

✔ Informal Assessment Opportunity

SELECTION OVERVIEW

Derived from the Greek words meaning "for" and "struggle," the word protagonist is the main character or hero of a story. The protagonist is faced with and must resolve the main conflict of the plot. In an effective story, the protagonist is a believable character with human characteristics with which we can identify. His or her conflict hooks our interest, creating suspense as we wait for the outcome.

Sometimes, the protagonist is matched against another major character—the antagonist. The conflict that must be resolved results from the struggle between these two. The suspense is greatest when both the protagonist and the antagonist are strong characters.

"One of These Days" is an excellent example of conflict between a protagonist and an antagonist. Both the dentist (the protagonist) and the Mayor (the antagonist) are strong-willed. Each has achieved a position of power in the town. The protagonist's authority comes from his ability to heal; the antagonist's power is based on the threat of suffering. The protagonist's conflict is internal as well as external. Will his faith in the power of healing overcome his hatred of the Mayor's violence? To win the struggle, the protagonist must remain true to his beliefs.

This story, in which a dentist is forced to treat the Mayor whom he hates, explores the power struggle between two men in a small Colombian town.

ENGAGING THE STUDENTS

Ask students to offer opinions on these two questions: Why do individuals become dentists? Why do so many people fear a visit to the dentist? Ask a volunteer to list responses on the board. Guide students toward understanding that dentists, like doctors, want to stop suffering and heal patients. Then, ask students to speculate about how dentists feel when they cause their patients temporary discomfort. Ask students to consider the points that are raised as they analyze the internal and external conflicts of Aurelio Escovar in the selection.

BRIDGING THE ESL/LEP LANGUAGE GAP

This selection presents a good opportunity for students to focus on the protagonist and antagonist. Suggest that as they read, students list their impressions of the dentist (the protagonist) and the mayor (the antagonist). Tell them to use the following questions to guide their thoughts: What kind of person is the dentist? In what ways are he and the Mayor alike? How are they different?

Encourage students from Latin America to share their observations about the role of government officials including the police, mayors, or presidents in their country.

Lead students into a discussion about what kind of power these officials have.

☑ PRETEACHING
SELECTION VOCABULARY

Have students create a three column chart based on the dentist and the Mayor. Tell them that one column should contain words and phrases about the dentist. (Examples: *erect*, **tranquil**, **cautious**, *pressure*, **rancor**, *bitter tenderness*.) The second column should contain words and phrases about the dentist's profession. (Examples: **anesthesia**, **abscess**, *pedal drill*, *bridge*, *sterilized instruments*, *tweezers*, *spittoon*). The third column should contain words and phrases about the Mayor. (Examples: *swollen*, *desperation*, *dull eyes*, *icy breath*). When they have finished the chart, use the questions listed below to generate a discussion about creating suspense:

- How do the terms in the first column show that the dentist is struggling with an internal conflict?
- How do the dental terms help to build an atmosphere of uncertainty and fear?
- How do the terms in the third column show that the Mayor has been struggling with an internal conflict?

The words printed in boldfaced type are tested on the selection assessment worksheet.

PREREADING

Reading the Story in a Cultural Context

Help students to read for purpose by asking them to consider how the details in the story illustrate the effect that political conflict and economic depression had on the lives of people in Colombia at the time of the story. Students should be able to point out that the town dentist, though capable and compassionate, does not have a degree. He must use a foot pedal to power his drill. He sterilizes his instruments by boiling them in a basin of water. His office needs repairs. Ask: What kind of local government would provide adequate facilities and the most modern equipment for the local dentist? What kinds of activities would such a government consider most important? What happened to the twenty dead men Escovar mentions?

Focusing on the Selection

On the chalkboard, write the words *power* and *strength*. Ask: Do you think these words mean the same thing? In what ways are power and strength alike? How are they different? Tell students to consider

the points raised in the discussion as they read the selection. Afterward, use the following questions as the basis for further discussion: Which character do you think is more powerful? Which character do you think is stronger? Who do you think won the struggle for power? Why? Challenge them to support their conclusions with details from the selection.

POSTREADING

The following activities parallel the features with the same titles in the Student Edition.

Responses to Critical Thinking Questions
Possible responses are:

1. García Márquez hints that the town is small and impoverished: The dentist is poorly equipped, and his office is shabby. The author also suggests that the political situation is unhappy: The Mayor feels that he *is* the town and can threaten people to get their cooperation. He apparently has killed 20 people who displeased him.

2. The story suggests that the government abuses power when it uses violence to control the people or when it allows its members to have great personal power. It also suggests that the common people show that they, too, have power when they stand up to such authority.

3. Answers will vary. Encourage students to think about what Escovar says just before pulling the tooth and whether he is telling the truth about the anesthesia. As students suggest courses of action, ask them to consider the likely results in each case.

☑ Guidelines for Writing Your Response to "One of These Days"

Have students share their journal entries with a partner. Or, as an alternative writing activity, ask each student to briefly summarize the selection and explain why they think readers care about the character of Aurelio Escovar. Next, have students exchange their writing with a partner. Ask them to collaborate to produce a single summary and explain how caring about Escovar increases the suspense of the story.

☑ Guidelines for Going Back Into the Text: Author's Craft

One way the author creates suspense in this story is by developing believable characters to whom readers relate. Help students understand how writers develop believable characters. **Round characters** seem like real

200

people. They are complex with typical strengths and weaknesses. **Flat characters**, on the other hand, do not seem real; they lack depth. A flat character has only one personality trait. In a flat protagonist, that quality may be a strength like courage or compassion. In a flat antagonist, that quality may be a weakness like cowardice or cruelty. Flat characters are not believable.

Use questions like these to guide class discussion about the two characters: Are Escovar and the Mayor round or flat characters? What qualities in Escovar do you find admirable? What imperfections, if any, must he struggle to overcome? What traits in the Mayor do you find objectionable? Does he show any strengths or admirable qualities at any point? Explain. How does the character development increase the suspense in the story?

Possible answers to the questions in the Student Edition are:

1. Curiosity begins when Escovar tells his son to lie to the Mayor about his whereabouts and the Mayor responds with a violent threat.

2. Tension is created when Escovar says, "O.K. . . . . Tell him to come and shoot me." That tension increases when Escovar states that he cannot use anesthesia. His refusal to look at the Mayor and the Mayor's refusal to stop looking at him adds suspense. When Escovar says, "Now you'll pay for our twenty dead men," there is a momentary surge in suspense.

3. Suspense is resolved when we see the outcome of the confrontation—when Escovar pulls the Mayor's tooth without anesthesia, but the Mayor does not respond violently.

☑ FOLLOW-UP DISCUSSION

Use the questions that follow to continue your discussion of "One of These Days." Possible answers are given in parentheses.

Recalling

1. What does the Mayor threaten to do if Escovar will not pull his tooth? (He threatens to shoot the dentist.)

2. What does Escovar say when he grips the Mayor's infected tooth with forceps? ("Now you will pay for our twenty dead men.")

3. What does the Mayor reply when Escovar asks if he should send the bill to him or the town? ("It's the same thing.")

Interpreting

4. Why are buzzards sitting on the roof of a house in the town? (Buzzards are attracted to dead bodies. The presence of buzzards in the town is a sign that there have been corpses in a public place recently [the execution of twenty villagers].)

5. Why does Escovar say, "So much the better" after learning that the Mayor knows he is in his office? (Escovar prefers to let the Mayor know that he was trying to avoid him.)

6. Why does Escovar change his mind and decide to pull the tooth? (He sees the pain and desperation on the Mayor's face. Compassionate by nature, Escovar cannot ignore the suffering of another human being, even a person like the Mayor. Therefore, he closes the drawer in which he keeps a gun and tells the Mayor to sit down.)

Applying

7. In your opinion, why doesn't Escovar look at the Mayor before beginning to pull the tooth? (Answers will vary. Some students may suggest that the dentist is deliberately showing disrespect. Others may suggest that he can only go ahead with his compassionate act if he concentrates on what he is doing and not whom he is helping. Still others may infer that Escovar is lying about the anesthesia and is afraid the Mayor will realize that, if their eyes meet.)

8. In your opinion, what is the significance of the Mayor giving a "casual, military salute" as he leaves? (Answers will vary. Some students may suggest that after showing "weakness" by asking the dentist to help him, the Mayor is trying to regain respect by acting "cool" [casual] and "macho" [military]. Others may suggest that the "military" salute illustrates the lack of democracy in Colombia at the time. The Mayor is also the military representative of the government and has the power to order the executions of twenty villagers or shoot an uncooperative dentist.)

ENRICHMENT

Students may enjoy viewing *Gabriel García Márquez: Magical Realism*. The film is available from Films For the Humanities and Sciences, P.O. Box 2053, Princeton, NJ 08543-2053, (800) 257-5126.

INTRODUCING THE THEME

Before students read the thematic connection to "Rise of the People," have them work in pairs or small groups to make a cluster diagram around the word *oppression*. Allow students about five minutes to brainstorm for ideas. Then invite volunteers to contribute their opinions to the class web. As students suggest words and ideas, construct the web on the board. Here is a sample web:

You may wish to use the following discussion prompts to help students make connections among the theme, graphic organizer, fine art, and their own experiences.

Discussion Prompts

- How would you define oppression? (Possible responses: loss of freedom, abuse of authority or power)
- What connections can you draw between the word oppression and the title of this theme, "Rise of the People"? (Possible responses: When oppression becomes too great, people will rebel. If the group is strong enough, people will seek freedom.)
- Based on the theme title and the Diego Rivera mural, what do you predict the selections in this unit will be about? (Possible responses: fictional and real examples of people's attempts to obtain their human rights)

BRIDGING THE ESL/LEP GAP

Pair ESL/LEP students with proficient speakers to read "Rise of the People." Partners should take turns reading alternate paragraphs aloud and then briefly restate the main ideas in the paragraph. When partners have finished reading, have them write a paragraph summarizing what they learned about oppression from this feature.

In addition, you may wish to have ESL/LEP students create a word bank of unfamiliar words or phrases they encountered in their reading. Possibilities include *iron will, apartheid, brutal, vitally,* and *extent.* Partners can look up these words in a dictionary to find their meanings.

COMPLETING THE ACTIVITY

Before each committee develops a new set of rules, students may wish to write guidelines to help them work together smoothly as a group. Here are some guidelines that students may wish to consider:

- Only one person at a time should speak to the group.
- Group members should listen carefully and nonjudgmentally to each speaker.
- Comments should be phrased in a positive way. Speakers should avoid making hurtful comments.
- A reasonable time limit should be set for each comment so that everyone has a chance to speak.
- Everyone should have a say in the final decision.

The Book of Sand

by Jorge Luis Borges (pages 342–348)

OBJECTIVES

Literary

- to analyze symbols and their meaning in a short story
- to discuss the *conceit* and the *oxymoron* as examples of figurative language

Historical

- to analyze the influence of the Metaphysical poets of the 1600s on the author
- to discuss the author's criticism of Argentine national policy under Juan Perón

Cultural

- to discuss other cultural influences on the author's works
- to indentify the questions about the nature of reality raised in the author's works

SELECTION RESOURCES

Use Assessment Worksheet 53 to check students' vocabulary recognition, content comprehension, and appreciation of literary skills.

 Informal Assessment Opportunity

SELECTION OVERVIEW

The young Jorge Luis Borges joined a group of writers known as *Ultraists*. The Ultraists experimented with themes involving the irrational nature of human existence and with radical literary forms, including books in which the reader could reorganize the sequence of pages to change the outcomes. It was probably this influence that resulted in two of the recurring images in Borges's works: the universe as an endless book and human experience as a series of absurdities or contradictions. Both ideas can be found at work in "The Book of Sand."

Borges begins his tale with a series of mathematical theorems about infinity. This provides a scientific basis for his philosophical concept of life as an endless book. It also sets the stage for the narrator's irrational or absurd experience. In mathematics, an infinite decimal, in which no consecutive set of digits repeats itself, is called an *irrational number* or a *surd.*

The existence of the book contradicts reality. Borges insists that his tale is true, although we know it is fiction. A previous owner, who treasured it, was an Indian peasant who could not read. Though a bound volume, its contents are limitless. The pages are numbered, but the sequence is illogical. Owning it brings both pleasure and misgivings. (It is only after purchasing the rare treasure that the narrator realizes the seller desperately wanted to get rid of the book.) In the end, the narrator hides the work on a library shelf among other books. Like *The Book of Sand* itself, the meaning of the story is open to various interpretations.

In this selection, the narrator purchases *The Book of Sand* from a Bible salesman. Unlike any other book, *The Book of Sand* has an infinite number of pages. As the narrator becomes more obsessed with the book—both because of its infinite nature and his fear of having it stolen—the narrator becomes reclusive. When he realizes the effect that the book has had on him he decides to lose the book on the shelves of a library where he once worked.

ENGAGING THE STUDENTS

On the board, write the following words: *curiosity, determination, obsession, frustration,* and *dismissal.* Ask students if they have ever tried, without success, to solve a challenging puzzle. Have them comment on what the experience was like. Refer to the terms on the board. Guide a discussion of the emotional stages people often go through in this situation. Elicit the following kinds of responses: "I'm going to solve this." "I can't put it down." "This is a nightmare." "I'll put it someplace where I'll never see it again." Suggest that they think about this discussion as they read the selection.

BRIDGING THE ESL/LEP LANGUAGE GAP

The overall vocabulary, specialized terms, and academic references in this selection will be difficult for many students, and they will probably need to read the selection more than once. Before they begin, ask them to take notes. As they read the story the first time, tell them to summarize what they learn about the mysterious book. Questions like these can guide their reading: What are some unusual features of the book? How did the Bible salesman obtain it? How does the narrator's behavior change after he buys the book? What does he eventually do with the book?

After they have read the story once, have them work in mixed groups of both limited and proficient English speakers to discuss Borges's use of symbols and his themes. (They may need to read the story with this focus.) Ask them to respond to questions like the following: How is the book a symbol for life? Why is it called *The Book of Sand*? Why is the Bible salesman willing to sell the book? Why does the narrator first call it a "treasure" and later a "nightmarish object"? Why does he decide to hide it?

✔ PRETEACHING SELECTION VOCABULARY

List the following topics on the board and ask students to fill in each topic with words from the story:

BIBLE REFERENCES Examples: *Vulgate, Holy Writ, Book of Books, Word of God*

GEOGRAPHICAL REFERENCES Examples: *Buenos Aires, Orkneys, Bikaner, Bombay, Norwegian*

TERMS RELATED TO BOOKS Examples: *octavo, spine, typographically, versicles, flyleaf, bibliophile*

Lead a class discussion about why Borges includes so many references to these three categories.

The words printed in boldfaced type are tested on the selection assessment worksheet.

PREREADING

Reading the Story in a Cultural Context

Help students read for purpose by telling them that in England, in the 1600s, a group of authors wrote poems with religious or philosophical themes. They used startling images and paradoxes (or contradictions) to convey their messages. These writers, whom Borges read, are called the *Metaphysical poets*. Metaphysics is a branch of philosophy concerned with the nature and meaning of existence, including reality. Ask them to consider, as they read, ways in which these writers influenced Borges's themes and style.

Focusing on the Selection

Call the students' attention to the quote at the beginning of the story "Thy rope of sands." Note that George Herbert was an English pastor and a Metaphysical poet. The quote is from his poem, "The Collar." The title refers to the discipline that restrains a person from unholy or forbidden pursuits. Ask students to consider the following questions as they read: Is it possible to climb a "rope of sands"? How do you think the rope of sands is like *The Book of Sand*? How are they different? Herbert is certain of God's existence and love. Do you think Borges agrees? Explain your answer.

POSTREADING

The following activities parallel the features with the same titles in the Student Edition.

Responses to Critical Thinking Questions

1. Details include the narrator's pride in his collection of Bibles, his love for Scottish writers, and his having retired from a position at the Argentine National Library.

2. Sample response: Nothing in the book is the same way twice. The book is always changing and seemingly infinite. Such a book challenges any view that there are limits in life or that we can know anything with certainty.

3. Answers will vary. Some students may appreciate the humor of losing a book by putting it on a library shelf; others may feel that the narrator should have tried to make some money by selling the mysterious book. Invite students to share their own ideas about how they would set themselves free from such a book.

✔ Guidelines for Writing Your Response to "The Book of Sand"

If students wish, have them share their journal entries with a partner. As an alternative writing activity, have students think about the selection and then write three questions that they would like to ask the author if they could meet him. Form groups of three or four and suggest that students share their questions and reach consensus on the best ones. Then have group members take turns asking questions and role playing the author.

☑ Guidelines for Going Back Into the Text: Author's Craft

Help students understand how an author's technique can help support theme by discussing the *conceit* and the *oxymoron*. Tell them that these were two favorite devices of the Metaphysical poets. A *conceit* is a striking, often witty, figure of speech that is intended to surprise the reader. An example is John Donne's now familiar "catch a falling star" as an image for the impossible.

An *oxymoron* is a type of conceit that links two apparently paradoxical or contradictory ideas for literary effect. Herbert's "rope of sand" is one example. Thomas Wyatt's description of passion, "I burn and freeze like ice," is another. The title of Borges's story is a third example.

Help students find other paradoxical conceits in the work. Examples: claiming his made-up story is true (page 343); "nondescript features" (page 343); the salesman correcting the narrator by substituting one Scot, Burns, for another, Hume (page 346) hiding a leaf in a forest (page 347); hiding a book in a library (page 347). Ask: How do these contradictory images support Borges's theme?

Possible answers to the questions in the Student Edition are:

1. Sample response: Theoretically, it might be possible to count the number of grains of sand, but in a practical sense, it is beyond measure. Thus, sand is infinite. Calling the mysterious text *The Book of Sand* indicates that it, too, cannot be measured (as the narrator finds out).

2. Sample response: Perhaps it represents what we think is safe, measurable, or predictable in our lives. *The Book of Sand* is a challenge to the narrator's library, even as it challenges his views; he is unable to keep it hidden within his home library. Finally, he shelves the book in the Argentine National Library, where he feels no one will find it again, so he can return to "normal" life.

3. Students' symbols need not be original, but students should be able to explain why each is appropriate. Sample responses are given:

- love = a rose; a sunrise; a heart
- anger = a volcano; the color red
- honesty = the color white; boy scouts
- wisdom = a diploma; a jewel

☑ FOLLOW-UP DISCUSSION

Use the questions that follow to continue your discussion of "The Book of Sand." Possible answers are given in parentheses.

Recalling

1. From whom did the Scottish Bible salesman buy the book? (an illiterate Indian of the lowest caste)

2. What does the narrator give the salesman in exchange for *The Book of Sand*? (his monthly pension check and a valued Bible that he inherited)

3. In the end, where does the narrator hide *The Book of Sand*? (on a shelf in the basement of the Argentine National Library)

Interpreting

4. Why has the book "passed through many hands?" (The mystery of its infinite contents fascinates and attracts buyers, but its destructive influence on owners drives them to be rid of it.)

5. What is the source of the "gloom that emanated from" the salesman? (the disturbing power that the book has over all who come into its possession)

6. Why is the narrator's choice of a hiding place for the book ironic? (By placing it on a shelf in a library open to the public, he is "hiding it in plain view" of anyone who comes in search of a book.)

Applying

7. What is Borges suggesting by the different backgrounds of the three owners of *The Book of Sand*? (Each comes from a different ethnic background. Borges is suggesting that the fascination and fear the book inspires are universal traits of people.)

8. Do you think the narrator acted responsibly by disposing of the book as he did? (Students should recognize that his decision not to burn it was based on concern for others rather than self-interest. In addition, he does not trick another unwary person into buying the book. Hiding it where it would not attract attention may have been his only responsible recourse.)

ENRICHMENT

Students may enjoy viewing the video *The Inner World of J.L. Borges* about the author's home and life in Buenos Aires. This movie is available from Films For the Humanities and Sciences, P.O. 2053, Princeton, NJ 08543-2053, (800) 257-5126.

Continuity of Parks

by Julio Cortázar (pages 349–352)

OBJECTIVES

Literary

- to analyze the use of sensory details to create atmosphere or mood in a short story
- to explain how the author uses literary elements to encourage active reading

Historical

- to discuss political repression in Argentina between the 1940s and the 1970s
- to examine the effect of political repression on the lives of Argentinians

Cultural

- to discuss Argentinian exiles' support of individual rights throughout South America
- to analyze the cultural basis for literary experimentation throughout South America

SELECTION RESOURCES

Use Assessment Worksheet 54 to check students' vocabulary recognition, content comprehension, and appreciation of literary skills.

 Informal Assessment Opportunity

SELECTION OVERVIEW

The sights, sounds, and other sensory impressions the writer uses to describe the physical location of a piece of literature create emotional responses in the reader's mind called atmosphere or model. These setting details influence the characters and the way they live their lives. They also establish certain expectations about what kind of events will follow. If the atmosphere is tense or ominous for example, readers and characters alike may be anxious or fearful. In his fiction, Julio Cortázar likes changing the atmosphere unexpectedly. By breaking the reader's habitual expectations, he heightens the emotional effect of the climax and makes the reader think.

In "Continuity of Parks," Cortazar creates a tranquil atmosphere for the real world of the study. Because the tension is confined to a fictional world, both the man and the reader can relax. As the lover enters the house, however, Cortázar surprises us by revealing that the two worlds are one. Terror replaces tranquility as murder invades the peaceful setting of the study.

ENGAGING THE STUDENTS

On the board, write: "I should have seen it coming."

Allow students two minutes to recall a story or movie from their experience that had a surprise ending. Tell them to write a brief paragraph about clues the writer gave the audience. These might be plot events or dialogue that seemed to mean one thing at the time but later turned out to mean something else.

Ask volunteers to read their paragraphs aloud. Use these responses as the basis for a class discussion. Guide students to understand the concept that surprise endings are most effective when we "should have seen it coming." The writer gives the audience enough information to figure out the surprise. However, the information is presented in a way that leads us to draw an incorrect conclusion. Tell students to think about the information shared in the discussion as they read the selection.

BRIDGING THE ESL/LEP LANGUAGE GAP

Students may have difficulty understanding the meaning of *estate, power of attorney*, and *joint ownership*. Explain that estate has two different meanings. An estate can be the house and surrounding land on which a wealthy person lives. An estate also refers to the money and other valuables that a person leaves behind at death. Often, a married couple has joint ownership of their estate. This means that each partner has equal rights to ownership. Power of attorney gives another individual the legal authority to make decisions regarding that estate. Have your ESL/LEP students work with fluent speakers to write sentences using these three terms. Encourage them to base their sentences on events in "Continuity of Parks" to reinforce their understanding of the story.

✔ PRETEACHING SELECTION VOCABULARY

Discuss how writers use nouns, verbs, and adjectives to create atmosphere. Have students scan the story for words that Cortázar uses to build an atmosphere of suspense or fear. Guide them to create the following list: *sordid,* **dilemma,** **apprehensive,** *furtive,* **rivulet,** *writhed,* **dissuade,** *abominably, destroy,* **alibis,** *hazards, cold-blooded,* and *thudding.* Call on students to predict what will happen based on the vocabulary. Encourage them to use one of the words from the list as they express their thoughts. Tell them to confirm their predictions as they read.

The words printed in boldfaced type are tested on the selection assessment worksheet.

PREREADING

Reading the Story in a Cultural Context

Help students read for purpose by reminding them that Cortázar challenges readers to see his stories in different ways. Explain that under the repressive government, most of the Argentinean people were poor. Almost all of the country's wealth was concentrated in the hands of a few. These wealthy people supported the government's actions because they feared a revolution. Tell students to consider possible political symbolism in the story. Ask: Who might the man in the study represent? Who might the lovers secretly planning his destruction symbolize? To whom did the wealthy give 'power of attorney' to handle the country's affairs? How might the estate on which the man mistakenly thought he was safe represent the short-sighted view of those who supported political repression?

Focusing on the Selection

Discuss with the students the fact that Cortázar likes to challenge readers to think about things in different ways. The author provides no background information on the characters. Suggest that students create their own mental pictures as they read. Ask them to consider the following prompts:

• What do the characters look like? How old are they?

• What kind of background does each come from? How did they meet?

• What kind of person is each? How did the relationship between the characters reach the point that it has?

After reading is completed, you might have students work in small groups to compare their impressions and discuss different interpretations of "reality" in the characters' lives.

POSTREADING

The following activities parallel the features with the same titles in the Student Edition.

Responses to Critical Thinking Questions

Possible responses are:

1. It is "dangerous" for the man who is reading because he becomes so involved in the story that he winds up being the fictional murderer's victim. It might be "dangerous" for readers because it challenges them to use their imagination and to consider different ways of thinking about things that they take for granted.

2. By blending fantasy and reality, the story suggests that liberation of the mind or imagination is important, perhaps as important as political liberation.

3. Answers will vary. Some students may feel uncomfortable about the ending of the story because it is so unusual; others may find their own imagination sparked by the unexpected ending.

✔ Guidelines for Writing Your Response to "Continuity of Parks"

Have students share their journal entries with a partner. Or, as an alternative writing activity, suggest that students write a one-paragraph extension to the story. Suggest that Cortázar has one more surprise in store for the reader. The man in the study suspects that his wife and her lover are planning his murder. He has set a trap for them and is waiting to spring it. Tell them to begin at the point when the lover enters the study.

✔ Guidelines for Going Back Into the Text: Author's Craft

A **motive** is the reason that a character acts in a certain way. A character's background, nature, and beliefs influence motive. Discuss with students the fact that

Cortázar does not provide the reader with information on his characters' motives for their actions. Remind them that he liked to challenge readers to break free of habits and think in different ways. Direct students to consider different possible motives as they read. Ask them to consider if the sensory details and imagery in the story offer clues to the characters' motives. Afterwards, you might have students work in groups to discuss their speculations.

Possible answers to the questions in the Student Edition are:

1. Sensory details include the sight and texture of the green velvet upholstery, possibly the scent of nearby cigarettes, and the flickering of the afternoon air in the park. They create a sense of relaxed comfort, a feeling that life is good and need not change.

2. Sensory details include the touch of the woman's kisses, the sound of the dry leaves, the warmth of the dagger against the man's chest, the pounding of his heart, the sound of their "panting dialogue," the look of the woman's flying hair as she departs, and the sight of a "yellowish fog of dusk" into which the man passes.

3. Answers will vary. Some students, for example, may respond to details in the fictional scene in the cabin; others may be drawn in by the details that describe the murderer's approach to his victim.

✔ FOLLOW-UP DISCUSSION

Use the questions that follow to continue your discussion of "Continuity of Parks." Possible answers are given in parentheses.

Recalling

1. What issue does the man discuss with his estate manager? (the issue of joint ownership of the estate)

2. In the novel the man is reading, who met at a mountain cabin? (a woman and her lover)

3. What does the murderer see as he enters the study? ("the high back of an armchair covered in green velvet and the head of a man in the chair reading a novel")

Interpreting

4. What do you think the lover means by the "liberty" that pounds underneath the dagger? (If he uses the dagger to murder the woman's husband, then they will be free to marry.)

5. Why does the woman hurry away in the opposite direction from the lover as they leave the cabin? (They have set up an alibi. It requires that she be seen in a location far from the house at the time her husband is murdered.)

6. What do you think Cortázar is referring to by "the woman's words" that the lover hears in his mind as he enters the house? (He has not been in the house before. She has provided him with a description of the rooms so he can move quickly and quietly through the house to the study where he will find his victim.)

Applying

7. Why do you think Cortázar does not make any moral judgments about the characters in his story? (Answers will vary. Students may suggest that Cortázar wants readers to think for themselves. By not making any judgments, he frees the reader to look at the story in as many different ways as possible.)

8. Did this story help you to free your imagination? Explain. Do you prefer this type of story to a more traditional one? Why or why not? (Answers will vary. Encourage students to cite passages they found particularly engaging or challenging. Also encourage them to compare this story to other more traditional ones they have read.)

ENRICHMENT

Students may enjoy viewing the video *The Southern Plains* about Paraguay, Uruguay, and Argentina. This video is part of the South America series available from Social Studies School Service, 10200 Jefferson Boulevard, Room 12, Culver City, CA 90232, (800) 421-4246.

Homecoming
by Dennis Scott

The Child's Return
by Phyllis Allfrey

Jamaica Market
by Agnes Maxwell-Hall

On Leaving
by Gertrudis Gomez de Avellaneda

Zion, Me Wan Go Home
Anonymous   (pages 353–360)

OBJECTIVES

Literary
- to analyze standard meters used in poems
- to understand how rhythm in poetry affects its meaning

Historical
- to understand Caribbean development from colonies to independent nations
- to discuss the influence of the slave trade on Caribbean nations

Cultural
- to recognize European and African influences on Caribbean culture
- to discuss the blending of many traditions into a Caribbean identity

SELECTION RESOURCES

Use Assessment Worksheet 55 to check students' vocabulary recognition, content comprehension, and appreciation of literary skills.

 Informal Assessment Opportunity

SELECTION OVERVIEW

Rhythm occurs naturally in speech. As we talk, we stress different sounds. We may do this to give greater emphasis to certain words. We may change stress to keep speech from becoming monotonous.

Poets frequently repeat sounds in regular patterns to create rhythm. When poets stress the second syllable in a word, it creates a rising sound. When they stress the first syllable, it creates a falling sound. When they mix the pattern, they create an alternating rising and falling sound. This alternating pattern echoes the rhythm found throughout nature, such as ocean tides, phases of the moon, and breathing.

Rhythm helps create the distinctive sound that is one of poetry's pleasures. Rhythm is also related to poetic meaning. Poets stress certain words that help reinforce the message of the work. This is especially true of the many one-syllable words in the language. As a rule, poets place the stress in a line on nouns, verbs, and adjectives. Articles and prepositions are unstressed.

In these five poems, the poets use rhythmic patterns and evocative images to recall their homelands in the Caribbean.

ENGAGING THE STUDENTS

Tell students to imagine that they are describing a place they know to someone who has never been there. Have them jot down ideas for details they would include. Suggest that they think about the sights, sounds, smells, and emotions they associate with that place. Use student details as the basis for a discussion about poetry that describes places of special meaning.

BRIDGING THE ESL/LEP LANGUAGE GAP

The poetic style and vocabulary in these poems may be difficult for many students, and they will probably need to read the selection more than once.

After students have read the poem once, have them discuss, in mixed groups of limited and proficient

English speakers, lines or images they find particularly challenging. You might suggest that they pay particular attention to the importance of colors in "Homecoming" and "Jamaica Market." Also ask them to compare the emotions of the seemingly young speaker in "On Leaving" with those of the older speaker who is coming home to die in "The Child's Return."

✔ PRETEACHING
SELECTION VOCABULARY

Discuss the poets' use of words that appeal to the senses. Have them scan the five poems for adjectives that describe color: *coffee* (from "Homecoming"); *cobalt* (from "The Child's Return"); *pallid, saffron, ruby* (from "Jamaica Market"). Next have them find geographical terms that appeal to sight: **topographies** and *quadrant* (from "Homecoming"). Then, tell them to scan for adjectives and nouns that appeal to the sense of hearing: **dissonant** and **metronome** (from "Homecoming"); **babel** (from "Jamaica Market"). After reading the selection, have students use these words in sentences to describe the impressions the images created in their minds.

The words printed in boldfaced type are tested on the selection assessment worksheet.

PREREADING

Reading the Poems in a Cultural Context

Help students read for purpose by making sure that they appreciate the beauty of the sea and its importance to island cultures. You might also want to discuss the kind of open-air market catalogued by Maxwell-Hall. Ask: Why do you think a person far from his or her place of birth might look at maps or read about geography? Why do you think these people would occasionally think about the sights and sounds of their homeland?

Focusing on the Selections

As they read, guide students to compare the images the poets use to describe Caribbean culture. Ask: What kinds of scenes do the poets recreate when thinking about their homeland? Why do you think they chose those images? How do you think these images are related to a Caribbean person's sense of identity?

POSTREADING

The following activities parallel the features with the same titles in the Student Edition.

Responses to Critical Thinking Questions

Possible responses are:

1. Dennis Scott: To be Caribbean means to feel the islands inside you, wherever you go. Phyllis All-frey: To be Caribbean means to have a place of eternal rest. Agnes Maxwell-Hall: To be Caribbean means to rejoice in the richness of the islands' plants and animals. Gertrudis Gomez de Avellaneda: To be Caribbean means to have lived in paradise. "Zion, Me Wan Go Home": To be Caribbean means to have a strong African heritage.

2. Yes. "Homecoming," "The Child's Return," "Zion, Me Wan Go Home," and "On Leaving" suggest a longing for one's homeland and/or the pull that draws one back home. In "Jamaica Market" the long list of the island's bounty reveals the poet's appreciation for the richness of her homeland.

3. Answers will vary. Encourage students to support their responses with specific reasons and details from the poem.

✔ Guidelines for Writing Your Response to "Homecoming," "The Child's Return," "Jamaica Market," "On Leaving," and "Zion, Me Wan Go Home"

Have students share their journal entries with a partner. Or, as an alternative, have students select their favorite Caribbean setting from one poem in the selection. Tell them to write one paragraph explaining why they would like to visit that locale and describing what they would like to see while there.

✔ Guidelines for Going Back Into the Text: Author's Craft

A **foot**, the basic unit of meter in poetry, is made up of a group of syllables. Each foot (or group) contains a stressed syllable and one or more unstressed syllables. We name the meter according to (1) the pattern of stressed and unstressed syllables in each foot and (2) the number of feet in the poetic line. "Jamaica Market," for example, is composed in trochaic tetrameter. The stress pattern is a stressed syllable followed by an unstressed syllable (trochaic). There are four feet in each line (tetrameter). The fourth foot contains only a stressed syllable so that each line ends with a rising sound. Possible answers to the questions in the Student Edition are:

1. Answers will vary. Students are likely to find "Jamaica Market" and "Zion, Me Won Go Home" most predictable. "The Child's Return" also has a fairly consistent rhythmic pattern. "On Leaving" and "Homecoming" are more conversational, as

these poems lack a consistent rhythmic pattern and their thoughts are more fragmented.

2. Scott's rhythm sounds more conversational and Allfrey's more predictable or formal, particularly because of its rhyme scheme. The rhythm lends an inspirational feel to Allfrey's poem but makes Scott's poem seem more immediate and sincere.

3. Answers will vary. Encourage students to take turns sharing their rhythms with the class to see the different ways in which rhythm and words work together to express a common theme.

☑ FOLLOW-UP DISCUSSION

Use the questions that follow to continue your discussion. Possible answers are given in parentheses.

Recalling

1. In "The Homecoming," what does his heart tell the poet is "home?" (this arc of islands)

2. In "The Child's Return," when will the poet return to the Caribbean? (when it is time to die)

3. In "Jamaica Market," what kind of bird can be found in the market? (pigeons with scarlet beaks)

4. In "On Leaving," what two bright objects does "shining" Cuba bring to the poet's mind? (a sea pearl and a western star)

Interpreting

5. In "Homecoming," who and what do you think the image "paper in the Admiral's fist" refers to? (The Admiral is Christopher Columbus holding the chart he used on his voyage to the Americas.

6. In "Jamaica Market," how is the final image of the sun a reference to Caribbean culture? (The light and heat of the sun blend all the colors into one. Similarly, in the Carribean, many cultures blend together to create one Caribbean identity.)

7. In "On Leaving," why do you think the poet refers to Cuba as "Eden"? (Her life in Cuba was like the innocent happiness of life in Paradise.)

Applying

8. After reading these poems, what traditions and beliefs do you think Caribbean immigrants bring to the diverse culture of the United States? (Answers will vary.)

ENRICHMENT

Students may benefit from exploring *Poetry in Motion*. The CD-ROM is available from National School Products, 101 East Broadway, Maryville, TN 37801. (800) 251-9124

RESPONSES TO REVIEWING THE REGION

1. Sample answer: Octavio Paz evokes a "sense of place" in "The Street" by describing the setting and character. The "long and silent street" filled with "blackness" creates an eerie mood. This is heightened by the "dark and doorless" streets to create a feeling of anxiety. The character is caught up in this tense mood as he follows someone, or is followed.

2. Sample answer: The poem "Chilean Earth" made me think that Chile is a beautiful place. The lines "The land most green with orchards / the land most blond with grain, / the land most red with grapevines" evoke images of a rich, colorful countryside.

3. Sample answer: If I were to become Bouki in the Haitian folktale "Bouki Rents a Horse," I would not be as frightened as Bouki. Instead, I would be the character to come up with Ti Malice's clever plan to get Bouki's deposit—and more—returned.

☑ FOCUSING ON GENRE SKILLS

"Bouki Rents a Horse" is a classic example of a folktale. Many folktales such as this one are amusing stories that were first told to entertain people; often, they make fun of a human weakness. This folktale humorously points out Bouki's timidity and Toussaint's foolishness. Folktales such as this one entertain people, keep the stories and traditions of the past alive, and teach moral lessons. They also warn people about bad character traits, such as jealousy and greed. Have students select another folktale, such as "The Ch'i-Lin Purse," and identify the elements that make it a folktale.

BIBLIOGRAPHY
BORGES, JORGES LUIS. "The Book of Sand." In *The Book of Sand*, translated by Norman Thomas di Giovanni. New York: Penguin USA, 1977.

CORTÁZAR, JULIO. "Continuity of Parks." In *End of the Game and Other Stories*. New York: Pantheon Books, a division of Random House, Inc., 1967.

CORTÉS, ALFONSO. "The Great Prayer." In *Poets of Nicaragua,* translated by Steven White. Greensboro, NC: Unicorn Press, 1982.

HAROLD COURLANDER. "Bouki Rents a Horse." In *The Piece of Fire and Other Haitian Tales*. New York: Harcourt Brace & World, 1964.

MÁRQUEZ, GABRIEL GARCÍA. "One of These Days." In *Collected Stories*. New York: Harper & Row, 1984.

MENDIOLA, VICTOR MANUEL. "The Room." In *New Writing From Mexico*, translated by Reginald Gibbons. City TriQuarterly Books, 1992.

MISTRAL, GABRIELA. "Chilean Earth." In *A Gabriela Mistral Reader*. English translation by Maria Giachetti. Fredonia, NY: White Pine Press, 1993.

9 Canada

CHAPTER PREVIEW

Literature of Canada			
Selections	**Genre**	**Author's Craft/Literary Skills**	**Cultural Values & Focus**
"The Old Man's Lazy," Peter Blue Cloud, pages 362–365	poetry	dramatic monologue	conflict between Native American and European cultures; conflict between generations; preserving cultural traditions and the land
"All the Years of Her Life," Morley Callaghan, page 366–373	short story	characterization	family relationships; spiritual growth from conflict; impact of the Great Depression on Canadian life
MAKING CULTURAL CONNECTIONS: The Americas, pages 374-375			
from *Little by Little*, Jean Little, pages 376–383	autobiography	autobiography	overcoming disabilities; accepting differences in individuals; learning the power of words
"A Night in the Royal Ontario Museum," Margaret Atwood, pages 384–387	poetry	onomatopoeia; alliteration; assonance	cultural identity; understanding how literature helps shape national identity; recognizing the influences of the past
"My Financial Career," Stephen Leacock, pages 388–392	essay	humor	use of humor to evaluate Canadian institutions and ways of life

ASSESSMENT

Assessment opportunities are indicated by a ☑ next to the activity title. For guidelines, see Teacher's Resource Manual page xxxvi.

CROSS-DISCIPLINE TEACHING OPPORTUNITIES

Social Studies   To help students understand the history of Canada, work with a history teacher to identify major figures who led the nation on its journey from colony to independent nation as well as important contemporary leaders. Include the *metis* (mixed French and Native American) leader, Louis Riel. Have interested students research the lives and accomplishments of these individuals and present brief oral reports to the class. You could invite guest teachers to discuss contemporary political issues in Canada. Examples include the separatist movement among French-speaking people in Quebec and the proposal to form an autonomous Native American province in the northwest. You might also discuss new fiction and nonfiction with historical connections to the country.

Art   The Native American cultural groups of Canada have a long and varied artistic tradition that includes paintings, totems as well as other wood carvings, and sculpture in bone and soapstone. Work with an art teacher to create a lesson on this Canadian art. Relate it to "A Night in the Royal Ontario Museum" and the search for a Canadian identity through the arts. Consider having students illustrate different scenes from "The Old Man's Lazy" (e.g., hanging the miniature shield). Small groups might collaborate on a set of pictures that could accompany an illustrated edition of the poem. You might encourage students to create an original totem the grandfather makes as a gift for his grandchildren.

Geography   Work with a social studies teacher to create a lesson on the physical and cultural geography of Canada. You might focus on the Canadian Shield, the vast region that contains the oldest rock formations in North America. Discuss its natural resources and how this hostile terrain hindered transportation between regions. Relate the discussion to the search for a national identity.

Have students work in pairs or small groups to select one province in the country and create a travel brochure (with map) describing the physical and cultural geography found there. Ask a social studies teacher to help you gather resource materials to assist the class in their projects.

Languages   Invite a language teacher to provide a lesson on the French literature of Canada that has developed independently of the English. Work together to create a comparison/contrast chart focusing on genres, characteristics, and themes. Ask the class to discuss how the bilingual tradition has affected the search for a Canadian identity.

Science   With a science teacher, create a lesson on the geology of the Canadian Shield. Include discussion of its formation by retreating glaciers, its harsh environment, natural features, and its vast mineral wealth.

Economics   Work with an economics teacher to present a lesson about current economic issues in Canada. Include developments of importance in particular provinces as well as national issues.

SUPPLEMENTING THE CORE CURRICULUM

The Student Edition provides humanities materials related to specific cultures in Making Cultural Connections: Latin America and Canada on pages 374-375 and in The Art of The Tapestries on pages A14-A16. You might wish to invite students to pursue the following activities outside of class:

- Have students examine the artwork and captions on the Latin American and Canadian pages of the art insert. Though the works might at first appear quite different from one another, encourage students to look closely for unifying themes that reflect cultural heritage. Ask: "What do you notice about the people portrayed in the two Latin American paintings? How do they reflect the cultural heritage of the area?" "What connections can you draw between the ancient Mexican carved stone and the utensils and mask carved by Native Canadian peoples?" "How was the painter of 'Late Autumn' influenced by his homeland?" Challenge students to write a comparison-and-contrast of at least two works that appear on the Latin American and Canadian pages.

- Lead a class discussion about the search for a national identity as a dominant theme in modern Canadian literature. Discuss how European influences from the colonial period might have hindered this search. Ask students to consider what effect the economic and political power of the United States may have had on the development of an independent Canadian identity. Encourage discussion of similarities and differences in themes between the Canadian selections and United States works with which the students are familiar. Students who wish to explore this theme further could use library resources to find and read other works by the authors in the chapter and other Canadian writers that address this theme.

- Tell students that some geologists believe that rocks in the Canadian Shield may be five billion years old. Suggest that they work in small groups to prepare a written report on the rocks and minerals found there. Each group member could take responsibility for one specific kind. (Examples: cobalt, iron, copper, uranium.) Encourage them to illustrate the report with original drawings.

- Tell students that, in recent years, Canada has become one of the favorite sites for paleontologists in search of dinosaurs and other prehistoric fossils. Fifty different species of dinosaurs have been found in Dinosaur Provincial Park in the western province of Alberta. Students who wish to learn more about this subject may consult the wide range of literature available on these fascinating prehistoric animals. Encourage them to create a diorama showing a scene from Alberta during the Age of Dinosaurs or a modern "dig" in western Canada with examples of fossil bones. You might incorporate this activity after students read "A Night in the Royal Ontario Museum."

- Tell students that Canada, like the United States, is a democracy. Canada however, is a parliamentary democracy. Encourage interested students to learn more and create a chart comparing and contrasting Canada's parliamentary system with our form of government.

INTRODUCING CHAPTER 9: CANADA

Using the Chapter Opener

On the chalkboard, write: "What is a national identity?" Tell students that in the past some Canadians have criticized their country for imitating the United States too closely. They were especially critical of Canadians who adopted materialistic values found in the society of their wealthier, more economically developed neighbor. They suggested that Canadians act like "little brothers." Challenge students to identify ways in which younger children sometimes try to act just like older siblings. On the board, assemble as comprehensive a list as possible. Then discuss ways in which these children establish their own identity as they mature. (Examples: exploring different interests; developing personal talents; dressing differently; find-

ing other role models.) Modern Canadian writers have tried to establish a national identity independent of the influences of writers in the United States. Ask: "How do you think these writers would try to establish a Canadian national identity in literature?" Ask them to consider the points raised in the previous discussion as they respond. Suggest that they think about the works they are about to read in the context of their responses to this question.

✔ Developing Concept Vocabulary

Illustrate the concept of the search for a national identity in Canadian literature through a simple graphic representation. On the chalkboard, draw a Venn diagram and label the two segments "Me" and "A Friend."

Then, explain that the United States and Canada share the longest unguarded border between nations that is found anywhere in the world. Historically, the two countries have had very friendly relations despite occasional differences. Nevertheless, Canadians, understandably, wish to have their own national identity recognized. Ask students to draw their own Venn diagrams and label the segments with words they would use to describe the ways in which they and a friend are alike and words that express unique identities, based on their responses to the following questions:

- What are our cultural heritages? From what countries or areas of the world did our ancestors come? From what region of that country or area?

- What kinds of people do we admire? Why? Who are some examples?

- What are our goals? How do we hope to accomplish them?

- What kinds of things and ideas do we value?

- Do we prefer modern or more traditional styles and ideas?

- What are our interests? favorite subjects? favorite kinds of entertainment? favorite sports?

- What are our personalities like? (outgoing/quiet; serious/light-hearted; etc.)

- What are our favorite expressions? What expressions don't we like?

- What are our favorite places? What do we like about them?

The Old Man's Lazy

by Peter Blue Cloud (pages 362–365)

OBJECTIVES

Literary

- to identify the elements of a dramatic monologue
- to recognize the ways character is revealed in a dramatic monologue

Historical

- to examine relations between native peoples in Canada and the descendants of Europeans in Canada
- to discuss the way of life and the rights of native peoples in Canada today

Cultural

- to understand the conflict between traditional Indian ways and modern customs
- to discuss Indian beliefs concerning the land and property rights

SELECTION RESOURCES

Use Assessment Worksheet 56 to check students' vocabulary recognition, content comprehension, and appreciation of literary skills.

 Informal Assessment Opportunity

SELECTION OVERVIEW

Irony is a way of speaking in which the real meaning is different than what the speaker seems to be saying at first. Writers use irony for humorous effect and to reveal character in a surprising way. For example, one character acts less intelligent than he or she really is. This character reports another character's words or deeds without openly criticizing. Instead, the first character uses understatement to show that the other is a braggart or a fool.

Irony is often a characteristic of dramatic monologues. Peter Blue Cloud uses irony very effectively in "The Old Man's Lazy." The speaker never says that the Indian Agent is a fool. He only reports what the agent says and does. This understatement allows the other's own words and actions to reveal his shallowness and self-deception.

The agent says the old man is lazy because he does not cultivate his land. As the agent says this, he foolishly tramples plants that obviously have significance in Indian culture. The agent boasts that he understands Indians, yet he does not realize the old man would never have built a fence, nor does he appreciate the hawk shield. Ask students to find examples of irony in comments about the neighbor or his children's way of life."

In this poem, the narrator expresses the differences in perspective and values between himself and the Indian Agent.

ENGAGING THE STUDENTS

On the board, write: "Good fences make good neighbors." Tell students that this quote is from another dramatic monologue called "Mending Wall." In that poem, the speaker does not want to rebuild a wall that separates his farm from a neighbor's land. The neighbor replies with the quotation. Ask students to respond to questions like these: What do you think this quotation means? Why do you think someone would say this statement? What reasons do you think the speaker gives for not wanting to rebuild the wall? Ask students to consider the points that are raised in the discussion as they read "The Old Man's Lazy."

BRIDGING THE ESL/LEP LANGUAGE GAP

The historical background and cultural concepts in this poem may present an obstacle to full comprehension. Before students read, be certain that they understand the concept of "reserve lands," including how they came into existence and what they are like. Make sure that students understand that an Indian Agent is a representative of the federal government and has responsibilities to help Indians, especially those living on reservations. Ask why it is important that an Indian Agent truly understand and appreciate Indian culture.

Finally, be certain that students understand the Indian belief that all living things have spirits and that people can learn a lot from animate, as well as inanimate, objects. Objects like the hawk shield can help us find the spirit of the hawk within us. Ask the class to name the characteristics of a hawk that they think the old man believes human beings should try to acquire or emulate.

✔ PRETEACHING SELECTION VOCABULARY

On the board, write the following words in a column: *get up and go*, *milkweed* [a plant with milky juice and clustering flowers], *wormwood* [a plant that yields a bitter, strong smelling green oil], *Indian Agent*, *lichen*, and *bitter*). In a second column, list definitions in non-matching order. Have students scan the selection and locate the sentence containing each word. Ask volunteers to read the words aloud in context and to try to match vocabulary words with definitions on the board. After all are correctly identified, have students quickly write several statements predicting what the poem will be about. Tell them to confirm their predictions after reading the work.

The words printed in boldfaced type are tested on the selection assessment worksheet.

PREREADING

Reading the Poem in a Cultural Context

On the board, write, "The earth should be left as it was . . . The land was made without [property boundaries], and it is no man's business to divide it . . ."

Tell students that this quotation is from a speech by the famous Native American leader, Chief Joseph of the Nez Perces. Help students read for purpose by explaining that most Native Americans believe that people do not have the right to buy or sell land. They believe that the earth is a gift from the Creator and should be preserved the way it was, without fences or property lines. Ask students to consider this statement as they read the monologue.

Focusing on the Selection

Discuss with students other works they have read that examine Native American beliefs about land and na-

ture. Ask them to consider how opposing views may have contributed to conflicts between Native Americans and settlers over U.S. land. Ask them on what points about land use and nature they think both cultures agree? Do they think there is room for both sets of beliefs to exist side by side? Why or why not?

POSTREADING

The following activities parallel the features with the same titles in the Student Edition.

Responses to Critical Thinking Questions

1. Sample response: All three major topics that the speaker discusses relate to the fence: The Indian Agent urges him to fix it; the former neighbor built it; it tells the narrator stories that he passes along to his family. The old man calls the fence "a curving sentence" in an "old language." It is a reminder both of where he has come from and how he is different from the person who built it.

2. Sample response: He says that his children once found it odd that he would live "way out here" but that they now envy him. In fact, they would like to join him "but can't/for some reason, do it." His words seem to suggest a conflict within the hearts of many native people in Canada—a clash between two vastly different cultures (that of whites and that of his native heritage) and between the need to be a part of modern Canada.

3. Answers will vary. Some students may feel that the Indian Agent is, if not correct, at least consistent with his failure to understand "us Indians" and his seeming distaste for their traditions. Most students, however, will suggest that the old man is using his place well—being taught by the land and the cedar fence, passing those teachings along, and appreciating the power that the place has over his children and grandchildren.

✔ Guidelines for Writing Your Response to "The Old Man's Lazy"

If students wish, have them share their journal entries with a partner. As an alternative writing activity, challenge students to write a story that the fence may have told the old man about "this wonderful earth." Encourage them to include a moral or lesson that the old man would tell his children to help them remember a traditional belief about nature and the land.

✔ Guidelines for Going Back Into the Text: Author's Craft

In lyric poetry, the speaker usually represents the voice of the poet. In a dramatic monologue, the speaker is always a character with an identity that is independent from that of the poet. In some dramatic monologues, the poet sympathizes with the views of the character. In other works, the speaker unintentionally reveals character traits that the poet is criticizing through irony. Tell students that to understand the theme of a dramatic monologue, it is important to determine whether the poet sympathizes with the speaker. Ask students whether they think Peter Blue Cloud sympathizes with the old man. What information in the poem supports their conclusions?

Possible answers to the questions in the Student Edition are:

1. Sample response: The old man discusses his relationships with the Indian Agent, his former neighbor, and his children and grandchildren. His family may mean the most to him, for it is to them that he passes along the lessons that "this Creation" teaches him.

2. Sample response: The first few lines offer only the Indian Agent's opinion of the old man. As the old man continues to speak, however, he proves that the agent's opinion is unwarranted. He shows himself to care about life, his traditions, and his family; he seems more content with his life than anyone else whom he describes.

3. Sample response: The old man's words suggest that the Indian Agent doesn't really understand him. A dramatic monologue told by the Indian Agent probably would advance the opinion that the old man is a lazy and tired follower of outdated ways. The monologue might tell about why the Indian Agent would have that opinion and how he believes in "modern" ways.

✔ FOLLOW-UP DISCUSSION

Use the questions that follow to continue your discussion of "The Old Man's Lazy." Possible answers are given in parentheses.

Recalling

1. How did the white neighbor change over the twenty years that he lived next to the old man's place? (He grew old, angry, and bitter because he never found the gold he was looking for.)

2. How has his children's attitude toward the land changed over the years? (Years ago, they did not understand why the old man would want to live so far from town. Now, it seems as though they would like to move back to their traditional homeland but for some reason cannot.)

Interpreting

3. How does the incident of the "hawk feathers" illustrate the cultural misunderstandings that exist between the old man and the Indian Agent? (The Indian Agent says that the old man should "fix the fence." He means that the old man should repair the fence so that it properly separates his property from his neighbor's place. The old man's idea of fixing the fence is to decorate it with a symbol from nature so that it appears to be part of the land.)

4. Why do you think that the old man says he felt lucky to be on the outside of the fence? (Unlike the white neighbor, the old man sees the fence as an enclosure that imprisons its builder by separating him from the natural beauty and wonders of the land, as well as from other people.)

Applying

5. What did you learn about traditional Indian beliefs concerning land and nature? (Answers will vary. Lessons may include: love of the land; the land should be left in its natural state rather than developed; the land should be open to everyone and not enclosed by fences; people should respect nature and learn from plants and animals, and other objects; people should live close to the land not in urban centers; people should pass on their beliefs to their descendants through stories.)

6. What story, taken from an experience in nature or from a family tradition, would you preserve for your grandchildren? Why might it be important to preserve? (Stories will differ according to students' experiences and creativity. They may point out that their story teaches an important lesson or passes along an important tradition that should be preserved.)

ENRICHMENT

Students will benefit from viewing *As Long As the Rivers Flow* by James Cullingham and Peter Raymont. The video is available from First Run Icarus Films, 153 Waverly Place, New York, NY 10014, (800) 876-1710.

All the Years of Her Life

by Morley Callaghan (Pages 366–373)

OBJECTIVES

Literary

- to distinguish between round and flat characters
- to understand how writers reveal character

Historical

- to place the Great Depression in time and place
- to understand the impact of the Great Depression on the lives of Canadians

Cultural

- to discuss the cultural links between the literature of Canada and the United States
- to recognize universal elements in family relationships

SELECTION RESOURCES

Use Assessment Worksheet 57 to check students' vocabulary recognition, content comprehension, and appreciation of literary skills.

 Informal Assessment Opportunity

SELECTION OVERVIEW

Characters can be classified as round or flat. **Flat characters** are predictable. They generally have only one or two personality traits, and they rarely change during the course of a story. **Round characters**, like real people, round characters are capable of surprising us. They are complex, solid, and believable. Sometimes they change in some important way as a result of a story's action.

Writers reveal character in different ways. One way is through the character's own thoughts, words, and actions. Character may also be shown through the thoughts and words of others in the story.

In "All the Years of Her Life," Callaghan uses both techniques to make Mrs. Higgins a round character. Her words and actions, when speaking to the druggist, show her gentle sincerity. This is her defining trait. On the way home, she lashes out at her son, releasing years of pent-up frustration. Callaghan rounds her character by having her show this other side. Her bitterness surprises us. It also makes Mrs. Higgins more believable as a person.

Callaghan also uses Alfred's impressions to round the character of Mrs. Higgins. Alfred, at first, sees only her strength and her anger. He thinks she is naturally "smooth" and strong. In the kitchen, he gains new insight. At last, he understands how difficult it is for her

to be strong. He sees the toll that his irresponsibility has taken over the years. The surprising revelation makes Mrs. Higgins more human and more admirable.

Using the Depression-era as its backdrop, "All the Years of Her Life" explores how the realtionship between a mother and her son changes as a result of a difficult situation.

ENGAGING THE STUDENTS

On the board, write: "Courage is grace under pressure."

Tell students that Morley Callaghan's friend, Ernest Hemingway, wrote this sentence. Explain that "grace," in this context, means dignity, kindness, or doing the right thing.

Ask students to explain in their own words what they think the statement means. You might use these questions as prompts: Do you think that courage comes naturally to some people? Do you think that being courageous means overcoming fear? Ask students to consider the points raised in the discussion as they read the selection.

BRIDGING THE ESL/LEP LANGUAGE GAP

The vocabulary in this selection could hinder full comprehension. For ESL/LEP students, slang, especially 1930s slang that has fallen into disuse, may be particularly troublesome. Write the following words and phrases on the board: *sap, point-blank, swaggering, red-handed, jam, a bad lot, smooth, swell.* Have ESL/LEP students work with fluent English speakers, or another adult to locate these terms, discuss their use in context, and come up with a current idiom that has a similar meaning. Have them take turns reading sentences from the selection and substituting the familiar term for the obscure one to appreciate both the meaning and the flavor.

☑ PRETEACHING SELECTION VOCABULARY

Callaghan uses very different words and phrases to describe the characters in the selection. Make a list of words from the story that indicate traits of each character such as this one. (As an alternative, have students create the word lists as they read.)

ALFRED HIGGINS	SAM CARR	MRS. HIGGINS
blustered	confident	friendly
indignation	**brusquely**	calmness
arrogantly	hard-faced,	dignity
swaggering	stern	simplicity
		gentleness
		earnestness
		humility
		dignity
		composure
		dominant
		tolerance
		strength
		repose

Post the list for students to study before reading so that they can get a sense of each character. Ask them to add words and phrases to the list after reading. Have them draw some generalizations about which characters are flat and which are round based on these word lists.

The words printed in boldfaced type are tested on the selection assessment worksheet.

PREREADING

Reading the Story in a Cultural Context

Help students to read for purpose by explaining that this story is set during the worldwide Great Depression of the 1930s. During this terrible economic peri-

od, as many as one in four people in the United States and Canada were unemployed. Those who had jobs often had difficulty making enough to get by. They also lived daily with the fear of losing their jobs and being unable to find other employment. Ask students to consider this setting as they think about the characters in the selection.

Focusing on the Selection

Have students work in groups of three. Assign one of the three questions in the student text (page 373) to each member. When they have finished working individually, challenge them to collaborate on a single shared response to the following exercise: Alfred says that his father is a printer who works nights. Mrs. Higgins warns Alfred not to say a word to his father about the incident. What do you think can be inferred about the character of Mr. Higgins from this information? Use student responses as the basis for a class discussion.

POSTREADING

The following activities parallel the features with the same titles in the Student Edition.

Responses to Critical Thinking Questions

Possible responses are:

1. Callaghan is saying that family members must stand up for each other, especially in difficult times; he also suggests that family members can make inaccurate assumptions about each other and take each other for granted.

2. In this culture, it is wrong to steal, even if the stolen items are inexpensive. Alfred's stealing results in the loss of his job (which, in a depressed economy, is likely to create financial hardship) and the distress of his mother. At the same time, the way in which Mrs. Higgins successfully appeals for her son is admirable. Her appeal is probably the most riveting part of the story. It suggests that family unity and forgiveness important values.

3. Answers will vary. Encourage students to explain the connection between themselves and the character they would portray. Invite them to identify the characteristics they would look for in the other portrayals.

☑ Guidelines for Writing Your Response to "All the Years of Her Life"

Have students share their journal entries with a partner. As an alternative writing activity, ask each student to write a paragraph summarizing the effect that they think the final scene has on Alfred's character. Ask: What does Alfred now feel "that his mother had been thinking of as they walked along the street"? What does Callaghan mean by "his youth seemed to be over?"

✔ Guidelines for Going Back Into the Text: Author's Craft

Discuss with students the relationship between motive and character.

Motive is the reason or the emotion that causes a character to behave in a certain way. Generate a class discussion about the motives for each character's attitudes and actions as they relate to the incident in the drug store. Note that sometimes one character can bring about change in another. Ask: How does Mrs. Higgins change Alfred and Sam Carr? What are the motives behind their changed attitudes? Possible answers to the questions in the Student Edition are:

1. Callaghan presents Mrs. Higgins as a round character. While her son views her as highly emotional, she acts with calmness and dignity at the drug store. She is gentle, diplomatic, earnest, and patient. We learn that she has adopted these qualities to deal with Mr. Carr and save her son. Back at home she is frightened, and her anger with Alfred verges on hopelessness.

2. Mrs. Higgins's quiet dignity is very strong. She is also friendly, warm, and sincere. She has a strong love for her son that turns to fright and anger when he does wrong.

3. Students probably will agree that Sam Carr is a flat character, but they may differ in their description of Alfred Higgins. Alfred does not affect the reader as strongly as Mrs. Higgins does; however, by the end of the story he shows that he is more than a mere juvenile delinquent. While Alfred is never fully developed during the course of the story, he does appear to change in the end.

✔ FOLLOW-UP DISCUSSION

Use the questions that follow to continue your discussion of "All the Years of Her Life." Possible answers are given in parentheses.

Recalling

1. What does Alfred Higgins do that is wrong? (He steals inexpensive items from the drugstore where he works.)

2. What does Mrs. Higgins suggest to Sam Carr may be the best thing for a boy Alfred's age? (a little good advice)

3. What does Sam Carr do rather than have Alfred arrested? (He fires Alfred.)

4. What changes does Alfred see in his mother when he looks at her in the kitchen? (Her face looks frightened, her hands tremble, and she looks very old.)

Interpreting

5. Why does Sam Carr tell Mrs. Higgins, "I'm truly sorry"? (Mrs. Higgins's dignity and strength surprised Sam Carr. He had not expected her to be like that. He is so impressed by the way she conducts herself that by the end of the conversation he truly regrets having caused her pain.)

6. How does Alfred's use of the word "smooth" to describe his mother's behavior show that he does not understand her? ("Smooth" in its slang sense implies that the person is not sincere. By using that term, Alfred is suggesting that his mother's behavior was the same kind of "act" that he had tried unsuccessfully when he responded to Sam's accusation with feigned indignation.)

Applying

7. In your opinion, how does the historical setting of the story make Alfred's behavior even more irresponsible? (Answers will vary. Students may suggest that because jobs were so hard to find during the Depression, Alfred was foolish to risk losing the one he had.)

8. Do you think that Mrs. Higgins should keep Alfred's behavior a secret from her husband? Why or why not? (Answers will vary. Some students may suggest that she realizes telling Alfred's father would only make matters worse, and this justifies her attitude. Others may suggest that the father has a right to know. Keeping secrets from him undermines the trust on which solid family ties are based, especially during difficult times.)

ENRICHMENT

Students may benefit from exploring the *Great Depression*. This CD-Rom is available from Learning Services, P.O. Box 10636, Eugene, OR 97440-2636, (800)877-3278.

OBJECTIVE

Overall

- to forge links between several famous monuments in the Americas and the cultures of these lands

Specific

- to discover what parallels the speaker in "A Night in the Royal Ontario Museum" draws between herself and the monument in the poem's title
- to compare and contrast what the poets in "Chilean Earth" and "Homecoming" think of the natural monuments in their homelands
- to describe the contrasts between traditional and modern values in *Florinda and Don Gonzalo* and "The Old Man's Lazy"

ENGAGING THE STUDENTS

Invite students to write on this topic:

> The culture of a nation is defined by its monuments.

Allow students five minutes to write. Then invite volunteers to share their responses. Discuss with the class what they think the quotation means. Ask: How do monuments represent our important values? Explain to students that in this feature they will make connections between famous monuments and different cultures in the Americas.

BRIDGING THE ESL/LEP LANGUAGE GAP

Read the selection aloud as students follow along in their books. Start by writing the following questions on the board. Direct students to find the answers as you read.

1. What is Macchu Pichu? (an ancient Incan city in the Andes Mountains in Peru)
2. What is the name of Mexico's financial center? (the Mexican Stock Market Building)
3. What are some of the attractions in Banff National Park? (hot springs, glaciers, and endangered animals)

EXPLORING LANDMARKS

Mexico City is the capital and largest city in Mexico. It is located in the Distrito Federal, in the south central part of the county, at an elevation of 7,710 feet. Bounded by mountains on three sides, Mexico City is the second largest urban concentration in the Western Hemisphere and exerts unrivaled domination on the political, economic, and cultural life of Mexico. For example, more than half of Mexico's industrial output is produced in or near Mexico City. Major industries include textiles chemicals, pharmaceuticals, electronic items, steel, and transportation equipment. Mexico City is served by an efficient subway system; a huge international airport is located east of the city. The center of the city has historically been the Zocalo, or plaza of the Constitution, which occupies the site of the central square of the Aztec city, Tenochtitlan. Notable landmarks in the center of the town include the National Cathedral, the Municipal Palace, the National Palace, and Chapultepec Park.

- Have students write a brief research essay that explains NAFTA (North America Free Trade Agreement) and the impact of it on Mexico City. Have students include how the agreement has either improved or hindered the lives of people living and working in the city. Encourage students to support their opinions with facts and details.

LINKING LITERATURE, CULTURE, AND REGION

Guidelines for Evaluation: Sample Answers

The speaker in "A Night in the Royal Ontario Museum" observes that there is a connection between her own identity and past cultures.

The speaker in "Chilean Earth" views the monuments in her homeland with love and joy, "more beautiful than Lia and Raquel," for whose sake "we want to light up the fields with song."

Traditional and modern views clash in "The Old Man's Lazy," as the Indian Agent cannot understand why the old Native American man does not cut his milkwood and curing wormwood and repair the split cedar fence.

from *Little by Little*

by Jean Little (pages 376–383)

OBJECTIVES

Literary

- to identify the elements of an autobiography
- to analyze an autobiography for facts and perceptions

Historical

- to analyze the political relationship between Canada and Great Britain
- to explain how the author's childhood experiences influenced her writing career

Cultural

- to understand that age can affect how a person perceives other people and events
- to discuss changing attitudes toward individuals with disabilities

SELECTION RESOURCES

Use Assessment Worksheet 58 to check students' vocabulary recognition, content comprehension, and appreciation of literary skills.

 Informal Assessment Opportunity

SELECTION OVERVIEW

Canada, in 1939, was a land adjusting to change. Emerging from the economic turmoil of the Great Depression, the former colony also was adjusting to its new political status as a "dominion" in the British Commonwealth of Nations. A dominion is a self-governing nation pledging only allegiance to the British monarch. That nominal allegiance, however, drew a reluctant Canada into a World War for the second time in the twentieth century.

Against this backdrop of large-scale upheaval in another time and place, author Jean Little frames a personal experience that has a universal theme. Jean is different from the other fifth-graders in her Ontario classroom. Her family has just returned to Canada from Taiwan where Jean was born with sight problems. Placed in a "mainstream" classroom for the first time, she must cope with the taunting of insensitive classmates who think that because she is different, she must also be dull. In her attempt both to fit in and to get back at the children who taunt her, Jean discovers the power that words hold.

In this story Jean uses her vivid imagination and her way with words to weave an imaginary tale that enthralls her teacher and peers. Sensing the respect she has won, Jean employs this same skill to disarm a snowball-throwing bully the next day.

ENGAGING THE STUDENTS

Note that before the fifth grade, Jean Little had been educated in classes attended only by students with visual problems. Explain that schools today must show an educational justification before placing a person with a disability in a separate class. Ask students to share their thoughts on this issue. You might use the following questions as discussion prompts:

- What benefits can individuals with disabilities gain from being in a regular classroom?
- What benefits can other students gain from being educated with individuals with disabilities?
- What kinds of reasons would not justify placing a person in a separate class?
- Under what circumstances, if any, do you think placing an individual in a separate class can be justified?

BRIDGING THE ESL/LEP LANGUAGE GAP

Because the author speaks in the voice of a ten-year-old child, the vocabulary should not present a significant obstacle to ESL/LEP students' comprehension. (See Preteaching Vocabulary for classwide suggestions.) To help clarify the theme, you might suggest that ESL/LEP students copy the following questions and work in cooperative groups of three or four to answer them as they read:

- What happens at the breakfast table after Jean shows her anger by throwing a few drops of milk? (Pat throws milk at Jean, soaking her clothes.)

- What happens during "crack the whip" when Jean acts as though falling down is fun? (Her classmates continue placing her in the same position and teasing her.)

- How do her classmates react when Jean uses her word power to tell an imaginary tale? (They listen fascinated. Later, one girl smiles in a friendly way. No one teases Jean.)

- What happens after Jean uses her word power to respond when the bully calls her cross-eyed? (He throws snowballs that land near her but do not hit her.)

☑ PRETEACHING SELECTION VOCABULARY

You may wish to preview the medical terms used by the mother —**haematoma**, **abrasion**, and **pupils**— and their definitions for all students before they begin reading. Then, ask volunteers to use each in an original sentence. Next, list the following words on the chalkboard: *strabismus, nystagmus, corneal, opacity,* and *eccentric.* Explain that these are all words used to describe Jean's visual problems in technical terms. Ask volunteers to look up their pronunciations and definitions and read them to the class. Discuss how these conditions might affect her vision (crossing of the eyes, poor vision).

The words printed in boldfaced type are tested on the selection assessment worksheet.

PREREADING

Reading the Autobiography in a Cultural Context

Help students read for purpose by asking if they think attitudes toward individuals with disabilities have changed since Jean Little was a child. Ask: Do you think people who were different in some way were more likely to be teased or avoided during the 1930s? Why or why not? Has their treatment changed today? If so, what has helped bring about that change? If not, why not?

Focusing on the Selection

Remind students that we are witnessing events through the eyes of a ten-year-old child. Ask: Why do children sometimes think that a parent loves a brother or sister more? Is this perception always accurate? List the following characters on the chalkboard: mother, Hugh, Miss Marr, the big girl, the smiling classmate, the bully. Tell students to evaluate Jean's perceptions of these characters as they read. Which perceptions are supported by facts? Which are not? Which perceptions might change with maturity?

POSTREADING

The following activities parallel the features with the same titles in the Student Edition.

Responses to Critical Thinking Questions

Possible responses are:

1. Sample response: Little speaks of the situation as a child would, especially in her fear of being found a liar and in her pleasure that her teacher seems to believe her. Other strong feelings, such as her annoyance with her younger sister and her wish to get back at the seventh-grader who teased her, are expressed in the "now" of her childhood instead of being filtered through an adult's perspective.

2. The fourth-graders sing "God Save the King." The song suggests a country with strong ties to Great Britain. (In fact, Canada became a self-governing dominion just a few months before Little was born; still, British traditions ran deep. "God Save the King [Queen]" remained Canada's national anthem until 1980, when it was replaced with "O Canada.")

3. Answers will vary, but many students will suggest that they would step in either as Jean Little is on her way to school, planning her excuse, or as she decides how to confront the seventh-grader who has teased her. Encourage students not only to share what they would say but also to explain why they would say it.

☑ Guidelines for Writing Your Response to *Little by Little*

If students wish, have them share their journal entries with a partner. As an alternative to recalling personal experiences, you might suggest that students choose one of the following activities:

- Describe a situation in which a public figure has used word power to bring about change for the better. Be as specific as possible in citing words the individual used to persuade others.

- Select a worthwhile goal (as Jean Little sought to present disabilities accurately) and describe your feelings about the subject in writing. Use words with the power to teach, persuade, or encourage.

☑ Guidelines for Going Back Into the Text: Author's Craft

Discuss with students the difference between *omniscient* and *limited* point of view. Help students to understand how authors often use a limited point of view to achieve a desired effect on the reader. Note that Jean shares her thoughts with us, but we only learn about the other characters from the words Jean hears and the actions she observes. Suggest that students compare the mother's words and actions with Jean's perception of favoritism. Tell them to analyze Miss Marr's words and physical reactions to Jean's story with Jean's belief that she has fooled the teacher. Ask them to consider why the adult writer has included these details in the child's narrative.

Possible answers to the questions in the Student Edition are:

1. Sample response: We learn that the Littles are unusual in that both parents are doctors. In other ways, however, they are a normal family, complete with squabbles. They also appreciate accuracy and honesty, for Mother makes sure that Jean knows the medical terms relating to her eye problems.

2. Sample response: The exact names for Little's eye problems are given. However, Little shows a child's perspective when it comes to the medical details in her excuse to Miss Marr. For example, she knew "the right medicine" to revive someone who was almost dead; furthermore, as she admits to us, "I was not absolutely sure what a dead person looked like."

3. Sample response: We wouldn't have the information about what really caused Jean to be late. The selection probably would focus on Miss Marr's thoughts and feelings that day, especially her reactions to Jean's tardiness and the story that the child tells. Undoubtedly, we would know whether she believes Jean's excuse. We also might find out how Miss Marr feels about Jean's physical problems and if she knows about the teasing that the girl receives.

☑ FOLLOW-UP DISCUSSION

Use the questions that follow to continue your discussion of *Little by Little.* Possible answers are given in parentheses.

Recalling

1. What song did school children in the British dominion of Canada sing each morning? ("God Save the King")

2. What is Jean afraid will happen if she writes her name on the board differently than others? (She is afraid that the other students will think that she is "dumb.")

3. Why does Jean put Band-Aids on both of her knees? (She cannot remember which knee is supposed to have been cut.)

Interpreting

4. Why does Jean think it is essential that she be out of breath when she arrives at school? (For her story about the emergency to be convincing, she must appear as though she has run all the way from home to school.)

5. Why do you think her classmates are astonished as they listen to Jean's story? (They thought that because she was different, she also was dull. For the first time, they realize that Jean is a bright, interesting person.)

6. Why do you think that the seventh-grader continues to tease Jean after her classmates have stopped? (He was not present to hear her tale and does not have the awareness of Jean's ability that her classmates have gained.)

Applying

7. What does this selection teach us about the danger of stereotyping individuals? (The selection teaches us that we should judge each person on his or her own merits, not on inaccurate generalizations about groups.)

ENRICHMENT

Students may enjoy watching *The Canadians: Their Land.* This video is available from Encyclopaedia Britannica Educational Corporation, 310 South Michigan Avenue, Chicago, IL 60604, (800) 554-9862.

A Night in the Royal Ontario Museum

by Margaret Atwood (pages 384–387)

OBJECTIVES

Literary

- to understand the relationship between theme and symbols in a poem
- to analyze onomatopoeia, assonance, and alliteration in poetry

Historical

- to identify historical developments that have influenced modern Canada and its literature
- to discuss the issue of Canadian nationalism

Cultural

- to recognize the diverse nature of Canadian culture
- to discuss the search for an independent Canadian literary identity

SELECTION RESOURCES

Use Assessment Worksheet 59 to check students' vocabulary recognition, content comprehension, and appreciation of literary skills.

 Informal Assessment Opportunity

SELECTION OVERVIEW

Margaret Atwood believes that, in order to survive, Canada must establish its own national identity. Her beliefs are rooted in her country's history. Like the United States, Canada is a multicultural society. Native Americans, descendants of Europeans (especially British and French), and people of African and Asian heritage live side by side. Unlike the United States, separate literatures, especially in English and French, have developed.

This cultural fragmentation has shown itself politically. Canada, a former colony, is a member of the Commonwealth of Nations with a nominal allegiance to Britain. Some French-speaking people in Quebec, known as *Separatists*, want to secede from Canada and form an independent nation. As recently as 1995, secession was narrowly defeated by voters in Quebec.

In this selection, Atwood uses the Royal Museum as a symbol for her nation. Founded by the British monarchy, the museum is devoted to preservation of relics from the past. They include European, Asian, African, and Native American objects. Though individually valuable, the objects appear scattered at random with no sense of unity. Canadians, Atwood suggests, are trapped in this fragmented past. To survive, they must find a unifying identity independent of these outside influences and move forward.

ENGAGING THE STUDENTS

On the chalkboard, write:

"She is Mark and Brenda's daughter."

"He is Martin's little brother."

Note that people who say such things are trying to be helpful by establishing connections to a heritage or a relationship. Ask students: Have you ever been introduced this way? How did you feel? Did you sometimes think that you would like to have your own identity established, independent of these relationships? How would you go about doing this? Use student responses as a guide to discussing Atwood's belief that Canadians must find their own identity. Point out that in the past, Canada has often been seen as an American outpost of British ideas, or as a cultural and political extension of the United States. Ask students to relate this to Atwood's argument that *Survival*, her book of poetry, is a "case for nationalism."

BRIDGING THE ESL/LEP LANGUAGE GAP

The unusual structure, extended sentences, and specialized vocabulary of this selection will present difficulties for many students. Before the first reading, ask them to pause after each stanza and write one short sentence paraphrasing the main idea. You will need to preteach some vocabulary: *weathered, tarnished, dusty, wastes, embalmed, mummified, boneyard, fossil.* You might read aloud and model the first and/or second stanza by writing, "Who locked me in this crazy place? I am lost and cannot find a way out."

After students have read the poem once, have them work in mixed groups of both limited and proficient English speakers to list details supporting the main idea in each stanza. As needed, guide them toward the following perceptions: the exhibits are multicultural (a totem pole, a Byzantine dome, Greek, Roman, and Chinese sculptures, carved masks, a possibly Egyptian mummified child); There is no unifying theme or logical progression to the display.

Encourage and monitor group discussion of the relationship between the images and Atwood's themes of nationalism and survival.

✔ PRETEACHING SELECTION VOCABULARY

In this poem, terms referring to art and death play prominent roles in the effect Atwood seeks to create in the reader's mind. Have students copy the following lists of words. Column 1: **totempole,** *byzantine,* **mosaic.** Column 2: *embalmed, fossil.* Review the definitions as found in the text. As students read, encourage them to find other words in the poem related to these subjects and add them to their lists. "Art" lists might include *marble, bronze, carved masks,* and *plaster.* "Burial" lists might include *preserved, skeleton, boneyard,* and **mastodon.**

After students have completed their lists, ask, "Why do you think Atwood chose the Royal Museum as a symbol for Canada? Why do you think she selected these details of museum exhibits as images for the cultural problem she believes her country faces?"

The words printed in boldfaced type are tested on the selection assessment worksheet.

PREREADING

Reading the Poem in a Cultural Context

Help students read for purpose by reminding them that *Survival* was considered controversial at the time it was published. As they read, ask them to consider why Atwood's call for a "truly Canadian" literature and her support for nationalism might be debated in a multicultural society. Discuss the issue of separation in Canada. Ask, "How do you think Canadians who sympathize with the 'Separatists' in Quebec would react to Atwood's ideas? Why?"

Focusing on the Selection

Have students do a quick freewrite before they read the selection. Have them summarize what they have learned about diversity in the United States. Tell them to recall anything they might have learned in past classes or in prior readings. Ask them to compare the ideas in their freewrites with Atwood's position as they read. Ask: Do individual cultural groups always lose their identity when they become part of a larger cultural group? Have students then discuss similarities and differences between the United States and Canada.

POSTREADING

The following activities parallel the features with the same titles in the Student Edition.

Responses to Critical Thinking Questions

Possible responses are:

1. Students probably will notice that the exhibits focus on civilizations and things that have not survived. The fact that the speaker seems lost in the museum may mean that she is wondering about her own survival.

2. A Canadian reader might wonder where Canadian history fits in—why it doesn't get a bigger mention in the poem. A Canadian reader might feel a little lost, as Atwood's speaker does.

3. Answers will vary. Encourage students to explain their choices.

✔ Guidelines for Writing Your Response to "A Night in the Royal Ontario Museum"

Have students share their journal entries with a partner. As an alternative writing activity, tell students that Margaret Atwood has also used images of fossil remains and bones when writing about modern women and the search for identity. Have students work together as partners to write a short paragraph discussing how Atwood might relate the images in the poem to a modern woman's changing role (e.g., in personal relationships, the workplace, and the home).

☑ Guidelines for Going Back Into the Text: Author's Craft

Have students write descriptive phrases, using onomatopoeia, assonance, and alliteration. Encourage them to link these phrases to create a short poem.

Possible answers to the questions in the Student Edition are:

1. Other examples of alliteration include: "where the weathered/totempole" (lines 4–5), "golden ... gods" (lines 9-10), and "fur ... fire ... further" (lines 23-27). The other example of onomatopoeia is *thundering* (line 45).

2. There is assonance in *past, masks, plaster,* and *glass.* The words link details in the display of native peoples. The long *a* sound slows reading, giving emphasis to those words that signify the national heritage.

3. Sample responses: The *o* and *ah* sound in lines 40-42 (in *lost, mastodons, beyond,* and *fossil*) links the ancient items that confuse the museum's visitor. The resonance of the words suggests that they emerge from history. The short *i* sound in lines 46-47 (in *dwindling, pin-points,* and *in*) helps strengthen the poem's final image and reinforces the sharpness of the speaker's confusion.

☑ FOLLOW-UP DISCUSSION

Use the questions that follow to continue your discussion of "A Night in the Royal Ontario Museum." Possible answers are given in parentheses.

Recalling

1. For what sign is the museum visitor searching in vain? (EXIT)

2. Which signs, though meant to be helpful, provide no sense of direction for the visitor? (YOU ARE HERE).

3. By which exhibit does the visitor say, "I am far/ enough, stop here please/no more"? (the exhibit of a skeleton child, preserved in the desert air)

Interpreting

4. Which is the only exhibit that is clearly related to a culture that originally developed in Canada? (The totempole was used by Native American culture groups along the northwest coast of North America in what is now Canada and the United States.)

5. Why does the poet describe the prerecorded message that visitors can activate to hear exhibit information as "...an idiot/voice jogged by a pushed/ button, repeats its memories? (The voice is a function of the crazed man-made store brain of the museum. It repeats fragments of information without providing a context or a sense of continuity.)

6. How does the reverse chronological arrangement of the exhibits that the visitor passes suggest that she is actually becoming more lost in the labyrinth of the past? (The visitor begins at the most recent historic exhibits, moves steadily backward in time, passes prehistoric fossils, and in the last stanza, is among non-living rocks and minerals.)

Applying

8. Why would it be impossible for the visitor to hear the roar of mastodons? (Mastodons have been extinct since prehistoric times.)

9. Why do you think Margaret Atwood believes that survival is the central theme in Canadian literature? (Answers will vary. Some students may suggest it is because Canada has remained intact as a country despite cultural tensions. Others might infer from the poem that Canada must come to terms with the past and move into the future.)

ENRICHMENT

Students may benefit from viewing the video *Canada: A Nation's Quest for Identity,* available from Social Studies School Service, 10200 Jefferson Boulevard, Room 12, Culver City, CA 90232, (800) 421-4246.

My Financial Career

by Stephen Leacock   (pages 388–392)

OBJECTIVES

Literary

- to analyze techniques used to create humor
- to discuss the characteristics of wit, humor, and satire

Historical

- to discuss the changing popular attitudes toward banks
- to understand how the standard of living has changed in the twentieth century

Cultural

- to discuss Leacock's use of humor to evaluate the Canadian way of life
- to discuss the influence of Leacock's academic background on his writing

SELECTION RESOURCES

Use Assessment Worksheet 60 to check students' vocabulary recognition, content comprehension, and appreciation of literary skills.

 Informal Assessment Opportunity

SELECTION OVERVIEW

Wit and humor, which share the purpose of making us laugh, are two kinds of comic writing. Wit refers to clever remarks that are skillfully and originally stated. Often associated with the adjective "biting," wit frequently has a sharp or critical edge. Writers who use wit always want the audience to appreciate the intentional comedy and cleverness of the speaker.

Humor refers to comic writing that points out the absurd or ridiculous in human behavior. The often associated adjective, "gentle," implies that humor does not have the cynical quality frequently found in wit. The humorist looks at human frailty without bitterness. Sometimes, the speaker is a bumbler who turns the simplest task into a "nightmare." The character is not trying to be funny. It is the absurdity, not the cleverness, of the speaker's behavior that we find amusing. This makes it easier for us to laugh at our own imperfections.

In this selection, the narrator finds himself in an increasingly absurd situation while trying to open a bank account.

ENGAGING THE STUDENTS

Have students describe a scene from a story that they found particularly amusing. You might use the following questions as prompts: Were the characters trying to be funny, or were they funny in spite of themselves? Was the scene funny because of what happened to the main characters or because of what happened to others? Allow five minutes for students to write their responses. Then, call on volunteers to read their responses aloud. Be sure that each identifies the literary work being described.

Use the responses as the basis for a class discussion about what people find amusing and why. Ask them to consider the discussion points as they read.

BRIDGING THE ESL/LEP LANGUAGE GAP

Before students read this selection, make certain that they understood the banking concepts discussed. This is especially important because Leacock occasionally uses Canadian terms that differ from those common in the United States. You might have them role-play a banking transaction and use words from the selection to define what the students are doing. *Clerks* are tellers; the *wickets* are what we call bank windows. A *cheque* is a bank check. A deposit is money placed in a bank account. A *withdrawal* is money taken out of a bank account.

Write the words on the board and identify them with the action of the role-play. Encourage students to look for these words and visualize the action as they read.

✔ PRETEACHING SELECTION VOCABULARY

On the board, write the following words in a column (*wickets, sepulchral, conjuring, cheque, invalid*). In a second column, list definitions in reverse order. Have students scan the selection and locate the sentence containing each word. Ask volunteers to read the words aloud in context and try to match vocabulary words with definitions on the board. After all are correctly identified, have students write statements predicting what the selection will be about. Tell them to confirm their predictions as they read the work.

The words printed in boldfaced type are tested on the selection assessment worksheet.

PREREADING

Reading the Essay in a Cultural Context

Help students read for purpose by placing the essay in historical context. Explain that Stephen Leacock died in 1944. Although today most people in the United States and Canada have bank accounts, this was not true at the time Leacock was writing. Many people distrusted banks. They kept their savings in a secret place in their home where it did not earn any interest. Note that when Leacock accepted his first teaching position at McGill University in 1901, his starting salary was five hundred dollars a year (or less than fifty dollars a month). The deposit may not have seemed huge to a bank manager accustomed to large deposits, but it was a significant amount to the average person. Ask students to consider how these points contribute to the effectiveness of the work as they read.

Focusing on the Selection

Remind students that Leacock was a respected economist who understood the advantages gained from keeping money in bank accounts. Ask: Why do you think he would poke gentle fun at people's fear of banks? What message do you think he might want Canadians to learn about banks? Do you think portraying himself as somewhat ridiculous makes his humor more effective? Why or why not?

POSTREADING

The following activities parallel the features with the same titles in the Student Edition.

Responses to Critical Thinking Questions

Possible responses are:

1. We sympathize with Leacock because of his great nervousness about banks and his lack of understanding about how to function in one. The oddness of the circumstances and the way Lealock describes them make us laugh.

2. Most students will feel that a majority of Canadian readers would disagree with Leacock. It is logical to assume that Canadians would not share Leacock's fear of banks.

3. Answers will vary. Some students may suggest that they thought about humor through exaggeration or in everyday activities; they also may comment about Leacock's making himself the subject of his own humor.

✔ Guidelines for Writing Your Response to "My Financial Career"

Have students share their journal entries with a partner. As an alternative writing activity, have students work together as partners to write a short extension of the essay in which a bank employee who witnessed Leacock's visit describes it to another employee who was absent that day. Encourage partners to include gentle humor in their description of the very odd visitor and his antics.

✔ Guidelines for Going Back Into the Text: Author's Craft

Like humor, satire uses exaggeration, ridiculous behavior, and outrageous situations to amuse us. However, the purpose of satire goes beyond laughter. The satirist uses laughter to make the reader think about a situation or condition that should be changed or to criticize human failings. Ask: Do you think there are elements of satire in "My Financial Career?" Have students explain their answers.

Possible answers to the questions in the Student Edition are:

1. Sample responses are given for each bulleted entry. The accountant seems threatening and evil; he is "a tall, cool devil."

    • Because Leacock seems so secretive, the manager assumes that he is a Pinkerton detective, then a detective from another agency, and then the heir to a huge fortune.

    • Leacock attempts to deposit his relatively small savings as one ball of money, and he is physically pale and shaky as he does so.

    • He has to be told how to write a check. Then, when he realizes that he has filled it out incorrectly, he is too nervous to correct himself.

    • Leacock decides to keep his money in his pants pocket and in a sock (in silver dollars).

2. Sample response: From the beginning of the essay, Leacock tells us that everything about banking upsets him. His mistakes pile up on each other until he literally must flee the scene.

3. Answers may vary, but Leacock does choose himself (rather than the banking industry, for example) as the subject for humor. He seems intent on making fun of himself for our amusement.

☑ FOLLOW-UP DISCUSSION

Use the questions that follow to continue your discussion of "My Financial Career." Possible answers are given in parentheses.

Recalling

1. Why does Leacock insist on seeing the bank manager? (He believes that anyone who wants to open an account must consult the manager first.)

2. How much money does Leacock say that he plans to deposit on a regular basis? (fifty dollars a month)

3. What does Leacock do after depositing his money in the new bank account? (He withdraws it all.)

Interpreting

4. Why do you think the bank manager assumes that someone being so secretive is a detective? (The job of a detective is to investigate crimes. The manager assumes that he must have some confidential information to reveal in private.)

5. Why does the bank manager go to the door and announce the purpose of Leacock's visit? (Opening an account and depositing fifty-six dollars is a routine matter that often occurs in a bank. There is no need to keep the matter a secret.)

6. Why do you think the clerk is surprised when Leacock withdraws all the money that he has deposited? (Withdrawing all the money from an account closes it.)

Applying

7. Leacock behaves ridiculously. In your opinion, what kinds of information should a person opening a new bank account obtain? (Answers will vary. Students may suggest that a new customer should learn what fees are charged in connection with an account; whether interest is paid on the account; whether a minimum balance must be maintained.)

8. What would Leacock have to have done differently to make "My Financial Career" satirical rather than humorous? (Leacock would have had to change the focus of his writing from his bumbling attempts to the banking institution or system.)

ENRICHMENT

Students may benefit from viewing *Discovering Canada,* available from Social Studies School Service, 10200 Jefferson Boulevard, Room 12, Culver City, CA 90232, (800) 421-4246.

RESPONSES TO REVIEWING THE REGION

1. Students should realize that the *tone* of a literary work is the writer's attitude toward his or her subject matter. The tone of "My Financial Career" is humorous and self-deprecating as the writer shows us how a simple task can be complicated by a bumbling fool.

2. Sample answer: The poem "The Old Man's Lazy" reveals the poet's culture by showing the contrast between the Native American and Anglo cultures. Native Americans, represented by the poet, value harmony with nature; the Anglos, represented by the Indian Agent, value taming nature to create precision. The poet leaves the fence because it represents history; the Indian Agent sees the fence as a heap of sticks.

3. Sample answer: I would like to be friends with the Native American in "The Old Man's Lazy" because he is at peace with himself and his environment.

☑ FOCUSING ON GENRE SKILLS

Stephen Leacock makes effective use of the essay, combining elements such as fact, opinion, description, and narration. He opens the essay by clearly stating his purpose — to describe how the bank rattles him. He then describes an incident that shows his fear of banking and financial institutions. Leacock uses humor to convey his message. Select, or have students select, another essay, such as "A Winter's Tale." Invite students to analyze the elements used by the writer and evaluate the effectiveness of the essay.

BIBLIOGRAPHY

BLUE CLOUD, PETER. "The Old Man's Lazy." In *Clans of Many Nations*. White Pine Press, 1995.

LEACOCK, STEPHEN. "My Financial Career." In *The Leacock Roundabout*. New York: Dodd Mead & Company, 1972.

Unit 4
The Americas
Focusing the Unit (page 393)

COOPERATIVE/ COLLABORATIVE LEARNING

Individual Objective: to participate in an art review featuring art from Canada, Central America, or South America.

Group Objective: to develop a presentation inspired by art shown in the art review.

Setting Up the Activity

Have students work in heterogeneous groups of three. Stipulate that each group member is responsible for researching and explaining the significance of a piece of art and for making a contribution to the group presentation. The suggested format for the review is as follows: Student 1 introduces the area in the Americas on which the review will focus; Student 2 describes a particular kind of art from that area; Student 3 gives a personal response to the art; each student in turn presents an individual work of art.

When they have finished their preparation, have each group present the review for the entire class. After each group's presentation, use the questions below to discuss and evaluate their reports.

- What different kinds of art are represented in Unit 4?
- In your group's opinion, how do these art forms reflect the societies and cultures from which they come?

Assisting ESL and LEP Students

To give students with limited English proficiency more opportunity to join in a closing discussion of the unit, have them choose one selection on which to focus. Then ask them to think about the answers to these questions:

1. What social or cultural group does the selection deal with?
2. What kind of art does that group produce?
3. How does the group's art reflect its beliefs and traditions?

Assessment

Before you begin the group activity, remind students that they will be graded on both an individual and a group basis. Without individual contribution, the group presentation will not be complete. Monitor group progress to check that all three students are contributing and that they have selected a presenter.

Time Out to Reflect

As students do the end-of-unit activities in the Student Edition, give them time to make a personal response to the content of the unit as a whole. Invite them to respond to the following questions in their notebooks or journals. Encourage students to draw on these personal responses as they complete the activities.

1. What have I learned about the different cultural groups in the Americas?
2. How does the art of each cultural group reflect the group's beliefs and traditions?
3. In what ways are the groups and their art similar? How do they differ?

WRITING PROCESS: PERSONAL ESSAY

Refer students to the model of a personal essay found on pages 425–426 in the Handbook section of the Student Edition. You may wish to discuss and analyze the model essay if you are working with less experienced writers.

Guidelines for Evaluation

On a scale of 1-5, the writer has

- clearly followed all stages of the writing process.
- made clear and specific references to the chosen selections.
- described the meaning of a personal experience.
- made minor errors in grammar, mechanics, and usage.

Assisting ESL and LEP Students

You may wish to provide a more limited assignment for these students so that they can complete their first drafts somewhat quickly. Then have them work at length with proficient writers in a peer-revision group to polish their drafts.

PROBLEM SOLVING

Encourage students to use the following problem-solving strategies to analyze two or more of the tales, poems, plays, or short stories in Unit 4. Afterward, encourage students to reflect on their use of the strategies and consider how the strategies helped in their analysis.

Strategies (optional)

1. Use a semantic map or brainstorm to list cultural groups of the Americas treated in Unit 4 and the conflicts that diversity has brought to the region. Have groups of students choose the conflict they most want to investigate further and the selection or selections that best shed light on the conflict.

2. Use a second graphic organizer, such as a problem/solution chart, to explore in detail the topic they chose. Include information both from the selections and from outside research. This graphic organizer should be used to show problems caused by diversity and solutions offered by writers or students' own solutions.

3. Decide which topics need further research or discussion. Set up a plan that shares responsibility for doing the research if students are working with a partner or group. Students can use information from graphic organizers to create a skit, dance, musical arrangement, art composition, news show, debate, or poem expressing feelings about the problem and solution.

Allow time for students to work on their presentations.

Guidelines for Evaluation

On a scale of 1-5, the student has

- provided adequate examples, facts, reasons, anecdotes, or personal reflections to support his or her presentation.

- demonstrated appropriate effort.

- organized the presentation so that personal analysis is clear and easily interpreted.

- demonstrated an understanding of conflicts that have arisen in the Americas due to cultural diversity.

Assessment Worksheet Answer Key

WORKSHEET 1 from *Sundiata: An Epic of Old Mali*
Vocabulary 1. exemplary; 2. infirmity; 3. malicious; 4. innuendo; 5. humiliated

Understanding the Selection 6. he was lame and people made fun of him; 7. the village seer told him that his son would be a great leader; 8. the king died and she took over the rule for her son; 9. bring a baobab tree to his mother's yard; 10. the bar of iron he used as a staff magically became an iron bow

Author's Craft: Epic 11. c; 12. e; 13. a; 14. d; 15. b

WORKSHEET 2 *Owner of the Sky: Olorun the Creator*
Vocabulary 1. solid and true; 2. waste; 3. plant their feet; 4. Chameleon; 5. give them goods

Understanding the Selection 6. a shell with a small amount of earth, a pigeon, and a hen with five toes; 7. threw the earth from the shell and the pigeon and hen scratched it all over the marshy waste; 8. Olorun had it made especially for the Yoruba people; 9. bringing the still figures to life; 10. making parts of some people's bodies from earth

Author's Craft: Cause and Effect 11. the small amount of earth was distributed all over the marsh, making enough land on which people could stand; 12. on the first trip, the land wasn't dry enough for people to stand on; 13. humans would have something to drink; 14. tried to watch Olorun bring life to the humans; 15. knew that Great God was jealous and that he was spying to learn the secret of bringing humans to life

WORKSHEET 3 *The Sea Eats the Land at Home, Song for the Sun that Disappeared Behind the Rainclouds*
Vocabulary 1. eternal; 2. hearth; 3. mourning; 4. dowry; 5. lamentations

Understanding the Selection 6. his home town which is located on the sea; 7. in the dead of night; 8. shout and call on all the gods they know; 9. the rain; puts out the fire and turns the wood black; 10. stars; overflows with light

Author's Craft: Sensory Details 11. sight: the sea is in the town/Running in and out of the cooking places; 12. hearing: and the mourning shouts of the women, calling on all the gods they worship; 13. touch: … shivering from the cold; 14. sight: the fire darkens, the wood turns black; 15. sight: He walks along the milky way, he collects the stars …, until the basket overflows with light.

WORKSHEET 4 *The Prebend Gardens, Interior, All That You Have Given Me, Africa*
Vocabulary 1. lagoons; savannahs; 2. pigments; 3. indelible; 4. obsession; 5. lamenting

Understanding the Selection 6. his continent has given him a rich heritage; 7. many of Africa's cultures are a mixture of Arab and African influences; 8. African culture groups have committed good and bad acts, just as other culture groups have; 9. were negative influences that hurt native African cultures; 10. build a sense of pride and joy in Africa and being African

Author's Craft: Nationalism in Poetry 11. T; 12. F; 13. T; 14. F; 15. T

WORKSHEET 5 *The Toilet*
Vocabulary 1. boutiques; 2. alternative; 3. premises; 4. Johannesburg; 5. knocked off

Understanding the Selection 6. be a nurse or teacher or learn the skills needed to be a wife and mother; 7. do something different, such as acting; 8. it was a small and private place; 9. her sister scolded her for being caught by Mistress; 10. the public toilet was locked and she wrote her story on a park bench

Author's Craft: Point of View 11. O; 12. O; 13. O; 14. F; 15. F

WORKSHEET 6 *A Chip of Glass Ruby*
Vocabulary 1. disarmed; 2. morose; 3. scandalous; 4. bewildered; 5. reproach

Understanding the Selection 6. are black South Africans; 7. become part of the protest movement to overthrow the government's policy of apartheid, or class and racial segregation; 8. they should protest themselves rather than allowing others to protest on their behalf; 9. joins a hunger strike; 10. cares about and remembers everybody, which are the qualities that make her so special

Author's Craft: Conflict 11. I; 12, I; 13, E; 14. E; 15. I

WORKSHEET 7 *Marriage Is a Private Affair*
Vocabulary 1. vehemently; 2. dissuasion; 3. commiserate; 4. implore; 5. remorse

Understanding the Selection 6. he himself has chosen the girl and arranged the marriage; 7. once she and he are married; 8. he doesn't love her; 9. continually talking to them and showing them that she is an excellent housekeeper; 10. Nene writes a letter telling him he has two grandsons that want to meet him.

Author's Craft: Conflict 11. NC; 12. C; 13. C; 14. C; 15. NC

WORKSHEET 8 from *The Dark Child*
Vocabulary 1. ecstatic; 2. blithely; 3. veranda; 4. millet, pestle and mortar

Understanding the Selection 5. getting his father's permission and telling his mother; 6. his destiny as decreed by the gods; 7. she will argue heatedly and be hurt by the decision; 8. she is afraid he will never return and she will have no one to care for her; 9. sobbing, then feeling excitement as he fingers the metro map in his pocket

Author's Craft: Dialogue 10. a; 11. c; 12. e; 13. b; 14. d; 15. e

WORKSHEET 9 *The Chair Carrier*
Vocabulary 1. inclination; 2. contemplate; 3. archaeology; 4. cartouche; 5. topple

Understanding the Selection 6. a religious object being carried in a holy parade; 7. the man smiled at him and greeted him; 8. it sounded as if it belonged to an ancient time; 9. before the Nile was called the Nile and before the capital of Egypt was moved to Cairo; 10. the man who gave the porter the order to carry the chair

Author's Craft: Irony 11. no; 12. yes; 13. yes; 14. no; 15. no

WORKSHEET 10 *The Marks of the Wise Man, of the Half Wise, and of the Fool*
Vocabulary 1. despairing; 2. illuminated; 3. blind; 4. halting; 5. degradation

Understanding the Selection 6. he will never be truly wise; 7. he can't acquire wisdom when he follows his own desires; 8. follow in the footsteps of his guide; 9. guide and protect his followers; 10. gaining wisdom, the wise man's "sight"

Author's Craft: Didactic Poetry 11. to use it to seek full and total light; 12. to lead others by one's acquired wisdom; 13. to avoid all efforts not directed by wisdom; 14. to avoid eternal death by seeking wisdom; 15. to acquire wisdom from one who is truly wise

WORKSHEET 11 *The House on the Border*
Vocabulary 1. nocturnal; 2. fazed; 3. gendarmerie; 4. jurisdiction; 5. collaborate

Understanding the Selection 6. his house is especially attractive to thieves; 7. are jealous and want the house for themselves; 8. shoot them; 9. he knows that the police won't do anything to help the renters; 10. handle it in a wise but not quite moral way (Accept other reasonable responses.)

Author's Craft: Satire 11. Nesin might be pointing out that people should be more astute when entering into contracts. 12. He may want the husband to rely more on his own good sense than on any government "protectors." 13. He may want the police to shape up and not shirk their responsibilities. 14. He probably wants the police to have to answer for their actions. 15. He probably believes that the neighbors should either be more helpful or should mind their own business.

WORKSHEET 12 *4+1=1*
Vocabulary 1. din; 2. disciplined; 3. imperative; 4. current; 5. stupefied

Understanding the Selection 6. He thinks he bumped his broom handle into it; 7. He fears that he will lose his job and have to pay for the machines; 8. He blinks, shakes, sweats, stammers, and drops his broom; 9. The oldest worker has the decisiveness to solve the problem; 10. The factory owner makes them fear that they will lose their jobs if they do anything wrong.

Author's Craft: Dialogue 11. description; 12. external dialogue; 13. description; 14. internal dialogue; 15. external dialogue

WORKSHEET 13 *A Lover from Palestine, Warmth of Blood*
Vocabulary 1. wilderness; 2. stoked; 3. orphanhood; 4. radiant; 5. restore

Understanding the Selection Possible answers are given. Accept reasonable responses. 6. "I saw you yesterday at the harbor,/Leaving without a people, without supplies," or "I saw you wandering in the streets,/In the songs of orphanhood and misery"; 7. bread and salt, the two most necessary things (besides water) to sustain life; 8. an abandoned child running hopelessly after his mother; 9. coldness and warmth; 10. dreams, memories, and hopes

Author's Craft: Figurative Language Possible answers are given. Accept reasonable responses. 11. songs of comrades, memories of love, the beloved's voice, fire; 12. "memories of love rising/in the branches of embrace" or "Your longing voice, a stoked and radiant fire. . ." 13. mountains of thorns, a shepherd without sheep, a wilderness, a cave; 14. orphanhood, a stranger, an orphan's songs of misery, orphan's garments, a shepherd without sheep, being chased away; 15. real fires, embers, woolen garments

WORKSHEET 14 *In This Valley, Once a Great Love, Late in Life*
Vocabulary 1. filtered; 2. afresh; 3. profiles; 4. spectacles; 5. destined

Understanding the Selection 6. to late in his life; 7. can't see the sea, but knows it's there somewhere; 8. "healing to my heart and rest to my eyes"; 9. "voices of men and machines wrecking and building"; 10. "die at their place and in their time"

Author's Craft: Figurative Language 11. metaphor; 12. simile; 13. hyperbole; 14. hyperbole; 15. metaphor

WORKSHEET 15 *You Can't Fool Menashe*
Vocabulary 1. offing; 2. languid; 3. checkered; 4. intimation; 5. contorted

Understanding the Selection 6. the Repertory Committee to decide whether they would stage his play; 7. breaking into giggles from time to time and threatening to emigrate; 8. Menashe's extraordinary ability to know how successful people are, or will be, in their careers; 9. know the level of a person's success even before it happened; 10. won 4,000 shekels in the lottery

Author's Craft: Characterization 11. T; 12. F; 13. F; 14. T; 15. F.

WORKSHEET 16 from *A Book of Five Rings*
Vocabulary 1. archery; 2. dexterously; 3. halberd; 4. invincible; 5. sieges

Understanding the Selection 6. spear; 7. favorite; 8. timing; 9. nine; 10. invincible

Author's Craft: Didactic Writing 11. T; 12. F; 13. F; 14. T; 15. T

WORKSHEET 17 *Till the Candle Blew Out*
Vocabulary 1. abalone; 2. sesame; 3. thatched; 4. abode; 5. abacus

Understanding the Selection 6. hunchback; 7. music; 8. art; 9. the rice crop fails and they cannot support themselves; 10. the supplies to make a kite

Author's Craft: Motivation 11. F; 12. T; 13. F; 14. T; 15. T

WORKSHEET 18 *The Ch'i-Lin Purse*
Vocabulary 1. matchmaker; 2. benefactor; 3. Buddha; 4. matchmaker; 5. benefactor

Understanding the Selection 6. spoiled; 7. promising male offspring; 8. a poor bride who is crying/Mrs. Lu; 9. great flood; 10. be the governess for their young son

Author's Craft: Moral 13. X; 15. X

WORKSHEET 19 *Hearing of the Earthquake in Kyoto (1830)*
Vocabulary 1. sunder, chaos; 2. flats; 3. multitudes, cower; 4. entreat, beseech; 5. dirge

Understanding the Selection 6. roof tiles; 7. the river sands; 8. wading through a stream; 9. his nurse's back; 10. dragons

Author's Craft: Point of View 11. X; 13. X; 14. X; 15. X

WORKSHEET 20 *A Call to Action, To the Tune "The River Is Red"*
Vocabulary 1. dragons; 2. waves; 3. flowers; 4. swallows; 5. perfume

Understanding the Selection 6. scholars, women; 7. heroes; 8. full of blood; 9. spare no effort, struggle unceasingly; 10. jeweled dresses and deformed feet

Author's Craft: Author's Purpose 11. F; 12. T; 13.T; 14. T; 15. T

WORKSHEET 21 *No Way Out*
Vocabulary 1. desolation; 2. predicament 3. furtively; 4. surveillance; 5. bourgeois

Understanding the Selection 6. any effort to bring about change; 7. mountains between China and Burma; 8. his signature on a bank withdrawal slip; 9. an enemy of the revolution; 10. relocation to a labor camp.

Author's Craft: Autobiography 11. F; 12. T; 13. F; 14. T; 15. T

WORKSHEET 22 *He-y, Come on Ou-t!*
Vocabulary 1. meters, kilometers; 2. cohorts; 3. corpses, vagrants; 4. plausible; 5. counterfeit

Understanding the Selection 6. a shrine was swept away by a landslide caused by a typhoon; 7. to see if it could be heard hitting bottom; 8. the hole; 9. nuclear waste, unnecessary classified documents, bodies of animals used in contagious disease experiments, the corpses of vagrants, old diaries and photographs, and counterfeit bills; 10. responsible ways of solving pollution problems

Author's Craft: Surprise Ending 11. b; 12. c; 13. a; 14. b; 15. c

WORKSHEET 23 *Savitri*
Vocabulary 1. contemplative; 2. ordained 3. pious; 4. equity; 5. alms

Understanding the Selection 6. he had lived a life of spirituality coupled with poverty; 7. the gods have ordained that Satyavant will die within a year of their wedding; 8. she is a woman.; 9. the wisdom of the gods; 10. to the highest heaven

Author's Craft: Theme 11. T; 12. T; 13. T; 14. T; 15. F

WORKSHEET 24 *This World Lives Because, Children, Tirumāl*
Vocabulary 1. wrath; 2. ghee; 3. tainted; 4. Vedas; 5. ambrosia

Understanding the Selection 6. Vishnu; 7. everything; 8. honorable, pious; 9. anger; 10. children

Author's Craft: Symbols 11. d; 12. e; 13. a; 14. b; 15. c

WORKSHEET 25 *The Tiger*
Vocabulary 1. b; 2. e; 3. d; 4. c; 5. a.

Understanding the Selection 6. becomes an angry roar; 7. mood in the animal's eyes; 8. it is far out of the men's reach; 9. her own labor pains; 10. it was protecting three newborn cubs

Author's Craft: Suspense 11. atmosphere; 12. sympathize; 13. relieve ; 14. fulfill; 15. plot twist

WORKSHEET 26 *Forty-Five a Month*
Vocabulary 1. cynically; 2. wry; 3. laboriously; 4. excruciating; 5. vermilion

Understanding the Selection 6. makes her figure it out herself; 7. her best dress and pants and puts a red dot on her forehead; 8. asking a servant from a neighboring house to take her home; 9. cash and accounts; 10. wake Shanta up and take her to the movies

Author's Craft: Plot 11. climax; 12. characters; 13. central conflict; 14. resolution; 15. rising action

WORKSHEET 27 from *When Heaven and Earth Changed Places*
Vocabulary 1. karma; 2. spouses; 3. altar; 4. colander; 5. rituals

Understanding the Selection 6. pray to the gods, help ensure good health, help ensure the war would end; 7. why the Vietnamese have to work so hard harvesting their rice; 8. water buffalo; 9. seed; 10. the farmers themselves

Author's Craft: Setting 11. T; 12. T; 13. F; 14. F; 15. T

WORKSHEET 28 *Tangaroa, Maker of All Things*
Vocabulary 1. d; 2. a 3. e; 4. b; 5. c

Understanding the Selection 6. no voice replied; 7. overturned; 8. he was still angry; 9. human beings; 10. water and plants that spring from it

Author's Craft: Figures of Speech 11. c; 12. e; 13. d; 14. a; 15. b

WORKSHEET 29 *Maui and the Great Fish*
Vocabulary 1. wrenched; 2. spells; 3. turmoil; 4. screeching; 5. bait

Understanding the Selection 6. special fishing hook; 7. under the floorboards of the boat; 8. makes the land look further away than it is; 9. New Zealand; 10. fight over the land

Author's Craft: Repetition 11. "I tricked you! I tricked you!" 12. "Look back! Look back … Look …" 13. pulled and pulled; 14. half man and half god; 15. many magic spells … many magic powers

WORKSHEET 30 *Family Council*
Vocabulary 1. unanimously; 2. plaintiffs; 3. arbitration; 4. grievance; 5. overrule

Understanding the Selection 6. pull her weight; 7. lets the animals out of their traps; 8. Spitfire; 9. carry home the dead animals; 10. The narrator

Author's Craft: Personal Narrative 11. T; 12. F; 13. F; 14. T; 15. T

WORKSHEET 31 *Butterflies*
Vocabulary 1. plaited; 2. hatch; 3. hoeing; 4. footpath; 5. plaited

Understanding the Selection 6. "Go to school. Listen to the teacher. Do what she say."; 7. picking beans; 8. killed all the butterflies; 9. she buys her cabbages from the supermarket; 10. her story reflects their way of life

Author's Craft: Setting 11. T; 12. F; 13. F; 14. F; 15. F

WORKSHEET 32 *The Servant*
Vocabulary 1. almshouse; 2. ingratiated; 3. disheartened; 4. charwoman; 5. downcast

Understanding the Selection 6. Moscow; 7. for military duty; 8. tells on the other servants; 9. ten-kopeck piece (money); 10. sin

Author's Craft: Historical Context 11. T; 12. T; 13. F; 14. F; 15. F

WORKSHEET 33 *If Not Still Higher*
Vocabulary 1. supplication; 2. studded; 3. broods; 4. dogged; 5. pious

Understanding the Selection 6. early Friday morning; 7. heaven; 8. under the Rabbi's bed; 9. to chop wood for the poor; 10. Vassil

Author's Craft: Writing Style 11. X; 12. X; 13. X; 14. X

WORKSHEET 34 *And When Summer Comes to an End …, Please Give This Seat to an Elderly or Disabled Person*
Vocabulary 1. b; 2. d; 3. a; 4. e; 5. c

Understanding the Selection 6. elderly person; 7. wrote during Stalin's oppressive government; 8. a dead end or death; 9. her feelings of alienation, betrayal, and aloneness; 10. Pride, Loneliness, and Art

Author's Craft: Free Verse 11. T; 12. T; 13. F; 14. T; 15. T; 16. F; 17. T; 18. T.; 19. T; 20. F

WORKSHEET 35 *Random Talk, The Heirs of Stalin, Refugees*
Vocabulary 1. c; 2. e; 3. d; 4. a; 5. b

Understanding the Selection 6. knowing that she will never return to her homeland; 7. "words of passage," they are spoken before going to the next place, which is death; 8. he feared the people; he believed in a great goal but forgot that the means must be worthy; 9. the oppression, beliefs, and power that Stalin held are still alive in some people; 10. "they want to live" in peace and freedom from oppressive government; 11. death and dying

Author's Craft: Author's Purpose 12. F; 13. F; 14. T; 15. F

WORKSHEET 36 *The Bicycle*
Vocabulary 1. partook; 2. gazed; 3. Tatras

Understanding the Selection 4. mountain goats; 5. leader; 6. grass; 7. the silver trophy of its horns; 8. heaven

Author's Craft: Fantasy and Realism 9. F; 10. R; 11. F; 12. R; 13. R 14. F; 15. R

WORKSHEET 37 *The Monster*
Vocabulary 1. grievous; 2. perplexity; 3. mangy; 4. dolefully; 5. frenzied

Understanding the Selection 6. blew hard to make them

freeze; 7. touching his pot (which he had forbidden them to do); 8. animal, in the wild; 9. remained standing, leaning against the stove and staring him straight in the eye; 10. freak show; 11. put a spell on them

Author's Craft: Metaphor 12. yes; 13. yes; 14. no; 15. yes; 16. yes

WORKSHEET 38 *A Winter's Tale*
Vocabulary 1. carnage; 2. abstract; 3. meticulously; 4. rations; 5. gulag

Understanding the Selection 6. Vienna, Austria; 7. potatoes; 8. packages; 9. innocent; 10. helpless

Author's Craft: Comparison 11. filled with pain, fear, and suffering; 12. sad, dangerous, sorrowful; 13. rationed; in short supply; 14. afraid; fearful; 15. the same; cold and clear

WORKSHEET 39 *The Oath of Athenian Youth*
Vocabulary 1. civic duty; 2. incite, annul, naught; 3. revere

Understanding the Selection 4. "We will;" 5. the city-state of Athens; 6. committing any act of dishonesty or cowardice; 7. greater, better, and more beautiful; 8. honesty, obedience, loyalty, duty, and civic pride; 9. Students' responses will vary. Accept all reasonable answers.

Author's Craft: Author's Purpose 10. F; 11. T; 12. T; 13. F; 14. F; 15. T

WORKSHEET 40 *The Nightingale's Three Bits of Advice*
Vocabulary 1. agape; 2. stove-in; 3. fluttered; 4. defy; 5. stifle

Understanding the Selection 6. small birds; 7. "don't go after what's beyond your reach"; 8. it has a big pearl in its breast; 9. stone; 10. ashamed of himself

Author's Craft: Sequence 11. 2; 12. 4; 13. 5; 14. 3; 15. 1

WORKSHEET 41 *Paying on the Nail*
Vocabulary 1. innate; 2. rogue; 3. demurred; 4. bade; 5. sleight-of-hand; 6. avail, forge,

Understanding the Selection 7. trading and straight dealing take place; 8. trader; 9. drink of water to give himself time to think; 10. only a few farmers shod their horses, but many would like the opportunity to have their own nails to pay on; 11. by cheating farmers

Author's Craft: Trickster Folktales 12. d; 13. b; 14. c; 15. a

WORKSHEET 42 *Death Seed, Woman, You Are Afraid,* from *My Mother's House*
Vocabulary 1. reaper; 2. stern; 3. sows; 4. expunged; 5. resemble

Understanding the Selection 6. "My mother's mother died/in the spring of her days"; 7. although she does not consider herself beautiful, the granddaughter discovers an inner beauty inherited from her grandmother; 8. life is a cycle—although there is death, there is also new life and growth; 9. Accept all reasonable answers. Students may suggest that women have probably feared finding out who they really are and what their feelings, hopes, and dreams are, they also may have feared challenging their traditional roles.

Author's Craft: Imagery 10. F; 11 T; 12. T; 13. F; 14. F; 15. T

WORKSHEET 43 from *Survival in Auschwitz*
Vocabulary 1. disconcerted; 2. phantoms; 3. demolition; 4. livid; 5. writhe

Understanding the Selection 6. twenty minutes; 7. hell; 8. translate from German to Italian; 9. he is a criminal; 10. prisoner (or Haftling)

Author's Craft: Personal Narrative 11. T; 12. F; 13. T; 14. F; 15. T

WORKSHEET 44 *Action Will Be Taken*
Vocabulary 1. aptitude; 2. vigorous; 3. pregnant; 4. delegated; 5. pensively

Understanding the Selection 6. pensive; 7. Broschek; 8. "Let's have some action!" 9. eleven; 10. a wreath of artificial roses

Author's Craft: Irony 11. N; 12. I; 13. N; 14. I; 15. I

WORKSHEET 45 *The Return*
Vocabulary 1. a; 2. d; 3. b; 4. c; 5. e

Understanding the Selection 6. Christmas; 7. Rosa, reminded him of his wife Herminia; 8. gasoline shortage; 9. garage; 10. responsibilities, worries

Author's Craft: Foreshadowing 11. N; 12. N; 13. F; 14. F; 15. N

WORKSHEET 46 from the *Popol Vuh*
Vocabulary 1. clay; 2. wood 3. gold; 4. flesh; 5. flesh … gold

Understanding the Selection 6. it dissolved in water and could not stand upright; 7. when tested with fire, it burned; 8. it was cold to the touch and could not speak, feel, or worship them; 9. making offerings of gratitude to them; 10. the kindness of the men of flesh.

Author's Craft: Myth 11. M; 12. F; 13. M; 14. M; 15. F

WORKSHEET 47 *The Great Prayer*
Vocabulary 1. L,F; 2. F, L; 3. F, L; 4. L, F; 5. L, F

Understanding the Selection 6. hunger; 7. cold; 8. quiet the anguish of the void; 9. on a solitary rock; 10. dream away your everyday life.

Author's Craft: Imagery 11. A; 12. A; 13. C; 14. C; 15. C

WORKSHEET 48 *Bouki Rents a Horse*
Vocabulary 1. e; 2. c 3. d; 4. b; 5. a

Understanding the Selection 6. more to rent the horse than the yams are worth; 7. Moussa's donkey, which he can borrow, has returned; 8. neither one of them has a baby in the family at that time; 9. "Where will we put Grandmother?"; 10. they could have put Grandmother on the horse.

Author's Craft: Characterization 11. b; 12. a; 13. d; 14. e; 15. c

WORKSHEET 49 *The Street, The Room*
Vocabulary 1. stumble; 2. turning; 3. rise; 4. lost; 5. bewildered

Understanding the Selection 6. "you" closing the windows; 7. "goes off with the dogs and howls"; 8. long and silent; 9. stones and leaves; 10. "forever to the street"

Author's Craft: Mood 11. b; 12. c; 13. a; 14. b; 15. a

WORKSHEET 50 *Keeping Quiet, Chilean Earth*
Vocabulary 1. The moment would be unusual because it is completely different from normal human activity and exciting because of its potential for improved understanding. 2. The poet will not compromise his belief in peace by making any agreements with death. 3. The Chilean landscape and the hard work necessary to make things grow forms the strong character of the people. 4. The feel of the earth under people's feet is like the gentle caress of a kiss. 5. The song of the people, celebrating the beauty of the landscape, will bring joy to the earth.

Understanding the Selection 6. the enjoyment and meaning of life; 7. winter and spring; 8. not understanding ourselves and threatening each other's lives; 9. the people's cheeks and their laughter; 10. beauty and its freedom

Author's Craft: Lyric Poetry 11. N; 12. L; 13. L; 14. N; 15. L

WORKSHEET 51 *Florinda and Don Gonzalo*
Vocabulary 1. consolation; 2. suitors; 3. pessimist; 4. Don; 5. remedy

Understanding the Selection 6. feels lonely; 7. being a burden to his own wife; 8. do something on his/her own; 9. she marry him; 10. let him know when they reach the other shore

Author's Craft: Dialogue 11. F; 12. G; 13. B; 14. G; 15. F

WORKSHEET 52 *One of These Days*
Vocabulary 1. rancor; 2. anesthesia; 3. abscess; 4. tranquil; 5. cautious

Understanding the Selection 6. the dentist will pull his tooth; 7. "to come and shoot me"; 8. changes his mind and decides to pull the tooth; 9. the deaths of 20 townsmen; 10. to whom he should send the bill for the extraction.

Author's Craft: Suspense 11. protagonist; 12. antagonist; 13. suspense; 14. character; 15. conflict

WORKSHEET 53 *The Book of Sand*
Vocabulary 1. e; 2. a; 3. d; 4. c; 5. b

Understanding the Selection 6. new pages keep growing between the cover and his thumb; 7. the salesman was determined to sell the book; 8. The Thousand and One Nights; 9. dreams of the book; 10. the smoke from infinite fires will suffocate the planet

Author's Craft: Symbolism 11. S; 12. N; 13. N; 14. S; 15. S

WORKSHEET 54 *Continuity of Parks*
Vocabulary 1. dissuade; 2. dilemma; 3. alibis; 4. apprehensive 5. rivulets

Understanding the Selection 6. reading a novel; 7. a mountain cabin; 8. to murder the woman's husband; 9. the husband's estate; 10. reading the novel in which he is now the victim.

Author's Craft: Sensory Detail 11. c; 12. b 13. c; 14. a; 15. a.

WORKSHEET 55 *Homecoming, The Child's Return, Jamaica Market, On Leaving, Zion, Me Wan Go Home*
Vocabulary 1. babel; 2. topographies; 3. dissonant; 4. cobalt; 5. metronome

Understanding the Selection 6. stop journeying and to consider the islands to be home; 7. "stiff rich grass", "volcanic stones"; 8. rhyme; 9. soothe her ear; 10. Ethiopia, Africa

Author's Craft: Rhythm 11. c; 12. d; 13. a; 14. e; 15. b

WORKSHEET 56 *The Old Man's Lazy*
Vocabulary 1. c; 2. e; 3. b; 4. a; 5. d.

Understanding the Selection 6. to grow naturally on the land; 7. a curving sentence of stick writing; 8. for the hawk, his spirit animal; 9. find gold on his property; 10. the rain and wind and snow,/the sun and moon shadows,/ this wonderful earth/this Creation.

Author's Craft: Dramatic Monologue 11. T; 12. T; 13. F; 14. F; 15. T

WORKSHEET 57 *All the Years of Her Life*
Vocabulary 1. brusquely; 2. dominant; 3. composure; 4. contempt; 5. indignation

Understanding the Selection 6. take a few things out of his pocket; 7. Mrs. Higgins come down to the store in a hurry; 8. they are friends; 9. disgraced her again and again; 10. the first time he had ever looked at his mother.

Author's Craft: Characterization 11. F; 12. R; 13. F; 14. R; 15. F

WORKSHEET 58 from *Little by Little*
Vocabulary 1. ominously; 2. stupendous; 3. petticoat; 4. pupils; 5. abrasion

Understanding the Selection 6. mental arithmetic; 7. his daughter was dying; 8. to be on time for school; 9. the words that the doctors use; 10. "what mere words could do"

Author's Craft: Autobiography 11. P; 12. F; 13. F; 14. P; 15. P

WORKSHEET 59 *A Night in the Royal Ontario Museum*

Vocabulary 1. mastodons; 2. embalmed; 3. totempole; 4. fossil; 5. mosaic

Understanding the Selection 6. a crazed man-made stone brain; 7. chronologically; 8. a labyrinth; 9. the mastedons and fossils; 10. the size and shape of the museum

Author's Craft: Onomatopoeia, Alliteration, and Assonance 11. assonance; 12. onomatopoeia; 13. alliteration; 14. alliteration and onomatopoeia; 15. alliteration

WORKSHEET 60 *My Financial Career*

Vocabulary 1. d; 2. e; 3. a; 4. c; 5. b

Understanding the Selection 6. in a crumpled ball in his pocket; 7. a Pinkerton detective; 8. writes a check withdrawing the entire amount; 9. "fifties" and "sixes"; 10. in cash in his trousers pocket; in silver dollars in a sock.

Author's Craft: Humor 11. the manager alone; 12. a huge fortune; 13. the safe; 14. a conjuring trick; 15. insulted him.

Literary Skill Answer Key

LYRIC POETRY *All That You Have Given Me, Africa*

Possible responses are given:

1. c; 2. e; 3. a; 4. c; 5. d; 6. a; 7. c; 8. d; 9. b; 10. c

METAPHOR AND SIMILE *In This Valley*

Possible responses are given:

1. "is a hope/of starting afresh without having to die first."

2. Amichai sees the valley almost as a promise of rebirth, a place where both positive and negative things can occur. The metaphor helps the reader to understand that this place is more than just a physical landscape; it is also a symbol of expectation or anticipation.

3. ". . . like the breeze that passes through it now without being destined for it."

4. This simile, comparing the hope to a breeze, shows that the poet is refreshed and perhaps motivated by the thought that both good and bad can pass through his valley without either one being permanent. Like the larger metaphor that begins the stanza, this comparison reinforces the poet's desire for relief from what bothers him.

FORESHADOWING *No Way Out*

Possible responses are given:

1. Wu makes plans to escape from China, but before he can do so, he is denounced and sentenced to reeducation through labor.

2. Comrade Ma and the other party members are closing in on Wu. It foreshadows the fateful meeting in which Wu is expelled from the Party.

3. This foreshadows the fact that Ning is the only Party member who understands Wu's plight. When Wu is called before the committee, none of the others speak for him or show him any kindness.

4. This foreshadows that this meeting will be different from other criticism meetings. Rather than just having his hand slapped, he is denounced, expelled, and arrested.

5. This quotation returns to and reinforces the foreshadowing of the title. The writer knows that his luck and his chances have run out. There's no escape.

SHORT STORY *The Tiger*

Possible responses are shown:

I. Plot

Fatima, a young pregnant woman, is bathing in the river, when she encounters a tiger. Although frightened by its presence, she notes that it doesn't seem to want to attack her. After swimming back to the village, she tells her story. When the men go out to hunt and kill the tiger, Fatima is upset. She feels labor pains at the moment she learns the tiger is dead and its three cubs were discovered.

II. Characters

Fatima: a young pregnant Malaysian woman who, despite her fear, is extremely sensitive and observant. Knowing that she has a baby to protect, she thinks out a strategy for escaping the tiger. In spite of the headman's persuasion, she doesn't want the tiger killed, though she is at first unaware of her own reasons. She feels the pain of another mother when the beast is killed.

Fatima's mother: an old woman given to telling exaggerated tales. She enjoys being the center of interest and is quite self-involved, believing that the tiger may attack her out of all of the other villagers. Although she is sympathetic to her daughter's labor pains, she dismisses Fatima's concerns about the tiger as those of a crazy person.

III. Settings

The story begins at a river surrounded by a forest and follows Fatima back to the village. From her hut, Fatima can hear the sounds of the hunt coming from the forest.

IV. Climax

Fatima learns that the men found three tiger cubs that were only a few hours old.

V. Resolution

There really is no satisfying end to the conflict. Fatima, we can assume, will soon give birth. We can infer that she has discovered a bond with nature, realizing that both she and the tiger share a desire to protect their children.

VI. Theme

Despite their differences, people and animals can play similar roles and experience similar instincts.

SEQUENCING *The Servant*

Possible responses are given:

1. **Setting:** Moscow just before Christmas (with a mention that the main character had returned to his village for military service, had found it dull, and had decided that Moscow, his boyhood home, offered better job prospects)

Summary: Gerasim, the main character, returns to Moscow just before Christmas in order to find work. He stays with friends and pursues every possible avenue of finding a job.

2. **Setting:** Yegor Danilych's place of employment at the extreme outer edge of Moscow, near Sokolnik

   Summary: Gerasim goes to Yegor Danilych, a friend who works as a coachman to a merchant, to ask him if Sharov might employ him. Gerasim has to listen to his friend's boasting as well as his lectures about being a good worker.

3. **Setting:** same as Chapter 2

   Summary: Yegor asks Sharov for a job for Gerasim. In order to make a good case for hiring his friend, Yegor diminishes the age and abilities of the present servant, Polikarpych.

4. **Setting:** same as Chapters 2 and 3

   Summary: Sharov interviews and hires Gerasim, but the servant overhears a conversation between Polikarpych and his wife about their having to go to the poorhouse.

5. **Setting:** same as Chapters 2, 3, and 4

   Summary: Gerasim feels incredible guilt and goes to Yegor to tell him that he can't take the job. Even though he is still unemployed, Gerasim feels happy and lighthearted.

CHARACTERIZATION *If Not Still Higher*

Possible responses are given:

1. **Personality traits:** The rabbi is a reliable religious force who will help his people remain good and pious and save them from evil.

   Technique: the reactions of the other characters

2. **Personality traits:** The rabbi takes his role and his job seriously. He doesn't sleep particularly well because he is weighed down by the troubles of the people of Nemirov.

   Technique: the author's direct statements

3. **Personality traits:** The rabbi is sensitive. He doesn't want others to know about his charitable acts.

   Technique: the character's own actions

4. **Personality traits:** The rabbi is sympathetic and giving. He tries to put the woman at ease and diminish her guilt over accepting charity.

   Technique: the character's own words

5. **Personality traits:** The rabbi is genuinely good and kind. No task is too low for him to perform if it will help someone.

   Technique: the character's own words

6. **Personality traits:** The rabbi is such an exceptional man that even heaven is not enough of a reward for his good deeds.

   Technique: the reactions of other characters

SENSORY DETAIL *Chilean Earth*

Possible responses are given:

1. We dance on Chilean Earth/more beautiful than Tia and Raquel

   Land most green with orchards, blond with grain, red with grapevines

   We will open its rocks; we will create vineyards and orchards

   Today we need only dance

2. Its rivers [molded] our laughter

   And it kisses our feet with a melody/that makes any mother sigh

   We want to light up fields with song

   to bathe its face in music

3. We dance on Chilean Earth

   the Earth kneads men

   how sweetly it brushes our feet

   Its dust molded our cheeks

   And it kisses our feet with a melody

4. Mistral creates a beautiful, colorful portrait of her native land. By comparing it to the beauty of two women and then focusing on the green, yellow, and red of the landscape, she helps us to understand why its inhabitants celebrate their happiness.

5. The people of Chile appreciate their home. Strongly influenced and molded by the land, they react with joy and laughter, not with bitterness. They appear to be hard-working and loyal; they do not forget the importance of honoring their land.

6. Mistral has strong, positive feelings about Chile that she wants to share with her readers. She particularly revels in the freedom that allows her people to celebrate their appreciation of their land. In addition to her aesthetic appreciation, she also communicates her nationalistic pride.

DRAMA *Florinda and Don Gonzalo*

Possible responses are given:

1. **Don Gonzalo:** predictable

   Florinda: adventurous

2. **Don Gonzalo:** pessimistic

   Florinda: romantic

3. **Don Gonzalo:** timid

   Florinda: bold

4. **Don Gonzalo:** uncertain

   Florinda: determined

5. **Don Gonzalo:** practical

   Florinda: romantic

AUTOBIOGRAPHY from *Little by Little*

Possible answers are given:

1. Jean probably didn't hate her little sister or hold her responsible for the trouble. It was easier to blame the youngest child in the family than it was to face the arithmetic test and having to wear the knitted suit. She probably was a bit jealous of her sister, wishing that she herself could stay home and be spoiled.

2. This was most likely a valid feeling on Jean's part. Fitting in was extremely important to her, and she had already experienced teasing.

3. As a child, Jean probably did believe that she had fooled her teacher. Writing as an adult, however, Jean includes numerous hints for her readers that Miss Marr really didn't buy the story.

4. This was undoubtedly a valid feeling for Jean as a child. She was looking for signs of acceptance and got one in the girl's smile.

5. Jean probably knew even then that the boy's aim wasn't off. Instead, he was so surprised at her having confronted him that he chose not to hit her.

6. This is a valid feeling based on her experiences. She learned that she could change the outcome of a situation with a story or with a fact.

Assessment Worksheets
Literary Skills Worksheets

There are sixty assessment worksheets, one for each lesson plan in the Teacher's Resource Manual. There are nine literary skills worksheets. Although the literary skills worksheets are each based on a specific selection in the Student Edition, these worksheets are generic in nature and can be used with other selections to which they apply.

Name _____   Date _____

Assessment Worksheet 1

from *Sundiata: An Epic of Old Mali* edited by D. T. Niane   (pages 7–18)

Vocabulary   The sentences below are based on descriptions or events in the selection.
Look for context clues to help you find the best word below to complete each sentence.

exemplary   **innuendo**   **humiliated**   **infirmity**   **malicious**

1. Sundiata owed much of his strength and power to his mother's _____ behavior.

2. Sundiata had to overcome his _____ of stiff legs before his people would accept him as their leader.

3. The king's first wife, Sassouma Bérété, caused great unhappiness and distress for Sogolon Kedjou by spreading _____ gossip.

4. Through _____, Sassouma hinted at Sundiata's unfitness to rule because he couldn't walk.

5. Sassouma carried her jealousy to extremes when she _____ Sogolon Kedjou by allowing villagers to look at and ridicule her and her son.

Understanding the Selection   Complete each sentence by adding appropriate information from the selection.

6. Sundiata had a slow and difficult childhood because _____
_____.

7. The king reinstated his second wife, Sogolon Kedjou, after _____
_____.

8. Sassouma Bérété gained power when _____
_____.

9. Sundiata finally stood up and walked so that he could _____
_____.

10. People knew that Sundiata would make a great Mali leader because _____
_____.

Author's Craft: Epic   The selection contains the following elements. Match the element to its example.

   a. great hero's deed   b. desirable quality   c. proverb   d. undesirable quality   e. poetic language

_____ 11. The future springs from the past.

_____ 12. Arise, young lion, roar, and may the bush know that from henceforth it has a master.

_____ 13. With all of his might, the son of Sogolon tore up the tree, put it on his shoulders, and went back to his mother.

_____ 14. People recalled Sassouma Bérété's scenes of jealousy and the spiteful remarks she circulated about her co-wife and her child.

_____ 15. It was said, the more a wife loves and respects her husband and the more she suffers for her child, the more valorous will be the child one day.

Name _____   Date _____

Assessment Worksheet 2

Owner of the Sky: Olorun the Creator retold by Virginia Hamilton   (pages 19–22)

Vocabulary   The sentences below are based on descriptions or events in the selection. Look for context clues to help you find the best word or phrase below to complete each sentence.

waste   give them goods   plant their feet   Chameleon   solid and true

1. Olorun wanted to provide humans with land, _____, on which to stand.

2. Because they were gods, Olorun and the other gods had no trouble playing on the earth, which was only a watery, marshy _____.

3. Olorun knew that humans would need wide, solid ground on which to _____.

4. Olorun asked _____ with his slow walk and large eyes to check Great God's creation of land carefully.

5. Olorun sent Great God to Ifé to plant trees, to feed humans, and to _____ they would need to survive.

Understanding the Selection   Complete each sentence by filling in the appropriate information from the selection.

6. To help Great God create hard ground, Olorun gave him _____
_____.

7. To make hard ground, Great God _____
_____.

8. The city of Ile-Ifé is sacred to Olorun's people because _____
_____.

9. Olorun's part in creating people was _____
_____.

10. Great God's part in creating people was _____
_____.

Author's Craft: Cause and Effect   This African myth explains the earth's creation through a series of causes and effects. Use the text to identify the element missing in each of the following statements.

11. Because the hen and the chicken scratched and scratched, _____
_____.

12. Chameleon had to make a second trip to the earth because _____
_____.

13. Great God planted palm trees so that _____
_____.

14. Because Great God was jealous of Olorun, he _____
_____.

15. Because Olorun knew everything, he _____
_____.

Assessment Worksheet 3

The Sea Eats the Land at Home by Kofi Awoonor
Song for the Sun that Disappeared Behind the Rainclouds an oral poem of the
Khoikhoi   (pages 23–26)

Vocabulary   The sentences below are based on descriptions or events in the poems.
Read for context clues to help you find the best word below to complete each sentence.

lamentations   mourning   hearth   eternal   dowry

1. The villagers in Kofi Awoonor's home town hear the never-ending, _____ sounds
   of the sea.

2. The villagers see things from their homes floating on the water, even the firewood from the

   _____.

3. Kofi Awoonor describes the villagers' cries and tears of _____ as the sea destroys
   the town.

4. Adena lost the jewelry that was her _____ for the man she married.

5. The Hottentots' _____ over the loss of the sun were so loud that God gave them a
   rainbow and a basket of stars.

Understanding the Selections   Complete each sentence by adding appropriate
information from the selections.

6. In his poem, Kofi Awoonor is recalling _____

   _____.

7. The flood began _____

   _____.

8. As the water washes through the village, the village women _____

   _____.

9. In the Hottentot song, the rainclouds cover the sun and bring _____ that

   _____.

10. After hearing the lamentations of his people, God collects _____ in a basket

    until it _____

Author's Craft: Sensory Details   To make experiences and events real, writers use
carefully chosen language to compose details appealing to the readers' senses. Read each
detail below. Identify the sense to which it appeals, then find the sensory language that the
authors use to describe it. Write the words or phrases in the blank.

11. You can see the flood waters everywhere in the town. Sense: _____
    Sensory language: _____

12. You can hear the grief of the villagers. Sense: _____
    Sensory language: _____

13. The children are cold and wet. Sense: _____
    Sensory language: _____

14. It gets very dark in the Hottentot village just before it rains. Sense: _____
    Sensory language: _____

15. After it rains in the Hottentot village, God searches for the sun. Sense: _____
    Sensory language: _____

Assessment Worksheet 4

The Prebend Gardens and
Interior by Léopold Sedár Senghor
All That You Have Given Me, Africa by Anoma Kanié   (pages 27–31)

Vocabulary   The sentences below are based on descriptions or events in the selections.
Look for context clues to help you find the best word below to complete each sentence.

pigments   savannahs   lamenting   lagoons   indelible   obsession

1. Among the many beautiful kinds of geography that Africa offers are misted _____ surrounded by lush greenery and grassy, golden _____ stretching to far horizons.

2. Anoma Kanié celebrates the rich, dark _____ that color his skin.

3. Kanié's pride in being African is as _____ a feeling as is the skin color passed down from his ancestors.

4. The tenderness Senghor sees in the "friendly lamp" softens his _____ with Africa.

5. Senghor feels sadness in describing how his African spirit is lost, _____ that other nations have repressed it.

Understanding the Selections   Complete each sentence by filling in the appropriate
information from the selections.

6. Kanié repeats the line "All that you have given me, Africa" to stress his feelings that _____
_____.

7. Léopold Senghor talks about the mix of Arab and African furnishings to show that _____
_____.

8. When Kanié talks about "praising my race which is no better or worse than any other," he means that ____
_____.

9. These poems give the feeling that foreign rule and foreign interference in Africa _____
_____.

10. Both poets are writing poems that _____
_____.

Author's Craft: Nationalism in Poetry   The poets have used languages and imagery
to express some of their feelings about their continent and cultures. Investigate the
meanings of the poems by marking each statement **T** for true or **F** for false.

_____ 11. Kanié feels that being African is a quality that inspires pride.

_____ 12. Senghor enjoys going to the Prebend Gardens because they remind him of all the things that the Europeans have done to help Africa.

_____ 13. Both poets celebrate the beauty of Africans in the phrases "pigments of my ancestors" and "softens my obsession with this presence so/black, brown, and red."

_____ 14. Senghor denies that African cultures have any Arab influence.

_____ 15. Both poets tell of Africa's geographical beauty with phrases such as "misted lagoons," "savannahs gold in the noonday sun," and "red as African soil."

Name _____   Date _____

Assessment Worksheet 5

The Toilet by Gcina Mhlope   (pages 34–42)

Vocabulary   The sentences below are based on descriptions or events in the selection. Look for context clues to help you find the best word below to complete each sentence.

> **Johannesburg**   **alternative**   **knocked off**   **boutiques**   **premises**

1. _____ in South Africa sold the ladies' clothing, which Mhlope helped to make.

2. Mhlope stayed in her sister's locked room during the week because she didn't have an _____ place to stay.

3. Mhlope had to be very quiet and careful so the white South African family would not know she was on the _____.

4. The story is set in the city of _____, the capital of South Africa.

5. Mhlope and her sister couldn't do much after her sister _____ work.

Understanding the Selection   Complete each sentence by filling in the appropriate information from the selection.

6. Mhlope's mother and sister wanted her to _____
   _____.

7. Mhlope wanted to _____
   _____.

8. Mhlope found a public toilet to use as a place "made just for her" because _____
   _____.

9. Mhlope cried herself to sleep one night after _____
   _____.

10. She found she could write anywhere when _____
    _____.

Author's Craft: Point of View   In a first-person narrative, an author often includes facts and opinions about the society in which he or she lives. Write **F** if the statement tells a fact about South African life; write **O** if the statement is an opinion about the life.

_____ 11. I was really lucky to have found that toilet.

_____ 12. I was getting bored with the books I was reading—the love stories all sounded the same.

_____ 13. How stupid it was for me not to cut myself a spare key long ago.

_____ 14. If my sister's employers were to find out that I lived with her, they would fire her.

_____ 15. For the first time, I accepted that the toilet was not mine after all.

Name _____   Date _____

Assessment Worksheet 6

A Chip of Glass Ruby by Nadine Gordimer   (pages 43–54)

Vocabulary   The sentences below are based on descriptions or events in the selection. Look for context clues to help you find the best word below to complete each sentence.

disarmed   morose   scandalous   bewildered   reproach

1. Mrs. Bamjee _____ her husband by always completing her duties as wife and mother, in addition to her political activities.

2. Mrs. Bamjee's work to end apartheid made Mr. Bamjee _____.

3. Although Mrs. Bamjee's activities were illegal, she was doing nothing _____ that would disgrace the family.

4. Mrs. Bamjee's arrest confused and _____ Mr. Bamjee.

5. Mr. Bamjee's silence after his wife's arrest was filled with pity for himself and _____ for his wife at leaving him in such a bad way.

Understanding the Selection   Complete each sentence by adding appropriate information from the selection.

6. Mrs. Bamjee is helping South Africa's natives, who _____
   _____.

7. The South African government's policy of apartheid compels Mrs. Bamjee to _____
   _____.

8. Mr. Bamjee's opinions about the natives and their situation is that _____
   _____.

9. While in prison, Mrs. Bamjee _____
   _____.

10. Girlie explains to Mr. Bamjee that her mother _____
    _____.

Author's Craft: Conflict   The selection is filled with many examples of both internal and external conflict. Write **I** if the conflict described is internal; write **E** if the conflict described is external.

_____ 11. . . . the resentment that he [Mr. Bamjee] had been making all day faded into a morose and accusing silence.

_____ 12. . . . he thought bitterly [that] his wife was not like other people.

_____ 13. . . . the policemen were searching through a soapbox of papers beside the duplicating machine.

_____ 14. . . . he had not recognized the humble, harmless and apparently useless routine tasks—the minutes of meetings being written up . . . , government blue books that were read . . . , the employment of the fingers . . . —as activity intended to move mountains.

_____ 15. The lump of resentment and wrongedness stopped his throat again.

Name _____   Date _____

Assessment Worksheet 7

Marriage Is a Private Affair by Chinua Achebe   (pages 55–62)

Vocabulary   The sentences below are based on descriptions or events in the selection.
Look for context clues to help you find the best word below to complete each sentence.

commiserate   dissuasion   implore   remorse   vehemently

1. Nnaemeka's father, who is against women teaching, speaks _____ against church leaders who encourage them to do so.

2. Okeke tries many methods of _____ to convince Nnaemeka that marriage to Nene is wrong.

3. Many members of the Ibo come to _____ with Okeke when they hear of his son's willful behavior.

4. Nene writes a letter to _____ Okeke to let Nnaemeka and their sons visit him while she remains in Lagos.

5. Okeke's dream fills him with sadness and _____ about the way he has treated his son and grandsons.

Understanding the Selection   Complete each sentence by filling in the appropriate information from the selection.

6. Nnaemeka's father doesn't want his son to marry a girl unless _____
   _____.

7. Nene thinks that Nnaemeka's father will forgive him _____
   _____.

8. Nnaemeka says he can't marry the girl his father has chosen because _____
   _____.

9. Nene overcomes the prejudice of Ibo women in Lagos by _____
   _____.

10. Okeke finally decides he will see his son when _____
    _____.

Author's Craft: Conflict   The sentences below identify the conflicts in the selection as
internal or external. Write **C** if the statement correctly identifies the type of conflict. Write
NC if the type of conflict is identified incorrectly.

_____ 11. Nnaemeka's conflict with his father and his father's beliefs is internal.

_____ 12. Nnaemeka and Nene's marriage, in conflict with Ibo marriage customs, is external.

_____ 13. The conflict between Okeke's feelings and beliefs is an example of internal conflict.

_____ 14. Church leaders encouraging Ibo women to teach in schools is part of an external conflict.

_____ 15. Okeke's dream is part of an external conflict with nature and the storm.

Assessment Worksheet 8

from *The Dark Child* by Camara Laye   (pages 63–71)

Vocabulary   The sentences below are based on descriptions or events in the selection. Look for context clues to help you find the best word or words below to complete each sentence.

    pestle and mortar   **veranda**   **millet**   **blithely**   **ecstatic**

1. Proud of his success at school, the villagers in Laye's home town welcomed him back with joyful and _____ greetings.

2. Before coming home, Laye _____ accepted a scholarship to a French university without a thought to how his parents might react.

3. On his first night home, Laye sat on the _____ in front of his father's hut and discussed his decision.

4. Mrs. Laye angrily ground the _____ with a _____.

Understanding the Selection   Complete each sentence by filling in the appropriate information from the selection.

5. Although Laye was happy about receiving a scholarship, he was also apprehensive about _____

_____.

6. Mr. Laye feels that his son's pursuing an education is _____

_____.

7. Mr. Laye and Camara go together to talk with Mrs. Laye because _____

_____.

8. Mrs. Laye doesn't want her son to go away because _____

_____.

9. On the plane, Camara demonstrates his mixed feelings about leaving home by _____

_____.

Author's Craft: Dialogue   An author uses dialogue for the following reasons: (a) to give background information; (b) to reveal character; (c) to reveal character relationships; (d) to advance the story's action; (e) to reveal characters' feelings and emotions. Match the reason with the dialogue that demonstrates that purpose. One reason will be used twice.

_____ 10. "For the last four years our son has been with us only on holidays."

_____ 11. "But how are we going to break the news to your mother?"

_____ 12. "I knew quite well that eventually you would leave us . . . And gradually I resigned myself to it."

_____ 13. "This opportunity is within your reach. You must seize it."

_____ 14. "By myself? No, my son. Believe me, even if we both go we'll be outnumbered." We went to look for my mother.

_____ 15. "You are nothing but an ungrateful son. Any excuse is good enough for you to run away from your mother."

Assessment Worksheet 9

The Chair Carrier by Yusuf Idris   (pages 72–78)

Vocabulary   The sentences below are based on descriptions or events in the selection. Look for context clues to help you find the best word below to complete each sentence.

contemplate   archaeology   inclination   cartouche   topple

1. The narrator has no _____ to speak to the porter, but he is drawn to him by simple curiosity.

2. It is impossible for the narrator to _____ the idea of carrying a chair around for thousands of years.

3. Because he is familiar with Egyptian history and _____, the narrator believes that the porter might really belong to another era.

4. The _____ under the letter or announcement attached to the chair is the ancient Egyptian signature of Ptah-Ra'.

5. The narrator is so frustrated by the porter's refusal to put the chair down that he has a terrible urge to _____ it from his shoulders.

Understanding the Selection   Complete each sentence with information from the story.

6. When he first saw the chair, the narrator thought it was _____
_____.

7. Despite his curiousity, the narrator might have let the porter go by except that _____
_____.

8. The strange thing about the porter's language was _____
_____.

9. The porter mentions that he has carried the chair since _____
_____.

10. Uncle Ptah-Ra' is _____
_____.

Author's Craft: Irony   Decide whether the people, objects, or situations named below are part of the irony of the story. Write *yes* in the blank if it is, and *no* if it is not.

_____ 11. The story takes place in Cairo, Egypt.

_____ 12. The porter doesn't know how to read.

_____ 13. The narrator manages to read the announcement attached to the porter's chair.

_____ 14. The porter was given the chair to carry because that was the work that porters did.

_____ 15. The narrator wonders whether he should feel sorry for the porter.

Name _____   Date _____

Assessment Worksheet 10

The Marks of the Wise Man, of the Half Wise, and of the Fool by Rumi   (pages 80–82)

Vocabulary   The sentences below are based on descriptions or events in the selection. Look for context clues to help you find the best word below to complete each sentence.

blind   illuminated   degradation   despairing   halting

1. The fool, who does not know where he wants to go, turns a _____ face toward the light but does not follow it.

2. The wise man is _____ inwardly by the torch of wisdom.

3. The half wise does not fear being _____ because he knows he will someday have his own light.

4. The fool is forever starting out and _____, because he has no idea where to go or how to acquire a light.

5. Even a man who has reached the depths of _____ can still hope for wisdom if he tries hard enough.

Understanding the Selection   Complete each sentence by using information from the selection.

6. The fool may have worldly wisdom, which he uses to acquire material wealth, but _____ _____.

7. The fool is pictured as wandering in a desert because _____ _____.

8. The half wise is not ashamed to _____ _____.

9. The wise man uses his torch to _____ _____.

10. The half wise "clings" to the wise man in hope of _____ _____.

Author's Craft: Didactic Poetry   What lessons are taught in the images below? In each blank, briefly describe the appropriate lesson.

11. having half a lamp: _____

12. leading a caravan: _____

13. traveling but never arriving: _____

14. springing downward: _____

15. being nurtured by another's light: _____

Assessment Worksheet 11

The House on the Border by Aziz Nesin   (pages 83–91)

Vocabulary   The sentences below are based on descriptions or events in the selection.
Look for context clues to help you find the best word to complete each sentence.

jurisdiction   **gendarmerie**   **collaborate**   **fazed**   **nocturnal**

1. The thief pays a _____ call on the renters' house on the first night that they moved in.

2. The thief is so confident that he is not even _____ by the renters' threats to shoot him.

3. The commandant of the _____ used maps to prove that their authority did not extend to the renters' house.

4. "Only a part of your garden is within our _____," said one police chief. "The thief didn't enter your house through the garden, did he?"

5. "The only way I can live with this situation," thought the husband, "is to _____ with our friendly thieves against the thieves that we don't know."

Understanding the Selection   Complete each sentence by adding appropriate information from the story.

6. The husband, who has just rented the house, is annoyed when his neighbors keep telling him that _____
   _____.

7. The wife tells her husband not to get upset, however, because the neighbors _____
   _____.

8. Just the same, in case any thieves show up, the husband plans to _____
   _____.

9. The thief allows himself to be tied up while the renters go to the police because _____
   _____.

10. The renters' solution to their problem at the end of the story shows that they _____
    _____.

Author's Craft: Satire   Satire is ridicule that is meant to change or improve the person or institution being ridiculed. Write the change or improvement that Nesin was aiming for in each situation below.

11. When the story begins, the renters seem stupid and gullible for moving into a house with such low rent.
    _____.

12. The husband is portrayed as an incompetent fool. _____
    _____.

13. The police are described as clowns and buffoons. _____
    _____.

14. The three chiefs seem much too sure of themselves. _____
    _____.

15. The neighbors have an "I told you so" attitude. _____
    _____.

Assessment Worksheet 12
4 + 1 = 1 by Ismail Fahd Ismail   (pages 94–99)

Vocabulary   The sentences below are based on descriptions or events in the selection.
Look for context clues to help you find the best word to complete each sentence.

disciplined   imperative   current   stupefied   din

1. With all the machines working at once, the _____ in the factory is ear-splitting.

2. Although they are _____, the factory workers are quicker to blame the cleaner than to solve the problem when the machines break.

3. The _____ tone in one worker's voice shows his insistence that something be done at once.

4. When a new wire is attached to the fuse box, the _____ again flows into the machines.

5. The cleaner, _____ by the fact that he has apparently broken the machines, is relieved but still confused when they are repaired.

Understanding the Selection   Use information from the selection to answer each of the following questions.

6. How does the cleaner think he broke the machines? _____
   _____

7. What is the cleaner's greatest fear when the machines brake? _____
   _____

8. What actions of the cleaner show how afraid he is? _____
   _____

9. What quality does the oldest worker have that the others lack? _____
   _____

10. How does the factory owner keep control of his workers? _____
   _____

Author's Craft: Dialogue   Write *description, external dialogue,* or *internal dialogue* to
identify the type of each quotation below.

_____ 11. "Puffs of smoke. Power failure."

_____ 12. "That's right. What are we going to do?"

_____ 13. All he could do was blink.

_____ 14. "My whole body's shaking!"

_____ 15. "What are you standing there for?" he shouted at the top of his voice.

Assessment Worksheet 13

A Lover from Palestine by Mahmud Darwish
Warmth of Blood by Ali al-Sharqawi   (pages 100–103)

Vocabulary   The sentences below are based on descriptions or events in the selections.
Look for context clues to help you find the best word below to complete each sentence.

stoked   radiant   wilderness   orphanhood   restore

1. Although his homeland may still be a lush and productive area, Darwish views it as a

    _____.

2. To the prisoner, thoughts of Palestine are _____ by vivid memories of past sights

    and sounds.

3. Since he has lost his homeland, Darwish's feelings of belonging have been replaced by a sense of

    _____.

4. Al-Sharqawi's dreams are full of voices and visions of the past, as warm and _____

    as real fire.

5. To _____ Darwish's life would be to give him back his country and all it means to him.

Understanding the Selections   Complete these sentences with information from the poems.

6. The image of Palestine as a homeless person is captured in the lines _____

    _____.

7. Darwish speaks of the "taste" of his homeland in terms of _____

    _____.

8. Darwish's view of himself as an orphan is captured in his image of _____

    _____.

9. Al-Sharqawi uses images of _____

    to contrast the prisoner's actual life with his dreams and memories.

10. Instead of a woollen garment, the prisoner would prefer that his visitor bring him _____

    _____.

Author's Craft: Figurative Language   Because poetry is meant to be short, poets condense
lengthy descriptions and feelings into images and use figurative language to suggest extended
ideas. Write which images and/or figurative language stands for each of the ideas below.

11. dreams and memories of home: _____

12. thoughts of shared love: _____

13. Palestine as a desolate place: _____

14. feelings of being lost and alone: _____

15. things that bring physical comfort: _____

Name _____   Date _____

Assessment Worksheet 14

In This Valley, Once a Great Love, and *Late in Life* by Yehuda Amichai
(pages 104–107)

Vocabulary   The sentences below are based on descriptions or events in the selections.
Look for context clues to help you find the best word below to complete each sentence.

filtered   spectacles   profiles   afresh   destined

1. Something that is _____ has passed through some sort of sieve.

2. The expression _____ means "all over again."

3. Silhouettes are cutouts showing people's _____ instead of their faces from the front.

4. An old-fashioned word for eyeglasses is _____.

5. People who believe "whatever will be, will be" feel that they are _____ to have a particular future or experience.

Understanding the Selections   Complete each sentence using information from the poems.

6. The "surprised woman" is the love to whom the poet came _____
_____.

7. The poet says that someone in the desert reading a sign that says "Sea level" _____
_____.

8. The effect of the passing years has brought the poet _____
_____.

9. From the hills the poet hears _____
_____.

10. Loves which cannot be moved to another site must _____
_____.

Author's Craft: Figurative Language   On each line write the kind of figurative
language used in each example. Choose from among simile, metaphor, and hyperbole.

_____ 11. "But this valley is a hope/of starting afresh...."

_____ 12. "They must die at their place and in their time/like an old clumsy piece of furniture...."

_____ 13. "Once a great love cut my life in two."

_____ 14. "Thus I remember your face everywhere...."

_____ 15. "[You are] a wild woman wearing spectacles—/those elegant reins of your eyes."

Name _____   Date _____

Assessment Worksheet 15

You Can't Fool Menashe by Ephraim Kishon   (pages 108–112)

Vocabulary   The sentences below are based on descriptions or events in the selection. Look for context clues to help you find the best word below to complete each sentence.

   contorted   languid   checkered   intimation   offing

1. None of Menashe's acquaintances ever knew what was in the _____ for them when Menashe approached.

2. A _____ wave with two fingers waist-high meant that the one whom Menashe greeted this way was in trouble.

3. A writer or producer with a _____ past in his field was likely to receive a cold stare from Menashe.

4. When Menashe approached Tola' at Shani in the café, the writer had absolutely no _____ about what was going to happen.

5. However, the _____ expression on Menashe's face and his icy "Hi!" told Tola' at Shani more than he wanted to know.

Understanding the Selection   Complete each sentence with information from the selection.

6. Tola' at Shani was a playwright who was waiting for _____
   _____.

7. Two of Tola' at Shani's actions that indicated how tense he felt were _____
   _____.

8. As Ervinke described it, the successometer was _____
   _____.

9. A surprising fact about the successometer was its ability to _____
   _____.

10. At the end of the night, Menashe greeted Ervinke with a broad grin, after which Ervinke learned that he had _____
    _____.

Author's Craft: Characterization   Which of the following quotations help Kishon build his characters? Write **T** on the line provided if the quotation helps build the characters or **F** if the quotation does not.

_____ 11. "Menashe is a born barometer."

_____ 12. "One of those wet evenings we were again sitting."

_____ 13. "Then something strange happened."

_____ 14. "He has an uncanny ability to make snap decisions on the success coefficient of the person he is meeting."

_____ 15. "What's the matter? What's … the matter … ?"

Name _____   Date _____

Assessment Worksheet 16

from *A Book of Five Rings* by Miyamoto Musashi   (pages 119–123)

Vocabulary   The sentences below are based on descriptions or events in the selection.
Look for context clues to help you find the best word below to complete each sentence.

halberd   **sieges**   **archery**   **invincible**   **dextrously**

1. _____ is the skill of shooting with a bow and arrow.

2. By following Musashi's expert advice, a person can learn how to handle _____ the
   conflicting needs of large groups of people.

3. A spear is a better choice than a(n) _____ on the battlefield because the spear is an
   offensive weapon.

4. Mastering timing can make a warrior _____, too strong or powerful to be defeated.

5. During the four centuries of fighting under the feudal lords, there were a great many
   _____ in Japan, as the armies blocked towns and fortresses.

Understanding the Selection   Complete each sentence by filling in the appropriate
information from the selection.

6. On the battlefield, the halberd is inferior to the _____.

7. You should not have a _____ weapon: it is important to select and use a variety of
   weapons that you can handle well in different circumstances.

8. The most important element in strategy is _____.

9. Musashi gives _____ rules to help warriors master strategy.

10. If you learn all these rules, you can become _____ and will not be beaten in a battle.

Author's Craft: Didactic Writing   To convey a lesson to their readers, authors will
often use writing that teaches and instructs. This is called didactic writing. Examine the
elements of didactic writing in this selection by marking each of the following statements
T for true or **F** for false.

_____ 11. Musashi addresses his book to a student, intending it to be a guide for life.

_____ 12. Musashi teaches that it is important to master only a few skills, especially fighting with weapons.

_____ 13. The author instructs his readers on the modern values of the business world, especially strategy
         and patience.

_____ 14. The author's advice can be applied to many leaders who are trying to govern and preserve
         discipline.

_____ 15. Musashi teaches that people should pay attention to even the smallest concerns.

Name _____   Date _____

Assessment Worksheet 17

Till the Candle Blew Out by Kim Yong Ik   (pages 124–131)

Vocabulary   The sentences below are based on descriptions or events in the selection. Look for context clues to help you find the best word below to complete each sentence.

thatched   abode   abacus   abalone   sesame

1. Life-Stone was jealous when Sunny-Tiger gave Gentle-Flute a(n) _____ shell whose shiny surface glittered in the sun.

2. Sunny-Tiger liked to eat spinach sprinkled with _____ seeds.

3. Life-Stone lived in a house with a(n) _____ roof made of reeds and straw.

4. Sunny-Tiger's _____, in contrast, had a tile roof.

5. The boys used a(n) _____ in school to help them figure out difficult math problems.

Understanding the Selection   Complete each sentence by filling in the appropriate information from the selection.

6. Gentle-Flute's mother suffered from a medical condition that made her a(n) _____.

7. Sunny-Tiger is very skilled in _____.

8. Life-Stone, on the other hand, is very good at _____.

9. Gentle-Flute and her mother have to leave the village because _____.

10. Life-Stone wants his aunt to give him money so that he can buy _____.

Author's Craft: Motivation   The author probes the characters' motivations, the reasons why the characters act as they do. Examine the characters' motivations by marking each of the following statements **T** for true or **F** for false.

_____ 11. When the story opens, Life-Stone and Sunny-Tiger fight with each other because Life-Stone is so much richer than his friend and feels superior to him.

_____ 12. The boys compete with each other in school, too.

_____ 13. Gentle-Flute gives the boys pencils to thank them for their gifts of food.

_____ 14. Sunny-Tiger's mother beats him to get him to behave and stop stealing honey from the house.

_____ 15. Life-Stone pretends to starve himself so his mother will give him money.

Assessment Worksheet 18

The Ch'i-Lin Purse retold by Linda Fang   (pages 132–139)

Vocabulary   The sentences below are based on descriptions or events in the selection. Look for context clues to help you find the best word below to complete each sentence. Two words will be used twice.

matchmaker   benefactor   Buddha

1. Hsiang-ling's marriage was arranged through a _____; Hsiang-ling would meet her husband for the first time at their wedding.

2. Mrs. Lu felt that Hsiang-ling was her _____ because the purse brought the Lu family good fortune.

3. _____ was the Indian philosopher and founder of the religion that bears his name.

4. The _____ considered Hsiang-ling's family background, education, and income when arranging her marriage.

5. Hsiang-ling really was Mrs. Lu's _____ because the purse contained a valuable piece of jade that financed the Lu's business.

Understanding the Selection   Complete each sentence by filling in the appropriate information from the selection.

6. At the beginning of the story, Hsiang-ling is beautiful and intelligent, but very selfish and

   _____.

7. According to Chinese tradition, the ch'i-lin is the symbol of _____.

8. Hsiang-ling gives her purse to _____.

9. Hsiang-ling and her family are separated by a(n) _____.

10. The Lu family hires Hsiang-ling to _____.

Author's Craft: Moral   "The Ch'i-Lin Purse," as with many folktales, has a moral or an instructive message. Put a check next to any of the following statements that express the moral of this story.

_____ 11. A penny saved is a penny earned.

_____ 12. The early bird catches the worm.

_____ 13. Do good deeds because your kindness will be returned.

_____ 14. Hire people who are down on their luck.

_____ 15. Goodness will be rewarded, so it pays to be nice to people.

Name _____   Date _____

Assessment Worksheet 19

Hearing of the Earthquake in Kyoto (1830) by Rai Sanyō   (pages 140–142)

Vocabulary   The sentences below are based on descriptions or events in the selection. Look for context clues to help you find the best word or words below to complete each sentence.

sunder   beseech   cower   flats   chaos   entreat   multitudes   dirge

1. The force of the earthquake made the ground _____, creating complete _____ and terror.

2. The poet thought his wife and children might be fleeing to the distant _____.

3. The crowds of injured _____ tried to draw back and _____ under any shelter they could find.

4. With their hands held in prayer, the people tried to _____ and _____ uninjured people for help.

5. The low moaning of the frightened and injured people was like a funeral _____.

Understanding the Selection   Complete each sentence by filling in the appropriate information from the selection.

6. Families crouch in the streets to avoid _____.

7. The poet's wife and sons flee to _____.

8. The poet's oldest son escapes by _____.

9. The youngest child was taken to safety on _____.

10. At the end of the poem, the poet compares the noise of the sea and rain to _____.

Author's Craft: Point of View   The point of view of a piece of literature is the perspective from which the story or poem is told. Put a check next to any of the following statements that correctly describe the point of view in "Hearing of the Earthquake in Kyoto (1830)."

_____ 11. The narrator is telling the story of the earthquake.

_____ 12. The narrator primarily uses the pronouns *he, she,* and *they.*

_____ 13. The narrator looks through the eyes of all the characters to show their feelings.

_____ 14. The narrator uses the first-person pronouns *I* and *me.*

_____ 15. This poem is written primarily in the third-person point of view.

Assessment Worksheet 20

A Call to Action and *To the Tune "The River Is Red"* by Ch'iu Chin
(pages 143–146)

Vocabulary   Poets choose vivid comparisons to convey meaning and to paint word pictures
in the reader's mind. The sentences below are based on interpretations of the poems. Look for
context clues to help you choose the word that best fits into each sentence.

waves   swallows   dragons   perfume   flowers

1. The swords of the women generals made a shrill, clear sound resembling the breathing of mythological

   _____.

2. Foreigners repeatedly threaten China like destructive _____, beating against the nation's

   shores.

3. When women are free, they will appear fresh and vigorous like row after row of _____

   growing in abundance.

4. China should be like a warm, secure home; the Chinese people, like _____, resting there.

5. The thought of freedom excites the poet in the same way that _____ stimulates the sense

   of smell.

Understanding the Selections   Complete each sentence by adding appropriate
information from the selections.

6. In "A Call to Action," the poet tries to persuade _____ and

   _____ to join the revolution.

7. In "A Call to Action," the poet believes that China can only be saved by _____

   _____.

8. In "To the Tune 'The River Is Red,'" the hearts of the heroine generals were _____

   _____.

9. In "To the Tune 'The River Is Red,'" the poet states that peace will come to China if the people _____

   _____.

10. If the revolution succeeds, Chinese women will be free to abandon symbols of their oppression such as

    _____.

Author's Craft: Author's Purpose   The purpose is the reason why the author wrote the
work. Examine each of the statements below. Write **T** to identify statements about the author's
purpose that are true. Write **F** to identify statements about the author's purpose that are false.

_____ 11. The poet simply wants to entertain her audience with tales of the past.

_____ 12. The poet wants to persuade readers that revolution is needed to save China.

_____ 13. The poet wants to persuade women that they must throw off oppression.

_____ 14. The poet uses vivid comparisons as part of her persuasive efforts.

_____ 15. The author uses rhetorical questions to add dramatic effect to her appeal.

Name _____   Date _____

Assessment Worksheet 21
No Way Out by Harry Wu   (pages 147–157)

Vocabulary   The sentences below are based on descriptions in the selection. Look for context clues to help you find the best word below to complete each sentence.

surveillance   predicament   bourgeois   furtively   desolation

1. Squatting alone and depressed in the detention center, Harry feels a sense of _____.

2. Innocent of theft, but afraid that denying it will lead to more questions, Harry is faced with a _____.

3. Ignoring the rules, Harry leaves campus _____ on Saturday evenings to see Li.

4. Escaping the guard's _____, Harry runs to the basement and burns the map of the Burmese border.

5. To some in the party, anyone who did not grow up poor but came from a _____ background is a suspect.

Understanding the Selection   Complete each sentence by adding appropriate information from the selection.

6. Harry Wu decides he must leave China because the Communist Party resisted and punished _____
_____.

7. Harry and three others plan to escape by crossing the remote _____
_____.

8. Harry is accused of theft when one of the others, Wang, forges _____
_____.

9. Later, Harry is summoned to a group criticism meeting where he is accused of being _____
_____.

10. Arrested for unspecified crimes, Harry is taken to a detention center to await _____
_____.

Author's Craft: Autobiography   "No Way Out" is an example of an autobiography. Examine each of the statements below. Write **T** to identify statements about the selection that are characteristic of an autobiography. Write **F** to identify statements that are not characteristic of an autobiography.

_____ 11. "No Way Out" is a third-person account of someone else's life.

_____ 12. "No Way Out" reveals insights into Harry Wu's life and times.

_____ 13. "No Way Out" is a bad source of information about China during the 1950s and 1960s.

_____ 14. By sharing his experiences, Harry Wu informs his audience about human rights violations in China.

_____ 15. The author reveals his character through introspection, the examination of his thoughts and feelings.

Assessment Worksheet 22

He-y, Come on Ou-t! by Shin'ichi Hoshi   (pages 158–163)

Vocabulary   The sentences below are based on descriptions or events in the selection. Look for context clues to help you find the best word or words below to complete each sentence.

> **kilometers   meters   cohorts   corpses   vagrants   plausible   counterfeit**

1. The hole was 5000 _____ deep. This would be 5 _____.

2. The concessionaire ordered his _____ to advertise the hole.

3. The _____ of homeless _____ were dumped in the hole.

4. The scientists had a perfectly _____ explanation.

5. The police used the hole to get rid of _____ bills.

Understanding the Selection   Complete each sentence by adding appropriate information from the selection.

6. In the opening of the story, a hole is discovered when _____

_____.

7. A pebble is thrown into the hole to _____

_____.

8. The mayor gives the concessionaire the rights to _____

_____.

9. The hole is ideal for getting rid of such things as _____

_____.

10. The hole causes people to stop thinking about _____

_____.

Author's Craft: Surprise Ending   When something unexpected happens at the conclusion of a story, it is called a surprise ending. Authors use different elements to bring about a surprise ending. Match the elements below to their examples. Two elements will be used twice.

> a. foreshadowing   b. repetition   c. science-fictional occurrence

_____ 11. a person calling "He-y, come on ou-t!" into a hole

_____ 12. the idea of a hole being above this town

_____ 13. a character warns the other townspeople that throwing their garbage into

  the hole "might bring down a curse on us"

_____ 14. a person dropping a pebble into a hole

_____ 15. the idea of a multi-level universe in which each universe uses another as a

  garbage dump

Assessment Worksheet 23
Savitri retold by J. F. Bierlein   (pages 165–170)

Vocabulary   The sentences below are based on descriptions or events in the selection. Look for context clues to help you find the best word below to complete each sentence.

> **pious   alms   ordained   contemplative   equity**

1. Satyavant lives the _____ life of a hermit, meditating on spiritual matters.

2. Unlike other young women whose marriages are _____, Savitri is allowed to choose her own husband.

3. Savitri surprises her father by choosing a _____ man who would rule in accordance with religious teachings.

4. Savitri and Satyavant rule the land with _____, treating all fairly and justly.

5. Savitri, who believes wealth is an illusion, gives _____ to the poor.

Understanding the Selection   Complete each sentence by adding appropriate information from the selection.

6. Satyavant could see through illusions and judge people fairly because _____
_____.

7. Savitri's father opposes the marriage because _____
_____.

8. When Yama tells Savitri that no man has ever entered his kingdom, she replies that _____
_____.

9. Yama's blessings go with Savitri always because she has learned _____
_____.

10. Yama tells Savitri and Satyavant that after their deaths, as a reward for their virtue, they are to go _____
_____.

Author's Craft: Theme   A theme is the main or central idea in a literary work. In fiction, the theme is almost always implied. Write **T** to identify statements illustrating how the author uses literary elements to imply the theme of this selection. Write **F** to identify statements that do not illustrate how the author uses literary elements to help readers understand the theme.

_____ 11. Savitri's wisdom and courage earn her the love and admiration of the people.

_____ 12. Savitri is more interested in philosophical questions than she is in the princes who visit her as suitors.

_____ 13. Savitri's resolution of a plot conflict proves love is stronger than death.

_____ 14. Their virtuous lives earn Savitri and Satyavant the highest salvation.

_____ 15. A one sentence moral at the end summarizes the theme of "Savitri."

Assessment Worksheet 24

This World Lives Because by Iḷam Peruvaḷuti
Children by Pāṇtiyaṇ Aṛivutai Nampi
Tirumāl by Kaṭuvaṇ Iḷaveyiṇaṇár   (pages 171–175)

Vocabulary   The sentences below are based on descriptions or events in the selections.
Look for context clues to help you find the best word to complete each sentence.

    Vedas   ambrosia   tainted   ghee   wrath

1. In the poem "Tirumāl," the poet says that the god Vishnu can transform furious _____
   into soothing calmness.

2. Many Indian cooks prefer clear _____ to solid butter because the fat has been removed.

3. In "This World Lives Because," the poet talks about great men who will not touch a gift that has been
   _____ by something spoiled or undesirable.

4. The _____ are the holy Hindu hymns and prayers.

5. Food of the gods, _____, is supposed to be indescribably delicious.

Understanding the Selections   Complete each sentence by filling in the appropriate
information from the poems.

6. "Tirumāl" is a hymn to the Hindu god _____.

7. In "Tirumāl," the poet concludes that Vishnu is _____.

8. "This World Lives Because" talks about _____ men.

9. In the second stanza of "This World Lives Because," the poet says that these men have no _____
   _____.

10. According to the poem "Children," no matter what a man has earned, the most important thing he can
    have is _____.

Author's Craft: Symbols   A symbol is a person, place, or object that represents an
abstract idea. Poets often use symbols to convey a great deal of meaning in a brief space.
Match each symbol on the left with its meaning in the poems on the right. Write the
correct letter in the blank.

_____ 11. Vishnu   a. food of the gods

_____ 12. children   b. truth

_____ 13. ambrosia   c. selfishness

_____ 14. Vedas   d. heat of fire

_____ 15. eating alone   e. love and the meaning of life

Name _____   Date _____

Assessment Worksheet 25

The Tiger by S. Rajaratnam   (pages 178–184)

Vocabulary   Match each vocabulary word in the column on the right with its definition in the column on the left. Write the correct letter on the lines provided.

_____ 1. a kind of very tall, thick grass   a. **sarong**

_____ 2. a piece of woven material used as a bed   b. **lalang**

_____ 3. a village chief in Malaysia   c. **betel**

_____ 4. a climbing pepper plant whose nuts are chewed d. **headman**

_____ 5. a simple, wraparound dress or skirt   e. **mat**

Understanding the Selection   Complete each sentence by adding appropriate information from the selection.

6. Fatima realizes that the tiger is not part of her dream world when the low growl _____

    _____.

7. Fatima becomes puzzled when she notices surprising changes of _____

    _____.

8. In the village, thinking about the tiger, Fatima hopes that _____

    _____.

9. When she hears the rifle report and the tiger's howl, Fatima feels the onset of _____

    _____.

10. The boy who brings the news suggests that the tiger fought so hard because _____

    _____.

Author's Craft: Suspense   A feeling of strong curiosity or uncertainty about the way that events will turn out is called suspense. Choose the correct word from the list to complete each of the sentences below concerning how writers create suspense.

plot twist   relieve   fulfill   atmosphere   sympathize

11. Writers use _____ to build suspense.

12. Suspense is strongest when we _____ with a character.

13. Writers _____ the tension created by suspense in one of two ways.

14. They may _____ our expectations by showing how what we anticipated happens.

15. They may also shatter our expectations by surprising us with a _____.

Assessment Worksheet 26

Forty-Five a Month by R. K. Narayan   (pages 185–191)

Vocabulary   The sentences below are based on descriptions or events in the selection. Look for context clues to help you find the best word below to complete each sentence.

> **laboriously   vermilion   wry   cynically   excruciating**

1. Shanta's mother looked at her daughter _____, doubting that her husband would be home in time to take the child to the movies.

2. Twisting her mouth to one side, to show her doubt, she gave a _____ smile.

3. Meanwhile, Venkat Rao worked _____, desperately trying to get out of the office on time.

4. Unfortunately, he faced two hours of _____ work going through the pay vouchers.

5. Shanta painted a _____ dot on her forehead with bright red makeup.

Understanding the Selection   Complete each sentence by filling in the appropriate information from the selection.

6. Rather than telling Shanta the time, the teacher _____.

7. To get ready for her father, Shanta dresses herself in _____.

8. Shanta gets back to her house by _____.

9. Shanta's father works in the _____ section of the company.

10. At the very end of the story, Rao wants to _____.

Author's Craft: Plot   The plot is what happens in a story. Identify each section of the story's plot by writing the correct word next to the description.

> characters   rising action   central conflict   climax   resolution

_____ 11. The manager gives Venkat Rao a raise just as he is about to resign.

_____ 12. Shanta, Mr. and Mrs. Rao, the office manager

_____ 13. Venkat Rao is torn between his duties at the office and his desire to spend time with his daughter.

_____ 14. Venkat Rao accepts the raise.

_____ 15. Mrs. Rao and Shanta argue about Mr. Rao coming home in time to take Shanta to the movies.

Assessment Worksheet 27

from *When Heaven and Earth Changed Places* by Le Ly Hayslip
(pages 192–196)

Vocabulary   The sentences below are based on descriptions or events in the selection. Look for context clues to help you find the best word to complete each sentence.

spouses   rituals   colander   karma   altar

1. A person's ultimate fate or _____ can be good or bad; it depends on the god of nature.

2. When the harvest was over, the people in this village found _____ for eligible, single young people.

3. They also prayed to their gods by placing food and special objects on a raised platform called the

   _____.

4. A _____ is a useful kitchen utensil for draining liquids off from foods such as rice and vegetables.

5. _____ such as sacrafices made before planting and harvesting, help bind a community together.

Understanding the Selection   Complete each sentence by filling in the appropriate information from the selection.

6. On the fourteenth of every month, family members burned special objects to _____

   _____.

7. The legend cited in the story explains _____

   _____.

8. The stalk and rice are separated through the labor of a large animal called a(n) _____

   _____.

9. The best rice is used for _____

   _____.

10. Crop failures not caused by the soldiers are blamed on _____

    _____.

Author's Craft: Setting   The setting of a literary work is the time and place where the events occur. Analyze the setting of *When Heaven and Earth Changed Places* by writing **T** for statements that are true or **F** for statments that are false.

_____ 11. The writer sets part of the story in her house to give a sense of Vietnamese customs and culture.

_____ 12. The part of the story set in the rice fields shows the importance of rice to the community.

_____ 13. The story also is partly set in America, which provides a sharp contrast.

_____ 14. The story takes place in the present-day.

_____ 15. Understanding the story's setting helps explain why the farmers supported the Communists.

Name _____   Date _____

Assessment Worksheet 28

Tangaroa, Maker of All Things edited by Antony Alpers (pages 200–205)

Vocabulary   Match the definition on the right with the vocabulary word from the selection on the left. Write the correct letter in the blank.

_____ 1. **ridges**   a. flat, rigid plates covering the body of a fish

_____ 2. **scales**   b. soft, light outgrowths covering the body of a bird

_____ 3. **shells**   c. arcs in the sky containing the colors of the spectrum

_____ 4. **feathers**   d. long, narrow ranges of hills

_____ 5. **rainbows**   e. hard, outer coverings of animals, nuts, etc.

Understanding the Selection   Complete each sentence by adding appropriate information from the selection.

6. When Tangaroa stood upon his shell and called, _____

_____.

7. When Tangaroa used his shell to form a dome for the sky, he named it Rumia, which means _____

_____.

8. After making the sky dome, rock, and sand, Tangaroa continued creating because _____

_____.

9. The last creation that Tangaroa called forth was _____

_____.

10. The land is a shell to the stones and also to both _____

_____.

Author's Craft: Figures of Speech   Figures of speech describe one thing (the subject) in terms usually applied to another (the image). The image creates a vivid impression of the subject in the reader's mind. Match the image on the right with its corresponding subject on the left. Write the correct letter in the blank.

_____ 11. a mountain range   a. Tangaroa's feathers

_____ 12. mountain ridges   b. Tangaroa's blood

_____ 13. fish scales   c. Tangaroa's backbone

_____ 14. trees and shrubs   d. Tangaroa's fingernails

_____ 15. rainbows   e. Tangaroa's ribs

Name _____   Date _____

Assessment Worksheet 29

Maui and the Great Fish retold by Kiri Te Kanawa   (pages 204–207)

Vocabulary   The sentences below are based on descriptions or events in the selection.
Look for context clues to help you find the best word below to complete each sentence.

screeching   **turmoil**   **wrenched**   **bait**   **spells**

1. With great effort, one of the brothers _____ the slats of wood from the floor of the boat.

2. Maui knew many magic _____ and had many magic powers that he used to fool
   people—especially his brothers.

3. Often, his tricks caused great _____ and upheaval, as shown in this story.

4. He tricked his brothers into thinking that his voice was the loud _____ of the seagulls
   flying overhead.

5. Since his brothers would not give him any _____ to use to catch fish, Maui put his own
   blood on the tip of his fish hook.

Understanding the Selection   Complete each sentence by filling in the appropriate
information from the selection.

6. When he hears that his brothers are going fishing, Maui takes out his _____
   _____ and heads for the boat.

7. Maui's brothers don't want to take him along, so Maui hides _____
   _____.

8. Maui's brothers agree not to turn the boat back to the shore because Maui _____
   _____.

9. Maui catches _____
   _____.

10. At the end of the story, Maui's brothers _____
    _____.

Author's Craft: Repetition   Kiri Te Kanawa, like many great storytellers, uses
repetition to emphasize meaning, link ideas, and create rhythm. Underline the repetition
in each of the following examples.

11. There was Maui, laughing loudly and boasting, "I tricked you! I tricked you!"

12. But Maui said, "Look back! Look back to the land! Look how far away it is!"

13. He pulled and pulled. The sea was in a turmoil and Maui's brothers sat in stunned silence, marveling at
    Maui's magic strength.

14. Maui was, they say, half man and half god.

15. He knew many magic spells and had many magic powers that his older brothers didn't know about.

Name _____   Date _____

Assessment Worksheet 30

Family Council by Oodgeroo   (pages 208–211)

Vocabulary   The sentences below are based on descriptions or events in the selection.
Look for context clues to help you find the best word below to complete each sentence.

overrule   **arbitration**   **unanimously**   **plaintiffs**   **grievance**

1. The family can only overturn the father's decision _____; everyone must agree to ask
   for a new hearing.

2. The brothers and sisters are the _____ since they brought the charges against the
   narrator.

3. Father is the _____ judge; it is his job to settle the conflict.

4. The _____ committee has met to discuss the narrator's problems with hunting animals
   for the family's meals.

5. Father listens to the complaints and the defense, then he decides whether to agree with the complaints or
   _____ them.

Understanding the Selection   Complete each sentence by filling in the appropriate
information from the selection.

6. The narrator's sisters and brothers complain that she does not _____
   _____ when it comes to bringing home food supplies from the hunt.

7. The second brother complains that the narrator gets up early and _____
   _____.

8. According to the younger sister, the narrator has trained her cat, _____ ,
   to frighten everyone away.

9. The narrator refuses to _____ because she does not like to do it.

10. _____ goes fishing most often and catches the most finfish and shellfish.

Author's Craft: Personal Narrative   Personal narratives allow authors to present
vivid descriptions of events and people that only an eyewitness or a participant can
provide. Examine the elements of personal narratives in this selection by identifying each
statement as **T** for true or **F** for false.

_____ 11. As shown in "Family Council," personal narratives are autobiographical incidents.

_____ 12. Personal narratives are written from the third-person point of view, using the pronouns *he*
      and *she.*

_____ 13. "Family Council" offers an objective account of a serious conflict experienced by one Australian
      Aboriginal family.

_____ 14. Since "Family Council" is a personal narrative, readers can assume that the author Oodgeroo is the
      narrator of the story.

_____ 15. The writer selected this incident because it shows how conflict is resolved in Aboriginal families.

Name _____   Date _____

Assessment Worksheet 31

Butterflies by Patricia Grace   (pages 212–214)

Vocabulary   The sentences below are based on descriptions or events in the selection. Look for context clues to help you find the best word below to complete each sentence. One of the words will appear in two of the sentences.

plaited   hatch   hoeing   footpath

1. The grandmother _____ her granddaughter's hair.

2. Butterflies _____ out and fly in the sun.

3. When the granddaughter came home from school, her grandfather was _____ cabbages.

4. The grandfather walked out to the _____ with his granddaughter.

5. The neighbor complimented the granddaughter's _____ hair.

Understanding the Selection   Complete each sentence by adding appropriate information from the selection.

6. Both the grandmother and the grandfather tell their granddaughter to _____

    _____.

7. When the granddaughter returns from school, her grandmother is _____

    _____.

8. In her story, the granddaughter _____

    _____.

9. The grandfather responds to the teacher's remarks by saying that _____

    _____.

10. The grandparents are proud of their granddaughter because _____

    _____.

Author's Craft: Setting   In literary works, setting is very important to the overall meaning of the story. Investigate the setting in the selection by marking each of the following statements **T** for true or **F** for false.

_____ 11. The grandfather and the grandmother lead traditional lives.

_____ 12. The granddaughter's teacher lives a similar life to the grandmother and grandfather.

_____ 13. The grandfather buys cabbage in the supermarket.

_____ 14. The only place the granddaughter learns is at school.

_____ 15. The grandmother and the grandfather have a gardener tend to their garden.

Assessment Worksheet 32

The Servant by S.T. Semyonov   (pages 221–228)

Vocabulary   The sentences below are based on descriptions or events in the selection.
Look for context clues to help you find the best word below to complete each sentence.

> **downcast**   **charwoman**   **almshouse**   **disheartened**   **ingratiated**

1. The Polikarpychs will have to live with other poor people in the _____ if Mr. Polikarpych loses his job with Sharov.

2. Gerasim _____ himself with Yegor Danilych by flattering him.

3. Gerasim is discouraged and _____ when he cannot get a job.

4. Mrs. Polikarpych earns money by working as a _____, cleaning other people's homes.

5. Mr. and Mrs. Polikarpych are _____ and sad when they realize they might be out on the street.

Understanding the Selection   Complete each sentence by filling in the appropriate
information from the selection.

6. Right before Christmas, Gerasim returns to _____ from the countryside.

7. Gerasim lost his last job when he was called back to his village _____.

8. Sharov values Yegor Danilych because the coachman _____.

9. At the end of their first meeting, Yegor Danilych gives Gerasim a(n) _____.

10. Mr. Polikarpych believes that it is a(n) _____ for Mrs. Polikarpych to tell Sharov about Yegor Danilych's thefts.

Author's Craft: Historical Context   The author uses the political, cultural, and
economic conditions of Russia during the 1920s as a backdrop for the story. This historical
context often motivates the characters to behave in a specific way. Examine the historical
context by marking each statement **T** for true or **F** for false.

_____ 11. It is very difficult for Gerasim to find a job because the upheavals in Russian society brought about widespread starvation, unemployment, and disease.

_____ 12. Gerasim approaches Yegor Danilych rather than Sharov for a job because peasants would never directly speak to rich landowners.

_____ 13. Yegor Danilych gets Gerasim a job because, in the 1920s, Russian servants always took care of each other.

_____ 14. Polikarpych is not worried about what will become of him and his wife because, in the 1920s, the Russian government took care of elderly people.

_____ 15. Gerasim gives up the job because he knows that he will be able to get another one easily.

Name _____   Date _____

Assessment Worksheet 33

If Not Still Higher by Isaac Loeb Peretz   (pages 229–233)

Vocabulary   The sentences below are based on descriptions or events in the selection.
Look for context clues to help you find the best word to complete each sentence.

pious   **dogged**   **broods**   **studded**   **supplication**

1. The rabbi heard frequent cries of _____ as the poor, sick people asked God for help.

2. When he disguised himself as a peasant, the rabbi wore a thick leather belt ornamented and

   _____ with brass nails.

3. It is plain that the rabbi _____ about the problems of the poor people, their sorrow

   hanging over him like a dark cloud.

4. The Lithuanian was _____ in his pursuit of the rabbi, determined to find out his secret.

5. By the end of the story, readers are convinced that the rabbi is a deeply religious and

   _____ man.

Understanding the Selection   Complete each sentence by filling in the appropriate
information from the selection.

6. The rabbi of Nemirov disappears every week _____.

7. The people of Nemirov are convinced that the rabbi is going to visit _____.

8. To find out where the rabbi is going, the Lithuanian first hides _____.

9. The Lithuanian discovers that the rabbi is going _____.

10. While away, the rabbi calls himself by the name _____

    so the peasant woman will not be able to trace him.

Author's Craft: Writing Style   The way in which an author tells a story is called style.
Write a check mark next to each of the following items that is part of an author's
individual writing style.

_____ 11. diction, or word choice

_____ 12. rhythm and rhyme

_____ 13. verb tense

_____ 14. repetition

_____ 15. autobiography

Name _____   Date _____

Assessment Worksheet 34

And When Summer Comes to an End …
Please Give This Seat to an Elderly or Disabled Person by Nina Cassian
(pages 234–236)

Vocabulary   Match each word with its meaning in the selection. Write the correct letter in the blank.

_____	1. **affliction**	a.	broad, flat, thick pieces
_____	2. **dignity**	b.	condition of pain, suffering, or distress
_____	3. **slabs**	c.	time of loss when something is ending
_____	4. **dejected**	d.	feeling of self-respect
_____	5. **decline**	e.	depressed or in low spirits

Understanding the Selections   Complete each sentence by adding appropriate information from the selections.

6. The image in the second stanza of "And When Summer Comes to an End …" is that of a _____
_____.

7. Cassian could not write openly about her feelings because she _____
_____.

8. "Winter Street on the corner of Decline" is a metaphor for _____
_____.

9. The title "Please Give This Seat to an Elderly or Disabled Person" refers to _____
_____.

10. In "Please Give This Seat to an Elderly or Disabled Person," the poet describes her three afflictions as _____
_____.

Author's Craft: Free Verse   A poet uses form to convey meaning. Free verse can help a poet express what he or she is trying to say. Indicate ways Nina Cassian used free-verse techniques in her poems by marking each statement **T** for true or **F** for false.

_____ 11. Mixture of line lengths.

_____ 12. Informal, everyday speech

_____ 13. End-rhyme

_____ 14. Repetition of words

_____ 15. Sudden and abrupt shifts

_____ 16. Regular, rhythmical meter

_____ 17. Irregular stanza length

_____ 18. Variety of punctuation marks

_____ 19. Irregular line breaks

_____ 20. Regular stressed and unstressed syllables

Assessment Worksheet 35

Random Talk by Raisa Blokh
The Heirs of Stalin by Yevgeny Yevtushenko
Refugees by Ilya Krichevsky   (pages 237–243)

Vocabulary   Match each word on the left (from "The Heirs of Stalin") with its definition on the right. Write the letter in the blank.

_____   1. **sortie**   a. large tomb

_____   2. **henchmen**   b. guards

_____   3. **pallbearer**   c. armed attack

_____   4. **mausoleum**   d. person who carries the coffin

_____   5. **sentries**   e. obedient followers

Understanding the Selections   Complete each sentence by adding appropriate information from the selections.

6. In "Random Talk," Raisa Blokh deals mostly with the emotional trauma of _____
   _____.

7. Blokh refers to "random talk" as _____
   because _____.

8. According to Yevtushenko, Stalin lost his way because _____.

9. The question "How do we remove Stalin from Stalin's heirs?" tells us that the author believes that _____
   _____.

10. According to Krichevsky, the refugees in Russia must continue their struggle because _____
    _____.

11. Ironically, even though Krichevsky speaks of going forward and the will to live, most of the poem is
    about _____.

Author's Craft: Author's Purpose   The poets use language and imagery to express
their feelings about oppression and to send a message to the reader. Examine the author's
purpose in each poem by marking each statement **T** for true or **F** for false.

_____   12. For Raisa Blokh, reminiscing about her homeland helps her survive the concentration camps.

_____   13. According to Yevtushenko, tyranny died in the USSR with Stalin's death.

_____   14. "Heirs of Stalin" is a warning that Stalinism may return to Russia.

_____   15. Krichevsky sees no reason to keep on living because "fate is harsh."

Name _____ Date _____

Assessment Worksheet 36

The Bicycle by Jerzy Harasymowicz   (pages 246–248)

Vocabulary   The sentences below are based on descriptions or events in the selection.
Look for context clues to help you find the best word below to complete each sentence.

   partook   gazed   Tatras

1. The bicycle _____ in romps with the mountain goats.

2. On a mountain high, the bicycle _____ at the walking people.

3. The sparkling sky was seen above the _____.

Understanding the Selection   Complete each sentence by adding appropriate
information from the selection.

4. The bicycle joined a herd of _____.

5. The bicycle became the _____ of the mountain goats.

6. The bicycle never nibbled at _____.

7. The poacher shot the bicycle because he was tempted by _____.

8. The bicycle died and went to _____.

Author's Craft: Fantasy and Realism   Imagery is a very important element of poetry.
In "The Bicycle," Harasymowicz uses both realistic and fantastic images to convey
character, mood, and theme. Identify the kind of images listed below as either realistic (**R**)
or fantastic (**F**).

_____   9. A bicycle gazed from above

_____ 10. Forgotten by tourists

_____ 11. A poacher shot it

_____ 12. The snow covered glade

_____ 13. … people walking

_____ 14. It warned them of danger with its bell.

_____ 15. It never nibbled at grass or drank from a stream.

Name _____   Date _____

Assessment Worksheet 37

The Monster by Nina Katerli   (pages 249–257)

Vocabulary   The sentences below are based on descriptions or events in the selection.
Look for context clues to help you find the best word below to complete each sentence.

grievous   dolefully   frenzied   perplexity   mangy

1. The government would not assign the monster to his own apartment because he had done no
   _____ , or serious, bodily harm.

2. The monster was confused and puzzled; he asked in _____ for someone to help him
   find his bone.

3. The monster's fur turned gray, and his tail, no longer well-groomed, became _____ .

4. Aunt Angelina was sad, moaning _____, shivering, and jumping in place to keep
   from freezing.

5. The two women obeyed the monster and began leaping about the apartment in a _____
   dance.

Understanding the Selection   Complete each sentence by adding appropriate
information from the selection.

6. Because the monster felt that the women had been picking on him, he _____
   _____ .

7. The women were turned into stone for thirty-five minutes for _____
   _____ .

8. Anna Lvovna felt no pity for the monster and considered him to be an _____
   that should live _____ .

9. When the monster ordered their legs to give way beneath them, two of the women collapsed at once, but
   Anna Lvovna _____ .

10. Anna Lvovna protested that life with him earlier had been like a _____
    _____ , but could be tolerated because he was useful.

11. The monster told the women they had no choice but to obey his orders because he had _____
    _____ .

Author's Craft: Metaphor   In this story, the metaphor of the monster is extended
throughout the selection. For the following statements, write *yes* if the words helped create
a visual picture of the monster in your mind or *no* if they do not.

_____ 12. The monster was a shaggy creature with a crimson eye.

_____ 13. He turned Anna Lvovna's husband into a saucepan.

_____ 14. I annoyed the monster very much.

_____ 15. He sat for days in his room, just hissing occasionally.

_____ 16. He blew so hard that his cheeks turned blue and his head trembled.

Name _____   Date _____

Assessment Worksheet 38

A Winter's Tale by Slavenka Drakulić   (pages 258–262)

Vocabulary   The sentences below are based on descriptions or events in the selection.
Look for context clues to help you find the best word below to complete each sentence.

> meticulously   gulag   carnage   rations   abstract

1. The bloody battles and _____ in Bosnia have resulted in the deaths of many people
   and the despair of many more.

2. The concept of 6.5 grams of potatoes or 600 grams of bread is _____ and difficult
   to understand.

3. The war in Bosnia has been documented _____ by writers, artists, and film makers who
   are careful and precise in recording their observations.

4. Food is in short supply because of the war, and people have been given small _____
   of only the most essential items.

5. The author compares what is happening in her country to the Russian system of labor camps called the
   _____.

Understanding the Selection   Complete each sentence by filling in the appropriate
information from the selection.

6. The author is writing this essay from _____
   _____.

7. The food shortages in her country make her think about the _____
   _____ she is planning to cook as a side dish for her lunch.

8. When the author was a child, her relatives in America used to send _____
   _____ filled with wonderful things.

9. According to the author, no one can remain _____
   _____ regarding what is going on in the war because of all the attention it has gotten.

10. For the first time, the author feels _____
    _____ because she thinks that her words do not have the power to make her country better.

Author's Craft: Comparison   Authors often use comparisons to show how elements
of a situation are similar and different. Complete the following chart to analyze the
comparisons in "A Winter's Tale."

The West	Sarajevo
The day is quiet and ordinary.	11. The day is _____.
Christmas is a happy time.	12. Christmas is a _____ time.
There is much food.	13. Food is _____.
People relax.	14. People are _____.
The weather is cold and clear.	15. The weather is _____.

Assessment Worksheet 39

The Oath of Athenian Youth by Anonymous   (page 264–266)

Vocabulary   The sentences below are taken from the selection. Look for context clues to help you select the best word below to complete each sentence.

> **revere**   **civic duty**   **incite**   **annul**   **naught**

1. "We will try always to improve the public's sense of _____."

2. "… [we] will do our best to _____ … respect in those above us who might try to _____ them [the laws] or set them at _____."

3. "We will _____ and obey the community's laws …"

Understanding the Selection   Complete each sentence by adding appropriate information from the selection.

4. The words "_____" are repeated five times in "The Oath of Athenian Youth" in order to emphasize the solemn promise being made.

5. In the oath, the words "the community" refers to _____
   _____.

6. The youth promise not to disgrace their community by _____
   _____.

7. Those taking this pledge hope to leave their community _____
   _____.

8. The values that Athenian youth held highest were _____
   _____.

9. The priority of the Athenian youth that I admire most is _____
   because _____.

Author's Craft: Author's Purpose   An oath often promises to protect the people or individuals who belong to a certain group. Examine the author's purpose in "The Oath of Athenian Youth" by marking these statements **T** for true or **F** for false.

_____ 10. "The Oath of Athenian Youth" was written to protect the city-state of Sparta from invasion.

_____ 11. The purpose of the oath was to preserve the ideals of Athenian democracy.

_____ 12. Ideally, by taking this oath, the young men of Athens would grow to be good citizens.

_____ 13. "The Oath of Athenian Youth" is written in the third-person point of view for emphasis.

_____ 14. The author of the oath mentions only those actions that the youth must avoid.

_____ 15. Before being entrusted with the protection of Athens, young men were required to take the oath.

Assessment Worksheet 40

The Nightingale's Three Bits of Advice by Henri Pourrat   (pages 267–270)

Vocabulary   The sentences below are based on descriptions or events in the selection. Look for context clues to help you find the best word below to complete each sentence.

stifle   defy   agape   stove-in   fluttered

1. Astonished, the villager stood with his mouth _____ when the nightingale started to speak.

2. The villager was as foolish as a _____ basket when he ignored the bird's advice.

3. The nightingale's wings _____ in the air as the bird hovered above the villager.

4. It was so incredible as to _____ belief that the nightingale could have a huge pearl in its breast.

5. The man wanted to _____ the small bird by crushing it with his thumb.

Understanding the Selection   Complete each sentence by filling in the appropriate information from the selection.

6. At the very end of winter, the villager set out traps to catch _____.

7. The nightingale's first piece of advice is _____.

8. The villager is beside himself when the bird tells him that _____.

9. To recapture the bird, the man first thinks of throwing a(n) _____ at it.

10. At the end of the story, the villager feels _____.

Author's Craft: Sequence   Authors often use key words to let readers know the sequence or order of events in a story. Below are five events from the story. Number the events from 1 to 5 to place them in the correct sequence.

_____ 11. The nightingale promises the villager three pieces of wonderful advice.

_____ 12. The nightingale flies up to the tree.

_____ 13. The villager tries to get the nightingale to come down from the pine tree.

_____ 14. The man frees the nightingale.

_____ 15. The villager catches a nightingale.

Name _____   Date _____

Assessment Worksheet 41

Paying on the Nail by Padraic O'Farrell   (pages 271–274)

Vocabulary   The sentences below are based on descriptions or events in the selection. Look for context clues to help you find the best word or words below to complete each sentence.

innate   rogue   bade   avail   demurred   forge   sleight-of-hand

1. Shynail's _____ superstitions make him fear cheating at market crosses.

2. Shynail was considered a _____, the kind of person who is difficult to trust.

3. Shynail _____ at the farmer's refusal to make any transactions.

4. The farmer _____ him to mount a horse.

5. Shynail uses _____ methods to deceive farmers.

6. Believing that many farmers would _____ of the opportunity to have their own nails to

   pay on, Shynail starts up a _____.

Understanding the Selection   Complete each sentence by adding appropriate information from the selection.

7. Market crosses are places where _____
   _____.

8. Shynail is a horse _____.

9. As Shynail and the farmer approach Fethard, the Shynail wants a _____
   _____.

10. Shynail is honest to the farmer because he realizes that _____
    _____.

11. In Killenaule, Shynail makes more money fitting horse shoes than he can _____
    _____.

Author's Craft: Trickster Folktales   Trickster folktales contain the following elements. Match the elements to their example from "Paying on the Nail."

a. Oral tradition

b. Conflict resolution through cleverness

c. Character with desirable qualities

d. Character with undesirable qualities

_____ 12. Shynail perfected a sleight-of-hand technique while paying for the stock.

_____ 13. Shynail realized that a few farmers shoed their horses at that time.

_____ 14. The farmer refused to take any money until they went to Clonmel.

_____ 15. It is called the "bargain store" by some.

Assessment Worksheet 42

Death Seed by Ricarda Huch
Woman, You Are Afraid by Maria Wine
from *My Mother's House* by Leah Goldberg   (pages 275–278)

Vocabulary   The sentences below are based on descriptions or events in the selections. Look for context clues to help you find the best word below to complete each sentence.

   sows   stern   resemble   expunged   reaper

1. The _____ in "Death Seed" was probably using a scythe or a sickle to cut the stalks of grain.

2. The reaper frightened the speaker because of the _____, serious look on his face.

3. The reaper scatters, or _____, the seeds over the earth.

4. All portraits of her grandmother had been _____, or removed completely, from the speaker's mother's house.

5. The granddaughter claimed that she did not _____, or look like, her grandmother.

Understanding the Selections   Complete each sentence by adding appropriate information about the selections.

6. The words in *My Mother's House* that tell the reader that the speaker's grandmother died young are

   _____.

7. The point that the author is making in *My Mother's House* is that _____

   _____.

8. The paradox, or double meaning, of the poem title "Death Seed" is that _____

   _____.

9. Considering the obstacles women have had to overcome throughout history, what are some fears women most likely faced during Maria Wine's lifetime? _____

   _____

Author's Craft: Imagery   A poet uses imagery to convey tone or mood. Knowing the tone helps the reader figure out the poet's message. Write **T** for those sentences that are true or **F** for those that are false.

_____ 10. The image of women staring into a dark forest helps create a humorous tone in the poem "Woman, You Are Afraid."

_____ 11. The serious image of the reaper sowing seeds helps to portray the author's message about life and death in "Death Seed."

_____ 12. The mirror in *My Mother's House* is compared to a lake hiding treasures because the speaker finds unexpected answers within it.

_____ 13. The speaker in "Death Seed" seems terrified by an encounter with Death.

_____ 14. The speaker in "Woman, You Are Afraid" sounds bitter and critical.

_____ 15. The speaker in *My Mother's House* can imagine what her grandmother looked like.

Name _____   Date _____

Assessment Worksheet 43

from *Survival in Auschwitz* by Primo Levi   (pages 279–286)

Vocabulary   The sentences below are based on descriptions or events in the selection.
Look for context clues to help you find the best word below to complete each sentence.

   writhe   livid   phantoms   disconcerted   demolition

1. The prisoners were confused and _____ when their clothing was removed and their
   hair shaven off.

2. Stripped of their clothing and hair, the men were as deathly pale as _____.

3. By taking away the men's possessions, the Nazis were responsible for the _____
   of their identity.

4. Standing in the icy water, the men were _____, deathly white with fear.

5. The cold made them twist and _____ with pain.

Understanding the Selection   Complete each sentence by filling in the appropriate
information from the selection.

6. The journey to the death camp lasted a short time, only about _____
   _____.

7. Levi compares his experience in the death camp to being in _____
   _____.

8. The SS man asked one of the prisoners to _____
   _____ so that everyone could understand what he was saying.

9. The dentist is not in the camp because he is Jewish; he is there because he _____
   _____.

10. When Levi gets his number tattooed on his arm, he fully understands that he is a(n) _____
   _____.

Author's Craft: Personal Narrative   Levi tells about his experiences in a personal
narrative, a nonfiction account of events. Examine the elements of a personal narrative by
marking each of the following statements **T** for true or **F** for false.

_____ 11. Levi uses techniques such as dialogue and characterization to help the reader understand the
            true horror of his experiences.

_____ 12. Since a personal narrative does not have to be historically accurate, Levi can invent details
            to include.

_____ 13. Levi occasionally comments on events to evoke a strong response in his readers.

_____ 14. Personal narratives such as this one are rarely presented in the form of a story.

_____ 15. A historian could verify Levi's account of events by comparing it to other factual accounts
            of concentration camps during the war.

Assessment Worksheet 44

Action Will Be Taken by Heinrich Böll   (pages 287–293)

Vocabulary   The sentences below are based on descriptions or events in the selection. Look for context clues to help you find the best word below to complete each sentence.

   aptitude   pregnant   vigorous   delegated   pensively

1. To get the job, the narrator had to take a(n) _____ test that will reveal his strengths and weaknesses.

2. The personalities of the workers are described as _____ because of the number of tasks they can accomplish simultaneously.

3. In the coffee shop the narrator is _____ with action and anxious to get started.

4. The narrator is _____ to carry flowers at the funeral.

5. The narrator _____ examines the dead Mr. Wunsiedel wondering what could have happened.

Understanding the Selection   Complete each sentence by adding appropriate information from the selection.

6. The narrator's personality is referred to as _____.

7. Wunsiedel's right-hand man is called _____.

8. Mr. Wunsiedel's first words to his secretary are _____.

9. The narrator had _____ phones by the end of the first week.

10. The narrator carries _____ behind his boss's coffin.

Author's Craft: Irony   Irony refers to a situation in which the intended meaning is the opposite of the usual meaning. Authors often use irony to help them make a point. The following descriptions, which are based on "Action Will Be Taken," may or may not be ironic. Write **I** on the line provided if the statement is ironic or **N** if the statement is not ironic.

_____ 11. The narrator can answer 13 phones at once.

_____ 12. The title is "Action Will Be Taken," even though there is very little action in the story.

_____ 13. Wundsiedel's right-hand man, Broschek, made a name for himself by supporting seven children and a paralyzed wife while going to school at the same time.

_____ 14. The narrator gets the job at the factory even though, by his own admission, he is more inclined to inaction.

_____ 15. The narrator answers phones by saying, "Action will be taken," without knowing what is produced in the factory.

Name _____   Date _____

Assessment Worksheet 45
The Return by Carmen Laforte   (pages 296–302)

Vocabulary   Match each vocabulary word on the left with the appropriate meaning from the selection on the right. Write the correct letter in the blank.

_____ 1. **asylum**

_____ 2. **refuge**

_____ 3. **straight jacket**

_____ 4. **acolyte**

_____ 5. **prattle**

a. where Julian found salvation

b. device used to constrain Julian

c. an altar boy

d. another word for asylum

e. silly talk

Understanding the Selection   Complete each sentence by adding appropriate information from the selection.

6. Julian believes it is a bad idea to send him home for _____

_____.

7. Julian did not like Sister _____ very much because she

_____.

8. Julian had been out of work for months because of a _____

_____.

9. Julian began imagining that his poor flat was a _____

_____.

10. Julian felt his shoulders sag under a load of _____ and

_____.

Author's Craft: Foreshadowing   Foreshadowing is something that is suggested or indicated before it actually happens. Authors often use foreshadowing to build suspense or to prepare the reader for what is going to happen. Write **F** on the line provided if the statement about the story foreshadows something or **N** if it does not foreshadow anything.

_____ 11. Julian leaves the asylum in time to spend Christmas with his family.

_____ 12. Before the gasoline shortage, Julian had been a good provider for his family.

_____ 13. The title, "The Return," may refer to the fact that Julian's madness will return.

_____ 14. Julian's realization that the nun he disliked and attacked reminds him of his wife, Herminia.

_____ 15. Julian loves Sister María de la Ascunción.

Assessment Worksheet 46

from the *Popol Vuh* edited by J. F. Bierlein   (pages 309–311)

Vocabulary   The sentences below are based on descriptions in the selection. Look for context clues to help you find the best word or words below to complete each sentence. Two words appear twice.

gold   clay   flesh   wood

1. The yellow god made a man out of yellow mud, or _____.

2. The red god made a man from hard plant fiber, or _____.

3. The black god suggested that they make the man out of a yellow metal called _____.

4. The colorless god made men from soft animal tissue or _____.

5. The men of _____ taught the man of _____ the meaning of kindness.

Understanding the Selection   Complete each sentence by adding appropriate information from the selection.

6. The man of clay was unsatisfactory because _____

_____.

7. The man of wood did not meet the gods' standards because _____

_____.

8. The man of gold displeased the gods because _____

_____.

9. The men of flesh filled the hearts of the gods with joy by _____

_____.

10. When he comes to life, the man of gold offers thanks to the gods for _____

_____.

Author's Craft: Myth   The selection from the *Popul Vuh* is an example of a type of folklore called myth. Write **M** to identify statements that characterize a myth. Write **F** to identify statements that are characteristic of other types of folklore.

_____ 11. The tale explains the unknown origins of people.

_____ 12. The plot describes the exploits of a great hero that may or may not be true.

_____ 13. Its account of creation has elements found in cultures from around the world.

_____ 14. The characters in the tale include supernatural beings or gods.

_____ 15. The characters in the tale are animals that talk and behave like people.

Name _____   Date _____

Assessment Worksheet 47

The Great Prayer by Alfonso Cortés   (pages 312–314)

Vocabulary   Below are five words from the selection. Write **L** to identify words that are defined literally. Write **F** to identify words that are used figuratively.

1. **time:**   _____ the point or period when something occurs

      _____ a craving that can never be satisfied

2. **space:**   _____ the human mind

      _____ the physical boundaries of the universe

3. **void:**   _____ the pain caused by loneliness

      _____ an empty space

4. **dream:**   _____ thoughts and images that occur during sleep

      _____ the home of the soul

5. **soul:**   _____ spiritual force

      _____ a majestic, soaring bird

Understanding the Selection   Complete each sentence by adding appropriate information from the selection.

6. Time is _____.

7. Space is _____.

8. Only prayer can _____.

9. Like an eagle, the soul makes its home _____.

10. The key to inner peace is to _____.

Author's Craft: Imagery   Concrete imagery is description that appeals to the senses. Abstract imagery is description that appeals to the mind. Write **C** to identify images that are concrete. Write **A** to identify images that are abstract.

_____ 11. time is hunger

_____ 12. the anguish of the void

_____ 13. dream is a solitary rock

_____ 14. the eagle of the soul

_____ 15. the soul's nest

Assessment Worksheet 48

Bouki Rents a Horse retold by Harold Courlander   (pages 315–318)

Vocabulary   Match the explanation for its French origins on the right with the vocabulary word on the left. Write the correct letter in the blank.

_____	1. **Malice**	a. money unit from the word for "water-bottle"
_____	2. **Madame**	b. a masculine suffix shows this is a male child
_____	3. **Boukinette**	c. a title meaning Mrs. or wife of
_____	4. **Boukino**	d. a feminine suffix shows this is a female child
_____	5. **gourde**	e. a noun meaning "mischief" or "trick"

Understanding the Selection   Complete each sentence by adding appropriate information from the selection.

6. Bouki is concerned that Toussaint will charge him _____

_____.

7. The reason that Bouki no longer needs Toussaint's horse the next day is _____

_____.

8. Bouki is surprised at Ti Malice's mention of a "baby" because _____

_____.

9. Toussaint gives Ti Malice fifteen gourdes after Bouki asks _____

_____.

10. We realize that Bouki did not understand Ti Malice's trickery because he does not think that _____

_____.

Author's Craft: Characterization   The audience anticipates a certain kind of behavior and humor when stock characters appear or are discussed. This familiarity helps us concentrate on the lesson to be learned from the story. Match the expected behavior on the right with the character on the left. Write the correct letter in the blank.

_____	11. **Bouki**	a. the clever prankster who outwits others
_____	12. **Ti Malice**	b. the prankster's simple but honest accomplice
_____	13. **Toussaint**	c. an imaginary character invented by the prankster
_____	14. **Moussa**	d. the dishonest fool outwitted by the prankster
_____	15. **Baby**	e. the friendly or helpful neighbor

Name _____ Date _____

Assessment Worksheet 49

The Street by Octavio Paz
The Room by Victor Manuel Mendiola   (pages 319–321)

Vocabulary   Poets choose the exact term they want to convey meaning and to paint a word picture in the reader's mind. The sentences below are based on interpretations of the poems in this selection. Look for context clues to help you choose the word below that best completes each sentence.

lost   bewildered   stumble   rise   turning

1. Unable to see his way clearly, the narrator can't help but to _____ as he tries to find direction in his life.

2. Although he keeps _____ corners in hopes of finding an escape, the narrator inevitably finds himself back at the same place.

3. Despite his frustration, the narrator is able to _____ each time he falls and continues his search for his identity.

4. The barking dogs, heard at a distance, represent a _____ connection with nature and the past.

5. _____ by the modern world, the dogs represent our instincts howling for attention in the darkness of the subconscious mind.

Understanding the Selections   Complete each sentence by adding appropriate information from the selections.

6. In "The Room," the subconscious "you" of the poem watches the conscious _____
   _____.

7. Unable to ignore basic emotional needs, the "you" of the poem _____
   _____.

8. According to the first line in the poem, "The Street" is _____
   _____.

9. Both the narrator of "The Street" and the Someone who follows him step on _____
   _____.

10. All of the corners the narrator comes upon lead _____
    _____.

Author's Craft: Mood   Each of the poems contains the following elements that help to create mood. Match the element to its example. Elements may be used more than once.

   a. repetition   b. unusual word choice   c. alliteration

_____ 11. "this camp of the hours exposed to all weathers"

_____ 12. "where you watch yourself closing the windows"

_____ 13. "if I slow down, he slows;/ if I run, he runs"

_____ 14. "the deaf shadow"

_____ 15. "nobody waits for . . . nobody follows me . . . nobody."

Assessment Worksheet 50

Keeping Quiet by Pablo Neruda
Chilean Earth by Gabriela Mistral   (pages 322–326)

Vocabulary   Explain the figurative meaning of each boldfaced word as it is used in the line of the poem identified in parentheses.

1. "It would be an **exotic** moment." ("Keeping quiet") _____
_____

2. "I want no **truck** with death." ("Keeping quiet") _____
_____

3. "The earth that **kneads** man." ("Chilean Earth") _____
_____

4. "And it **kisses** our feet with a melody." ("Chilean Earth") _____
_____

5. "We want to **light up** fields with song." ("Chilean Earth") _____
_____

Understanding the Selections   Complete each sentence by adding appropriate information from the selections.

6. In "Keeping Quiet," Neruda suggests that frantic activity distracts people from _____
_____.

7. In "Keeping Quiet," Neruda suggests that we can learn from the seasonal cycles of _____
_____.

8. In "Keeping Quiet," the silence would interrupt the destructive activities of _____
_____.

9. In "Chilean Earth," the dust and rivers of the Chilean landscape have molded _____
_____.

10. In "Chilean Earth," the "song," and the "music," will celebrate the land's _____
_____.

Author's Craft: Lyric Poetry   Lyric poetry is any poetry that reminds us of songs and expresses strong, personal feelings. On the lines provided, write **L** if the statements about the poems are characteristic of lyric poetry or **N** if they are not.

_____ 11. Both poems celebrate the beauty of nature.

_____ 12. Both poems have characteristics that remind us of songs.

_____ 13. In both poems, the speaker expresses strong personal feelings.

_____ 14. Both suggest that society's activities distract us from the meaning of life.

_____ 15. Both contain many imaginative details to express the speaker's emotion.

Name _____   Date _____

Assessment Worksheet 51

Florinda and Don Gonzalo by Luisa Josefina Hernández   (pages 327–334)

Vocabulary   The sentences below are based on descriptions or events in the selection. Look for context clues to help you find the best word below to complete each sentence.

Don   **remedy**   **suitors**   **pessimist**   **consolation**

1. Don Gonzalo finds _____ in Florinda's confident approach to life.

2. In his youth, Don Gonzalo was one of two _____ who courted a family friend.

3. A _____ by nature, Don Gonzalo worries that his wheelchair will fall apart.

4. The polite Florinda always uses _____, a title of respect, when speaking to her neighbor.

5. Florinda believes that love is a _____ for loneliness.

Understanding the Selection   Complete each sentence by adding appropriate information from the selection.

6. Florinda says that she wanted to speak to Don Gonzalo because she, too, _____

_____.

7. Don Gonzalo agreed that his first love should marry someone else because he could not have endured

_____

_____.

8. Florinda believes that life can be miraculous but only if a person is willing to _____

_____.

9. The only thing Don Gonzalo asks of Florinda is that _____

_____.

10. Florinda tells Don Gonzalo to imagine the street is a river and she will _____

_____.

Author's Craft: Dialogue   In a play, the author most often reveals character through dialogue, or conversation. The adjectives below identify character qualities revealed through the dialogue in the selection. Write **F** to identify adjectives that describe Florinda. Write **G** to identify adjectives that describe Don Gonzalo. Write **B** if the adjective describes both characters.

_____ 11. adventurous

_____ 12. pessimistic

_____ 13. lonely

_____ 14. hesitant

_____ 15. optimistic

Name _____   Date _____

Assessment Worksheet 52

One of These Days by Gabriel García Márquez   (pages 335–339)

Vocabulary   The sentences below are based on descriptions or events in the selection. Look for context clues to help you find the best word below to complete each sentence.

tranquil   cautious   rancor   anesthesia   abscess

1. Escovar speaks without _____ although he bitterly resents the political killings.

2. We do not know if Escovar is telling the truth when he says that he cannot use _____ to deaden the pain.

3. Yellowish pus around the infected tooth indicates that the mayor has an _____.

4. Calm and unhurried, Escovar goes about his work in a _____ manner.

5. Escovar is _____ as he inspects the tooth because he does not like to inflict unnecessary pain.

Understanding the Selection   Complete each sentence by adding appropriate information from the selection.

6. The Mayor comes to Aurelio Escovar's office to ask if _____
_____.

7. Upon hearing that the Mayor has threatened to shoot him, Escovar says to tell him _____
_____.

8. When he sees the pain and desperation in the Mayor's eyes, Escovar _____
_____.

9. Escovar believes that the Mayor's suffering is payment for _____
_____.

10. The Mayor indicates that he "is the town" by his response to Escovar's question about _____
_____.

Author's Craft: Suspense   The story contains the following literary elements. Match the element to its description by writing the correct answer in the blank provided.

suspense   character   conflict   protagonist   antagonist

11. The _____ is the main character in a story.

12. Sometimes, suspense involves a struggle between the main character and another major character known as the _____.

13. _____ is a feeling of strong uncertainty about the outcome of the story.

14. The tension is strongest when it involves a _____ that we care about.

15. Our anxiety is relieved at the climax when the _____ between the major characters is resolved.

Assessment Worksheet 53

The Book of Sand by Jorge Luis Borges   (pages 342–348)

Vocabulary   The vocabulary words below are all related to books and book collecting. Match each definition on the right with the vocabulary word on the left. Write the correct letter in the blank.

_____   1. **octavo**

_____   2. **spine**

_____   3. **typographically**

_____   4. **flyleaf**

_____   5. **bibliophile**

a. the supporting back portion of a book cover

b. a lover or collector of books

c. a blank page at the beginning or end of a book

d. with respect to printing or typing

e. a book whose size is that of a piece of paper cut
    eight from a sheet

Understanding the Selection   Complete each sentence by adding appropriate information from the selection.

6. When the narrator tries to open the book to the first or last page, _____
   _____.

7. The narrator later realizes that the reason the salesman immediately accepted his offer is because _____
   _____.

8. The first night the narrator hides the Book of Sand behind a book of fantastic tales titled _____
   _____.

9. During the few hours of sleep that he gets each night, the narrator _____
   _____.

10. The narrator fears that if he tries to destroy the book by burning it, _____
    _____.

Author's Craft: Symbolism   A symbol is something that stands for or represents something other than itself. The symbol is something real and familiar. What the symbol represents is abstract and different from the symbol. Write **S** to identify statements below in which the underlined word is used as a symbol. Write **N** to identify statements in which the underlined word stands for itself without symbolic meaning.

_____   11. The narrator hides the book in a <u>library</u>, the storehouse of all that is safe and measurable in
            our lives.

_____   12. The narrator hides the book in a <u>library</u>, a building containing a large collection of books.

_____   13. It is the Book of <u>Sand</u>, small coarse granules of matter.

_____   14. It is the Book of <u>Sand</u>, infinite matter without beginning or end.

_____   15. The book is a never-ending <u>nightmare</u> from which the narrator cannot escape.

Name _____ Date _____

Assessment Worksheet 54

Continuity of Parks by Julio Cortázar   (pages 349–352)

Vocabulary   The sentences below are based on descriptions or events in the selection. Look for context clues to help you find the best word below to complete each sentence.

> **dilemma**   **apprehensive**   **rivulet**   **dissuade**   **alibis**

1. Danger is not enough to _____ the lovers from their murderous plan.

2. The fact that the woman is married to another man presents a _____ for the lovers.

3. After leaving the cabin, the two go in opposite directions to establish _____.

4. In the study of his estate, the man is not _____ about his safety.

5. The dialogue in the fast-paced novel seems to run down the page like a _____ of snakes.

Understanding the Selection   Complete each sentence by adding appropriate information from the selection.

6. After a business trip to town, a man relaxes in his study by _____
_____.

7. In the novel, a married woman and her lover meet in _____
_____.

8. The two lovers in the fictional work are planning _____
_____.

9. After dark, the lover in the novel sneaks into _____
_____.

10. The real and fictional worlds merge when the lover from the novel enters a room and finds the man
_____.

Author's Craft: Sensory Detail   Cortázar uses sensory details to draw us into the character's world. Match the senses below to the sensory details that follow by writing the correct letter in the space provided.

> a. sight   b. hearing   c. touch

_____ 11. "he let his hand caress the … upholstery"

_____ 12. "the thudding of blood in his ears"

_____ 13. "the dagger warmed itself against his chest"

_____ 14. "a blue chamber, then a hall, then a carpeted stairway"

_____ 15. "the avenue of trees which led up to the house"

Assessment Worksheet 55

Homecoming by Dennis Scott
The Child's Return by Phyllis Allfrey
Jamaica Market by Agnes Maxwell-Hall
On Leaving by Gertrudis Gomez de Avellaneda
Zion, Me Wan Go Home by Anonymous   (pages 353–360)

Vocabulary   Poets choose words that appeal to the senses to create impressions in the reader's mind. The sentences below are based on images from the poems that appeal to sight or hearing. Look for context clues to help you choose the word that best fits into each sentence.

cobalt   topographies   dissonant   metronome   babel

1. In "Jamaica Market," the many different voices heard in the marketplace sound like _____.

2. In "Homecoming," the poet dreams of the island _____, as though seeing the features on a detailed map.

3. In "Homecoming," the poet wants to guide the children away from _____ places, filled with unpleasant sounds.

4. In "The Child's Return," the poet paints the Caribbean waters as _____, a dark, metallic blue.

5. In "Homecoming," the poet's heart beats with the steady ticking of a _____ whenever he thinks of the Caribbean.

Understanding the Selections   Complete each sentence by adding appropriate information from the selection.

6. In "Homecoming," the poet believes that it is time to _____
   _____.

7. In "The Child's Return," the poet will be buried on _____ by
   _____.

8. In "Jamaica Market," the pagan fruits have names that _____
   _____.

9. In "On Leaving," no matter where the poet goes, the sound of Cuba's name will _____
   _____.

10. In "Zion, Me Wan Go Home," the poet wants to return to his home in _____
    _____.

Author's Craft: Rhythm   The following is a list of poetic elements related to sound patterns. Match the element with its definition below.

   a. rhythm   b. meter   c. anapestic   d. trochaic   e. foot

_____ 11. a rhythmic pattern that sounds like da da DUM, da da DUM, da da DUM

_____ 12. a rhythmic pattern that sounds like DUM da, DUM da, DUM da

_____ 13. the pattern of stressed and unstressed syllables in writing

_____ 14. the basic unit of meter

_____ 15. any regularly repeated rhythmic pattern

Name _____   Date _____

Assessment Worksheet 56

The Old Man's Lazy by Peter Blue Cloud   (pages 362–365)

Vocabulary   Match each vocabulary word in the column on the right with its definition in the column on the left. Write the correct letter in the blank.

_____ 1. a government official who works with Native Americans

_____ 2. resentful

_____ 3. a plant with a strong-smelling green oil

_____ 4. ambition and energy

_____ 5. a plant that consists of a fungus and algae

a. **get up and go**

b. **wormwood**

c. **Indian Agent**

d. **lichen**

e. **bitter**

Understanding the Selection   Complete each sentence by adding appropriate information from the selection.

6. The old man believes that he is making use of his place by allowing plants _____

_____.

7. To the old man, the broken fence lying on the ground looks like _____

_____.

8. The old man thinks the Indian Agent should have looked within himself _____

_____.

9. The former neighbor dug holes all over his place in a futile attempt to _____

_____.

10. The old man is told stories by the fence and by _____

_____.

Author's Craft: Dramatic Monologue   "The Old Man's Lazy" is a dramatic monologue. Write **T** to identify statements that are characteristics found in dramatic monologues. Write **F** to identify statements that are not typical of a dramatic monologue.

_____ 11. It presents the thoughts of one person, an elderly Native American.

_____ 12. The old man is speaking at an important moment in his life.

_____ 13. Another character, an Indian Agent, asks questions that the old man answers.

_____ 14. Although he speaks, the old man reveals nothing about his own personality and beliefs.

_____ 15. The poet uses irony in the old man's words to reveal the Indian Agent's character.

Assessment Worksheet 57

All the Years of Her Life by Morley Callaghan   (pages 366–373)

Vocabulary   The sentences below are based on descriptions or events in the selection. Look for context clues to help you find the best word below to complete each sentence.

indignation   **brusquely**   **contempt**   **composure**   **dominant**

1. Although he speaks _____ to Alfred, Sam Carr is friendly to Mrs. Higgins.

2. When his mother tells him to go to bed, Alfred's meek obedience shows that she is the _____ person in their relationship.

3. In the end, Alfred realizes how difficult it was for his mother to keep her _____ under the circumstances.

4. Mrs. Higgins reveals her _____ for her son's actions by telling him to have the decency to be quiet.

5. The blustering Alfred fakes _____ when he is caught stealing.

Understanding the Selection   Complete each sentence by adding appropriate information from the selection.

6. As Alfred is leaving work, Sam Carr asks him to _____

_____.

7. Before reporting the theft to the police, Sam calls Alfred's home and suggests that _____

_____.

8. Mrs. Higgins's dignity so impresses Sam Carr that soon they are behaving almost as if _____

_____.

9. On the way home, Mrs. Higgins bitterly tells Alfred that he has _____

_____.

10. As his mother sits trembling in the kitchen, it seems to Alfred that this is _____

_____.

Author's Craft: Characterization   As the plot develops, a round character reveals different sides to his or her personality. Flat characters continue to show only one or two traits. Read the sentences below. Write **F** (for flat) to identify statements that show only a basic trait first identified with the character. Write **R** (for round) to identify statements that show a new side of the character that we did not see before.

_____ 11. Sam Carr tells Mrs. Higgins that he ought to get a cop.

_____ 12. Alfred understands what his mother has been thinking, and it seems his youth is over.

_____ 13. Mrs. Higgins tells Alfred that he is a "bad lot" and has caused one problem after another.

_____ 14. Mrs. Higgins, looking very old and tired, sits trembling at the kitchen table.

_____ 15. Alfred, blustering, thanks God that things turned out the way they did.

Assessment Worksheet 58

from *Little by Little* by Jean Little   (pages 376–383)

Vocabulary   The sentences below are based on descriptions or events in the selection.
Look for context clues to help you find the best word below to complete each sentence.

abrasion   petticoat   ominously   stupendous   pupils

1. At this late hour, the street was empty and seemed _____ quiet to Jean.

2. Jean would not forget the _____ lesson she had learned about the power of mere words.

3. The milk soaked through Jean's dress and wet the cotton _____ beneath.

4. Eccentric, or off-center, location of the _____ made it difficult for the child to focus her vision.

5. Mother's word, _____, made the scrape sound more serious than it was.

Understanding the Selection   Complete each sentence by adding appropriate information from the selection.

6. Jean did not want to go to school that morning because the teacher was giving a test on _____
   _____.

7. Jean tells Miss Marr that she was late for school because a man called her home and said that _____
   _____.

8. In her tale, Jean tells the sick girl's relatives that, more than anything else, she wants _____
   _____.

9. Jean astonishes the seventh-grade bully by describing her visual problems, using _____
   _____.

10. From her experiences in the story, Jean found out _____
    _____.

Author's Craft: Autobiography   The autobiography contains statements that are facts
and others that are perceptions. Write **F** to identify statements that are based on facts.
Write **P** to identify statements that express Jean's perceptions about matters.

_____ 11. It is her little sister Pat's fault that Jean is late for school.

_____ 12. Jean is late for school because she must take time to change her clothes.

_____ 13. Other students tease and play tricks on Jean when the teacher is not nearby.

_____ 14. Miss Marr is almost speechless because she is in awe of Jean's heroic deed.

_____ 15. The bully's snowballs miss Jean because he can only hit a running target.

Assessment Worksheet 59

A Night in the Royal Ontario Museum by Margaret Atwood (pages 384–387)

Vocabulary   Poets often choose words that help reinforce images they wish to create in the reader's mind. The sentences below are based on dictionary definitions and the image the poet wants to convey of Canadian culture. Look for context clues to help you find the best vocabulary word to replace the italicaized word or phrase in each sentence.

totempole   mastodons   mosaic   embalmed   fossil

1. Canada's past is like *large, extinct animals* roaring at the poet from a graveyard. _____

2. The museum exhibits are *preserved like a corpse* with the hollow appearance of life. _____

3. This Native American *pillar, with its natural images,* seems at odds with the ornate European dome.

   _____

4. Canadian literature too often resembles the traces of a *long-dead being, hardened* and *preserved.*

   _____

5. Canada's diverse culture is like a *design formed from various materials and colors* set in a pattern.

   _____

Understanding the Selection   Complete each sentence by adding appropriate information from the selection.

6. In the first stanza, Atwood suggests that she is locked inside _____

   _____.

7. Beginning with the most recent and moving backward, the curators have arranged the exhibits _____

   _____.

8. Despite numerous signs giving directions, the poet feels as though she is lost inside a _____

   _____.

9. The poet cries out that she has gone far enough and wants to stop before she gets to _____

   _____.

10. The poet feels overwhelmed by _____

    _____.

Author's Craft: Onomatopoeia, Alliteration, and Assonance   Poets use techniques like alliteration, assonance, and onomatopoeia for the poetic effects of the sound and also to link and emphasize ideas. Decide whether each example from the selection represents **alliteration**, **assonance**, or **onomatopoeia**. Write your answer(s) in the blank. One example contains two of these poetic devices.

_____   11. dwindling to pinpoints in …

_____   12. the roar of the boneyard

_____   13. dragged to the mind's deadend

_____   14. the thundering tusks

_____   15. crazed man-made stone brain

Assessment Worksheet 60

My Financial Career by Stephen Leacock   (pages 388–392)

Vocabulary   Match each definition on the right with the corresponding vocabulary word from "My Financial Career" on the left. Write the letter in the correct blank.

_____ 1. **wickets**

_____ 2. **sepulchral**

_____ 3. **conjuring**

_____ 4. **cheque**

_____ 5. **invalid**

a. of the process of performing magic

b. a sick, injured, or disabled person

c. a written order to pay a bank money from an account

d. grilled windows through which business is transacted

e. gloomy

Understanding the Selection   Complete each sentence by adding appropriate information from the selection.

6. When he enters the bank, Leacock has his money rolled up _____
   _____.

7. Leacock's secretive behavior convinces the bank manager that he must be _____
   _____.

8. After depositing fifty-six dollars, Leacock, in a panic, mistakenly _____
   _____.

9. Leacock asks to have his fifty-six dollars returned to him in _____
   _____.

10. After his experience at the bank, Leacock keeps his money _____ and his savings
   _____.

Author's Craft: Humor   Humorous writing appeals to our sense of the ridiculous. Below are descriptions of ridiculous situations from the selection. Fill in the blank with a word or a short phrase to complete the statement.

11. Opening a routine bank account, Leacock insists on seeing _____
   _____.

12. He acts in a way that leads the bank manager to believe that he is a detective or the heir to a _____
   _____.

13. Attempting to leave the manager's office, he steps into _____
   _____.

14. He pokes a ball of money at the accountant as though he were doing a _____
   _____.

15. Rather than admit that he wrote the wrong amount on the check, he tries to act as though something has
   _____.

Literary Skill: Lyric Poetry

All That You Have Given Me, Africa

by Anoma Kanié (translated by Kathleen Weaver) (pages 28-29)

A **lyric** is a poem that focuses on expressing strong, personal feelings or thoughts rather than on telling a story.

A **lyric poem** reminds us of a song sung by one person, the **speaker**. This individual may be thinking aloud, talking directly to another person, or addressing an abstract idea. He or she uses vivid images to express powerful emotions or important thoughts. The speaker may also use a refrain, a phrase that is repeated, sometimes with slight changes. This adds to the melodic quality of the poem, as do the musical effects of rhyme, rhythm, alliteration, and onomatopoeia.

Lyric Poetry "All That You Have Given Me, Africa" contains the elements of a lyric poem. Use the list below to identify these elements. Some may appear more than once.

a. the speaker   b. abstract idea   c. vivid images   d. powerful emotion   e. refrain

1. _____ Music, dances, all night stories around a fire

2. _____ All that you have given me, Africa

3. _____ And I go forward

4. _____ Savannahs gold in the noonday sun

5. _____ A pride that is evident in the way I walk

6. _____ I bear it…

7. _____ Feet large with journeys

8. _____ A desire to protect you from harm

9. _____ Pigments of my ancestors/Indelible in my blood

10. _____ All that you have etched in my skin

Literary Skill: Metaphors and Similes

In This Valley

by Yehuda Amichai (page 105)

A **simile** is a comparison of two dissimilar things using the linking words *like* or *as* to show the connection. A **metaphor** is a comparison of two dissimilar things in which the connection is implied rather than stated by linking words.

Similes and metaphors are figures of speech used widely in prose and poetry because they help readers discover surprising connections or understand ideas in a new way. These two kinds of comparisons also create vivid and memorable images.

Metaphors and Similes In the third stanza of the poem "In This Valley," Yehuda Amichai uses a metaphor to describe the valley. He then uses a simile to compare the metaphorical image to something else. These comparisons reinforce the writer's feelings for his homeland.

Find the figurative comparisons in the third stanza of "In This Valley." Write the figures of speech indicated and then interpret their meanings in your own words.

1. **metaphor**: "This valley _____

   _____"

2. Interpret this description in prose and then explain how this metaphor adds to your understanding of the poem.

   _____

   _____

   _____

   _____

3. **simile**: "...of being _____

   _____"

4. Interpret this description in prose and then explain how this simile adds to your understanding of the poem.

   _____

   _____

   _____

   _____

Literary Skill: Foreshadowing

No Way Out

by Harry Wu (pages 147-157)

Authors sometimes **foreshadow** plot events, or give readers clues to what will happen later in the story.

These hints are intended to create suspense, increasing our curiosity and leading us deeper into the plot so that we can discover the outcome. Foreshadowing can also lay a believable, logical foundation for what will follow. Giving readers clues that prepare them for the climax and resolution adds to the structural unity of a plot.

Foreshadowing In "No Way Out," foreshadowing begins with the title. As we read about Harry Wu's desperate attempts to escape political oppression, its words echo in our minds, hinting at and preparing us for the climax.

Read the following quotes from the selection. In the space provided, describe later plot events that are foreshadowed by each quotation.

1. "I could see no role for myself in my country's future . . ."_____

_____

_____

2. "The day before my expected departure for home, Comrade Ma appeared in my dormitory . . . 'Your permission to travel to Shanghai has been denied.'"

_____

_____

3. "I had always known him to be a fair and kind man, but I was amazed when [Ning] poured me a cup of tea."

_____

_____

4. "Then Wang Jian strode to the front of the room. Normally Kong and his fellows from the Youth League branch office chaired these criticism meetings themselves."

_____

_____

5. "This can't be happening," I thought to myself again. "There must be some way out."

_____

_____

Name _____ Date _____

Literary Skill: Short Story

The Tiger

by S. Rajaratnam (pages 178-185)

A **short story** is a brief work of fiction.

Short stories usually have one or two **settings** and only a few **characters** who are involved in the **plot**, or central conflict. The conflict usually involves a series of complications until it reaches a **climax**, or point of highest tension. The climax is usually followed by the **resolution**, or end, of the conflict. All of these elements of the short story contribute to its **theme**, the central idea or insight, that the writer wants to convey.

Short Story In the story "The Tiger," S. Rajaratnam develops great tension in two important scenes. The reader learns a great deal about several characters through dialogue and the author's third-person omniscient point of view.

Complete a story outline of "The Tiger" by describing the following elements.

I.   Plot

_____

_____

II. Characters

   A. Fatima

_____

_____

   B. Fatima's mother

_____

_____

III. Settings

_____

_____

IV. Climax

_____

_____

V.   Resolution

_____

_____

VI. Theme

_____

_____

Literary Skill: Sequencing

The Servant

by S. T. Semyonov (pages 221-228)

Sequencing is the order in which the major incidents of the plot take place.

Writers carefully plan the sequence of events in a story so that readers can follow the action and make sense of it. The most common method of organization is **chronological order**, which shows how one event follows another in time.

Ways of showing sequence Writers have different ways of showing chronological sequence. In "The Servant," S. T. Semyonov uses words like *finally, one day, inside of half an hour, then*, and *the next evening* to make transitions between major incidents. He also divides his story into chapters to show the passage of time. In addition, Semyonov changes the setting in which incidents take place when moving the plot forward.

Trace the sequence of incidents in "The Servant." Complete the outline below by identifying the setting and summarizing what the writer tells you at each stage.

1. Chapter I **Introduction**—gives background information and catches the reader's interest

   Setting _____

   Summary _____

2. Chapter II **Major Incident**

   Setting _____

   Summary _____

3. Chapter III **Major Incident**

   Setting _____

   Summary _____

4. Chapter IV **Major Incident**—the high point or *climax*

   Setting _____

   Summary _____

5. Chapter IV **Resolution**—the main problem is resolved or settled

   Setting _____

   Summary _____

Name _____   Date _____

Literary Skill: Characterization

If Not Still Higher

by Isaac Loeb Peretz (pages 229-233)

Characterization is the way writers create the people who inhabit the world of a story.

Writers have numerous ways to develop and reveal their characters. Sometimes, the writer speaks directly to the reader, telling us exactly what a person is like. At other times, the characters themselves provide us with specific information through their own thoughts, words, and actions. Finally, writers may indicate the personality of their characters by showing their effect on other people, demonstrating how other characters feel or behave toward them.

Characterization In the short story "If Not Still Higher," the author uses the different techniques described above to reveal the character of the rabbi. Complete the character analysis below. Describe the personality traits that the author is revealing. Then, identify the technique the author uses to reveal this information. You may refer to the preceding paragraph to guide you in deciding how the information is revealed.

1. "Satan . . . sees and accuses and tells tales. Who shall help if not the rabbi? So think the people of Nemirov."

Personality traits: _____

Technique: _____

2. "Whoever has heard the groaning of the Rabbi of Nemirov knows what sorrow, what distress of mind, was in every groan."

Personality traits: _____

Technique: _____

3. "The rabbi keeps to the street side and walks in the shadow of the houses."

Personality traits: _____

Technique: _____

4. "You are a poor, sick woman, and I am willing to trust you . . . I believe that in time you will repay."

Personality traits: _____

Technique: _____

5. "I will light the stove for you."

Personality traits: _____

Technique: _____

6. "When anyone tells how the rabbi . . . flies up to heaven, the Lithuanian, instead of laughing, adds quietly, 'If not still higher.'"

Personality traits: _____

Technique: _____

Name _____   Date _____

Literary Skill: Sensory Detail

Chilean Earth

by Gabriela Mistral (page 323)

Sensory detail is language that appeals to one or more of our five senses.

Writers use sensory detail to create vivid impressions in the reader's mind. They do this by describing how something **looks**, **sounds**, **feels**, **tastes**, or **smells**. By appealing to our senses, writers can almost transport us into the heart of the scene or experience they describe.

Sensory Detail In "Chilean Earth," Gabriela Mistral uses sensory details to bring her poetic scene to life. Conduct a search through the poem for sensory images that appeal to **sight, hearing**, or **touch**. Some images appeal to more than one of these senses and may be repeated when responding to the questions. Then describe the impressions created by these sensory details.

1. What images of the Chilean landscape appeal to our sense of sight?

   _____   _____

   _____   _____

   _____

2. What images of the Chilean landscape appeal to our sense of hearing?

   _____   _____

   _____   _____

   _____

3. What images of the Chilean landscape appeal to our sense of touch?

   _____   _____

   _____   _____

4. Describe the picture created in your mind of the Chilean Earth.

   _____

   _____

5. Describe the picture created in your mind of the Chilean people.

   _____

   _____

6. What do you think are the strong personal feelings that the poet wanted to express about the land of her birth?

   _____

   _____

310

Literary Skill: Drama

Florinda and Don Gonzalo

by Luisa Josefina Hernández (pages 327-334)

A **drama** is a literary work written to be performed by actors on a stage.

The playwright develops the story through **dialogue**, or the conversations of the characters. In conventional drama, the author may include **stage directions** that give instructions about props, lighting, costumes, scenery, and the gestures of the characters. In **experimental drama**, the playwright may rely on dialogue alone to tell the story and to reveal the thoughts, feelings, and motivation of the characters.

Drama In the experimental play *Florinda and Don Gonzalo*, dialogue alone reveals the personalities of the characters and the conflicts that they must resolve.

For each item below, read the dialogue and write one quality it reveals about each character. Each segment of dialogue may reveal a different characteristic. The following list contains suggested qualities you may find.

(un)conventional	adventurous	lonely	(in)dependent
romantic	timid	pessimistic	compassionate
uncertain	understanding	determined	bold
optimistic	apologetic	practical	predictable

1. FLORINDA: . . . Don Gonzalo spends every afternoon seated in the doorway reading. Perhaps a bit of conversation might suit him.

   Don Gonzalo _____   Florinda _____

2. DON GONZALO: . . . What kind of life would she have had at my side?

   FLORINDA: If the two of you loved one another, a lifetime of love.

   Don Gonzalo _____   Florinda _____

3. DON GONZALO: Then it's . . . a proposal of marriage?

   FLORINDA: Only in case you wanted to see it that way. I'll be satisfied just with your coming to my house.

   Don Gonzalo _____   Florinda _____

4. DON GONZALO: And when . . . when are you coming for me?

   FLORINDA: Well, now. The truth is that I was coming now to pick you up, and I intended to return home with you.

   Don Gonzalo _____   Florinda _____

5. DON GONZALO: Be careful in getting off the sidewalk because this wheelchair is getting shakier by the minute.

   FLORINDA: Don't worry, Don Gonzalo. Close your eyes and think that the street is a river. I'll let you know when we reach the other shore.

   Don Gonzalo _____   Florinda _____

Name _____   Date _____

Literary Skill: Autobiography

Little by Little

by Jean Little (pages 376-383)

An **autobiography** is a form of nonfiction in which a person tells his or her own life story. An autobiographer may trace this life story from birth to the moment of writing or may choose to highlight turning points, happiest memories, or important decisions. Regardless of the writer's focus, however, he or she will make use of **introspection**.

It is by examining thoughts and feelings about past experiences that the autobiographer is able to reveal both the significance of his or her life and the uniqueness of his or her personality.

Autobiography In the excerpt from *Little by Little,* the autobiographer describes incidents that took place when she was nine years old. Looking back from an adult's perspective, the author may still hold some of her childhood beliefs, but others may no longer be true.

Analyze the thoughts and feelings of the child, Jean Little. Find the quotes below in the story and reread them in context. Identify which childhood perceptions you believe were valid, and explain why you think so. Identify those you think were invalid and explain why.

1. "... hating my little sister who was the cause of all the trouble and who got to stay home and be spoiled by everybody."

    _____

    _____

2. "If I wrote my name up there differently than the others did, they would have a new thing to tease me about."

    _____

    _____

3. "She [Miss Marr] had believed me. I was sure of that."

    _____

    _____

4. "One girl had even smiled at me, as though she might be my friend."

    _____

    _____

5. "Perhaps his aim was off because he was so used to firing his missiles at a running target."

    _____

    _____

6. "But I had found out what mere words could do. I would not forget."

    _____

    _____